THE DUBLIN & SOUTH EASTERN RAILWAY

An Illustrated History

Ernie Shepherd and Gerry Beesley

Midland Publishing
Limited

This book is dedicated
to our wives and children
for their patience and understanding.

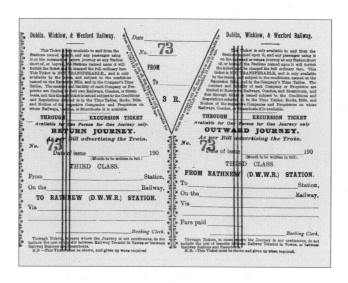

Copyright 1998
W Ernest Shepherd and Gerry Beesley
ISBN 1 85780 082 6

Published by
Midland Publishing Limited
24 The Hollow, Earl Shilton
Leicester, LE9 7NA
England
Tel: 01455 847 815 Fax: 01455 841 805
E-mail: midlandbooks@compuserve.com

Printed and bound by
WBC Book Manufacturers Limited
Bridgend, Mid Glamorgan
CF31 3XP

Designed by
Midland Publishing
and Stephen Thompson Associates.

Typeset in
ITC Garamond and Gill Sans

Illustration on this page:
**An example of a through excursion ticket
issued by the DW&WR in the early years
of the century.**
W E Shepherd collection

CONTENTS

Harcourt Street 1859, G. Wilkinson Arch.

Title page:
Pictures of Merrion are most rare, particularly when open. This view, taken before the turn of the century, shows a down train entering the station.
IRRS collection

Front cover, top:
The mail train at Waterford, Abbey Junction, in 1905. 0-4-2 No 39, later named *Suir*, leads kitchen van No 11, bogie open first No 12 and bogie open second No 42. H Fayle - IRRS collection

Front cover, bottom:
Greystones station, looking north from the Wexford end with Bray Head in the background. The line diverging to the right fans out into sidings with a turntable at the inner end. Note the bathing boxes.
K A Murray - IRRS collection

The illustration on this page is from a drawing of the D&SER's Harcourt Street terminus in Dublin.
W E Shepherd collection

ACKNOWLEDGEMENTS

AS ALWAYS, it would have been impossible for the authors to have written such a history without considerable and generous assistance from many sources. First and foremost, the authors owe a great debt of gratitude to the Secretary of Córas Iompair Éireann, the holding company for the present Irish railway system, and the custodian of the statutory records of all the Irish railways which came under its control via the Great Southern Railways. The various minute books of the Dublin & South Eastern Railway and its predecessors have been made freely available, as have those of other companies which had dealings or disputes with the D&SER. The Director and staff of the National Library of Ireland provided access to newspaper files, including a few remaining issues of the *Irish Railway Gazette*, an Irish equivalent of the *Railway Times*. In addition, the NLI hold copies of many of the Board of Trade Accident reports. Further copies of these and the Inspecting Officers' reports of line inspections prior to opening were kindly made available by the Public Records Office in London. The Librarian and Archivist of the Irish Railway Record Society have allowed access to the vast store of material in the Society's care at Heuston station. This includes a large collection of Ordnance Survey maps and files originally belonging

to the Dublin Wicklow &Wexford Railway and D&SER from 1900 onwards. Regrettably only a fraction of these files has survived.

Many individual members of the IRRS have assisted in numerous ways. Among these must be mentioned the late Robin Clements who took such an interest in all matters relating to the locomotives and rolling stock. Eugene Field is an expert on tickets and kindly provided the appendix dealing with these. Clifton Flewitt kindly loaned files of the late George Wild, the last Locomotive Superintendent of the D&SER. Ken Manto is particularly interested in signalling on Irish railways and gave of his expertise in this context. Kevin Murray has spent a lifetime researching the history of the Dublin & Kingstown Railway and has had his own history of that line published by the IRRS. Inevitably, his researches also extended into D&SER territory and he has given freely of these. Herbert Richards has assisted by making his work on D&SER wagon stock available to us and has also read the manuscript making a number of constructive points as a consequence. Peter Rowledge, who has spent considerable time researching the BoT records as well as having recently published a record of Irish railway locomotives, has freely allowed access to this material. Tom Wall kindly allowed the

authors access to records in the Archives of Telecom Éireann.

In 1895 the DW&WR drew up a new register of its carriage stock and about 1908 this was carefully copied by the late Canon T W B Nicholson, an early Irish railway enthusiast. He added considerable data from his personal observations in the early 1900s, and this comprehensive record, supported by other contemporary documents, has enabled the preparation of an almost complete schedule of the company's carriages which is given in Appendix E.

Others who have provided valuable assistance include Jimmy Cleary of the Wicklow Press, Ron Hamilton, Reg Jarvis of the Maritime Museum in Kilmore Quay, Carmel Moore of Wicklow County Library, Celestine Rafferty of the Wexford County Library and Jim Scannell. John Kennedy of the Green Studios provided photographic prints for this work, and a look at these speaks for itself in terms of John's commitment to producing a fine product. Photographs are acknowledged individually. In the event that the authors have omitted to mention anyone, please accept our apologies and our regrets. Any such omission is entirely unintentional.

Last, but not least, we must express our thanks to the publishers for having faith in the results of our labours.

AUTHORS' NOTE

AS IN THE companion volume on the Midland Great Western Railway, the spellings of place names are those used by the company. These spellings may not always agree with those used by the Ordnance Survey. Kilcool was in fact sometimes shown by the company with a final 'e', while both Sidney and Sydney have been used for Sydney Parade, the latter being more correct. Corbawn Lane in Shankill is shown as such on OS maps although the company invariably referred to it as Cawbawn Lane. OS spellings are adopted in this instance.

The names of some stations changed over the years. That which is known today as Greystones was variously called in the past Delgany, Delgany & Greystones and Greystones & Delgany. Bray was renamed Bri

Chuallan in 1922, this latter title being used for many years by the GSR. Kingstown, the title granted to the town to commemorate the departure of King George IV through the port in 1821, reverted to the Irish Dun Laoghaire one hundred years later. Reference will be found in the text to Dunleary, this being the name of the original town near the West Pier, and still used today. Ovoca was so named until 1912, being renamed Avoca in that year. Both spellings are used as appropriate.

The Great Northern Railway (Ireland) was generally shortened simply to the Great Northern, abbreviated to GNR(I). Likewise, the MGWR was generally referred to in Ireland as 'the Midland'. It had no connections with the English railway of that name.

The 24-hour clock has been used throughout, except in direct quotations from other sources. References to monetary values have been expressed in the currency of the period. Prior to 1970, the pound (£) consisted of 20 shillings, each of 12 pennies, there being thus 240 pennies to the pound. A current penny is therefore worth 2.4 old pence. The abbreviations used were 's' for shillings and 'd' for pence, as in the example £234.11s.6d.

SOURCES

I N RESEARCHING a history such as that of the D&SER, reference had to be made to many and varied sources. As regards official records, the authors extensively trawled the Board and Traffic minutes of the D&SER and its predecessors, including the City of Dublin Junction Railway, from 1845 to 1925. In addition, reference was made to the records of the Great Southern & Western Railway, MGWR and the Waterford & Limerick Railway for additional background information. Weekly reports submitted to the Board by the Locomotive Superintendent and the Chief Engineer for a part of the above period are still extant as are letter books of George Archer, one time Chief Permanent-way Inspector at Bray. Some of the Secretary's files are still available, and these in conjunction with the GNR(I), GS&WR and MGWR correspondence files gave additional insight into the building of both the Loop Line, the Link Line and other matters.

The papers of George Wild, the company's last Locomotive Superintendent, shed an interesting light on the proposed electrification of the Amiens Street to Bray section, subsequent plans for petrol motors, and the events leading up to the amalgamation.

Other official records include station layout diagrams, signal cabin diagrams, drawings of locomotives and rolling stock, public and working timetables and appendices there-to and the DW&WR and D&SER tourist guides for 1895 and 1914 respectively.

In addition, Parliamentary papers, Acts of Parliament, BoT reports on inspections and accidents, Ordnance Survey maps and reports of arbitration proceedings proved useful. The minute books of the Wexford Harbour Commissioners were kindly made available by Reg Jarvis, Curator of the Maritime Museum in Kilmore Quay, County Wexford.

Newspapers referred to, included: *Freemans Journal, Irish Independent, Irish Press, Irish Times, Saunders Newsletter, Wicklow Newsletter.*

Railway periodicals included: *Engineering, Herepath's Railway Journal, Irish Railfans' News, Irish Railway Gazette, Journal of the Irish Railway Record Society, The Locomotive, Railway Gazette, Railway Magazine, Railway News, Railway Times.*

Other printed sources referred to:
A History of Railways in Ireland: Conroy, J C; Longmans, Green & Co Limited, 1928.
A Sketch of the Early History of the Dublin & Kingstown Railway: Grierson, T B.
Ireland's First Railway: Murray, K A; Irish Railway Record Society, 1981.
Irish Steam: Nock, O S; David & Charles, 1966.
Irish Railways Today: Pender, B & Richards, H; Transport Research Associates, 1967.
Irish Steam Locomotive Register: Rowledge, J W P; Irish Traction Group, 1993.
Locomotive & Train Working in the Latter Part of the Nineteenth Century, Vol.6: Ahrons, E L; W Heffer & Sons Ltd, 1953.
Midland Great Western Railway of Ireland: Shepherd, W E: Midland Publishing Limited, 1994.
Railways in Ireland, 1834 to 1984: Doyle, O & Hirsch, S; Signal Press, 1983.
Railway Lines of Córas Iompair Éireann & Northern Ireland Railways: Doyle, O & Hirsch, S; Signal Press, 1985.

ABBREVIATIONS

B&WR	Bagenalstown & Wexford Railway
BoT	Board of Trade
BoW	Board of Works
C&HR	Chester & Holyhead Railway
CB&SCR	Cork Bandon & South Coast Railway
CIE	Córas Iompair Éireann
CofDJR	City of Dublin Junction Railways
CofDSPC	City of Dublin Steampacket Company
CTC	Centralised Traffic Control
DART	Dublin Area Rapid Transit
D&BR	Dublin & Bray Railway
D&BST	Dublin & Blessington Steam Tramway
D&DR	Dublin & Drogheda Railway
D&KR	Dublin & Kingstown Railway
D&NDLR	Drumcondra & North Dublin Link Railway
D&SER	Dublin & South Eastern Railway
D&WR	Dublin & Wicklow Railway

DD&RR	Dublin Dundrum & Rathfarnham Railway
DGJR	Dublin Grand Junction Railway
DP&DB	Dublin Port & Docks Board
DSDT	Dublin Southern Districts Tramway
DTCR	Dublin Trunk Connecting Railway
DUTC	Dublin United Tramways Company
DW&WR	Dublin Wicklow & Wexford Railway
ETS	Electric Train Staff
F&RR&H	Fishguard & Rosslare Railways & Harbours Company
GCS	Grand Canal Street Works
GNR (I)	Great Northern Railway (Ireland)
GPO	General Post Office
GS&WR	Great Southern & Western Railway
GSR	Great Southern Railways
GWR	Great Western Railway (England)
IREC	Irish Railways Executive Committee
ISER	Irish South Eastern Railway
K&BR	Kingstown & Bray Railway
K&KJR	Kingstown & Kingsbridge Junc Rly

L&NWR	London & North Western Railway
LB&SCR	London Brighton & South Coast Rly
LMSR	London Midland & Scottish Railway
MGWR	Midland Great Western Railway
NR&WER	New Ross & Waterford Extension Railway
PWLC	Public Works Loan Commissioners
RDS	Royal Dublin Society
SWR	South Wales Railway
TPO	Travelling Post Office
W&ER	Wexford & Enniscorthy Railway
W&LR	Waterford & Limerick Railway
W&WR	Waterford & Wexford Railway
WC&DJR	Wexford Carlow & Dublin Junc Rly
WD&LR	Waterford Dungarvan & Lismore Rly
WHC	Wexford Harbour Commissioners
WL&WR	Waterford Limerick & Western Rly
WNR&WJR	Waterford New Ross & Wexford Junction Railway
WWW&DR	Waterford Wexford Wicklow & Dublin Rly (also appears as 3Ws)

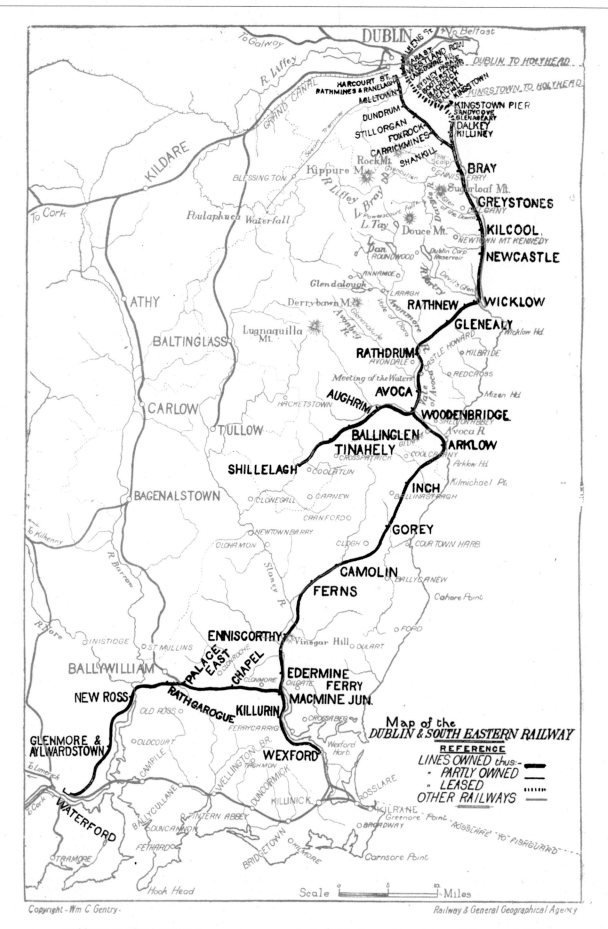

Dublin & South Eastern Railway system map as included in the company's Annual Report of 1916.

Chapter One

IN THE BEGINNING

THE Dublin & South Eastern Railway, as its name suggests served the area to the south-east of Dublin. Whilst the southern terminus of the completed system was in Waterford city, the line in fact did not serve the county of Waterford at all. The station in Waterford is situated on the north bank of the River Suir and is thus in County Kilkenny.

The counties of Wicklow and Wexford through which most of the line runs are predominantly agricultural, the only industries being centred around two or three towns in each county. The Wicklow mountains form the largest single group of mountains in Ireland, extending from the Dublin foothills almost to the Wexford boundary. The highest peak, Lugnaquilla, at 3,039ft, is in fact Ireland's third highest mountain. Further south in Wexford, the Blackstairs mountains extend across into Waterford and these two ranges presented a formidable barrier to transport.

In consequence, the larger towns tended to be situated either on or close to the coast or alongside rivers. In County Wicklow, there are Bray (population about 12,000), Wicklow (3,000) and Arklow (6,000), while in County Wexford are Gorey (3,000), Enniscorthy (6,000) and Wexford (12,000).

Prior to the advent of the railway, many now well-established towns were but hamlets. As an example, at the close of the 18th century, Greystones consisted of some six to eight fishermen's cottages. Bray was little better, with only two houses on the sand dunes forming the Esplanade. It remained for half a century practically no more than a fishing village and posting town.

The coming of the railway and the energy and ability of William Dargan saw Bray develop at such a rate that by 1857 the population had risen to more than 3,000.

The D&SER's 1914 Tourist Guide refers to the district through which the system ran in the following glowing terms:

'It would be difficult to find elsewhere contained within so limited a space such a combination of scenery – high rugged mountains, wild glens, wooded valleys, lakes, rivers and waterfalls – all bounded by a varied and picturesque coast. It also abounds in objects of Antiquarian interest, ruins of castles, abbeys, round towers and Celtic churches'.

The county of Wicklow has been justifiably dubbed the 'Garden of Ireland' and amongst the famous resorts are Powerscourt Glen and Waterfall, Glendalough, Glenmalure and the Avoca Valley.

The towns of Wicklow, Wexford and Waterford are all of Danish origin, and were known respectively as Wykinlo, Weisfiord and Vedifiord. Rathdrum, situated at the junction of the Avonmore and Avondale valleys, was at one time the centre of a thriving flannel industry. The Irish statesman, Charles Stewart Parnell, lived in the nearby Avondale House. Rathdrum was the nearest station to Glendalough (Glen of the two lakes), as described by Sir Walter Scott as 'the inestimably singular scene of Irish antiquity'. Further south, Avoca was famous for its mines which produced large quantities of copper, iron and sulphur ores. Arklow was chiefly a centre of fishing, with a sizeable fleet, although in later years it boasted a large explosives factory set up just to the north of the town by Messrs Kynochs. The town was of Scandinavian origin, being variously referred to as Arn-Kell's Lo, Her-Keloo and Arclo.

The now small town of Ferns was once the city of the Kings of Leinster and dates from the sixth century. The Abbey was plundered by the Norsemen and the town burnt in 930. Enniscorthy is a thriving town surrounded by rich lands on the banks of the River Slaney, which is never far from the railway from here to Wexford. New Ross was and is a prosperous town on the River Barrow; Waterford, on the south bank of the River Suir, was a walled city (as was Wexford) and was founded by King Sitric in 853. Today it is a busy port and is the home of the world famous Waterford Crystal.

With much of County Wicklow being wild and mountainous, it was an ideal area for insurgents to hold out for long periods. In particular, the Rebellion of 1798 was largely centred on south Wicklow and north Wexford, involving such places as Glenmalure, Arklow and Enniscorthy. In an attempt to open up the vast expanses of Wicklow, the Military Road was constructed in the early years of the nineteenth century from just south of Dublin to Glenmalure. It is today one of the main tourist routes into the interior of the county.

The Civil War in 1922-23, although affecting Dublin and Wicklow to a small degree, was mainly centred on the Wexford and Waterford area as far as the D&SER was concerned, and details of its effects on the railway are chronicled later in this history.

With such towns as Bray, Wicklow and Arklow developing on the east coast, it was natural that some means of communication should be set up. To the north, in and around Dublin, the commercial interests of the city were concerned at the damage being done to the city's trade by the lack of suitable shipping facilities. Passenger and mail vessels successively operated from Ringsend (up to 1796), the Pigeonhouse (1796 to 1818) and Howth (from 1818). By 1800 no vessel of more than 200 tons was safe in the port of Dublin, larger vessels grounding at low tide. In an attempt to improve the situation, Sir Thomas Page, an eminent engineer, suggested the construction of a canal from Ringsend docks, via Milltown, Stillorgan and Monkstown to a new deep-water harbour at Sandycove Point. Various other schemes were put forward including that of Sir John Rennie who suggested a large new harbour at Dunleary and a ship canal thence to the River Liffey. This latter would have been 80ft wide at the bottom, twice this width at water-level and had a mean depth of 20ft, whilst the harbour itself would have had a depth of 14ft of water at low tide. The entire scheme was estimated to cost £489,734. At that period there was but a small harbour at Dunleary with a short pier constructed in the mid-18th century. In 1815, an Act of Parliament established a Board of Commissioners for an Asylum Harbour at Dunleary and within two years construction of what is now the deep-water harbour was commenced, not being finally completed until 1859 at a cost of about £825,000. During its construction, thousands of tons of granite were brought down from Dalkey quarries by means of a tramway about two miles in length with cast-iron rails on stone sleepers. Even before the harbour was completed, ships were calling to lighten their loads so as to be able to cross the shallow bar into the port of Dublin. As a natural consequence of this, the population of Kingstown began to grow and the question of providing access to the city again came to the fore.

An early view of Carlisle Pier with one of the paddle steamers berthed alongside. The left hand of the three railway vehicles is a former D&KR three-compartment first. Photographer unknown

It was quickly realised that the cost of constructing a canal would be prohibitive and attention was turned to a new mode of transport. Possibly because it was so new and largely untried, a Bill submitted to Parliament in 1825 for a 'Railway or Tramroad from the Royal Harbour of Kingstown ... to or near Mount Street' was strenuously opposed, not least by the proprietors of the Grand Canal Company who still saw merit in a canal. Ireland's first successful Railway Act was that for the Limerick & Waterford Railway, passed in the following year, the scheme failing for lack of finance. When the Kingstown promoters tried again success was achieved with the incorporation of the Dublin & Kingstown Railway to construct a line of railway from or near Trinity College to the (West) pier at Kingstown. The Act received Royal Assent in September 1831.

The story of the D&KR has been adequately told elsewhere (see *Ireland's First Railway* by K A Murray: IRRS; Dublin, 1981). However as the history of the D&SER was closely tied up with that of the Kingstown company, it is necessary to briefly outline the latter's beginnings at this point.

The Kingstown Line

The provisional committee of the new company held its first meeting on 25th November, 1831. The committee included Edward Alexander, James Perry, John Barton, Thomas Pim, James Ferrier, Robert Roe and Joseph Kincaid, all men of considerable business acumen in the city. At a further meeting early in December, James Pim of the Dublin banking firm of Boyle, Low, Pim & Company was appointed to the post of Company Secretary. He has been described as being a man of rare ability and was to prove

his worth in future negotiations with the Great Western Railway (of England). At the same meeting, Thomas Pim was appointed Chairman. On 30th May 1832 the Board of Works instructed the eminent Irish engineer Charles Vignoles to report on the line and he was later to be appointed to the position of Company Engineer. His estimate amounted to £150,000 but the Board of Works felt that this was on the high side and requested a cheapening of the work before it would be prepared to grant a loan to the company. Vignoles therefore reduced his estimate to £126,406, whereupon the BoW granted a loan of £50,000, increased in the next year to £75,000 at 4% interest repayable in half-yearly installments over a period of 25 years.

Considerable difficulty was encountered with the purchase of land, particularly around Blackrock where opposition came from Lord Cloncurry and his neighbour, Sir Harcourt Lees. These gentlemen eventually agreed to accept financial compensation as well as the erection, at the company's expense, of fishing and bathing lodges, a camera obscura tower and a boat slip with a pier. Having overcome this opposition, the company accepted the tender of William Dargan at £83,000 for the main construction work, the permanent-way materials to be supplied by Messrs Lee, Watson & Company of St Helens. The length of line to be built was 5 miles and 43 chains from the east side of the present Westland Row to the pier of the old harbour at Dunleary, beside the level crossing which existed prior to electrification; the gauge to be 4ft 8½ins. The line opened on 17th December 1834, the first timetable being introduced in January 1835.

Even before the line was opened, plans had been drawn up for an extension to the

south. The Admiralty originally intended to construct a wharf for the mail and other steamers at the west pier but subsequently the new wharf was constructed further to the east. A Bill to extend the line to the east end of the harbour was thrown out in the 1833 session but in the following year success was achieved, the contract being awarded to Dargan, the cost including land to be about £21,500. The line as opened on 13th May 1837 ran to what is now the terminal section of the present Dun Laoghaire station behind the down platform. As opened, the station did not have any coverings over the platform, these being provided in November 1845.

Atmospheric to Dalkey

In 1839, a patent was obtained by Samuel Clegg and the Samuda Brothers for an invention which was to result in the extension of the D&KR to Dalkey. It is a scientific fact that nature abhors a vacuum and as long ago as 1685 Denis Papin came up with a means of transporting goods based on this principle. Nothing came of Papin's invention until in the 19th century when the idea was once again explored.

One of the big problems faced was the forming of an airtight connection between the cylinder in which the vacuum is created and the vehicle moving along on the surface above it. Messrs Clegg and Samuda invented a leather flap-valve which partially overcame the problem and a short stretch of line was laid at Wormwood Scrubs on the Birmingham, Bristol & Thames Junction Railway. Some of the directors and officers of the D&KR were present at the demonstration and were persuaded that this was a proposition worthy of consideration. The township of Dalkey was at this time increasing in population and the Kingstown directors decided that the time was right for extending their line to this point.

Construction of the great new harbour at Kingstown was by now nearing completion. The materials used in its construction came from a quarry at Dalkey and were transported by means of a tramway with horse-drawn wagons. The Board of Works was approached and readily agreed to lease one line of the tramway and in addition grant a loan of £25,000 towards the construction and equipment of the atmospheric railway.

Top right: **Work in progress on the doubling of the Kingstown to Dalkey section in 1881-82.** IRRS collection

Below: **An up train comprised of a motley collection of carriages enters Salthill from Kingstown. The first and second vehicles are a D&KR large third and a D&WR five-compartment Brown-Marshall third respectively, and the sixth vehicle is a D&KR open second. The magnificent Salthill Hotel dominates the background.** Photographer unknown

The new line was first tested on 19th August 1843 when a train reached Dalkey in four minutes. The line was officially opened to the public on 29th March 1844.

The atmospheric principle was employed only for the uphill run to Dalkey, where the power house was situated. Trains returned to Kingstown by gravity. During off-peak hours trains consisted of the piston carriage and one other carriage, but at busy periods as many as nine vehicles might be used. It has to be said that the atmospheric, whilst it operated for ten years, did not live up to the directors' expectations, in part due to the disastrous effects of the famine which struck the country some three years after its opening. Any defect in the pumping system put the line out of action. On one such occasion in December 1848, the company found it necessary to modify its locomotive *Princess* to conform to the atmospheric section's restricted loading gauge, and the line was steam worked for almost two months.

The terminus at Dalkey was situated about half a mile north of the present Dalkey station.

Chapter Two

RIVAL SCHEMES FOR WEXFORD

BRAY, by its position, is the gateway to County Wicklow and its importance as such was recognised in a railway context as far back as 1832 when Vignoles was carrying out his survey for a possible Dalkey extension to the D&KR. He was requested to survey a line to Bray, although this came to nothing at this time. At one point, the promoters of the atmospheric system were so confident in their mode of traction that they announced their intention of extending to Bray and approached the D&KR for their support. The matter was considered but rejected by the Kingstown directors. Following the opening of the atmospheric railway, many eminent railway people visited this unique mode of traction. In August 1844, the chairman, two directors, the secretary and engineer of the Great Western Railway (of England) came over to inspect the line. During the course of this visit, their engineer, the famed Isambard Kingdom Brunel, spoke to James Pim to the effect that the GWR were interested in con-

structing a line to the port of Fishguard with a view to opening up another cross-channel steamer service. Holyhead had been used as the port for the Irish mail traffic since the time of Queen Elizabeth I, the destination on the Irish side alternating between Rings-end, the Pigeonhouse, Howth and, gradually after 1827 with the completion of the East Pier, Kingstown. The GWR had in mind the creation of a new port south of Wexford at a point then known as Greenore Bay, later Rosslare. It was felt that the D&KR might be interested in the construction of a line of railway from Kingstown to Wexford and Waterford. The matter was discussed by the Kingstown board in the following month, and after much correspondence between Westland Row and Paddington, the D&KR expressed their intention of going as far as Wicklow.

The GWR obviously felt that the D&KR having reached Wicklow, would probably lose interest in going any further south. Nevertheless in November 1844 it was decided

to publish Notice of Intention to apply for an Act. It was hardly a coincidence that on the very day that the D&KR had their notice published in the *Dublin Gazette*, the GWR also published a notice for a line from Kingstown to Wexford and Waterford with branches. An urgent meeting of D&KR shareholders was called, and Brunel, who was in Dublin, endeavoured to reassure those present that the GWR had no ulterior motives, suggesting that the GWR notice would serve both interests. However, by mid-December it became clear that the necessary plans were not ready for presentation to Parliament. With this setback, the D&KR now turned back to their plans for a Bray extension. At the end of the year, the D&KR board received a letter from the GWR seeking confirmation that their Bray extension would form part of a line being submitted to Parliament under the title of the Waterford, Wexford, Wicklow & Dublin Railway. The D&KR replied to the effect that the Bray extension was to be constructed by a separate company, the Kingstown & Bray Railway - it was separate in name only as the Kingstown directors had appointed themselves as a provisional committee to the K&BR. The D&KR however offered the Bray extension to the new company and this was embodied in Section 40 of the Act for the Bray extension which received Royal Assent on 16th July 1846. It should be stated that because of pressure from Paddington, the K&BR Bill was defeated in the Commons and it thus fell to the D&KR to seek the extension.

· Details of the WWW&DR, or the 3Ws as it came to be known, had emerged in April 1845. Capital was to be £2 million comprised of 100,000 shares. The provisional committee included the Earl of Courtown, Thomas Meagher, Chairman of the W&LR,

Left: **Probably one of the earliest Irish railway photographs, taken in 1853-54 during the construction of the line, this shows the original lattice girder bridge across Dartmouth Road, Ranelagh, prior to track laying. The lattice girder bridges between Harcourt Street and Milltown were replaced in 1892-94 by plate girder bridges constructed by Andrew Handyside of Derby.** D H Gillman collection

and Lord Viscount Barrington MP, a director both of the GWR and the South Wales Railway. The object of the line was to connect the metropolis with the important ports of Wexford, Waterford and Cork, the latter via the Cork & Waterford Railway, a line also promoted by the GWR. It is interesting to note that no reference whatsoever was made of the D&KR, a fact which must have disturbed some of the latter company's directors. The prospectus went on to state that the importance of the port of Waterford was too well known to need any detailed account. The portion of line connecting Wexford and Waterford would receive a very large traffic from the W&LR and the Waterford & Kilkenny Railway. Nobody apparently queried how this could be if the port of Waterford was so important. Alluding to the short sea passage, the prospectus finally referred to the 'very romantic and justly celebrated beauties of County Wicklow (which) will probably attract a larger passenger traffic than any other railway in Ireland'. A month later, a committee of management was appointed, including the Earl of Courtown, Viscount Duncannon MP and Sir Thomas Esmonde, Bart MP. In all, there were two viscounts, a baronet and seven members of parliament. Brunel was appointed engineer to the new company at a meeting held at their offices at 449 West Strand, London on 27th May. At the same meeting, it was agreed that accounts should be opened with the Bank of Ireland at its Waterford and Wexford branches.

There are three gaps through the Leinster mountain chain, one along the coastal strip by way of the town of Arklow and two inland routes via the Slaney and Barrow rivers. Coincidental with the projected plans for a coastal communication between Dublin and Wexford, proposals were put forward for an inland connection. This was the Wexford, Carlow & Dublin Junction Railway which was proposed to connect with the GS&WR's Carlow branch at the latter point. The GS&WR had been promoted in 1843 to connect Dublin with Cork, along with a branch to Carlow. The WC&DJR was to pass through the Slaney gap via Newtownbarry to Wexford. By June 1845, the WC&DJR Bill was in Committee; in support of the scheme it was reported that almost all of the landed proprietors on the course of the line were in favour of it. The lime trade from County Carlow would be very extensive and Sir John Macneill expected no particular engineering difficulties. It was admitted that the harbour at Wexford was in poor shape, but vessels sailing from there to Liverpool would enjoy a considerable time advantage over vessels using the port of Waterford. The Committee in due course decided that the Preamble to the Bill had not been proved and went on to comment that before sanctioning any similar railway project, the harbour at Wexford

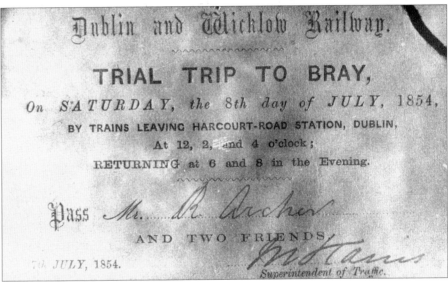

Above: **An invitation to a trial trip over the Dublin & Wicklow Railway two days before the official opening. It is signed by the first Traffic Superintendent, Mortimer Harris.**
H Richards collection

Top: **Although the nameboards proclaim this station to be Rathmines & Ranelagh, it was always simply known as Ranelagh by public and railway alike. Opened on 15th July 1896, its construction was part of a deal with Rathmines Town Commissioners which allowed the company to use intermediate supporting pillars in conjunction with the renewal of the girders of Ranelagh Road bridge in 1894. Originally built with timber platforms, the majority of the up one was renewed in concrete in 1943. The small section of the down side building nearest the camera was at one time the signal cabin.** J Langford

would require improvement. With this in mind, the managing committee announced that they had made arrangements for a separate company to be formed for the purpose of 'making the most eligible and permanent improvements in that harbour'.

Meanwhile, negotiations had been taking place between the D&KR and the 3Ws. The latter had suggested that they should construct an inland route from Dublin to Bray as part of their line to Wexford, and the D&KR should extend their line to join the 3Ws near Bray. These ideas prompted the D&KR board to suggest a lease of their line to the Wicklow company. At the 3Ws board meeting on 3rd December 1845, Brunel advised that a measure of agreement had been reached in this regard. In return for accepting the lease the 3Ws were to pay to the D&KR a fixed annual rent of £34,000 plus 50% of the annual gross receipts of the D&KR portion of the line in excess of £55,000 per annum. In the event of a double line of Atmospheric being laid by the 3Ws, the above mentioned additional rent was to be calculated only on receipts in excess of £58,000. The lease was to be for a term of 35 years with a compulsory renewal or amalgamation of the two companies at its termination on conditions to be mutually agreed in the 30th year of its duration; in the event of disagreement, the matter was to be referred to arbitration. An agreement was signed on 10th March 1846 and suitable clauses were to be inserted in both companies' Bills.

The Act for 'making a railway and branch railway to be called the Waterford, Wexford, Wicklow & Dublin Railway' received Royal Assent on 16th July 1846, the same day as the D&KR obtained their Act for the extension to Bray. It should be noted that this latter extension would have terminated at the Dublin end of the Main Street in Lower Bray, rather than close to the sea. The WWW&DR Act laid down the capital as £2 million, with additional borrowing powers of £666,000. Initially there were to be 14 directors, although this number could be altered to any number between ten and 20. The line of railway was to run from Dundrum, connecting near Bray with a line from the D&KR terminus at Kingstown and terminating at Grannagh or Granny Ferry at Waterford, where it would form a junction with the W&LR. Branches were to run from the main line to or near the seashore at Wicklow, to a pier at Grenore (sic) Bay, later known as Rosslare, and from Foxrock to or near Victoria Square in Kingstown. It is interesting to note that the Wexford line was to run down the east bank of the River Slaney to Ferrycarrig where it would cross to the opposite bank on a bridge with an opening span for

river traffic. By an Act of 1847 this bridge was authorised to carry both rail and road traffic, the existing road toll bridge was to be closed and demolished. The usual periods of three and seven years were allowed respectively for purchase of lands and completion of the railway.

There were a number of important provisions laid down in the Act in relation to agreements with other companies. Section 23 referred to the WC&DJR, with which a junction was to be formed at Scarawalsh; the 3Ws would have running powers to Carlow and the WC&DJR between Enniscorthy and Wexford, although there would be separate stations at the former point. Powers were granted for the D&KR to sell their Bray extension to the 3Ws and for the latter to lease the D&KR.

A third Act was passed on the same day, namely that of the Dublin, Dundrum & Rathfarnham Railway for the connection from Harcourt Road to Dundrum. This company had first been promoted as the Dublin, Dundrum & Enniskerry Railway, but had been persuaded by Parliament to restrict their line to Dundrum with a branch from Ranelagh to Rathfarnham. Running powers were

granted to the 3Ws. Section 27 of the DD&RR Act empowered the 3Ws to take over the construction of the line between Dublin and Dundrum should the DD&RR not complete it within two years. In 1847, the DD&RR obtained a further Act for an extension to St Stephen's Green.

Shareholders' Dissension

Although the 3Ws Act of incorporation had received Royal Assent, other views were being expressed as to the future prospects of the company. To this end, a committee of shareholders was set up in August 1846 to look into matters and report back. At a meeting held at Radley's Hotel in College Green, Dublin on Tuesday 8th September, a Dr Gray read the committee's report which basically recommended that 'the most energetic means should be adopted by the shareholders to break up the company'. Two days later, with no decision taken, a long letter was penned to the shareholders by the chairman, the Earl of Courtown. He was fearful that the recent meeting might have the effect of causing serious injury to the company and he went on to review the reasons for its suggested dissolution. In the first instance,

Left: **Bray station in April 1927 during construction of the second platform on the down side. The company hotel can be seen in the background. The original signals and scissors crossover are still in situ. Note the milk churns, a feature of railway life which has disappeared.** J M Robbins - IRRS collection

Below: **The south end of Bray station, looking north, in the 1890s. The south cabin, a standard McKenzie & Holland structure, is clearly visible, as is one of the gas tank trucks on the left of the picture. The three locomotives, resplendent in green livery are, from left to right, No 9 a 2-4-0T of 1890, No 12 a Fairbairn 2-4-0 of 1860 and No 18, one of the large Sharp 0-4-2 goods engines of 1864.** R N Clements collection

the shareholders complained that no statement of accounts had been laid before them - this was true as no detailed financial statement had yet been prepared. The second point was on the question of a proposed leasing of the line by the GWR, as no approaches had been made to the latter company. Despite all the difficulties facing the company, the Earl was confident that 'this great undertaking will go on and prosper'. Unmoved by this letter, another meeting of shareholders was held at the end of September. One of the arguments put forward by the Chairman was that the construction of the new line would provide much needed employment – as worthy a cause as this might be, the shareholders should not be compelled to construct what they believed to be an unproductive line for such a purpose. At the end of this meeting, it was proposed that contact should be made with the directors and if they responded in a positive manner, then the shareholders should be prepared to make a sacrifice and go on.

At a further meeting in October, reference was made to a meeting held the previous May at Paddington, when the directors, finding it necessary to obtain the support of the shareholders for the third reading of the Bill, had pledged that no calls would be made during the year and no calls in 1847 unless permitted by the money market. It was also understood that as soon as the Act was passed, the line would be leased to the GWR. On the strength of these two undertakings, approval for the Bill had been granted. Now a call was being made on the shares and there was no hint of an agreement to lease the line. The Chairman attempted to state that the shareholders had misinterpreted the remarks made in May; a decision was however taken to make a petition to Parliament by the most 'united and vigorous action to break up or at least suspend the bad activity of the directors'. It was proposed to issue Notice of Intention for a private Bill to break up the company; this Bill was in due course withdrawn.

The first ordinary meeting of the shareholders was convened in December 1846. The directors now suggested that the section from Kingstown to Bray, which had been staked out, be forthwith carried out and then an extension to Wicklow. The section of line from Wexford to the point of junction with the WC&DJR should then be completed, leaving the section from Wicklow to Scarawalsh to be constructed at some future date. To enable the necessary land to be purchased, it was now proposed to make a call of £1.10s.0d per share forthwith and a second call of £1 in November 1847. The meeting turned out to be a long one, with many of the shareholders voicing their opposition to the actions of the directors. It was absolutely essential, if the line was to survive, that it be leased to the GWR. In due

course the meeting was postponed until 17th February 1847. In the interim, a deputation was appointed for the purpose of ascertaining whether any means could be devised either by sale or lease of the line to the GWR or any other company for enabling the dissenting shareholders to withdraw from the undertaking. At the adjourned meeting, attempts were made to replace the directors, particularly those representing the GWR and South Wales Railway, who were accused of interference. When a vote was taken, it was discovered that the directors had been buying up shares enabling them to win the vote and hold on to their seats on the board. A Mr Reynolds then made reference to each item of expenditure in the accounts, 'persisting with great vehemence' in being satisfied on each point.

On the occasion of the next half-yearly meeting in March, the shareholders were informed that the preliminaries for setting out the line between Enniscorthy and Wexford and between Kingstown and Wicklow were complete. In the latter case, it only required a contract to be let and construction could proceed. The next three years were to see many meetings of the shareholders held to express dissatisfaction with the activities of the directors. An Act was passed on 30th June 1848 empowering the SWR to subscribe to the WWW&DR, and to appoint seven directors thereto. The same Act gave powers for the re-gauging of the D&KR section, to be completed at the expense of the 3Ws. The lease of the D&KR was not to commence until the line between Wicklow and Kingstown was completed and open for traffic, but the 3Ws might take over the Kingstown to Dalkey section. At a shareholders' meeting in February 1849, only some twelve shareholders turned up. After an hour, when no directors had put in an appearance, the company solicitor's clerk arrived to inform those present that there being an insufficient number present, the meeting was adjourned, whereupon the shareholders decided to hold a meeting of their own and appointed one of their number, a Mr Nash, as Chairman. He was immediately seized by the clerk and a scuffle ensued. Nash was to be one of the leading figures amongst the dissentients. At a subsequent meeting, he advised those present that he had recently attended a meeting of the SWR shareholders, where he learned that company was in default by twelve months in calls on 3Ws shares and he wondered exactly what were their intentions. It also appeared that the SWR were themselves finding difficulty in raising monies to go beyond Swansea. Lest it be thought that such meetings were the sole preserve of the 3Ws, similar acrimonious meetings were taking place involving the DD&RR, which were sufficiently boisterous to keep the citizens of Dublin entertained.

At the September 1848 meeting, Nash made a 'voluminous and somewhat personal attack on the 3Ws directors'. He endeavoured to propose a resolution to the effect that the salaries of the Secretary and officers of the company be reduced; this was ruled out of order by the Chairman. It is of interest to note that the Secretary, Muggeridge, wrote to the board in the following July suggesting that his salary be reduced from £1,000 to £600. In the meantime, the ceremony of turning the first sod was carried out at Bray Head by the Earl of Courtown on 25th August on the property of Lord Meath, who had most generously presented the company with all the land required on his estate.

The company allotted some contracts to several firms and work was commenced at Bray Head by a Mr James Grogan and between Dalkey and Bray. Whilst initially good progress was made, shortage of finance soon hampered the works.

Early in 1849, with Dalkey tunnel completed and some heavy works carried out at Bray Head, construction ceased. In the interim, the contract for the DD&RR had been awarded to William Dargan, who commenced work near Churchtown in April 1849. This three mile stretch of line from the city to Dundrum included stone walled embankments for the first mile from Harcourt Road, and a nine-arched viaduct over the River Dodder at Milltown.

At the August 1849 meeting, the 3Ws directors advised that after careful consideration, they had decided that it would not be desirable to proceed beyond Wicklow and this decision had been conveyed to the SWR. The latter in fact had problems of their own, with construction apparently stopped. They wrote twelve months later recommending that the 3Ws be wound up or allied to some other company. To give effect to this decision to restrict the line to Wicklow, a Bill was submitted to Parliament in the 1851 Session. When the Bill came before the shareholders for their approval in June 1851, it was reported that while the dissenting shareholders mustered strongly, the directors succeeded in carrying the resolution. From this point onwards, the shareholders appeared to have rowed in behind the directors. The Act repealed the powers for the line as between Wicklow and Waterford with the branch to Greenore Bay. A diversion was approved over the last two miles into Wicklow. It was stipulated that the line from Dundrum to Bray should not be opened for traffic for two years from the passing of the Act, unless the Kingstown to Bray line be previously opened. The company title was altered to the Dublin & Wicklow Railway, to better reflect the shortened line. Capital was reduced to £500,000.

Another Act passed on the same day was that of the DD&RR which authorised that company to construct a line from Dundrum to Bray. It was however stipulated that should the D&WR within one year of the passing of the Act either contract for the purchase or have taken possession of the lands for this section, and complete same within two years, then the powers granted to the DD&RR should cease. The powers for the branch to Rathfarnham were repealed and the company changed its title to the Dublin & Bray Railway. Finally, it was agreed that two D&WR directors should in due course step down and make way for two D&BR directors on the former's board. The contract for the works on the D&WR was now awarded to William Dargan, who was also entrusted with the construction of the D&BR. By the shareholders' meeting in February 1852, the Chairman was able to state that the line should be completed by July 1853. In fact, at the August 1853 meeting, it was reported that the line between Dundrum and Bray was now ready for traffic, and that the D&BR not having completed their line from Dublin, the powers were thereby transferred to the D&WR.

Opening to Bray

The *Saunders Newsletter* for 25th July 1853 reported that the completed line had been inspected on the previous Thursday by the Government Inspector, who expressed himself totally satisfied with the entire works. Two days later, the directors accompanied by the company officials and about 30 ladies and gentlemen, proceeded in a first and second class carriage from Dundrum to Bray, which they reached in half an hour 'without the slightest obstruction or accident'. After partaking of refreshments at Quin's Hotel, the party returned to Dundrum. An even longer account was given of a further experimental trip made from Dublin to Bray in March 1854, 'for the purpose of inspecting the condition of the works'. As the last quarter mile into the Dublin terminus awaited completion, the train commenced from Charlemont Bridge, 'hauled by the (Fairbairn?) engine *Avoca*. As the company did not possess an engine so named, we must assume that this was one of Dargan's engines. *The Railway Times* for 1st July 1854 reported the most active measures in progress to have the line opened for traffic as from Monday 10th July. In accordance with the agreement with the D&KR, it was arranged that a train should leave Bray for Dalkey at 06.30 so that this section might technically speaking be the first opened. On the inland route, stations were provided at Dundrum, Stillorgan, Carrickmines and Shankill, while those on the coast route were at Dalkey and Killiney.

Saunders Newsletter for 8th July 1854 gave details of the train service to be provided. Trains would depart Bray at 07.00, 09.00, 11.00, 14.00, 16.00 and 19.00 and trains left Harcourt Road at 08.00, 10.00, 13.00, 15.00, 17.00 and 20.00. There were to be seven trains each way on the Dalkey line, all stopping at Killiney. There were five trains each way on Sundays on both lines. Within a month of the opening to Bray, it was reported that some of the platforms on the inland route were being lengthened. At Bray, it would appear that the practice was to allow the public to cross the railway line by means of the level crossing. This was found to hinder rail movements as it was ordered on 22nd September that a wooden bridge be erected over the level crossing and that the gates be kept closed and only opened for the passage of carriages and other conveyances. Public access to the station itself also appears to have been a problem as it was stipulated that the platform should be kept closed from the public at the north end and a gate placed across the yard at the south end.

At the shareholders' meeting within six weeks of the opening, the Chairman reported that traffic receipts up to the previous Saturday showed an average of £406.13s.9d per week or £25.7s.2d per mile per week. This translated into an average of 8,218 passengers per week. In regard to the extension works, Brunel reported the completion of the embankments and masonry between Bray and the cliffs at Bray Head. Around the Head itself, the tunnels, embankments and excavations were sufficiently far advanced to allow for ballasting. Brunel was hopeful that fewer difficulties would be encountered with the soft ground at Morris's cliffs near Greystones than had previously been anticipated. By the time of the February meeting, the average weekly number of passengers, exclusive of subscription ticket holders, was 6,251 or 9,450 including subscribers. Average working expenses were 8.57d per mile. Brunel reported steady progress on the works at Bray Head, with only two ravines to be crossed by timber bridges, one of which was far advanced towards completion. Work would begin on the stations once the very severe winter weather had passed. Plans were submitted in March for the proposed station at Greystones, to include residential accommodation for the station master. The company's architect, George Wilkinson, was also requested to prepare plans for the station at Wicklow, 'as near as may be similar in extent and style to that at Shankill'. At this same meeting, Purdon, the resident engineer, was requested to prepare and submit the best plan in his opinion for the working of goods traffic between Dublin and Wicklow with the existing appliances. Tenders for the construction of the two stations were read at the board meeting on 13th April, that of Mr Cockburne being accepted if he agreed to complete the work within four months. Unable to give such a guarantee, the work was given to Messrs Crowe & Sons at £3,000. By August, the section around Bray Head was virtually complete, with the line south of there being ready for opening, although the stations were reportedly still not completed. Dargan had announced his intention in March 1855 of doubling the section of line from Shanganagh to Bray by 1st July, but in the event it was 29th October before the BoT inspected and gave approval for the second track from Bray to the 'Dalkey Junction'.

Atmospheric problems

While these various works were proceeding on the Wicklow extension, the atmospheric section had been handed over to the D&WR on 12th April 1854, the £50,000 contract for the conversion being awarded to Dargan. Brunel reported on 23rd February 1855 that it was a task requiring 'considerable management and contrivance to alter it at the lowest possible cost'. Up to that date, some 70,000 cubic yards of excavation had been completed, representing about 90% of the total. By early August, it was hoped to open the line within two to three weeks. However, when Captain Wynne made his inspection on behalf of the BoT on 3rd September, he reported unfavourably as the line did not conform with the Parliamentary plans, particularly in regard to the curves which were as sharp as ten to 20 chains. A copy of the report having been sent to the D&KR, their engineer also condemned it, although Vignoles, their consulting engineer, expressed the view that it could probably be worked safely if proper precautions were taken.

At the D&KR half-yearly meeting on 5th October, reference was made to the line from Dublin to Kingstown being used 'by the highest dignitaries and most exalted salaries in the land, including the Lord Chancellor, the Judges of the land and others whose income depended on their lives. Were one of these gentlemen killed, it would be a very serious matter'. It presumably did not matter if the ordinary traveller were to be killed or seriously injured. Four days later, the line was again inspected by Wynne, who saw little change but nevertheless gave qualified approval. Trains were to occupy 12 minutes between Kingstown and Dalkey, all being required to stop at the new station of Kingstown Sandycove. Operation was to be by single engine in steam while the line remained single and all carriage windows were to have bars on them in view of the restricted clearances. The line was hurriedly opened for traffic on 10th October, but the D&WR directors were in for a surprise. When the first train arrived at Kingstown, the passengers were refused the use of the station there, and apart from a few who availed of a ladder to climb up to the street, they had to return whence they came. Dargan now agreed to reconstruct the line to the satisfaction of the D&KR engineer.

Above: **A turn of the century view of Greystones station looking towards Bray. The footbridge that replaced the level crossing is in the background, and the original DW&WR signal cabin, which was replaced by the GSR in 1926, is visible on the down platform.** Lawrence collection - courtesy NLI

The line was again closed and it was not until Monday 30th June 1856 that *Saunders Newsletter* announced the re-opening from the following day.

Opening to Wicklow
The extension to Wicklow was inspected by the BoT and found in order, enabling the directors to make an experimental trip on Saturday, 13th October 1855, a lengthy description of this trip being recorded in the *Railway Times*. It was stated that the stations, whilst not yet complete, 'will be greatly admired for their simple and useful style of architecture and are most creditable to the architect'. The stations were located at Greystones, Kilcool, Killoughter and in Wicklow at the Murrough. That at Newcastle was in due course opened on 1st August of the following year. With everything ready, the line was formally opened on 22nd October by the Lord Lieutenant and to the public eight days later. It was reported that both goods and passengers were carried and the directors expressed satisfaction with the results as regards the latter.

With the line now open to Wicklow, the way was clear for the company to take a lease of the D&KR. Although chronologically out of place at this point, it is a convenient time to detail the various agreements up to 1866. By an agreement dated 17th March 1854, the D&WR had been obliged to alter the gauge of the D&KR within six months of the latter handing it over. The principal rent was to be reduced to £32,000 and the contingent rent to be 30% rather than 50% of the surplus revenue over £55,000. The compensation rent from the June 1846 agreement was retained. The D&WR were to at once pay £5,000 towards the cost of the new station required at Kingstown and £16,000 half-year's rent in advance, in due course to be deducted from the final year's rent. The actual lease was not formally signed on behalf of both companies until 30th June 1856 due to a legal complication regarding the D&KR's title to the Atmospheric. The D&WR were obliged to maintain separate accounts. The term of the lease was to be for 35 years from the date of assignment. Provision was made for a renewal of the lease, the terms of renewal to be agreed on or before the determination of the first thirty years. In the event of the lease not being renewed, the D&WR were obliged to hand over a 'competent and sufficient plant, or stock of carriages and locomotive engines to enable the Kingstown company ... to carry on the traffic on the Railway from Dublin to Kingstown, with the extension thereof to

Dalkey in a full and efficient manner'. A schedule to the agreement listed all of the assets being handed over.

By an Indenture dated 1st October 1859, the terms of the lease were retrospectively altered to the previous January to remove the compensation rent. This latter rent was introduced to safeguard the D&KR in the event of the 3Ws diverting traffic from the Kingstown line. The amount to be paid for any loss so suffered was to be decided by arbitration.

As from 1st January 1865, the lease was further altered to a term of 980 years (999 years from the date of the 1847 Act). The fixed rent was increased to £36,000 per annum and the contingent rent done away with. This agreement was given effect to by Act of 18th May 1866. Section 6 of this Act contained an important provision in that should any railway or tramway capable of competing with the D&KR traffic be made and opened for public traffic, and the DW&WR in good faith oppose it, then the lease should revert to the position pertaining in 1859.

To complete the story as regards the D&WR, some additional items require mention at this stage. In May 1856, it was decided to dispense with Brunel's services as consulting engineer to the company as from 30th June, although later in the year the directors decided to appoint Barry Gibbons at a salary of £300. He in turn was replaced

Left: **Newcastle looking towards Greystones with the down island platform on the right. The signal cabin is the 1923 replacement of the 1888 McKenzie & Holland cabin which was destroyed in September 1922.**
T Cott - IRRS collection

Bottom: **Wicklow Junction, looking south, with the main line to Wexford curving to the right away from the line straight ahead to Wicklow old station. The headshunt in the foreground was part of the original double line and later formed part of the Chemical Company sidings. The 1877 signal cabin, which was dispensed with in 1927, is visible on the left.**
T Cott - IRRS collection

by William Le Fanu, who in July 1857 was ordered to prepare plans for a terminus at Harcourt Street, as it had been decided to abandon the proposed extension to St Stephen's Green. In due course these were approved and tenders accepted from John Cunningham for the building of the new station at £8,502 and from Messrs Courtney & Stephens at £1,666 for the bridge over Harcourt Road. Cunningham was censured for delays in completion of the work, but the station was finally opened on 7th February 1859 after an inspection by Captain Ross of the Board of Trade. In November 1858, the company applied to the BoW for permission to lay rails from Kingstown station to the new pier in connection with improved postal services. The work was carried out at the expense of the BoW, Colonel Yolland inspecting the works on 9th September 1859. He laid down some requirements,

including signalling, before he would approve it for use. The line was duly opened for traffic on 23rd December, following a further BoT inspection. It was agreed to work the single line section on the basis of one engine in steam.

In March 1859, following a report from the Traffic Manager on improving the service between Dublin and Dundrum, the decision was taken to double this section of line. Although completed in February 1860 and instructions being given for its immediate use, it does appear to have been brought into use until the Dundrum to Shanganagh doubling was completed on 15th July 1861. The decision to double the latter section had been taken on 30th March 1860. The work was initially carried out by the company's own men but was transferred on 6th July to Thomas Edwards who was to be paid not more than £5,000 for the work.

Suggestions were made to the board in October 1859 regarding an extension into the county of Wexford, Gorey being suggested. The plans for, and the construction of the various extensions to Wexford will be considered in the next chapter.

In conclusion, it may be of interest to note the figures quoted in April 1859 for passenger traffic between Dublin and Bray as between the two lines for the period 1st July 1858 to 2nd April 1859:

Passengers	Receipts
Harcourt Street to Bray – 55,354	£2,607.15s. 1d.
Bray to Harcourt Street – 44,458	£2,245.16s.11d.
Westland Row to Bray – 8,257	Not quoted.
Bray to Westland Row – 5,327	Not quoted.

Chapter Three

FURTHER EXPANSION

EVEN before the line was open to Bray, plans were being formulated for an extension from Wicklow to Woodenbridge, a point forming 'an intersection of the leading roads of the county and well calculated to embrace both the mineral and ordinary traffic of the county'. Delays in the opening to Bray and the lack of a final agreement with the D&KR obviously persuaded the directors to forego the extension at this time. The only item of note in relation to the extension plans was that there would have been a short spur joining the Wicklow terminus to the new line near Broadlough, thus creating a triangular junction. In December 1854, the Wicklow Mineral Railway made a brief appearance with plans for a railway from Newbridge (Ovoca) to Wicklow. Powers were to be sought for the D&WR to subscribe to and make traffic arrangements, as well as supplying engines and rolling stock. Within two months however, the Bill had been withdrawn and no more was heard of the project.

A more serious proposal came to light in 1858 under the title of the Wicklow & Enniscorthy Junction Railway Company, a project which had the support of a number of the principal landowners. Obviously anxious to avoid serious competition, the directors now turned their thoughts to an extension of their own, Gorey being suggested in November 1858. Terms were agreed with Le Fanu to act as engineer for the extension line and he was directed to prepare the necessary plans in connection with the parliamentary application. Whilst these preparations were being made, the directors had other pressing matters to worry them. At the March 1858 shareholders' meeting, the Chairman, Joseph Hone Jnr, had reported a falling off in passenger traffic on the Wicklow line, which he attributed to a reduction in pleasure traffic. Whilst goods traffic was showing a considerable increase, the facilities for dealing with it were far from adequate and would remain so until the new station at Harcourt Street was completed. The matter was again referred to at the September meeting, when the Chairman pointed out that they were almost obliged to discourage goods traffic for want of accommodation at Harcourt Road. As against this, new houses were springing up in Killiney, Bray and Dun-drum, auguring well for an increase in passenger traffic.

A shareholder, a Mr Smith, referred to apparent omissions in the Chairman's report. Was the work at Harcourt Street being done by contract and what was the estimated cost of this work? Though the number of passengers on the Wicklow line had increased by some 11,000 in the half year, the income of the shareholders had actually decreased. He also referred to a steamer service put on by the British & Irish Steampacket Company between Dublin and Wexford, which must be diverting traffic from the line. Matters took a sinister turn in November, when a special meeting was held in Dublin to consider the removal of some or all of the directors and also the propriety of extending to Gorey. Smith again led the questioning, enquiring as to those directors who held a similar position with the D&KR. In reply to various queries in relation to the current position of the company, Hone pointed out that when he joined the board in 1855 the affairs of the company were in 'the greatest confusion and difficulty', whereas they were now in a more prosperous condition. An attempt by Smith and others to have some of the directors removed from office proved unsuccessful. *The Railway Times* commented that 'the agitation which has for some time disturbed this company, harassed the board and weakened the management generally, has at length been finally and completely disposed of'. The matter of the Gorey extension was postponed for further consideration.

At an adjourned meeting held on 19th November, the chairman spelt out the reasons why the directors had unanimously concluded that the Gorey extension was a most desirable measure. By going inland from Wicklow, the line would pass through a rich agricultural tract of land and furthermore, the country was thickly populated with a vast number of resident gentry. At a conservative estimate, the whole line would bring in £6,000 per annum from passengers, while 100,000 tons of minerals from Ovoca would give a minimum of £15,000. With easier access to the sea, this latter tonnage could increase considerably. Other goods traffic would add an additional £13,000, and with working expenses calculated at 40%, there would be sufficient to provide a 9% dividend. A Mr Samuels disputed Hone's remarks in that whilst the line as far as Arklow would undoubtedly provide a good income, there was not a more bleak and unprofitable road than that from Arklow to Gorey. If the landed gentry of Counties Wicklow and Wexford wanted railway accommodation, let them put their hands in their pockets. Another shareholder, Martin Burke, said he believed the Wicklow company was 'the only one in the world that had never taken a carrier off the road'. His view was that they should not go beyond Woodenbridge. A Mr Flood went further, believing in the existing state of the company's affairs, that they should not think of any extensions until the original shareholders were in receipt of a 4% dividend.

Despite continuing reservations, the shareholders' approval was given for the Gorey extension at the half-yearly meeting in February 1859; in fact, at a shareholders' meeting in April, Smith actually urged the directors to proceed with all haste to Enniscorthy! The Gorey Extension Act received Royal Assent on 8th August 1859. Additional capital in an amount of £200,000 was authorised, along with further borrowing of £66,000. Section 18 of the Act recognised that it would be necessary for the company to take or affect portions of the private mineral tramway belonging to Henry Hodgson of Ballyraine House. An agreement with Hodgson was incorporated as a schedule to the Act. Before outlining the terms of the schedule, a brief background to the mineral tramway would be in order.

Mining in the Avoca area goes back to pre-Christian times, modern operations dating from the mid-eighteenth century. The mines were situated on both sides of the valley and as far as the Avoca Mineral Tramway is concerned, we are interested in the workings at Ballymurtagh and Ballygahan, both situated on the west, or right-hand, side as one travels towards Arklow. The Hibernian Mine Company was incorporated in 1792, powers being granted to 'hold and enjoy all powers and privileges of the harbour of Arklow' and to construct a canal thence to Ovoca; a branch was also envisaged to Aughrim and the coalfields at Kilkenny. There would seem to have been major differences between the proprietors, and production at the mine had ceased by about 1803, with no attempt having been made to construct the canal.

On 13th May 1822, the Hibernian Mine Company entered into an agreement with Cheyne Brady and Henry Hodgson (locally pronounced Hudson) to lease the mine for 31 years. Hodgson in particular saw great potential in the mine and in due course succeeded in turning the operation into a profit-making venture. The Wicklow Copper Mine Company was incorporated in June 1827 to take over the working of the Ballymurtagh mine. At this period, due in part to the inadequacies of the port of Arklow, ores could be held for as long as four months in winter, while the smelting works in South Wales ran short. In addition, all of the Ovoca mines were in an area ill-served by roads. Minerals were transported by road to either Arklow or Wicklow and, up until the time of the Great Famine, as many as 2,000 people gained employment carrying ores to the ports. The large de-population arising from the famine led Hodgson to consider an alternative means of transport and the idea of a tramway was born. It is not clear exactly when the tramway was opened, but suffice to say that it ran initially from Ballygahan, later with a branch from Ballymurtagh, to the South Quay at Arklow, a distance of about eight miles. The gauge was 3ft 6in. Initially horses were used on the tramway hauling two trucks, each holding two tons of ore. Locomotives able to take 18 laden wagons each were later employed. It may be of interest to note that the output of Ballygahan mine in 1855 was 12,200 tons, while three years earlier, Ballymurtagh produced 30,763 tons. The importance of the tramway is evident from these figures.

The schedule to the 1859 Act laid down that Hodgson was to be paid a sum of £16,000 on the company taking possession of the tramway and rolling stock. The latter is shown as consisting of two locomotives and 100 wagons. It was agreed that Hodgson would continue to work the tramway until 1st January 1862, or until the DW&WR were in a position to carry ores to the port of Arklow. The payment of the £16,000 was to be made on 1st January 1861, with the option to withhold it for a further year on payment of interest at 5%. On 29th April 1861 the company paid Hodgson £19,850 for the tramway and its rolling stock, the latter being handed over to Mr O'Connor of the Wicklow Copper Mine Company, who operated the tramway under contract for the company from 1st May 1861 at £3,000 per annum.

On 3rd May 1863 the company took up the working of the tramway from the Wicklow Copper Mine Co, retaining the services of the Tramway Manager, Mr O'Connor, and the rest of the staff of the tramway. At the same time, one further locomotive and 12 mineral wagons, belonging to the WCM Company, were purchased for £576.

The directors had already decided to extend the line through to Enniscorthy and prepared to lodge a Bill. This became law on 15th May 1860. Under this Act, the company changed its name to the Dublin, Wicklow & Wexford Railway, as more befitted its extended status, and it was authorised to raise additional capital up to £100,000, and borrow in addition up to one-third of this amount.

Opening To Rathdrum

In December 1859, Le Fanu submitted plans for the Gorey extension, to be completed in three divisions – Wicklow to Woodenbridge, Woodenbridge to Arklow and Arklow to Gorey. Reporting in February 1860, the *Railway Times* stated that the works were to be done as cheaply as possible, and that sufficient time needed to be allowed so that the company would be in a position to provide the necessary capital. In March, following correspondence with the BoT, it was agreed to substitute a wooden bridge at Broadlough at the Murrough in Wicklow in place of the iron bridge first proposed. Also in March, tenders were submitted for the first division of the extension, that of Thomas Edwards at £96,200 being accepted. It was agreed that plans and estimates be at once prepared for the second division. Meanwhile, in May it was ordered that two viaducts of stone, with five arches, each of 45ft span, be substituted for the iron-decked seven span viaducts planned near Rathdrum.

Also in May 1861, tenders were opened for station buildings at Glenealy and Kilcommon, that of James Douglas of Granville Street, Dublin, being the lowest, was accepted at £845 for the two. It was also arranged that an engine house be provided at the latter by re-erecting a wooden shed lately pulled down at Bray. By the following November, with about 1,000 men at work, Edwards advised that he was hopeful of having the line to Rathdrum ready for opening by 1st June 1861. In the event, it was to be 20th August before the line was opened to Kilcommon, a little over a mile north of the present Rathdrum station, following a BoT inspection by Captain Tyler. The section from Kilcommon to Rathdrum was being excavated in deep cutting and this, with the construction of Rathdrum viaduct, led to slow progress.

Stations were opened at Milltown and Foxrock, respectively in 1860 and 1861, the latter at the request of a Mr Bentley who provided the necessary land. He also agreed to guarantee minimum receipts of £300 per annum, and within a year of opening he was being asked for a shortfall of £74. Later in the year, a number of requests were made for sidings. The Mining Company of Ireland, who mined lead ore at Glendalough and Glenmalure, enquired about carrying ore from Rathdrum to Shankill for smelting at Ballycorus. Le Fanu was requested to prepare plans for the necessary siding at Shankill. It was estimated that this would cost £231.10s.4d and it was ordered to be constructed. Hodgson approached the board later in the year in connection with the carriage of ore from Rathdrum to Carrickmines, and was informed that a siding was being put in at Shankill and should be ready for use by 1st January 1862. A request was also received from the Hibernian Brick, Tile & Drain Pipe Works at Wicklow for a siding to their factory, which was provided.

Left: **The station house at Kilcommon, the site of the temporary station for Rathdrum prior to the completion of the Rathdrum viaduct, looking towards Wicklow.**
T Cott - IRRS collection

The Company Secretary, Arthur Moore, announced his resignation in February 1862 on his appointment to a similar post with the Bristol & Exeter Railway. A presentation of a mounted clock was made to Moore, on the occasion of which, comment was passed as to the manner in which he had zealously, ably and honourably carried out his duties during the past five years. He was replaced by Edward Maunsell, who had been the Secretary to the Limerick & Ennis and the Waterford & Limerick Railways. Later in the year, Mortimer Harris, the Traffic Manager from the beginning resigned on the grounds of ill health and was replaced by William L Payne from the W&LR at a salary of £400 per annum, plus house.

Edwards was given the £36,000 contract for the second division of the new line in May 1862. At the half-yearly meeting in August 1862, the Chairman reported that there was a desire on the part of the company to have a communication with the Quays at Kingstown. To give effect to this, an approach had been made to the BoW for liberty to lay down a tramway, so that ores could be carried direct to the ships' sides. Permission was readily given and the connection to the Traders' or Mineral Wharf was opened early in 1863. A rent of £100 per annum was payable, and the company were obliged, on a month's notice from the BoW, to remove the tramway and reinstate the quay as it was previously. Tenders were received in January 1863 for the stations at Rathdrum and Newbridge (Ovoca), those of Cockburne being accepted at £3,400 and £995 respectively. The tender of a Mr Byrne was also accepted for alterations required at Westland Row to cater for the English mails. On 13th February Wilkinson submitted plans for the station buildings at Arklow, Gorey, Ferns and Enniscorthy. Tenders for their construction were received in March, Cockburne once again being successful at £700, £1,510, £1,180 and £3,100 respectively. It was stipulated that these be completed by 1st August 1863. It was ordered that a footbridge be put in at Rathdrum; this was provided by Messrs Courtney & Stephens at a cost of £48. This bridge was the scene of a potentially serious accident described in Chapter Ten.

The 6¾ mile section from Kilcommon to Ovoca was opened for traffic on 18th July 1863, following an inspection by Captain Rich a week earlier. After the inspection, the entire party were entertained by the contractor at Avondale. It was hoped that this short extension would increase receipts considerably, particularly with the Mineral Wharf line also open. At the half-yearly meeting in August 1863, it was reported that Le Fanu had resigned as Consulting Engineer on his appointment as Engineer to the BoW. He was in due course succeeded by Messrs Cotton & Flemyng. Work proceeded rapidly

Above: **An 1860s view of the Rathdrum viaduct, just north of Rathdrum station. This impressive structure was built in lieu of an earlier design using wrought iron girders on stone piers. Early semaphore signals controlling the entry of trains to the station stand at the near end of the viaduct.** IRRS collection

with the section to Enniscorthy which had more engineering difficulties. Edwards had been granted the entire contract from Arklow to Enniscorthy for £73,000. Captain Rich was back in mid-November to inspect the Enniscorthy extension and being satisfied with this, the line was opened for traffic on 16th November. The *Railway Times* reported 'crowds of country people assembled at the various stations to witness . . . the evidently novel spectacle of the arrival of the train. It was Fair Day at Enniscorthy and about 1,000 congregated at the station'. While opened as a single line, provision had been made for doubling if found necessary. The only other significant event of 1863 was the fact that a plan and estimate were submitted for a house for the station master at Rathdrum. Michael Clarke was awarded the contract at £362. During the year, working expenses were 42% as against 45% for 1862. This was regarded as a very creditable performance, as all other companies' expenses had increased, most of the others ranging from 45 to 49%, although the Bagenalstown & Wexford figure was 133%!

The Shillelagh Branch

The first moves towards the construction of a branch to Shillelagh were taken in the autumn of 1862 when the directors agreed on the heads of a notice for a Bill to give effect to the planned line. At a poorly attended meeting of shareholders held on 27th October, the Chairman said he hoped

the small attendance was proof that shareholders were not opposed to the scheme. The proposed line would be 16 miles in length, of which the Earl of Fitzwilliam had generously given the land for 12, together with £1,000 towards the preliminary expenses. It was reported by Le Fanu that the line should not cost more than £4,000 per mile, and it would open up a district of great value to the company, serving the towns of Hacketstown, Newtownbarry, Tullow, Carnew and Tinahely. The original Act of 1863 authorised a line from the main line, with the junction facing south and situated in the townland of Kilcarra West. A further Act in 1864 settled the point of junction about a mile further north and facing north.

Construction was commenced in March 1864 with Thomas Edwards as contractor and had reached Aughrim by the following June and Ballinglen three months later. By September 1864, the Honourable Frederick Ponsonby, agent to the Earl of Fitzwilliam, was urging speedy completion of the line and the provision of a station at Ballinglen. By now, various estimates had been submitted and approved – £736.5s.11d for station works at Shillelagh, £490 and £530 respectively for stations at Aughrim and Tinahely, plans for which had been prepared by the company's Architect, George Wilkinson. In the previous July, the tender of Messrs Courtney & Stephens at £487.3s.9d for the erection of signals on the branch, was approved. Early in February 1865, the directors made a tour of inspection of their new line as far as Tinahely and expressed their satisfaction with the works. During the course of their visit, they approved a plan and estimate for works at the junction at Woodenbridge costing £246.15s.1d. Messrs Fogarty's Mills in Aughrim approached the board at an early stage requesting a siding from Aughrim station into their mills and it

was agreed in April 1865 that this should be provided. The line was opened throughout to Shillelagh on 22nd May 1865, with a service of two trains each way. *The Wicklow Newsletter*, reporting on the opening, commented that the event created much interest in the newly-opened district, a number of persons collecting at the three stations on the branch to view the opening train as it passed. The Aughrim town band turned out for the occasion and the Earl of Fitzwilliam addressed the assembled crowd at Shillelagh and thanked the directors.

It would appear from the board minutes that no more than a temporary station was provided at Shillelagh, as it was not until August 1871 that a plan was put to the directors for a new station house and it was to be a further two years before it was completed. Ponsonby approached the board in February 1873 offering a sum of £100 together with a rent of £5 per annum for the exclusive use of a waiting room at Shillelagh for the Earl. Subsequently, it was agreed that he have such a room, after he had agreed to contribute £150 towards the cost of the station.

Top: **A pre-1888 photograph of Woodenbridge Junction, showing the original signal cabin and Courtney & Stephens signals.** K A Murray - IRRS collection

Above: **A view of Avoca looking towards Woodenbridge, with the goods yard and store on the left and the horsebox siding at the Dublin end of the up platform on the right.** T Cott - IRRS collection

Heating, lighting and cleaning of the room were to be at the Earl's expense. In the interim, further requests were being made for a station at Ballinglen, or Drummin which was the local townland. The company continued to decline to provide such a station 'having regard to the requirements of the BoT'. In 1874, Ponsonby informed the company that an agreement existed whereby they were obliged to provide a station, the company informing him that they could trace no such agreement. However in March 1875, Maunsell, the Company Secretary, informed the board that he had found among other papers 'a certain letter regard-

ing a station at Ballinglen'. By the following December, it was reported that the station house at Ballinglen was ready for occupation, being opened for passenger and parcels business on Monday, 3rd January 1876. A request for the establishment of a goods station here in February 1876 was declined unless a sufficient sum was paid by the residents of the district. Various approaches were made and declined, the siding being eventually installed in February 1882. To control access to the siding, a set of points with Annett's lock were transferred from Bray Head.

During the late 1870s and 1880s, a number of schemes were put forward for extensions of the branch. In September 1878, Henry Brett CE, waited on the board suggesting a possible line from Tinahely to Hacketstown. At about the same time, a line was being proposed from Shillelagh to Castlecomer. Both of these schemes were considered undesirable by the company. A further such scheme was proposed by a Mr Strype CE in August 1882 for a line from Shillelagh to Newtownbarry and Tullow. This time, the company confirmed they would work the line if built, at a percentage of gross receipts. A year later, it was proposed to run the line on to Carlow, the company agreeing to work it. The scheme was foreshortened in October 1883, when the company offered to work a line from Shillelagh to Newtownbarry at 50% of receipts, if made to the satisfaction of the Company's Engineer. In the following December, Strype attended a board meeting and suggested an extension from Newtownbarry to either Scarawalsh Bridge or Ferns. A further suggestion in February 1884 was that the company should lease the entire line for 35 years, which they agreed to do.

Matters had progressed sufficiently by June 1884 for a special board meeting to be held 'to consider the draft agreement for working the Scarawalsh Light Railway'. It was decided to extend the period of working beyond 35 years, so long as the Baronies extended their guarantee. When the gross receipts exceeded £10,000 per annum, the DW&WR were to receive the entire of such excess, they providing the rolling stock and all necessary working staff, including gangers and milesmen. It was agreed that there would be stations at Carnew, Clonegal, Newtownbarry, Clohamon and Scarawalsh, the DW&WR to have power to close any station found not to pay. Nothing further happened as regards the light railway, it would appear due to the company losing interest in the scheme. However, an announcement in the *Evening Herald* for 29th July 1896 of a large and influential meeting in Enniscorthy to persuade the GS&WR to make an extension from their Tullow branch to Enniscorthy via Newtownbarry, spurred the company to action. An Act of 1897 empowered the company to construct a line from Shillelagh via Newtownbarry to Scarawalsh. The time for completion of the works was extended for five years under a 1902 Act, but this was to be the end of the proposal.

There is little else to report as regards the branch. In connection with BoT requirements for the interlocking of points and signals under the Regulation of Railways Act of 1889, estimates were prepared in a total amount of £1,353.2s.6d. In May 1891, Smith and Payne recommended that Aughrim, Tinahely and Shillelagh should be worked as single platform stations, with loops at the former two for crossing goods trains. It was also suggested that the signal cabins at these stations be placed adjacent to the passenger exit doors so that the, 'signal porters', might take up tickets. At this time, it was also proposed to make Ballinglen a block post, but this was not pursued.

Towards Wexford

Having decided to go as far as Enniscorthy, it was realised that the obvious goal should be Wexford which had a port, albeit not a good one from the point of view of cross-channel traffic. It is hardly surprising therefore to find the company obtaining an Act for such an extension in June 1864. The railway was to commence by an end-on junction with the Enniscorthy extension and terminate, 'at or near the North-west Side of Slaney Street in the Parish of Saint Selskar's'. The company was empowered to raise additional capital to the extent of £150,000 and borrowing up to £50,000. Obtaining an Act was one thing but the construction of the line was to be a different matter as it proved extremely difficult to obtain the necessary finances. Brief details are given in Chapter Five of the inland scheme of the Bagenalstown & Wexford Railway to reach Wexford. There is little doubt that it was this latter project which finally spurred the DW&WR to commence the last 15 mile section from Enniscorthy to Wexford. Even before tenders were sought for its construction, it was necessary to return to Parliament for powers to extend the time for construction. These were obtained by an Act of June 1868.

Orders were given in October 1864 for the mineral siding at Ovoca to be lengthened at a cost of £159.9s.4d. At the half-yearly meeting in February 1865, Dargan, who was by now Chairman of the Board, mentioned that a great deal of time and trouble had been devoted to making preparations for carrying the mineral traffic from the Ovoca mines, and a large sum expended in providing suitable rolling stock, sidings and platforms for it. However, the mining companies had not been sending forward their consignments with sufficient regularity to enable the company's staff to be kept fully employed. To meet this in some degree, rates were increased at the beginning of 1865, but

these were being resisted by the mining companies. Some measure of agreement was reached later in the year, although by now, the mines were past their best in terms of production and from this time onwards, carryings began to drop. This resulted in the conversion of mineral wagons for other uses.

Requests were made during 1864 for a station at Rathnew, approval being given in October. Three months later, the tender of Patrick Byrne at £398.9s.0d was accepted. The station was opened for traffic on 1st September 1866, the station at Killoughter being closed on 1st April 1867. Requests for the latter's re-opening were made both in 1871 and 1894, but were declined on both occasions. A Bill was put forward in 1865 for a railway to join the D&KR at Sydney Parade with the DW&WR near Ranelagh. Whilst it received Royal Assent in July 1865, nothing further was to be heard of it. In June 1865, an estimate for £419.2s.2d was submitted by Cotton & Flemyng for a short branch to the Connorree Mining Company; this was provided but was short-lived, being taken out in 1869 due to non-payment of charges: the rails were used for Davis's siding at St John's near Enniscorthy. Requests for stations at Inch and Camolin were declined though it was agreed to open a station at the latter location in July 1867 at an estimated cost of £105.

William Dargan, who had been a director since 1856 and Chairman for the years 1865-66, died early in 1867. Although in poor health, his death had obviously been precipitated by a fall from his horse in May 1865. The company had sought the closure of the station at Sandycove on a number of occasions, although the BoT had ordered that all trains should stop there as a condition of approval for opening the section of line from Kingstown to Dalkey following on its conversion from atmospheric working. Approval was finally granted by the BoT in May 1867. At the same time, plans were brought forward for a new station at Adelaide Road in Glenageary. Lords Longford and de Vesci gave land and a grant of £50 towards the works. It was agreed that a temporary station would be provided as soon as the resident engineer, Murphy, could have a platform and signalling erected. At Newcastle, a second platform was erected to allow trains to cross there. Following a collision at Bray early in 1868, Murphy was dismissed and was replaced by John Challoner Smith at a salary of £400 per annum. Smith had been resident engineer on the W&LR under George Hemans and in 1861 had moved to the W&KR. He was to remain with the DW&WR until 1894, a year before his death. In 1868, Messrs Shaw & McMullen & Company approached the board in connection with the establishment of a chemical works at Wicklow. It was agreed to allow them use

surplus water from Wicklow station and subsequently in May, it was agreed that a siding be put in to the factory at an estimated cost of £135. At the half-yearly meeting in June, Mr A Parker in the chair, apologised for the non-attendance of the Chairman and his deputy, who were in London seeking Government assistance. Parker also apologised that, despite promises made to the contrary, it would not be possible to repay the holders of 5% Preference stock, which was now due for redemption. The stock was a good and safe security, yet in the present state of the money markets, it had been impossible to repay them.

Tenders for the Wexford extension were submitted to the board on 22nd December 1868 and after being considered it was decided 'to postpone the subject of the extension for the present'. Reporting to the board in the following April, Sir James Power stated that he had had interviews with the greater number of the landed proprietors on the extension and all whom he had spoken to had agreed to give possession of their lands, postponing the time for payment for a year or eighteen months on being paid interest at 4%. The board met again on 14th April to consider the means of proceeding with the extension. Thomas Edwards attended this meeting and it was ordered that the necessary plans and valuations be lodged and application made to the BoW for the appointment of an arbitrator. Edwards having expressed his willingness to enter into a contract for execution of the works at cost price, he was requested to put forward a definite offer. His figure was £79,000, £20,000 for the Enniscorthy to Killurin section which was to be completed by 1st May 1870, and £59,000 for the balance to be completed by 1st December of the same year. On this basis it was ordered that a formal contract be drawn up, this being duly signed a fortnight later. It was agreed in April 1869 that work would commence at Killurin. Messrs Samuel & Abraham G Davis, who had a large mill at St John's, one mile to the south of Enniscorthy, wrote to the board in November 1869 offering to forego a claim for land compensation if the company would provide a siding to their mill. Further details appear in a later chapter.

As we shall see, the proposed dates were not met. In November 1869, the directors paid a visit to Wexford for the purpose of deciding on the site for the terminus there, this being approved as the piece of land between the New Road and the river. At the board meeting on 13th January 1870, Sir James Power urged the early opening of the extension to the tunnel at Carrig Bridge, a point 1¼ miles from the Metal Bridge at Wexford. A week later, Messrs Cotton & Flemyng wrote to the board suggesting that the most convenient site for a temporary station at Wexford would be at the western boundary of Cullentra, some three English miles from Wexford. The cost of providing a temporary terminus, including purchase of land, would be £1,650. Consideration of the matter was postponed, Cotton in the meantime being requested to report on the cost of completing the line from Enniscorthy to Cullentra.

Addressing the shareholders at the end of January, Waldron reported considerable progress with the extension, the tunnel at Ferrycarrig having been commenced at both ends and the earth works on the remainder of the line were also being pushed forward as much as possible. However, the company was still finding it difficult to raise the necessary finances. Negotiations had been taking place with the L&NWR seeking assistance, this being agreed in September 1869, when they confirmed that they would advance £30,000 towards the extension on the understanding that 600 fully paid-up Preference shares of 1865 be transferred to them. This agreement was incorporated in the Company's Act of 1870. In February the Wexford Harbour Commissioners had threatened to oppose powers being sought in a further Bill in connection with an extension 1 mile 4 furlongs and 85 yards in length from Carrick to a point at the southern approach to the old bridge at Wexford situated opposite to the county court house. The objection referred to a portion of the new extension where it was to cross the Cot Dock. It should be mentioned that a cot was a boat used for salmon fishers, a very primitive vessel, not unlike a canoe, propelled by paddles resembling a common spade. It was estimated that some 400 boats were operating on the river, giving direct employment to 800 people. A clause was inserted in the 1870 Act for the protection of Wexford Harbour. In April however, William Gaffney wrote to the company urging the directors to review the site of the proposed station as its location would involve the acquisition of his storage yard, but they declined to reconsider the matter.

Cotton & Flemyng reporting on progress in June stated that it would not now be necessary to line the tunnel at Ferrycarrig which would effect a saving of £298 but as against this there was a requirement for further expenditure of £500 in preparing foundations for Ardcandrish Bridge necessitated by a subsidence and slip of the embankment there. In January 1871, Edwards was summoned to the board room and was urged to greater speed in executing the works on the extension. Edwards complained that it was impossible to obtain a sufficient number of men without a considerable increase of wages and asked the assistance of the board. They were not very sympathetic to the problem and Cotton & Flemyng were requested to report on Edwards' efforts up to that time. Later in the month, Edwards suggested that he be paid a premium of £2,500 as a condition for undertaking to open the extension by 1st November. He requested that he be given possession of all lands before 1st March and that rails be delivered at the rate of 100 tons per week from 1st May. Orders were given for Keogh to obtain possession of any lands required. Plans for Killurin station were approved in May 1871, William Wardrop's tender at £481.16s.7d being approved in May 1872. At Wexford, Wakefield suggested the provision of an oil store, smithy and fitter's shop as an extension to the locomotive shed. It was agreed to transfer the turntable from Wicklow to the new temporary station at Wexford, that at Enniscorthy to be moved to Wexford when the permanent station was ready. Messrs Cotton & Flemyng's attention was called in July 1872 to the want of a locomotive shed and water tank, these and the forge being estimated to cost £311. This work was ordered to be undertaken at once, and two new water columns provided at Enniscorthy.

Also in July, Edwards was referred to the great importance of opening the extension as soon as possible. It was thought that greater exertions might be made on his part. The half-yearly report once again referred to the difficulty in procuring labour, but the Chairman confidently spoke of an opening by the end of the year. The end of the year came and the line was not completed. Cotton stated that it should now be open by 1st May 1872.

Meanwhile in October, it was ordered that a plan and estimate be submitted for a temporary station on the Enniscorthy side of the Free bridge. It would appear that this matter was not immediately followed through as it was not until the following February that a sketch of the proposed temporary wooden station was submitted along with Messrs T & C Martin's estimate for £104.10s.0d for its erection. Nor had the station been built at Killurin, for Smith was advised to await the laying of rails to that point before commencing to build the station there.

Both Cotton and Edwards attended the board meeting on 11th July 1872 and stated that the line would be ready for the Government inspection within a fortnight. In fact, Lieutenant Colonel Hutchinson inspected the extension to Carcur on 29th July but found a number of items requiring further attention. The permanent way consisted of 71lb flat bottomed rail in various lengths secured to transverse sleepers; ballast was of broken stone and gravel; in all there were 48 bridges, viaducts and large culverts, the Slaney Bridge at Enniscorthy consisting of seven spans of 30 ft each. Enniscorthy tunnel came in for criticism, where there were some projecting points of rock in the unlined portion. Ballasting was defective and the fencing was inadequate in some places. In addition, clocks were called for at Wexford and Killurin stations and the signalling at both ends of the line and at Killurin was also inadequate. Hutchinson returned again on 16th August and this time he pronounced the line fit for opening subject to a few minor matters. It was opened to traffic on the next day with a service of three trains each way on weekdays to and from Dublin. There was in addition a train from Ovoca.

Within two months of the Wexford extension being opened, Cotton & Flemyng were requested to report on the cost of laying down a tramway from the temporary terminus at Wexford into Gaffney's yard there. On receipt of this information, instructions were given for the tramway to be constructed as soon as possible. Permission was sought to lay the tramway for wagons along the public road outside Gaffney's yard. The Town Clerk replied in December enquiring whether the company would be prepared to make a new road if the present one were given up for the tramway. In reply, the company rightly pointed out that they did not require exclusive use of the road in question but only permission to lay down a tramway to be worked by horse power. Despite this, the corporation refused permission for the tramway.

The question of a joint station for the use of the company and the Waterford & Wexford Railway was also considered. In January 1873 an order was placed with Messrs Courtney & Stephens for a new wrought iron turntable at a cost of £365, to include erection. In April 1873, the agent of the Liverpool & Wexford Steamship Company had written asking that a further berth be assigned for vessels in the yard, this being refused but four months later, Smith was ordered to construct two timber jetties at Gaffney's Yard, subject to the approval of the Harbour Commissioners. These were agreed to subject to the company giving an undertaking not to charge dues for ships using them. On 17th April, Cotton & Flemyng submitted a plan for working traffic over the tramway. Edwards wrote on 22nd May stating that the tramway from the temporary station into Gaffney's Yard would be ready for opening by 10th June. Work was by now being carried out at the site of the permanent station in Wexford.

Complaints had been made in November 1873 of slow progress on the permanent station by Edwards, while in the following May, Smith, Payne and Wakefield were ordered to confer with the consulting engineers and fix up the exact site for this station so that the platforms might be proceeded with as soon as possible. From this it would appear as if the original plan was to have two platforms at Wexford but of course the station was constructed with only one on the up side of the line.

The question of the tramway was raised once again in May 1874 when a renewed application was made for permission to lay one along the Quay from the goods depot at the end of Monck Street. This time success was achieved, both the WHC and the Corporation consenting, the latter body asking that it extend as far as the Crescent which was agreed to. In June, Smith was authorised to arrange with a Mr Wardrop for the removal of the temporary station, his tender being accepted in July. The engine shed was actually removed to the new station by the company's men in September. Hutchinson inspected the new extension and reported on 17th August. The short line was 42 chains in length and the only work of note was an overbridge of 14ft span. His only criticism was in relation to signalling but he passed the line for opening, this taking place some days later. Messrs Cotton & Flemyng were also satisfied with the works, and recommended in September that the line be taken over from Edwards.

Another Rival for Wexford
To the south of Wexford, plans were put forward in 1863 for a railway from Ballyhack, the termination of the ferry from Passage East, via Duncormick to make a connection with the authorised extension of the DW&WR. In addition, a branch was proposed to Greenore Bay where a new harbour was to be constructed. In the previous year the Waterford & Passage Railway had been authorised and the two lines would therefore have provided through communication between Waterford and Wexford, apart from the short ferry crossing, although the parties involved even had a scheme for spanning this gap with a bridge. The Waterford & Wexford Railway was duly incorporated by Act of Parliament in July 1864.

Five years later and with no construction commenced, the line from Ballyhack or Arthurstown was abandoned. As originally planned, the W&WR was to run around the back of the town at Wexford, but in 1869 plans were put forward for a line along the Quays, necessitating the construction of a wharf. The Wexford Harbour Commissioners agreed to such a line being built. Also in 1869, application was made for the construction of the harbour at Greenore Bay, a harbour authority being set up to take over the powers of the W&WR in relation to its construction.

An Act was obtained in 1871 for an extension of time and the contract to build the Wexford to Rosslare railway was awarded in the following year to Messrs Barnett & Gale of London. Work commenced in March 1873 and by the following August, Rosslare Harbour was also under construction, although progress was slow on both fronts.

Application was made in 1874 to the Public Works Loan Commissioners for a loan but this was refused, a further application being made in the following year. This time the application was referred to the Treasury on the understanding that the GWR would agree to allow rebates on traffic brought to them via the new line. Despite this, the Treasury refused to sanction a loan, reportedly due to the extremely slow progress of the works.

As early as January 1871, the DW&WR had made an application for the right of user of the line along the Quay, this being granted by the WHC and by the W&WR, the necessary clauses being inserted in the latter's Bill. In June 1871, the WHC having further considered the proposed quay line, suggested that in addition to the running line, a siding should also be provided on the piled wharf so as to avoid any delay or danger if the one line was used for through traffic and for the loading and unloading of vessels at the Quay.

In May 1874 the DW&WR applied to run a horse tramway as a temporary measure along the Quay facilitating the loading of vessels.

Below: **A view of the north end of Enniscorthy station, taken from the water tower in GSR days, with the engine shed on the left and the goods store opposite. This scene with two goods trains present, portrays the busy nature of this station in earlier years.** IRRS collection

Having considered the plans submitted by Smith, the Harbour Commissioners agreed to the tramway on condition that it be removed on 30 days notice, the quay being restored to its original state.

By February 1876, some three miles of the DW&W line had been laid, a rather poor average of one mile per annum. In April the W&WR Secretary, H E Wynne, wrote to the DW&WR seeking a working agreement for their line when completed, based on a percentage of receipts. He was informed that in the absence of information as to the likely receipts of the line, it would not be possible to come up with an offer. In May following receipt of a deputation from the W&WR, the DW&WR expressed their willingness to enter into a twelve month working agreement at 50% of the gross receipts, provided a substantial guarantee be given that the gross receipts would be not less than £6,000 per annum. Nothing further transpired until November 1877 when Wynne wrote suggesting that the Wicklow company should purchase or amalgamate with the W&WR, a suggestion which was declined. At this point, the original contractors withdrew from the scheme and arrangements were made for one of the Wexford county surveyors, Mr M J Farrell, to oversee the works. However, work soon came to a halt due to the company's inability to raise finances and it was not until a loan of £25,000 came from the BoW that some further progress could be made. Suffice to say that the line was finally completed in 1882 after further Acts had been obtained for extensions of time, the contract for its completion having been given to William Murphy in May 1880.

In November 1881, the DW&WR agreed that the line between the south end of Wexford Quay and the south end of Ballygeary Pier would be worked on the basis of one engine in steam, the section from the south end of the Quay to their Wexford station being worked by train staff.

Agreement was reached between the two companies in February 1882 for the DW&WR to work the line for a payment of £30 per week, the service to be two trains each way daily, Sundays included. Either company was to be at liberty to terminate the agreement on a month's notice. Agreement was also reached for the use of Wexford station by the Rosslare company. Following a BoT inspection, the line opened for traffic on 24th June 1882. At the end of the month, the W&WR requested that a third train be run daily and this was agreed to at an additional cost of 18s per day.

Although the BoT had passed the line, Smith found defects and there was a suggestion that the working by the DW&WR might cease but this difference appears to have been overcome.

The DW&WR laid in a siding at Rosslare in August at the expense of the W&WR, at a cost of £121.11s.9d. In December, Wynne wrote requesting a reduction in the charge for working the line in the coming three months and this was agreed to in January. The Rosslare company endeavoured to have the reduction carried into the summer months but this was declined. A request for the hire of ballast wagons in February 1886 was turned down, the Wicklow company being unable to spare any.

Difficulties emerged in May 1889 as the result of non-payment for the hire of rolling stock and the DW&WR advised they would withdraw their rolling stock as from Friday 17th May if the debt remained unpaid or no guarantee of payment was forthcoming. The W&WR refused to take up either option and the line effectively closed on that date.

Appeals from the Rosslare company and letters from the Town Clerk of Wexford deprecating the DW&WR's stand were of no avail. Worthington approached the Wicklow Board in July 1890 seeking to hire rolling stock which was readily offered on the same terms as had applied to the railway but it was 6th August 1894 before the line was re-opened to public traffic, being worked by the Fishguard & Rosslare Railways & Harbours Company which had now entered the arena. Later, in 1898, the working of the line was taken over by the GS&WR.

The only other DW&WR involvement at this stage was the completion of an agreement for the use of their station at Wexford. Following the 1925 amalgamation, the Wexford to Rosslare section was worked as part of the South Eastern section as regards main line services.

The single platform station at Wexford, southern terminus of the main line. The engine shed and signal box are both visible in the background. IRRS collection

Chapter Four

NEW ROSS & WATERFORD

W E SAW in Chapter Two how the WC&DJR had proposed a line to run down the Slaney gap to Wexford. These plans were aborted when the company amalgamated with the Great Leinster & Munster Railway to form the Irish South Eastern Railway. As originally incorporated, the ISER was to construct a main line from Carlow to Kilkenny, with branches from Kilkenny to Clonmel and from Carlow to Enniscorthy, but under the prevailing circumstances the directors wisely decided to concentrate on the first of these lines. The main line was opened throughout for traffic on 14th November 1850 and worked by the GS&WR. In July 1854, the nominally independent Bagenalstown & Wexford Railway was incorporated basically reviving the powers of the WC&DJR scheme for a line from Bagenalstown to Enniscorthy. Two branches had been proposed, one from a point some three miles north of Ballywilliam to New Ross, the other along the Slaney from Scarawalsh to Enniscorthy, but in the event, Parliament did not sanction these.

The first sod was cut on 1st January 1855 and the contract for the first division from Bagenalstown to Borris was awarded to J J Bagnell. Capital was slow to come in and it was not until 20th December 1858 that this eight mile section opened for traffic. This reduced the journey time to Wexford from Dublin by two hours.

Another Act was required in 1859 to extend the time for purchase of lands and construction. The second division, from Borris to Ballywilliam, was awarded to a Peter O'Reilly in 1859. It would appear that O'Reilly had little or no experience of railway works and it is perhaps hardly surprising that he went bankrupt in April 1861. Bagnell took over the contract and the section was opened on 17th March 1862, being worked by the GS&WR as was the first part of the line.

In July 1863, the ISER, finding itself in financial difficulties, was taken over by the GS&WR. William Haughton, who had become Chairman of the latter company in November 1860, was vehemently opposed to the B&WR scheme and on 19th December notice was given that the GS&WR would cease to work it. Having no rolling stock of their own and being unable to persuade the

W&LR to hire any to them, there was no option but to close the line. It was declared bankrupt in June 1864 and the company was put up for auction in the Bankruptcy Court on 6th January 1866. It was purchased by a London barrister, Standish H Motte, for a sum of £25,000. Motte succeeded in having an Act passed in 1866 for the Waterford, New Ross & Wexford Junction Railway, empowering the new company to purchase the B&WR line from him and to construct 33 miles of extensions, 19¼ miles from Ballywilliam to Waterford via New Ross and 13¾ miles from Ballywilliam to Macmine, where it would form a junction with the authorised Wexford extension of the DW&WR.

The contract for the Macmine extension was given to Edgeworth & Stanford, who were also required to put the existing line into proper working order. It was 5th September 1870 before the line was re-opened as far as Borris, followed on 26th October by the section to Ballywilliam, along with a 10½ mile extension to a temporary terminus at Sparrowsland. The line was worked at this period by the contractors.

Notice for a further Bill was published in November 1868 which would have the effect of abandoning the Waterford extension and constructing an alternative line to Wexford and altering the name to the Wexford & Carlow Junction Railway. Motte approached the DW&WR board offering to abandon the portion of his Bill for the Wexford extension if the DW&WR would undertake that if their own Wexford extension was not proceeded with within twelve months, they would not offer any opposition to him obtaining his Act the next year. This they declined to do. In 1871, Motte tried again, this time seeking running powers over the DW&WR from Enniscorthy to Wexford and following determined opposition from the DW&WR, the Bill was thrown out on Standing Orders in March. By now the latter company was proceeding with its own Wexford extension which was opened in August 1872.

The final piece of the WNR&WJR, the 3¾ miles from Sparrowsland to Macmine, was opened for traffic on 1st May 1873, a short item in *The People* (Wexford) recording the event. However the line was closed on 30th September as the result of the GS&WR engineer reporting it as being unsafe.

In the meantime, discussions had been taking place regarding the junction at Macmine, it being agreed in March 1874 that the DW&WR should have the right to appoint the signalmen, the cost of any necessary labour being shared jointly on the understanding that the WNR&WJR would convey a piece of land for the building of two houses for servants, the houses to be built by and at the expense of the DW&WR. About this time, Motte returned to practice at the Bar in London and this might have spelt the end of the line were it not for Arthur MacMurrough Kavanagh, MP for Carlow, who took over as Chairman. He was a remarkable man, having been born without limbs, despite which he became an MP and a successful business man. Kavanagh approached the GS&WR in January 1874 asking them to work the line, which they declined to do, although they did offer an engine and rolling stock. Traffic was resumed on 9th February 1874 and worked by the company itself.

In February of the following year, with losses mounting, Kavanagh approached the DW&WR asking them to make an offer for the purchase of the line. No decision was taken and three months later it became clear that the PWLC, who were owed loan repayments and interest on their investment in the scheme, intended to sell it, Smith being asked to report on its condition. An auction was announced for Tuesday 11th June, subsequently postponed to 27th July. The matter was referred to Moon, Chairman of the L&NWR, for their views on purchasing the line, their advice being to steer clear of it. Nevertheless in October, following a further approach from Kavanagh for the DW&WR to purchase the Ballywilliam to Macmine section, a conference was arranged with the GS&WR when agreement was reached for them to purchase the entire line for not more than £40,000, with the DW&WR having the option to purchase the southern section.

An Act giving effect to this was obtained during 1876, pending which the DW&WR initially undertook the working of the entire line from Bagenalstown as from 1st March, the GS&WR later working their own section north of Ballywilliam. When the DW&WR wrote to the GS&WR in regard to the advisability of extending the line from Ballywilliam to New Ross, the latter company

Above: **Macmine Junction in 1904, looking south towards Wexford. The signal cabin is just visible behind the footbridge on the down platform; a Waterford branch train stands behind the up island platform.**
H Fayle - IRRS collection

declined to become involved but did agree to join in a guarantee to give a Mr Wallis £18 per week for running a three-horse car on the route. In due course the purchase price of £16,000 plus interest at 5% from 1st March, was paid to the PWLC on 25th September.

Agreement was reached in June 1883 for DW&WR engines to work through to Kilkenny with pig specials, and in this context it was ordered in October 1884 that a charge of 1s.3d per mile should be levied on the GS&WR for this service. In August 1884, Payne was instructed to try and arrange with the GS&WR that their carriages should run through between Bagenalstown and Macmine in the summer months and those of the DW&WR in winter, but nothing appears to have become of this proposal.

The GS&WR took over the working of the Bagenalstown to Ballywilliam section in October, at which time it was ordered that the DW&WR trains should not wait more than 15 minutes for late running GS&WR trains.

Towards New Ross and Waterford
As previously stated, the original intention of the 3Ws as incorporated in 1846 was to construct a line from Dublin to Waterford. This line was to have formed a junction with the infant W&LR at Grannagh or Granny Ferry, 'if such last-mentioned railway shall be authorised to cross the said river (the Suir) at or near the said Ferry'. The uncertainty lay in the fact that section 27 of the W&LR's Act of 1845 stated that, 'the part of the railway from the South bank of the Suir below Granny Castle to the town of Carrick-on-Suir shall not be commenced or contracted for until ... the Board of Trade shall determine whether a line South of the River Suir between Granny Castle and Carrick-on-Suir, or what other line shall be adopted by the said railway company'.

In the event, the proviso was academic as the 3Ws were not destined to reach Waterford for a further 60 years.

When the GS&WR refused to become involved in an extension to New Ross, the DW&WR decided to draw up their own plans and these were put before the board in August 1876. In October, a special board meeting was held to consider whether application should be made to the Baronies for a guarantee of interest on the cost of construction of the line, but after a very full discussion it was agreed that this would be inexpedient. This did not deter the directors from making contact with the Chief Secretary for Ireland some three years later seeking Government assistance in completing the Waterford extension, a request which was turned down as the area through which that line was to run was not categorised as being distressed. When notice for the Bill was issued in November, the New Ross Town Commissioners announced their intention to oppose it unless a guarantee was given that the line would be brought into the town and the company would undertake to sell to the Commissioners any wharves or quays which they might construct on the Rosbercon side of the river. The company refused to give any such guarantee. It should be mentioned at this point that the proposed location of the station at New Ross was situated across the river from most of the town it was intended to serve. In due course the Act for the New Ross extension was passed in August 1877. The authorised line was to be 7 miles 2 furlongs and 27 yards long. Powers were also obtained at the same time for the doubling of the line from Kingstown to Dalkey and a diversion at Breache's Bridge near Newcastle. Additional capital up to £120,000 was authorised along with borrowing powers up to £40,000.

Long before any tenders were sought for this extension, the company turned their thoughts towards Waterford and in September 1877 we find Cotton & Flemyng submitting an estimate of £105,000 for such an extension. The decision was taken to proceed with this at a special board meeting held on 21st September, while some two weeks later Cotton submitted plans showing the line approaching Waterford from the west side of the river. There was to be a bridge across the River Suir to give access to the Waterford, Dungarvan & Lismore Railway. Cotton and Payne were deputed to see the WD&LR to ascertain the terms for a joint bridge across the river. Various meetings were held with the Dungarvan directors, arising out of which a draft agreement was put forward. Briefly, the DW&WR was to construct the bridge and both companies would jointly construct and work the station. The WD&LR would pay half of the cost of the bridge and station. The traffic of both lines was to be free, tolls from all other traffic were to be divided equally. The Wicklow company was to bear the cost of the Bill in Parliament provided it was unopposed. If it was opposed, each company was to pay half of the extra cost. Denny, the Dungarvan Chairman, wrote in November asking the DW&WR to co-operate in extending their line into the city and also with an extension from Fermoy to Cork. As regards the latter, the DW&WR declined to become involved and in relation to the Waterford end they sought more details.

The Waterford Extension Act received Royal Assent on 22nd July 1878. Four lines were authorised. The principal one was almost 14 miles long, from an end-on junction at New Ross to a point close to Newrath House in Waterford. There was to be a branch some 5 furlongs long, crossing the Suir by means of an opening bridge and terminating by a junction with the WD&LR in the townland of Gibbet Hill. There was also to be a connection with the lines of the Waterford & Central Ireland Railway. Additional capital was to be £150,000 with additional borrowing powers of up to one-third of this amount. A clause in the Act gave the company powers to contribute half the cost of construction of the portion of the WD&LR between the junction of the DW&WR line and the Dungarvan company's terminus. Running powers were to be granted over this latter portion of line and the company might enter into working agreements with the WD&LR. The Waterford extension was of course not destined to proceed in this manner or at this time and we shall return to it later. The Dungarvan company wrote on a number of occasions enquiring when work was going to commence, finally announcing in desperation on 20th November 1884 that the powers obtained under their Acts of 1878 and 1882 were about to be abandoned.

With their Act obtained for the New Ross extension, the directors requested Cotton & Flemyng to prepare plans and specifications for the line in November 1877. Tenders were sought in March of the following year and by May it appeared that a successful contender had emerged in the form of Messrs D Laing & Company whose tender was for £74,392.2s.5d. Laings were unable however to provide the necessary sureties and fresh tenders were sought in July, but it was to be six years before Robert Worthington's tender at £52,520.5s.0d was accepted in March 1884. Plans and specifications for the Barrow Bridge were prepared in August and the tender for its construction given to Dixon & Thorne at £21,234 in November. Alluding to the decision not to proceed with the extension at the half-yearly meeting in February 1879, Foot said it had been deemed prudent not to make any progress 'until the state of the money market shall be more favourable to the issue of new stock'.

It was deemed necessary in March 1886 to draw Worthington's attention to the slow progress of the works and the fact that penalties would be enforced. About this time consideration was given to the provision of a station at the Wexford end of Mount Elliott tunnel north of New Ross, but this was never provided. Matters began to move forward in mid-1886, plans being submitted for New Ross station and a tender being accepted from Cowan & Sheldon for a 45ft turntable there at a figure of £235. Mann's tender at £1,033.7s.6d was accepted for the station buildings at New Ross and Macmine. Further correspondence with Worthington took place in August when he was informed that penalties were to be deducted from his next certificate.

Just before the line was opened, Smith made a report to the board to the effect that on the evening of 19th August 1887, one of Worthington's engines, which had been engaged on the construction works, had been run over the Ballywilliam branch without staff or ticket. His report went on 'I deeply regret to state that my two assistants, Messrs Grierson and Shannon, were present and assented to this being done... and I look upon their conduct as a gross infringement of discipline and duty'. The board took the same line and at the board meeting of 25th August, it was ordered that notice be given to the two gentlemen. Grierson applied for a testimonial for his 7½ years service with the company and this was supplied. A few weeks later however, having had time to reflect on their misdoings, the two men wrote letters

of apology, the board relented and ordered that the notices be withdrawn. One can but speculate at the future history of the engineering department of the company had they gone elsewhere.

With the New Ross extension approaching completion, Payne had an interview with the GS&WR secretary in February 1887 as to the latter company taking over the working of the Ballywilliam to Palace East section. In March, the GS&WR submitted a plan and report on various works required at Palace East as a condition of their working this section. Following some consideration, the DW&WR agreed to construct these works on condition the GS&WR paid two-fifths of the cost of the station, including 10% of the value of the alterations. They in turn were to be paid 10d per mile for each of their trains working into the station from Ballywilliam. In April 1887, tenders were accepted for a 45ft turntable for £235 from Cowan & Sheldon and the erection of a station house at Palace East from Thompson Brothers at £210.

Further correspondence followed and it was to be September 1902 before an agreement was finally reached enabling the GS&WR to take over the working of the Ballywilliam to Palace East section as from 1st October of that year.

The BoT inspection of the New Ross line was carried out by Hutchinson on 5th September 1887, official confirmation being obtained on 15th September, allowing opening of the line four days later. With the line barely open, letters were received from Messrs D & J Fitzgerald and Worthington giving notice of intention to take proceedings against the company on foot of the latter's contract. This matter was resolved in May 1888 when Worthington agreed to accept a sum of £6,700 in full discharge of all

claims against the company. Reference is made in March 1888 to a further inspection by the BoT, following which it was stated that a fresh undertaking had been given as to the mode of working the single line section from Ballywilliam to New Ross. A further reference in October 1895 states that the line was by then fitted with Webb & Thompson staff instruments and the line was then ready for working with them. From this it appears as if the branch was worked for the first eight years on the basis of staff and ticket or a single engine in steam. In November 1894, the BoT had agreed to certain changes in the operation of the Barrow Bridge and the signalling on the line, which would effect large savings in expenses. Some other alterations were proposed during this period, including the provision of a loop at Palace East to enable trains to pass there. This regrettably was never done and D&SER trains never crossed there. A memorial was received in March 1893 from the people in the neighbourhood of Rathgarogue praying that a station be erected. Smith estimated the cost of a passenger station at £250 and this was approved, the station being opened in March of the following year. Complaints were received in November 1897 of the locomotive shed at New Ross being left open to the weather in consequence of the removal of the cast-iron water tank which formed the roof and it was ordered that a cheap roof be put on it.

The System is Completed

We have already seen how the company obtained an Act in 1878 for a Waterford extension, but despite occasional reminders from the WD&LR, nothing further was done to construct the line. At one point, when the WD&LR wrote once again enquiring what

Right: **Palace East looking towards New Ross with the goods bank on the left. Trains for Bagenalstown used a bay on the far side of the platform. The signal cabin dates from 1923.** J Langford

Dublin, Wicklow, and Wexford Railway.

TIME TABLE
(WEEK DAYS)

On and after 1st MARCH, 1876.

Wexford, Bagnalstown, and Kilkenny Railway.

Trains to Bagnalstown and Kilkenny.

					A.M.	A.M.
D.W. & W. Railway.	DUBLIN	..	..	dep.	..	9 0
	Bray			,,	..	9 40
	Wicklow	..		,,	..	10 25
	Gorey	..	..	,,	6 40	11 55
	Enniscorthy	..		,,	8 30	12 55
	Wexford	..		,,	9 0	12 0
	Macmine Junction	..		arr.	9 20	12 55
	Macmine Junction	..		dep.	9 22	1 15
	*Sparrowsland	..	..		FLAG	FLAG
	*Chapel	..	..		FLAG	FLAG
	*Palace East ..	..			FLAG	FLAG
	Ballywilliam (for New Ross)	..		10 10	2 0
G.S.&W.Ry.	*Glynn	..	..	..	FLAG	FLAG
	Borris	..			10 40	2 35
	*Goresbridge..	..			FLAG	FLAG
	Bagnalstown ..	..			11 0	2 55
	Kilkenny	..	..	arr.	11 40	4 38

Trains to Wexford, Enniscorthy, and Dublin.

					A.M.	P.M.
G.S.&W.Ry.	Kilkenny	..	..	dep.	7 15	2 30
	Bagnalstown ..	..			11 15	4 0
	*Goresbridge ..	..			FLAG	FLAG
	Borris	..	..		11 35	4 30
	*Glynn	..	..		FLAG	FLAG
D.W. & W. Railway.	Ballywilliam (for New Ross)	..		12 10	5 0
	*Palace East..	..	..		FLAG	FLAG
	*Chapel	..	..		FLAG	FLAG
	*Sparrowsland	..	..		FLAG	FLAG
	Macmine Junction	..	arr.	12 45	5 40
	Macmine Junction	..	dep.	12 55	5 45
	Wexford	..	..	arr.	1 20	6 5
	Enniscorthy	..	..		..	6 0
	Gorey	..		..	..	6 55
	Wicklow	..		..	..	8 26
	Bray	..		..	..	9 20
	DUBLIN	..	..	arr.	..	10 0

* Stops on notice being given to the Guard.

Top left: **A rare timetable leaflet from the period when the DW&WR worked the Bagnalstown (*sic*) line, before the GS&WR takeover.**

Top right: **Isolation personified - a lone individual stands on the platform at Rathgarogue.** T Cott - IRRS collection

Above right: **Construction in progress on the New Ross extension at Ballyanne cutting in 1885.** W Cavanagh - James FitzGibbon collection

the company's plans were for Waterford, they appear to have replied in desperation to the effect that the question of a Waterford extension would nòt be considered until progress was made on the New Ross line. Correspondence was received in 1891 urging the company to construct the extension; they agreed on condition that they got a satisfactory guarantee as regards the necessary capital and if arrangements could be made for the use of the W&LR station. Grierson produced plans in April 1896 of a proposed route for a New Ross to Waterford line, which he estimated would cost £150,000 or £215,000 if a bridge was required across the Suir. The decision was taken to proceed and the necessary Act was obtained in August 1897. The principal line was to be 13 miles 6 furlongs and 3½ chains in length from New Ross to a junction with the Waterford Limerick & Western Railway, as the W&LR had by now become, at Ferrybank, to the east of Waterford. A short line was to run from the goods extension of the WL&WR to a junction with the said railway near the bridge carrying the Waterford to Clonmel road over the railway. The third line was to cross the Suir on a bridge with an opening span and form a

junction with the WD&LR. It was made clear by the Act that the authorised lines were to be constructed and worked as a separate undertaking. This fact was to play an important part in events some ten years later. Capital was to be £200,000. Negotiations had been entered into with the L&NWR seeking financial support, these being finalised in 1902 when the L&NWR subscribed a loan of £100,000 and also purchased £87,000 of the £100,000 Guaranteed Stock of the separate undertaking, the New Ross & Waterford Extension Railway.

In March 1898, it was ordered that the plans for the proposed line should be extended so as to provide for the purchase of sufficient land for a double line, likewise the bridges were to be so designed. Tenders were received in June 1899, that of Messrs S Pearson & Son Limited of 10 Victoria Street, Westminster, London being accepted. There were two contracts, 'A' from New Ross to the townland of Abbeylands worth £92,565 and 'B' from there to a junction with the WL&WR at Mount Misery for £4,935. Pearsons commenced work on 24th August, having been quickly put in possession of the first 9¼ miles of land from New Ross. Initially, they

employed 200 men and about 20 horses. They consistently complained of an insufficiency of men to carry out the works, which were also delayed by bad weather. Before proceeding any further with the history of the Waterford extension, it is necessary to briefly take a look at other developments in the area which were to have a profound effect from this point forward.

As already stated, the L&NWR had endeavoured to keep the GWR out of Ireland and in the previous chapter we saw how the W&WR had been incorporated to construct a line basically connecting the two places in its title. Only the section from Wexford to Rosslare was constructed by them. Going back to 1844, the reader will recall that the GWR were behind the original idea of a coastal line from Dublin to Wexford and Waterford as part of an overall scheme for a through service from London to Dublin. In 1844, the SWR, in effect a subsidiary of the GWR, was incorporated to construct a line from Chepstow to Fishguard. Whilst construction commenced in 1846, it was suspended as the result of the Famine in Ireland. A branch had been authorised from Clarbeston Road to Haverford West and rather than build to

Fishguard, the company chose instead to turn south for Haverford and then by a short extension to the port of Neyland, at the time the terminal for a steamer service to Waterford and Cork. This line was opened to Neyland in April 1856.

In 1872, a Mr Cropper, the proprietor of slate quarries at Rosebush some distance to the east of Fishguard, constructed a line 8¼ miles long from Rosebush to a junction with the SWR at Clynderwen, while seven years later, the Rosebush & Fishguard Railway was incorporated to provide a connection from Clynderwen to Fishguard. Construction commenced in August 1879 but ceased in June 1881 when the company, which had purchased the Rosebush line, went bankrupt. Renamed the North Pembrokeshire Railway in 1884, after being bought by Messrs Rowlands and Cartland, it was proposed to complete the line to Fishguard where a pier would be built and the newly completed pier at Rosslare purchased. The company was offered to the GWR who declined to purchase it. Rebuffed, the proprietors obtained an Act in 1895 for a line from Clynderwen to join the L&NWR at Abergwili. Now the GWR woke up and bought out the concern. In 1893 an Act had been obtained by the Fishguard Bay Railway & Pier Company for the construction of a pier and a mile of railway from Fishguard to Goodwick. The GWR in due course constructed a line to connect Clarbeston Road (on the original SWR line to Haverford West) to Letterston, from which point it would use another line from Clynderwen to Goodwick. The connection with Fishguard was now effectively complete.

By an Act of 1894, the W&WR and Rosslare Pier were vested in the FBR&PC whose name was now changed to the more familiar Fishguard & Rosslare Railways & Harbours Company. The GWR meanwhile had been negotiating with the GS&WR regarding the possible purchase of the WD&LR and the Fermoy & Lismore companies, thus giving the GS&WR direct access to Waterford. In fact the F&RR&H obtained an Act in 1898 for the same purpose and for the construction of railways from Waterford to a junction with the W&WR at Rosslare Strand and from Cork direct to Fermoy. In due course, the Dungarvan and Lismore lines were taken over and the contract for the Rosslare to Waterford line was awarded to Messrs Robert McAlpine & Son of Glasgow. Work commenced in June 1900 and the line was completed in August 1906.

At this point, it should be mentioned that the GS&WR absorbed the Waterford & Central Ireland Railway in 1900 and the WL&WR the following year. Under the F&RR&H Company's Act of 1898, provision was made for the section of line from Ferrybank, later Abbey Junction, to Waterford station to be jointly owned by the Fishguard and the Wicklow companies.

Returning to the NR&WER, in January 1900, Moore was able to report that the masonry of three bridges was in a forward state, although inclement weather and an insufficiency of men had kept the work back. At this time the contractors had 566 men (*viz* 11 carpenters, 28 gangers, 461 labourers, 15 boys, 9 smiths and strikers and 42 horse drivers) and 38 horses at work.

Five months later, there were 734 men, 54 horses, a locomotive, a steam navvy and one boat employed on the works.

In July 1900, the F&RR&H wrote enquiring whether the DW&WR wished to exercise their right under the 1898 Act to become joint owners of the line from Ferrybank into Waterford as well as the bridge across the Suir. The matter was postponed and it was not until July 1902 that it was agreed to serve formal notice of the company's intention to acquire the joint lines as set out in the Act. In reply, the F&RR&H undertook that the joint line would be ready by the time the Waterford extension was completed, provided the DW&WR agreed to alterations proposed in the siting and construction of the Suir bridge. Writing in December 1903, the Fishguard company intimated that before the DW&WR could be permitted to exercise any rights as joint owners or commence to run over the joint lines, they would be required to pay one-third of the cost of their construction. In the following February, an account was submitted for £39,371.14s.9d and further liability was expected to amount to £16,216, a remittance for one-third of the total being requested. The DW&WR offered to pay their proportion of the amount actually expended and to give an undertaking to pay the balance when incurred. This was not to the satisfaction of the F&RR&H and in due course the DW&WR portion of the balance was lodged in the bank.

Meanwhile, in August 1900, the GS&WR and WL&WR Amalgamation Bill received Royal Assent. In return for withdrawing their opposition to the Bill, the DW&WR were granted running powers between Waterford and Limerick, powers which were in due course to be exercised in part.

Early in October 1900, it was reported that Mr D E Burtchaell, who had been appointed resident engineer in charge of the extension works, was 'not looking after his work or taking the interest in same that he should do'. Having spoken to Burtchaell, Shannon, the Company's Engineer, recommended to the board that another person be sent to New Ross to take his place, Burtchaell to work under the new man. So in November, William Henn Hinde, who had recently completed work on a portion of the London Underground and also had considerable experience on the Liverpool Overhead Railway, was appointed at £250 per annum. Hinde however resigned early in July 1901, reportedly owing to ill health although only 36

years of age at the time, and was replaced by a Mr J C Martin. Burtchaell appears to have resented Martin's appointment and in an effort to resolve the situation, it was agreed to put Burtchaell in charge of half of the line northwards from Waterford, with Martin in charge of the northern half, Shannon undertaking to closely supervise the former's work. By August 1901 reports were being made of slow progress on the works between New Ross and Raheen Pill, although south of the latter point the line had been completed to formation level and ballasted for 3½ miles. At No 18 cutting, about five miles from Waterford, a steam navvy was reported to be at work with a large number of men and two locomotives.

Slow progress in November 1903 led to a complaint being made to Pearsons. A further complaint related to the unsatisfactory condition of the ballast. Pearsons complained at one stage that the quality of stone from rock cuttings was quite unsuitable for use in bridge arches and they were given permission to substitute bricks, but the company refused to admit liability for any additional costs involved.

More serious complaints were made as to the unsatisfactory surveys carried out by the company's engineers, large areas of rock having been encountered where they should not have been. It transpired that Burtchaell had not been present on a number of occasions when borings were being made. These difficulties undoubtedly increased the construction costs and, as will be seen shortly, caused even greater problems later on.

An intermediate station was to be built at Aylwardstown, a plan of the new station buildings and station master's house being shown to the board in March 1903. They ordered that a building of more solid construction be substituted and in due course, Martin Quin's tender was accepted at £760. Footbridges were ordered for both Aylwardstown and New Ross from Messrs Ross & Walpole at £225 each. A signal cabin was included in the plans for Aylwardstown and Quin quoted £100 for its erection. It would appear that Quin was somewhat tardy in constructing this as in March 1904 it was reported that the construction of the building as authorised would entail delay in opening the station for traffic, so the plans were altered to a corrugated iron structure. At the same time, a siding was sanctioned at Rathgarogue at an estimated cost of £280. At Waterford, work was proceeding on a locomotive shed, carriage shed, 50ft turntable and a cast-iron water tank, all at Abbey Junction.

The line opened for goods and cattle traffic on Monday 15th February 1904, the BoT having given permission without an inspection of the line. With the line almost ready for passenger traffic, the company wrote to the BoT early in April 1904 stating they would like an inspection carried out as soon as possible in view of the impending visit to Waterford of the King. Colonel von Donop inspected the line and reported back on 25th April. The report showed the line to consist of 85lb bull head rail in 30ft lengths with 10 sleepers per rail, ballast being of broken stone and gravel. At Aylwardstown, there were two platforms 400ft long and a signal cabin with 16 levers. It was pointed out that station nameboards and lamps, a shelter on the down side and some alterations to signalling were required. Similar requirements were ordered for New Ross. On the same day, the joint line was inspected and passed subject to a minor requirement regarding interlocking. Passenger services commenced on 27th April 1904.

Difficulties at Waterford

As early as February 1903, plans had been received from the GS&WR indicating the temporary accommodation for the company's traffic at Waterford. DW&WR trains would run round the back of the station and reverse into one of the bay platforms facing west. Various plans were passed back and forth between the two companies. In June 1904, the DW&WR complained of the inadequate accommodation provided for them; amongst other things, there was no roof on the bay platform. In the absence of any agreement by February 1905, the GS&WR announced their intention of applying to

Colonel Hutchinson of the BoT. In May, Reid wrote a memorandum to Pim, in which he pointed out that the company would be placed in a rather foolish position if the arbitration went ahead and suggested that the wisest course might be to write to the GS&WR accepting their proposals, subject to some minor alterations recommended by Shannon. In fact, Shannon had indicated that he now thought the GS&WR plans the best which could be put forward. Despite writing to this effect, the arbitration went ahead and in due course the DW&WR were requested to pay Hutchinson's fees, which they endeavoured to avoid on the grounds that they had not sought the arbitration. These fees were paid after the company sought counsel's opinion. Negotiations in relation to payment for the use of Waterford station rumbled on until agreement was finally reached in January 1907, with the DW&WR paying £2,000 per annum, the agreement to be for five years with provision for five year periods of renewal.

With the use of the station by two new companies, it became obvious that it was inadequate and would have to be rebuilt. Consequently, a contract was concluded with Messrs Collen Brothers for the provision of a new station at Waterford, which was opened in 1906. This was situated partly on the site of the former quay line and partly on space gained by blasting into the side of Mount Misery. Three through roads were

provided along with two bay platforms facing east and four more facing west. The through platform was the longest in Ireland at 1,210ft. The Newrath Road was altered to pass on the river side of the station building, the road having to be constructed on concrete piles out over the river.

At different times, requests were made for stations at Bree, Curraghmore, Rathpatrick and Ballyverneen, the latter suggestion due to the reportedly inconvenient position of Aylwardstown station. All of these requests were declined. Aylwardstown was renamed Glenmore & Aylwardstown in 1906 following a request from the Reverend P Feely. It was reported in February 1905 that negotiations were in progress with the Waterford Steamship Company regarding the withdrawal of their steamer service between Waterford and New Ross, this being effected as from 1st July 1905, from which date additional goods trains were put on experimentally. Resulting from a refusal on the part of the GS&WR to apply existing cross-channel through rates over the company's route and lack of agreement on payment for the use of Waterford station, it was decided to exercise the running powers granted by the GS&WR Act of 1900, these taking effect for goods traffic between Waterford and Limerick Junction as from 2nd May 1904. The GS&WR suggested referring the matter to arbitration in December 1904. These goods trains finally stopped running as from 1st July 1908. It is of interest to note that the DW&WR had at this time a goods store at Tipperary.

Even with the line open, problems still arose. As already mentioned, the contract for the Waterford extension had been granted to Pearsons of London, an agreement dated 30th December 1899 stating that the DW&WR were about to carry out the works 'acting under the authority vested in them by the Act' (of 1897). Subsequent to this agreement, it became clear that there was going to be a financial over-run. Initially in 1906, it was agreed that the amount in question was £20,921.18s.4d plus interest, but even this figure was to be substantially increased. In reply to this demand, the company stated that the debt was not their responsibility but that of the separate undertaking.

As it was clear that the D&SER were not going to discharge the debt, the matter was referred to the courts. Mr Justice Madden in November 1907, at the suggestion of the two

Great Southern and Western Railway.

GENERAL ORDER No. 90.   TRAFFIC MANAGER'S OFFICE,
KINGSBRIDGE, DUBLIN,
15th September, 1902.

Working between Ballywilliam and Palace East.

On and from the 1st proximo, the portion of the Dublin, Wicklow and Wexford Railway between Ballywilliam and Palace East will be taken over and worked by this Company. Ballywilliam Station will be closed, so far as traffic of all description is concerned, on and from the date mentioned.

The Dublin, Wicklow and Wexford Company will perform all terminal and transfer services for this Company at Palace East, where there is accommodation for passenger, goods, and live stock traffic, and a system of rates and fares between that station and stations on this railway and beyond will be put in operation on the 1st prox. All traffic for the Dublin, Wicklow and Wexford Railway should be booked to Palace East Station in the absence of through rates, unless otherwise consigned by the sender.

Rates and Fares will be supplied by the Goods Manager and Superintendent of the Line.

Be good enough to acknowledge receipt of this communication.

ROBT. G. COLHOUN,
Traffic Manager.

To the Station Master

*at*_____

Left: **A notice issued by the GS&WR Traffic Manager in September 1902 informing staff of their company taking over the working of the Ballywilliam to Palace East section from the DW&W.** W E Shepherd collection

parties, abstained from giving a judgement, referring the matter on to the King's Bench Division. This latter ordered judgement to be entered for the contractors but limited the judgement so as to operate against and be levied only out of the property of the separate undertaking. The case was now referred to the Court of Appeal in May 1908, the appeal being dismissed.

Not prepared to let the matter rest there, it was now appealed to the House of Lords. Following a meeting with Sir Weetman Pearson in January 1909, Reid, having requested reasonable time to find the money should the judgement go against the company, reported to the board that Pearson's reply was to the effect that 'I fancy 24 hours will be about the time we will give you'. Whilst the Act of 1906 empowered the company to avail of fresh capital and borrowing powers,

all the monies were earmarked for specific projects. The problem facing the company was the distinct possibility that a receiver/manager would be appointed, which would be nothing short of a disaster. It was made clear that this was the option being considered by the contractors, who also made the point that the GWR would be quite willing to purchase the line. Approaches to the company's bankers met with a refusal.

The House of Lords handed down their judgement in February 1909 in favour of the contractors, the debt up to the end of that month amounting to £44,931.15s.10d.

Another problem was that the L&NWR, having subscribed to the undertaking, would not allow further debts to be incurred without their approval, which they declined to give. In desperation, approaches were made to the GS&WR, who expressed their willing-

ness to assist if a way could be found. This may have led to rumours about this time that the D&SER was contemplating amalgamation with that company. In any event, this idea also foundered and with a deadline of 1st May set by Pearsons, the directors now sought to organise Lloyd's Bonds through a contact in Huddersfield. Before this arrangement was finalised, one of the directors, Richard W Booth JP along with some of his friends agreed to take up the entire debt at 5% interest, arrangements to be made for repayment at £5,000 per annum.

So came to an end a particularly stormy period in the company's history. The system was now complete, with a total worked mileage of 157 miles 31 chains. It had taken almost sixty years for the vision of a line from Dublin to Wexford and Waterford to be realised.

Right: **New Ross, looking towards Palace East, shortly after the opening of the Waterford extension in 1904.**
H Fayle - IRRS collection

Below: **Waterford, during re-construction of the GS&WR station in 1906. The main station building in the background is that constructed by the W&LR. The introduction of the two new bay platforms on the left allowed D&SER trains a direct entry to the station.** Sean Kennedy collection

Chapter Five

THE DW&WR 1870 TO 1890

THE PERIOD between 1870 and 1890 was one of extension and consolidation. The extensions to Amiens Street, Wexford and New Ross are dealt with in their respective chapters as also is the acquisition of the WNR&WJR jointly with the GS&WR. The Wexford chapter also relates the story of the W&WR in so far as it affected the DW&WR. In this chapter we deal with the various alterations which consolidated the position of the company leading up to the disturbed years after 1890. In Chapter Six, reference is made to plans for extensions to connect the system to the other railways serving Dublin.

The original contract for Westland Row station amounted to £1,700, from which Dargan agreed to allow a sum of £600 for part of the embankment it replaced. It was decided to cover over the line, the roof contract going to Messrs John Bradley & Company of Stourbridge at £950 for the necessary ironwork for two spans. The slating was to be undertaken by a John Wilson for £292.10s.0d. Extras brought the total cost to £2,551.14s.0d. Some improvements were carried out in 1863 to provide for the cross-channel traffic. As constructed, the station had three platforms including an island, access to which was provided from the up side by two raisable gangways. By the time of an inspection by the BoT, following the derailment of a local train on 31st January 1870, there were only two platforms. Colonel Rich also commented on the fact that on the approaches to the station there was a short single line section of about five yards in length. In 1878 the platform on the down side was used for departing local trains and the arrival of the mails, the latter because of the cab approach to the station from Great Brunswick Street. The down mails departed from the up side, the local trains also using this platform. The two platform lines were connected at the inner end by means of a turntable which acted as a locomotive release. It should be mentioned that when plans were being drawn up for the extensions in 1875, the possibility of a northwards extension was borne in mind.

By this time, Westland Row was handling approximately 4¼ million passengers per annum, around twice the number of 20 years earlier, and it was obvious that some drastic improvements were required. An Act of 1875 empowered the company to purchase the buildings between the station and Great Brunswick Street and also a good deal of property adjoining the station along Cumberland Place South (joining South Cumberland Street with Sandwith Street). By so doing, it would be possible to provide four platform faces, the outer lines being arrival and departure platforms, and the inner two for local trains. The new cab entrance was to be by means of a ramp from Sandwith Street. Access to the central island platform was to be by a footbridge, with the booking office and waiting rooms at the down side of the station rather than at the Westland Row end. Another plan drawn up by Grierson shows a cab exit on the up side. This plan also shows access to the island platform by means of raisable gangways. First and second class departing passengers were to be segregated from their third class brethren. Grierson, in an article in the *Journal of the Institution of Civil Engineers*, commented that the purchase of the necessary land enabled the clearing away of a number of disreputable houses, 'decidedly improving the sanitary conditions of that portion of Dublin in which the terminus is situated'.

To avoid as far as possible interfering with railway traffic, the works were divided into a number of contracts. No 1 was for the clearing of the site on the south side and the construction of concrete foundations, piers, arches, platforms and station walls. This contract went to Messrs Michael Meade & Son. The arches in question were subsequently let to Messrs John Power & Son, whiskey distillers. To give effect to the possibility of an extension towards Amiens Street, the entire station, including roofs and platforms, was built to a rising gradient towards Westland Row of 1 in 240, thus obviating the necessity to lower the street by 18in to give the necessary clearance under the bridge. In addition, the new offices were constructed to the side rather than at the end of the building. These latter formed contract No 3, also awarded to Meade, and had to be constructed with the approval of the L&NWR who were to occupy a portion of them at ground level. The main offices of the company were located on the first floor and included those of the Secretary, the Cashier and the boardroom, this level being in direct communication with the platforms by a footbridge at the city end of the station. The upper floor accommodated the accounts and audit offices and also included a large room where all used tickets were cut up. This operation had to be overseen by the Chairman and Deputy Chairman.

The iron roofs, arched girders and columns (contract No 2) were supplied and erected by Messrs Courtney, Stephens & Bailey of Blackhall Place. The roof design followed that of Lime Street station in Liverpool, being the work of the (then) late Richard Turner of Dublin. Messrs Courtney, Stephens & Bailey also supplied the timber and glass. Erecting the new roof caused great difficulties in endeavouring to avoid disruption of traffic. To erect the main 90ft span involved the provision of a moveable stage over the tracks. Later, when the loop line was being built, the gable at the west end was constructed of a strong bow-string girder to carry the roof. In reconstructing the station, Messrs McKenzie & Holland provided a new 40-lever signal cabin. The works, which were commenced in 1878, were finally completed in 1884, the year in which the City of Dublin Junction Railways was incorporated.

Co-incidental with the commencement of works at Westland Row, the BoT received a letter from Mr Maurice Brooks, MP for Dublin, bringing to their notice several, 'causes of complaint ... from which the inhabitants of Dublin, Kingstown and the intermediate stations suffer'. These included, inadequate facilities at Westland Row, the deficiency of footbridges at intermediate stations, the old and dilapidated condition of rolling stock and the excessive fares being charged. Subsequently, he wrote again regarding the condition of the underbridges on the Kingstown line which 'by reason of their darkness and the facilities they offer for the deposit of nuisance of a most objectionable nature, and the inadequate height of the arches (are) no longer tolerable in a great city and improving neighbourhood'. These complaints led to Major General Hutchinson being requested to hold an inquiry into the various matters raised. Hutchinson carried out an inspection of the line and rolling stock and subsequently held the inquiry at the City Hall in March 1878.

Reporting back to the BoT, Hutchinson stated that plans were already in hand for the rebuilding of Westland Row, which when completed would afford reasonable accommodation. Hutchinson agreed that facilities at a number of the intermediate stations were deficient as regards waiting rooms, water closets and platform shelters. There were no footbridges and these were essential, particularly at Booterstown where the up and down trains were timed to cross. Platforms at all intermediate stations, Lansdowne Road excepted, were too low and led to considerable difficulties for infirm people. This remained a problem, as a list prepared in 1901 shows platform heights varying from 1ft 8in to 3ft 2in. In relation to rolling stock, Hutchinson was unable to comment on allegations regarding leaky carriages as the weather was fine during the period of the inquiry. However, he did comment that there appeared to be an insufficiency of seating for first and second class passengers, necessitating them having to resort regularly to third class carriages.

The majority of the complaints received related to the high level of fares charged. Hutchinson, having compared the Dublin to Kingstown fares with those for roughly comparable journeys on English, Scottish and Irish lines, concluded that they were indeed high, particularly in relation to season tickets. As an example, annual tickets from Dublin to Kingstown were £14 first and £12 second class. These compared with figures between £6.10s.0d and £13 for first class and between £5.17s.0d and £9.15s.0d second on other lines. Finally, in relation to the condition of certain underbridges between Grand Canal Street and Westland Row, the only issue in relation to these bridges which might be imposed upon the company was the necessity to maintain them watertight.

In reply to the various allegations and comments in the report, Maunsell, the Company Secretary, replied to the effect that alterations at Westland Row were in hand, as was the doubling of the Kingstown to Dalkey section, both of which would improve the service. It was agreed that the sanitary arrangements at certain stations were not up to standard, but as Hutchinson had remarked, the drainage in the various townships needed improvements before the station facilities could likewise be improved. A footbridge was in course of construction at Booterstown. Had it been there earlier, it might have prevented an incident which brought the company before the House of Lords. Briefly, a Mr Slattery went to Booterstown with his wife and friends to see an intending passenger off by train. It appears that Slattery crossed the line by means of, 'a level pathway used by the public without objection by the defendants,' behind a train standing in the station and was run down by an express train coming from the opposite direction. There was some doubt as to whether the driver of the latter train blew his whistle on approaching the station. An action was taken against the company which after much legal wrangling ended up in the House of Lords, where the case went against the company. The company totally rejected the allegations regarding the condition of the rolling stock and high fares. Lastly, regarding the underbridges, the company submitted that this was a problem for Dublin Corporation, 'who have and exercise unusually extensive powers of taxation, and to this taxation the railway company are obliged very largely to contribute'.

As the result of slips in the Dalkey to Killiney section at the close of 1876, Smith recommended to the Board that the line between Kingstown and Ballybrack should be doubled. This suggestion was approved by the board and Smith was ordered in January 1877 to prepare the necessary plans. Claims were made by several persons for car hire and compensation resulting from the closure of the line but were declined, but it was agreed that for the months of January and February holders of Killiney and Ballybrack subscribers' tickets should be permitted to travel via the Harcourt Street line to Bray. In November 1877 Smith was ordered to prepare plans for submission to the BoW seeking their sanction for the proposed alteration of the section between Kingstown and Dalkey and also for laying a second line of rails to the Mineral Pier at the former point. Part of Smith's report recommended the substitution of one new station for those

Below: **2-4-0T No 41 stands at Dundrum with a down local. The leading carriage is one of the four-wheeled Metropolitan third brakes of 1878.** IRRS collection

Above: **A local train climbs the bank on the single line from Killiney as it approaches Shanganagh from where the Westland Row line ran alongside the double track main line from Harcourt Street into Bray.**
Sean Kennedy collection

currently existing at Ballybrack and Killiney. This proposal was to lead to opposition from some local residents. Co-incidental with the doubling proposals, plans were prepared for the provision of a second through platform on the up side at Kingstown. A booking office was to be provided on the footbridge giving access to the two platforms from Crofton Road. Similar plans were drawn up some 15 years later but it was not until 1957 that this facility was provided.

The second line between Ballybrack and Dalkey was opened to traffic on 15th September 1879, the *Daily Express* looking forward to an improvement in time-keeping as the up and down trains would now cross near Dalkey tunnel. The section between Dalkey and Kingstown, laid as it was on the site of the old atmospheric line with its sharp curves, was to take rather longer, being opened in two parts, Dalkey to Glenageary on 7th July 1881 and thence to Kingstown on Monday 8th May 1882. At Glenageary, a new road was constructed on the up side to improve vehicular access. Similarly at Killiney, where a new station was opened, access was provided by means of a new private road.

To accompany the improvement in journey times of up to ten minutes, fares between Kingstown and Bray were reduced - singles by 3d, 2d and 1d for first, second and third classes, returns respectively by 7d, 5d and 2d. Reductions were also made between Westland Row and Dalkey and between Harcourt Street and Stillorgan. These reductions temporarily had the desired effect, the Chairman being enabled to report increases of 83,304 in second class and 58,578 in third class passengers in the half year ending June 1882.

Total cost of the doubling, which was carried out by the company, was estimated at £50,000, this figure being exceeded by £6,460, due in part to additional works not originally included in the plans.

The 5½ mile Newcastle to Wicklow section was also doubled and opened on 19th July 1877. Consideration was also given to doubling northwards to Greystones but this was postponed and although once again briefly considered in the early years of the 20th century, was never to come to fruition. Going back some years, it will be recalled that the section between Dundrum and Shanganagh had been doubled in 1861 with the line from the latter point to Bray having been similarly treated six years previously. In June 1861 it was reported that a ticket platform was to be formed at Shankill *(sic)* Junction, along with two cottages for the accommodation of the ticket collectors. An extract from *The Irish Times* dated 11th December 1876 refers to the presence of the platform consisting of, 'a few planks laid between the up and down lines without any protection from the weather', and situated some yards from the site of a previous 'permanent platform'. It was reported that the line here was, 'laid in some points within 12in to 15in of the edge of the precipitous bank washed by the waves', a situation described as being a wreckless disregard of human life. A fortnight later, *Freemans Journal* announced that trains would no longer stop at the junction for the interchange of passengers.

In August 1868, it was decided not to have a station at Shanganagh Junction, Smith having recommended the provision of a third line to Bray and the removal of the junction. It was to be a further seven years before Smith was instructed to proceed on this basis, the third road being opened in May 1877, and the junction dispensed with.

Although the place continued to be referred to in official company circles as Shanganagh Junction, the situation now was that the up and down Harcourt Street lines ran through to Bray, as did the single Westland Row line on the seaward side, with no physical connection between them. This situation was to remain until a new junction was provided in 1915 as part of the diversions and doubling of the Westland Row line. Readers should bear in mind that the new junction was situated some quarter of a mile inland of the original line.

Consideration was given in June 1874 to the erection of a new station near the Brickfield at Wicklow. The directors inspected the area in the following November and subsequently ordered that plans be prepared for inclusion in the company's 1875 Bill, but nothing further was done for another ten years. The visit of the directors to Wicklow nevertheless led to a meeting of the Wicklow Township Commissioners who objected to the planned move in the strongest terms, opposition to the Bill being threatened. It was pointed out that the land at the Murrough had been granted to the company 'for a very small sum of money on the understanding that it should be used for railway purposes only'. If the station were moved to the proposed location further removed from the town, this would constitute a gross breach of faith. The matter was put in abeyance until March 1883 when Smith was instructed to proceed with the building of the new station. Hutchinson inspected the works in February 1885 but found them wanting in certain respects. The station was duly opened as from Wednesday 1st April. A notice in the *Wicklow Newsletter* advised passengers that the 'present' station would close except for goods and cattle traffic from that date. The new station was no sooner open than requests were received for a contribution towards the cost of widening a road for foot passengers, the company agreeing to give a subscription of £15. In response to memorials from the inhabitants of the town, it was agreed to put on an early train from the old station, the running of a late train into it being refused.

Additional stations were opened at Inch, Chapel and Lansdowne Road. In relation to Inch, opened in 1885, various requests for the provision of a station had been received over the previous 20 years. In December 1886 it was ordered that a siding be installed here at a cost not exceeding £190. The station at Chapel was opened in 1876, a siding being provided here two years later. The original station was obviously of a temporary nature as a new station house was built here in 1884.

A similar situation occurred at Camolin, opened in 1867, Smith being instructed in April 1872 to submit an estimate for improving the temporary station.

This matter dragged on until November 1875 when Smith was ordered to erect a station building for not more than £350. A goods platform for six wagons and a cattle bank were provided in 1878. In June 1884, it was ordered that a wooden shed at Bray be removed, half to Rathdrum and half to Camolin as a goods shed. A proper shed, costing £125, was provided in March 1888.

Like many other stations provided, requests were received over an extended period for a station in the vicinity of Haig's Lane or Lansdowne Road. In July 1869 a deputation from the Pembroke Township handed in a memorial from about 250 inhabitants seeking a station here. The deputation proposed that the company should work such a station on the condition that the cost of its erection should in the first instance be defrayed by the Trustees of the Pembroke Estate, with the company undertaking to repay half the cost in the case of it being remunerative. The subsequent agreement specified that the station would cost in the region of £1,000 to £1,200 and that the company would provide a service of at least twelve ordinary trains each way daily. Before Smith had prepared the necessary plans, a Mr Vernon, on behalf of the Pembroke Estate, asked that the station be provided on the Kingstown side of the River Dodder, the present site being agreed in March 1870. Tenders for the construction were considered at the board meeting on 21st July 1870, the contract being awarded to Thomas Tighe at £563. At about this time, Alderman Boyce wrote suggesting that the name should be altered to the Pembroke Township Station, a suggestion which was not taken up.

Consideration was briefly given to the provision of a new station at Milltown, a quarter of a mile nearer to Dublin, in 1877, but this was not pursued. Similarly in September 1884, a deputation met with the board suggesting the amalgamation of Stillorgan and Foxrock stations. A month later another large deputation opposed the idea which was allowed to lapse.

Whilst in this area, mention should be made of the Reverend John Sullivan. The gentleman in question approached the board in June 1872 asking for a level crossing for carts over the line between Carrickmines and Foxrock and a siding at the latter station. Two months later, Foxrock is mentioned as the location for both the siding and the crossing, while two months later again it was ordered that a level crossing be put in near Stillorgan station, 'at the place pointed out by the Reverend Mr Sullivan'. It

was agreed to provide a siding on certain conditions, Sullivan paying half the cost. In October 1875 it was ordered that Smith have liberty to negotiate with Sullivan regarding the making of a deviation road and stopping up of the old road and level crossing at Foxrock. This latter was most likely at the south end of the down platform. It was almost a year later before Smith was ordered to put in the siding at Foxrock, 'as long ago promised to the Reverend Mr Sullivan'.

A new station building was provided at Woodenbridge Junction in 1877 by Thomas Tighe at a cost of £148. Improvements at other stations included the provision of goods sheds at Kilcool and Newcastle, additional passenger shelters at Dundrum and Stillorgan and a second platform at Macmine, the latter to better accommodate branch trains. Macmine was purely an interchange point at this time, road access not being provided until 1888. Newcastle station was slated in September 1866 when the *Wicklow Newsletter* commented that, 'for dirt and inconvenience it is certainly unsurpassed by any other in Ireland'. It was reported that the station master, who had a large family, was accommodated in one small room serving as a parlour, kitchen and bedroom, the only means of access being through the waiting room. Three years later, Arklow received a superlative of its own when it was said that, 'there is not such an approach to a railway station in the world'.

Correspondents of the *Newsletter* were obviously widely travelled! Arklow came to the attention of the BoT in November 1878 when a complaint was made by a Captain Kiddle regarding the condition of the permanent way. Major General Hutchinson was sent to investigate, reporting that the 80lb bridge rail was in fair order although the joint bolts tended to work loose, while some of the sleepers were more or less decayed. In a follow-up letter to the BoT, Kiddle commented that, 'neither on the Grand Trunk, the Panama or the Barranquilla lines had I seen much worse parts'.

In this period a number of private sidings were provided at various locations, these being detailed in the chapter on services and traffic.

Tenders were sought in June 1870 for the construction of new offices at Harcourt Street for the Traffic Manager. In October, Smith submitted a report on the proposed alterations here, including the conversion of the parcels office into a first and second class waiting room, the waiting room on the platform to be changed to a parcels office. It was also decided to provide increased accommodation for goods traffic, siding room for 36 wagons being installed at a cost of £1,000. Further improvements were made in this regard by the taking down of four houses belonging to the company in Adelaide Road. The Harcourt Street goods shed came in for censure from the directors in January 1873, it being reported that the flooring was, 'in a fearfully dangerous state'. Smith was held personally responsible for the safety of the store. As part of the improvement to this store, approval was given in the following April for the addition of a loft at a cost, including machinery, of £2,232. A board minute of 8th July 1875 would indicate that the conversions proposed in 1870 for the accommodation of the Traffic Manager had not been put into effect as Smith was requested to estimate the cost of such alterations. Approval was finally given in May 1876 at a figure of £482. Plans were also drawn up for a new engine shed, the tender of Samuel Bolton for £2,000 being accepted in February 1877. In November of the same year, instructions were given for a further extension of the goods shed by 100ft while the engine shed was extended by a further 50ft in 1885.

Dundrum station came to the attention of the BoT in October 1871 when a Mr James wrote to them complaining of the inadequacy of the waiting room on the up platform and suggesting its enlargement. In fact a memorial had been received in the previous month for a number of improvements

Right: **The north end of Greystones prior to 1897, showing the level crossing which was replaced by a footbridge in that year.**
D Paine collection

and Smith had been authorised to close in with glass the waiting shed in question. James was politely informed that since he had adopted the course of writing to the BoT, the directors would now await the Government Inspector's report. Colonel Rich came to Dundrum at the end of October, following which it was ordered that ramps be made at the ends of both platforms. No mention was made of the waiting shed, but three months later following a further communication from James, this time direct to the company, the enlargement of the building was put in hand at a cost of £80. Not apparently having learnt anything from his previous experience, James wrote again to the BoT in July 1875, this time expressing concern at the alleged dangerous condition of the road overbridge. In due course, the company replied to the BoT. In November 1879 Smith and Payne were asked to consult and report on re-arranging the station with a view to avoiding the necessity for passengers crossing the rails. It was not until 1884 that instructions were given to erect a footbridge here at a cost of about £80. Other stations listed at the same time were Stillorgan, Greystones and Enniscorthy. Tenders were received in the following April, that of Messrs Morewood & Company being accepted at £638.10s.0d for the four bridges. Iron footbridges had previously been erected at a number of stations on the coast line in 1878.

In April 1877, Edward Hartigan offered for sale his interest in the lease of the premises known as the Boston Lime Works, near the Factory at Grand Canal Street. It was agreed to acquire the property at a figure of £2,000, subsequently reduced to £1,700. In November 1877, Keogh, the company solicitor, was ordered to make whatever arrangements he could for the purchase of additional land adjoining the site in anticipation of the Company's Act of 1878. However when a Mr Bewley asked a figure of £10,000 for his interest in a three acre site at the Sugar Refining Company there, the idea was shelved. A wall was placed around the site and the land filled in 1879 to enable carriage sidings to be built. Later, in November 1881, plans were drawn up for the erection of carriage sheds on the site. As regards Grand Canal Street, the engine shed was extended in 1875 at a cost of £1,394.4s.0d, while in January 1876 four turntables were provided for a new carriage shed. A new running shed was also provided about this time. Two tenders having been received in November 1877, these were adjudged to be too high and Smith was instructed to carry out the work himself.

A letter received from the BoT in June 1873 referred to a complaint from a Mr E L Griffin regarding the level crossing near Breslin's Hotel at Bray. The company's response was that the crossing was a duly authorised one. It is rather surprising to note a board minute of October 1874 calling on Smith to prepare plans for the substitution of the crossings at Bray and Dunleary by bridges. As regards the latter, a deputation from the Kingstown Township attended the board meeting on 4th February 1875 to explain the Township's opposition to such a move. The BoW also objected to the scheme, suggesting instead that a footbridge would suffice. In due course this idea was accepted.

As regards Bray, bearing in mind the levels of the road on either side of the crossing, it is interesting to note that the company proposed an underbridge. Again, objections were received from the Town Commissioners, the company's response being that the proposal was put forward in the interests of the public. In April 1876, the company offered instead to erect a footbridge and to close the wicket gates currently being used by foot passengers. Following on Rich's inspection in September 1876 of the third line from Shanganagh to Bray, he stressed that the company should give an undertaking to alter the level crossing gates so as to connect them with the signals and reconstruct them so as to cross the road and the railway. In due course the footbridge was put in, although at one stage Breslin offered to give land for a nominal consideration to form an approach for an underpass. The company at one point contemplated putting the footbridge on the station side of the crossing on their own land following Breslin's refusal to agree to a footbridge. When he did, he requested that it be of an ornamental design, the company refusing to accept any conditions.

In connection with the proposed relaying of the Kingstown line, Smith recommended in March 1870 that the flange rails in use should be replaced by double-headed section. A week later, he requested permission to purchase 200 tons of such rail, the cargo of a vessel wrecked at Wicklow a fortnight earlier. Authority was given subject to the price not exceeding £5.15s.0d per ton. At the half-yearly shareholders' meeting in February 1878, the Chairman reported that work was proceeding, with 23 out of 137 miles of track relayed to the new standard.

Reference has been made to a complaint regarding the state of the underbridge at Dundrum station. From about 1868, consideration was given to the replacement of wooden bridges by iron structures. The Bray River Bridge was among the first to be replaced, followed by the Brunel bridges around Bray Head.

In June 1875 the decision was taken to replace a further 13 wooden bridges as necessity arose. Broadlough Bridge at Wicklow (No160) was replaced in 1884. Further north, a Mr Keane was informed in April 1885 that the Breache's Bridge between Kilcool and Newcastle was not dangerous; it was however replaced by an iron structure eighteen months later. An advertisement in the *Wicklow Newsletter* for 11th June 1887 offered for sale a steam hoist, two ton derrick crane, a pile engine and 500 cubic feet of Riga timber on site, application to be made to the bridge manager at Kilcool. The original iron bridges at Dundrum and over the Grand Canal were in the news in May 1887 when Smith submitted plans for their replacement, the estimated cost of which was about £3,000. In fact that at Dundrum was replaced by the Darlington Wagon Company for £298, this figure including the extra drilling of rivet holes. Most of the remaining Harcourt Street line bridges were replaced during the 1890s. A number of iron footbridges were also put up during this period. At Bray Head, a wooden footbridge had been provided in 1861 for the use of the Earl of Meath to gain access to his private strand. His Lordship's agent requested the bridge's replacement in April 1885, along with the building of a boundary wall and footpath. These works were carried out, the bridge being finally removed ten years later.

The Avoca Mineral tramway was briefly mentioned in connection with the proposed extension of the line to Gorey. In October 1867, Murphy was requested to submit an estimate for the expenditure required to make the tramway suitable for to be worked by locomotive engine power to the bridge at Arklow. In February 1872, Hodgson complained to the board regarding delays in the movement of his ores along the tramway; he was advised that every exertion would be made to accommodate him. Three months later, Payne drew the board's attention to the great increase in the carriage of ores to Arklow and it was agreed that Payne should purchase a horse and hand it to Dunne 'who undertakes to repay its price in work'. It was reported that tramway engine No 3 was derailed about two miles south of Woodenbridge, blocking the main line and causing an hour's delay to traffic. Resulting from this derailment, Smith, Payne and Wakefield were instructed to jointly report on the condition of the tramway and as to any outlay necessary to enable trains to run over it at speeds of at least six or seven miles per hour.

Opposite page, top: **Morris' Bank, the scene of several diversions, on the south side of Bray Head, photographed prior to the major diversion of 1917 which included the construction of Bray Head No 4 tunnel. The leading carriage is a former D&KR, six-compartment, large third.** IRRS collection

Bottom: **No 14, one of the three Fairbairn 2-4-0s of 1860. This particular locomotive was reconstructed at Grand Canal Street in 1907 as No 31** *Glen of the Downs***, although it is generally assumed that in its new guise the locomotive embodied parts from all three of the original Fairbairns.**
H Fayle - IRRS collection

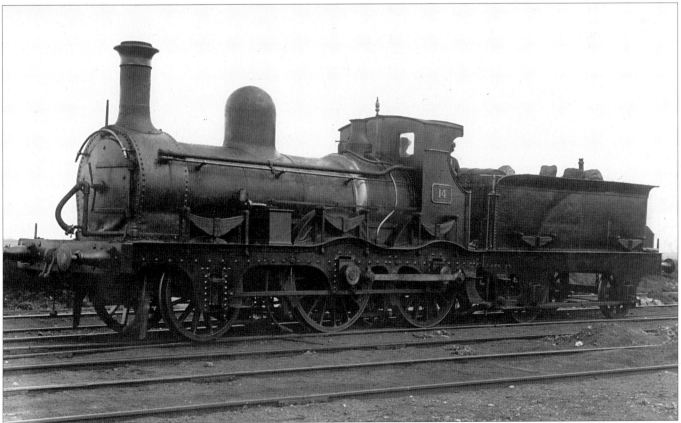

It was later ordered that the necessary repairs be carried out, rails required to be taken out of the main line.

Obviously concerned at the state of the tramway, the directors instructed Keogh to report on the company's liability. They also requested him to arrange for the giving up of a stable rented from Hodgson at Ballyraine for £10 per annum and also, if possible, the payment of 2s.6d per week to Lord Wicklow's watchman at Woodenbridge to be discontinued. When Hodgson wrote to the company in January 1877 requesting a renewal of the contract for the carriage of ores to Arklow, Payne was instructed to make the best arrangements he could, other than by the tramway. By this time, two of the three locomotives had been offered for sale. On the other hand, a letter was received from the secretary of the Wicklow Copper Mine Company five months later for the tramway to be put in order in connection with the carriage of ores to the Arklow Chemical Works. Hodgson drew the company's attention to flood damage to the embankment at Shelton Marsh in the following November. Keogh was again urged to report on the company's liability, but despite a number of reminders, he does not appear to have done so as Hodgson's representatives took an action against the company in November 1878 when the matter was referred to counsel for an opinion. Tenders were received in December 1880 for the purchase by two gentlemen of old tramway wagons, the offers being regarded as too low, Wakefield being ordered to break them up. The last reference made to the tramway in the board minutes was in January 1883 when the question of a level crossing at Shroughmore was referred to Keogh.

The 20-year period after 1870 saw a downturn in the company's financial position. After a brief peak in the dividends on the ordinary shares at 5½% during 1877, they gradually dropped back to 1% or 2% until 1895 when there was a short recovery to 2½%. Dividends on ordinary shares ceased altogether in the latter half of 1896. At the various half-yearly shareholders' meetings, a number of reasons were put forward for this downturn in the company's fortunes. These included the extreme wetness of the summer of 1878 and a resultant stagnation of trade. Weather again intervened in the following year, while an outbreak of foot and mouth disease in Britain in 1883 also had an effect, not obviously as serious as on some other lines, such as the Midland, heavily dependent as it was on cattle traffic. On the other hand, since the DW&WR was a carrier of large numbers of excursionists, they were bound to be adversely affected by weather. The general depression of trade was common to all the Irish railways, the DW&WR perhaps faring better than many others in these areas.

Reference has already been made earlier in the chapter to fare reductions on the suburban section, bringing about an increase in the numbers travelling. However, this did not convert itself into increased revenue. For example, 121,626 more passengers were carried in the second half of 1881, yet receipts on ordinary tickets were down by £729. During the same period, working expenses also increased substantially, and a number of unfortunate accidents led to the payment of compensation. The replacement of iron by steel rails, wooden by iron bridges and renewal of level crossings, plus the BoT requirements in respect of block signalling and the fitting of automatic brakes resulting from the Armagh accident, all contributed to a large expenditure in these areas and added to the problems facing the company.

TRAINS from DUBLIN (Harcourt-street) to WEXFORD.

FIRST, SECOND AND THIRD CLASS BY ALL TRAINS.

Passengers are requested to get Receipts in all cases when Excess Fares are paid.

Distance from Dublin	STATIONS	WEEK DAY TRAINS A.M.	A.M.	A.M.	A.M.	A.M.	A.M.	P.M.	P.M.	P.M.	P.M.	P.M.	SUNDAY TRAINS A.M.	A.M.	A.M.	P.M.	P.M.
—	Harcourt-street (dep.)	...	...	...	8 0	9 0	11 30	2 0	...	4 30	5 10	6 30	9 0	10 0	...	...	8 0
1¾	Milltown ...	...	...	...	8 5	9 5	11 35	...	...	4 35	...	6 35	9 5	10 5	...	...	8 5
3	Dundrum ...	...	...	...	8 10	9 10	11 40	2 10	...	4 40	...	6 40	9 10	10 10	...	...	8 10
5¼	Stillorgan ...	...	...	...	8 17	9 15	...	2 15	...	4 47	...	6 47	9 17	10 17	...	...	8 17
6	Foxrock ...	...	...	...	8 20	...	...	...	...	4 50	...	6 50	9 20	10 20	...	...	8 20
7¼	Carrickmines ...	...	...	...	8 23	...	...	...	...	4 53	...	6 53	9 23	10 23	...	...	8 23
9¾	Shankill ...	...	...	...	8 30	9 25	...	2 25	...	5 0	5 30	7 0	9 30	10 30	...	...	8 30
12¼	Bray (arr.)	...	...	...	8 40	9 35	12 0	2 35	...	5 10	5 40	7 10	9 40	10 40	...	...	8 40
12¼	Bray (dep.)	...	...	...	8 45	9 37	12 5	2 37	...		5 42	7 15	9 42	10 42	...	...	8 42
17	Greystones and Delgany ...	...	...	...	9 0	9 52	12 20	2 52	...	...	5 57	7 30	9 57	10 57	...	...	8 57
19¾	Kilcool, N. T. Mt. Kennedy ...	...	...	...	...	10 0	...	3 0	...	...	6 5	...	10 5	11 5	...	...	9 10
22½	Newcastle ...	...	...	...	...	10 7	...	3 7	...	...	6 14	...	10 15	11 15	...	...	9 20
28½	Wicklow ...	...	...	...	...	10 20	...	3 20	...	...	6 30	...	10 30	11 30	...	...	9 45
29¾	Rathnew (New-rath Bridge) ...	...	...	...	...	10 30	...	3 30	...	...	6 40	...	10 42	11 42	...	...	—
33¼	Glenealy ...	...	...	...	...	10 40	...	3 40	...	...	6 50	...	10 52	11 52	...	...	10 15
37¼	Rathdrum ...	...	...	...	...	10 50	...	3 50	...	...	7 5	...	11 2	12 2	...	...	10 25
42¾	Ovoca, Newbridge	5 45	...	...	...	11 5	...	4 5	...	...	7 20	...	11 20	12 20	...	...	10 40
44¾	Woodenbridge & Shil. Junc. (arr.)	5 50	...	...	...	11 15	...	4 15	...	...	7 30	...	11 25	12 25	...	...	10 45
44¾	Shillelagh Branch: Woodenbridge (dep.)	...	...	...	...	11 20	...	4 20	...	...	7 35	...	...	...	...	...	...
49¼	Shillelagh Branch: Aughrim ...	...	...	...	...	11 30	...	4 30	...	...	7 45	...	...	...	...	...	...
53¾	Shillelagh Branch: Ballinglen	...	...	...	...	FLAG	...	FLAG	...	...	FLAG	...	...	...	...	...	...
56¾	Shillelagh Branch: Tinahely	...	...	...	...	11 45	...	4 45	...	...	8 0	...	...	...	...	...	...
61¼	Shillelagh Branch: Shillelagh for Tullow ...	...	...	...	...	12 0	...	5 0	...	...	8 15	...	...	...	...	...	...
44¾	Woodenbridge & Shil. Junc. (dep.)	5 55	9 0	...	...	11 18	...	4 18	...	...	7 35	...	11 26	...	...	...	10 50
49	Arklow ...	6 10	9 15	...	...	11 30	...	4 30	...	...	7 45	...	11 36	...	...	...	11 5
59½	Gorey ...	6 45		...	...	11 50	...	4 50	...	...	8 5	...	12 0	...	...	...	11 30
67	Camolin ...	7 5	...	...	...	12 8	...	5 8	...	...	8 25	...	12 20	...	...	...	...
69¾	Ferns ...	7 15	...	...	...	12 15	...	5 15	...	...	8 32	...	12 25	...	...	...	12 0
77½	Enniscorthy ...	8 30	...	...	...	12 30	...	5 30	...	...	8 50	...	12 40	...	...	...	12 20
81	Edermine Ferry	FLAG	...	...	...	FLAG	...	...	...	...	FLAG	...	12 50	...	...	...	...
83¼	Macmine Junction (arr.)	8 55	...	...	...	12 45	...	5 45	...	...	9 5	...	1 0	...	...	...	12 35
83¼	Ballywilliam Branch D.W. & W.R.: Macmine Junc. (dep.)	9 0	...	...	...	1 0	...	6 0	...	...	...	...	...	...	...	...	...
89½	Ballywilliam Branch D.W. & W.R.: Chapel ...	FLAG	...	...	...	FLAG	...	FLAG	...	...	...	...	...	...	...	...	...
93¾	Ballywilliam Branch D.W. & W.R.: Palace East	FLAG	...	...	...	FLAG	...	FLAG	...	...	...	...	...	...	...	...	...
97¼	Ballywilliam Branch D.W. & W.R.: B'william for N. Ross (arr.)	9 55	...	...	...	1 45	...	6 45	...	...	...	...	...	...	...	...	...
97¼	G.S. & W.R.: Ballywilliam (dep.)	10 0	...	...	...	1 50	...	...	...	...	...	...	...	...	...	...	...
110	G.S. & W.R.: Borris ...	10 30	...	...	...	2 20	...	...	...	...	...	...	...	...	...	...	...
113¾	G.S. & W.R.: Goresbridge	FLAG	...	...	...	FLAG	...	...	...	...	...	...	...	...	...	...	...
118	G.S. & W.R.: Bagnalstown (arr.)	10 55	...	...	...	2 45	...	...	...	...	...	...	...	...	...	...	...
83¼	Macmine Junction (dep.)	9 0	...	...	...	12 46	...	5 46	8 0	...	9 6	...	1 1	...	...	...	12 36
86	Killurin ...	9 8	...	...	...	1 0	..	6 0	8 10	...	9 10	...	1 10	...	...	...	12 40
92¾	Wexford (arr.)	9 25	...	...	...	1 15	...	6 15	8 30	...	9 30	...	1 30	...	...	...	1 0

Passengers for Stations on Shillelagh Branch change Carriages at Woodenbridge Junction, and for Ballywilliam Branch at Macmine Junction.

Flag Stations—Passengers must notice the Guard at preceding Stations, as otherwise the Trains will not stop.

Return Tickets—Those for distances exceeding 15 Miles are available for Return day after date of the Ticket. Those for distances exceeding 25 Miles are available for Return two days after date; and exceeding 50 Miles, three days after date. Sundays not counted, except for distances under 15 Miles. (See page 2).

Left: **An extract from the DW&WR 'Time and Fare Tables' for August 1881, showing trains on the main line between Harcourt Street and Wexford.** W E Shepherd collection

Chapter Six

THE DUBLIN RAILWAYS

THE VARIOUS railway lines terminating in Dublin were constructed over a period of some twenty-five years, commencing with the Dublin & Kingstown Railway in December 1834 (Westland Row). It was followed by the Dublin & Drogheda (Amiens Street) in 1844, the GS&WR (Kingsbridge) in 1846, the MGWR (Broadstone) in 1847 and the D&WR (Harcourt Road) in 1854, the latter extending to Harcourt Street in February 1859, the last of the Dublin terminal stations to be opened. During this 25 year period, only the D&KR had suggested any connection between the various lines.

Below: **Railway and canal connections around Dublin in 1908.** IRRS collection

It had originally been proposed that the D&KR terminus would have been in Great Brunswick Street (now Pearse Street), but opposition from Trinity College led to the decision to locate it in Westland Row. Following on the death of Alexander Nimmo in January 1832, Charles Vignoles was appointed Engineer to the company. He suggested three separate Dublin extensions, the first shortly after his appointment being a resurrection of the earlier scheme, a 20 chain extension to Great Brunswick Street. In 1835, Vignoles proposed a rather more ambitious scheme for an extension from Westland Row across the city and a line to Valentia in Kerry, where a suitable harbour would be provided for the conveyance of the

American mails. Whilst receiving the warm approval of the D&KR directors, the scheme was too ambitious for the time and was soon forgotten. Three years later, Vignoles produced plans for a high-level railway from Westland Row to Barrack Bridge (now Watling Street bridge) on the River Liffey. The route of this line would have been along Great Brunswick Street, across Townsend Street, Hawkins Street, D'Olier Street and Westmoreland Street to Aston's Quay, where it was to run above the footpath on the river side to a central station at Barrack Bridge. Here, all the lines 'which were shortly to radiate through the country in every direction, with termini in Dublin, should converge'.

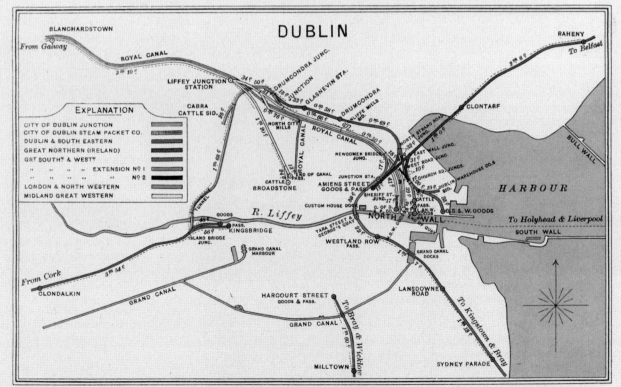

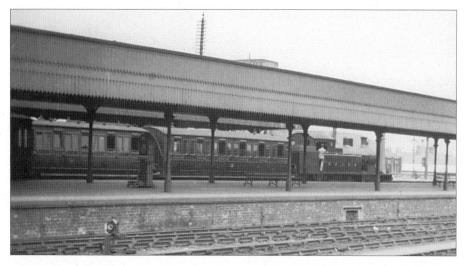

In 1859 the MGWR obtained an Act for a branch to the North Wall, deviating from their main line, 1 mile 33 chains from their Broadstone terminus, at a point subsequently known as Liffey Junction. The branch, which opened for cattle and goods traffic on Tuesday 1st March 1864, gave the Midland access to the River Liffey and was the first link in the chain which would join the various lines in Dublin. Also in 1859, a conference of the traffic managers of the various companies was held in Dublin, the result of which was that the D&WR Engineer, Le Fanu, drew up plans for a line from the South Quays to the D&KR at Sandymount, across the D&WR main line to the GS&WR, through the Phoenix Park to join the MGWR, along the Royal Canal to link up with the Dublin & Drogheda Railway and terminating in a large goods yard at the North Wall. During the next 20 years or so, many schemes were put forward to connect the various railways serving Dublin. It would not be possible to mention all of these

schemes, many of which in any event had no relevance to the DW&WR. We will however take a brief look at some of them.

In November 1860, Sir John Macneill put forward plans for the Metropolitan Junction Railway to run from the GS&WR at Inchicore, forming a double junction near Islandbridge, and further junctions with the DW&WR at Ranelagh and Mount Street. Powers were sought for the DW&WR and the GS&WR to contribute and make traffic arrangements. A year later the Dublin Metropolitan Railway briefly made an appearance. As far as the DW&WR was concerned, there was to be a line from Kingsbridge to Westland Row. Once again, powers were sought for traffic arrangements with the DW&WR. There was to be a central station over the Liffey extending from the west side of Carlisle Bridge (now O'Connell bridge) to a point 150 yards west of the Metal Bridge. November 1862 saw a similar scheme for a line from Kingsbridge to Westland Row but there was in addition to be a branch to the D&DR. The

year 1863 saw no less than five major schemes for Dublin. The simply titled Dublin Railway envisaged, *inter alia*, a line from Harcourt Street to the GS&WR and the D&KR at Ballsbridge; in addition a tramway was planned from Ranelagh to Rathmines Road. At the other extreme was the long winded Dublin, Rathmines, Rathgar, Roundtown, Rathfarnham & Rathcoole Railway, which was to have a central station at Trinity Street. A connection was to be made with the DW&WR main line near the Grand Canal overbridge. This company obtained an Act in July 1864, a further Act in the following year giving powers for an extension from Rathcoole through Blessington and Ballymore Eustace to Poulaphouca. Further expansion to Baltinglass was envisaged in 1866, with the company's title altered to the Dublin City Suburban & Wicklow Railway. All notions of construction were abandoned by an Act of August 1874.

In 1864 an Act was obtained for the Dublin Trunk Connecting Railway. A number of lines were envisaged, including Kingsbridge to the DW&WR near Serpentine Avenue. Despite strong opposition from the DW&WR, the Act received Royal Assent in July 1864. In the following year, a further Act granted powers for an extension to Lower Sackville Street (now O'Connell Street) with a pneumatic tube connection to the General Post Office. The company actually got as far as sinking shafts for the Liffey tunnel but these were abandoned in 1866 and despite Acts for extensions of time, the entire scheme (at one stage renamed the Dublin Port & City Railway) was abandoned. One other scheme was for the South Dublin Railway & Land Reclamation Company from Inchicore to the DW&WR at Milltown and Ballsbridge. Its promoter, Frederick Barry, who was behind a number of the Dublin schemes, approached the DW&WR enquiring if they would work his line. They initially refused to quote, stating that special rolling stock would be required in view of, 'the severe curves, gradients and junctions'. This company was dissolved in 1878.

Cotton, the DW&WR's consulting engineer, put forward proposals for an extension of the Kingstown line to D'Olier Street in October 1868.

Top: **A D&SER train stands at the loop line platforms of Amiens Street Junction. The locomotive, No 34, is one of the two Beyer Peacock 4-4-2Ts supplied in 1924.** J E Kite

Left: **The Loop Line Bridge over the river Liffey with the Custom House in the background. The competition to the railway is evident in the foreground.** From a postcard in the W E Shepherd collection

The new terminus, which was to be on a convenient and suitable site at the end of Great Brunswick Street near to D'Olier Street would be at street level with the line gradually ascending to Westland Row. *The Railway Times* reported that both the L&NWR and the City of Dublin Steampacket companies approved of the project and were willing to contribute. It was to be a further twelve months before Notice for a Bill for the D'Olier Street Extension & Terminus was published, a similar notice being published in November 1870 when it was stated that the CofDSP board had recommended its shareholders to subscribe £20,000 towards the project. Nothing further came of the scheme although a special meeting of the DW&WR board was held on 2nd October 1872, 'to consider the construction of a station at D'Olier Street and a connection with the D&DR'. The meeting passed a resolution calling on the Chairman to contact Murland and Watson, his opposite numbers respectively on the D&DR and the CofDSP. The former declined to take any part in the project while the CofDSP agreed, provided the L&NWR joined in. Meanwhile, Smith and Payne were requested to consider whether Westland Row could be improved at reasonable expense. A Charles Cummins approached the board in October 1874 advocating the promotion of a connecting line from the D&KR to the North Wall by means of a tunnel under the Grand Canal Dock and the Liffey but it declined to become involved.

With the need for carrying out improvements to Westland Row station becoming ever more necessary, Smith was authorised in March 1876 to ascertain the views of the other companies as to the possibility of connecting the D&KR with the North Wall and forming connections with the other companies. No progress was made in this regard and in the following year the company obtained powers to carry out the necessary improvements at Westland Row. These alterations are referred to in Chapter Five. In carrying out this reconstruction, the idea of a possible connecting line running towards Amiens Street was borne in mind. Brief reference is made in 1878 to an approach from James Price CE when he requested an interview with the board to explain a plan for a railway from Westland Row to Amiens Street, but the directors appear to have been singularly unimpressed.

Four years now passed by and in June 1882 the Dublin Chamber of Commerce invited the attendance of a deputation of DW&WR directors at a proposed conference of the Dublin railway companies relative to a junction being formed between them. It was by now clear that the time had come for the DW&WR to be connected with the remainder of the Dublin railway system. It will be recalled that the MGWR's Liffey branch was

opened for traffic in 1864. Conscious of the advantages to be gained from a direct connection with the River Liffey, the GS&WR obtained powers by Act of 1872 for a line leaving their main line immediately outside the Kingsbridge terminus, crossing the Liffey and tunnelling under the Phoenix Park to make a junction with the Midland's Liffey branch at Glasnevin. Running powers were obtained over the latter as far as Church Road, at which point the GS&WR were to lay a line into their own goods yard further down the North Wall. The GS&WR opened their connection in September 1877. Coincidental with its opening, the Great Northern Railway (Ireland), as successor to the D&DR, completed a short spur from East Wall Junction, thus effectively connecting three of the four Dublin railways. Financial assistance for both the GS&WR and the GNR(I) projects came from the L&NWR.

The opening months of 1883 were to prove critical in the later decision to connect the DW&WR with the remaining companies north of the Liffey and we must now devote a little time to review the postal connection between Britain and Ireland. A postal service between the two islands had been established as far back as 1572 when post stages were set up for a weekly service via Chester and Liverpool, the latter altered four years later to Holyhead. Steamers first appeared on the Holyhead route in 1819, operating to Howth. Due to difficulties in entering the latter harbour in certain tidal and weather conditions, its use was short-lived and with the completion of the deep-water jetty on the East Pier at Kingstown in 1827, some services were diverted here, Howth ceasing to be used by the mail packets as from January 1834. Completion of Carlisle Pier and the rail connection thereto in December 1859 saw the mail service moved to this location. When the postal authorities ceased to provide their own vessels, the seaborne portion of the contract was awarded to the City of Dublin Steampacket Company, a fact not entirely pleasing to the Chester & Holyhead Railway and its successor, the L&NWR. In an attempt to take this lucrative contract, the former company commenced a Holyhead to Dublin North Wall service in 1848.

This was the situation existing on 24th February 1883 when the Postmaster General was questioned in Parliament as to whether his attention had been drawn to a statement by the L&NWR chairman to the effect that his board had ordered the construction of two new steamers for their Holyhead to North Wall route. It was by now clear that the L&NWR intended to make an assault on the Dublin company's hold on the mail contract. Local authorities from as far afield as Bray and Limerick began a campaign against the L&NWR, despite which they were awarded the contract. *The Galway Vindicator* reporting on the award in March stated

that, 'perhaps no action of the Government has done so much for a long time to unite all classes in Ireland as the taking away of the contract… for the carriage of mails'. The success was short-lived however for such a campaign of vilification was mounted against the L&NWR that the contract was again put out to tender, reverting to the CofDSP, with whom it remained until 1920. However the pressure was now on to improve the connection across the city from Westland Row to the other railway termini. Up to now, the mails were brought by train to Westland Row from which point they were transferred to horse-drawn carts, while passengers, who did not really figure in the equation, had to make their own arrangements.

It is hardly surprising to find therefore in August 1883, Smith being directed to confer with W H Mills, Engineer of the GNR(I), and report on a plan for connecting Westland Row with the remainder of the Dublin rail network. Plans were duly prepared and copies sent not only to the various railway companies, but also to the CofDSP, Dublin Corporation, the Dublin Port & Docks Board and the Chamber of Commerce. All initially approved of the plans, although the GS&WR declined to provide pecuniary assistance, while the DP&DB subsequently declined to assent to the railway crossing the Liffey to the east of the Custom House. Smith, Payne and Wakefield reported in October as to the likely increase in traffic to be derived from the proposed line. The decision was taken to proceed with lodging a Bill, the relevant notice being published in November, at which time it became clear that there was a rival scheme in prospect. This was the Dublin Grand Junction Railway, promoted by Messrs Clay, Hassard and Worthington, for a line from Sandymount to Inchicore. This Bill was strenuously opposed by the DW&WR, although at one point its promoters approached the Wicklow board for their support. At the GS&WR half-yearly meeting in February, their Chairman referred to the two schemes, stating their preference for the Inchicore line which would give a faster transit for the American mails from Kingstown.

By March 1884, both the GNR(I) and the CofDSP had agreed to subsidise the interest on capital for the new line. The MGWR directors on the other hand did not see their way to recommend the scheme to their shareholders. It was obviously vital to the DW&WR and the CofDSP to have the line constructed if the mail contract was to remain at Kingstown in the latter's hands, the GNR(I) had an interest in it to prevent the possible diversion of the northern mails to the Larne to Stranraer route, and whilst the GS&WR might see a need for it, it was of little or no advantage to the Midland. Sir Ralph Cusack, chairman of the MGWR, commented that 'the citizens of Dublin would be just as well pleased to have their letters in Dublin at 8.30 as 7.30 (a.m.), as it is not pleasant to read business letters by candle light'. Initially the Dublin United Tramways Company announced their opposition to the Bill but having attended on the board on 24th April, they agreed to the inclusion of some protective clauses and duly withdrew their opposition. Having initially gone along with the scheme, Dublin Corporation now announced their opposition to the bridge over Beresford Place and went as far as requesting the BoW to construct and display a model of it to show how much it would disfigure the city. There is no evidence to suggest that such a model was ever built. Interestingly, it was reported at the board meeting on 3rd July that an anonymous letter had been received threatening to blow up the proposed junction railway if built – such threats are not the sole preserve of 20th century society!

The City of Dublin Junction Railways Act which received Royal Assent on 28th July 1884 made it clear that the C of DJR was to be a separate undertaking with a distinct capital proprietary and borrowing powers. Capital was to be £300,000 with additional borrowing of up to £100,000. Although the GS&WR had already notified their intention not to contribute financially to the scheme, Section 32 of the Act empowered not only the GS&WR, but also the DW&WR, CofDSP, GNR(I) and the MGWR to guarantee dividends and interest on the CofDJR capital to enable the company to pay dividends on the share capital not exceeding 4% per annum. The DW&WR could subscribe up to £6,000 per annum, the C of DSP £3,000 and each of the other companies £2,000. Two railways were empowered – No 1 commencing from an end-on junction with the D&KR at West-

land Row and terminating by a junction with the GNR(I) at Amiens Street, and No 2, commencing at a junction out of No 1 at Amiens Street and terminating in a connection with the MGWR at a point some 105ft from the south-east face of Newcomen Bridge carrying North Strand over the Royal Canal lock. Provision was made for the viaduct over Beresford Place and the bridge over the Liffey to be of ornamental character and design. In the case of the latter bridge, conditions were also laid down as regards the number and location of piers so as to interfere as little as possible with navigation of the river. Finally, in accordance with an agreement made with the DUTC, protective conditions were laid down regarding any works which might affect or disrupt the tramway.

With the Act gained, the Wicklow company requested the Midland to have their engineer prepare plans and estimates for a double junction at Newcomen Bridge and these were duly completed. In November, a conference was called of the managers of the guaranteeing companies at which a letter was read from the GS&WR declining to recommend to their shareholders to give any assistance to the project on the grounds that their Engineer, Bayley, had reported against the proposed junction at Newcomen Bridge. Sir Ralph Cusack undertook to consult his directors to consider whether, in these circumstances, they would join with the three remaining companies in continuing with the project. Only 24 hours later, the Midland wrote declining to take any further part in the negotiations, 'at least so long as there is any probability of a competing line or the GS&WR holding aloof'. This was a serious blow to the project and whilst one can

understand the GS&WR being strongly influenced by the L&NWR views on the matter, one wonders if they also persuaded the Midland not to become involved, although it has to be said that there is no hard evidence to suggest this. A week later, and possibly sensing that they might yet have an opportunity of proceeding with their own project, Messrs Caldbeck and Clay waited on the DW&WR board and suggested the introduction of a clause in their Bill for the DGJR to pay the DW&WR all the costs of the C of DJR Act. It was a most unusual offer and it is difficult to see how Parliament would have agreed to such a clause, but in the event they were politely informed that the C of DJR project was to proceed.

The C of DSP agreed in December to pay one-third of the expenses of preliminary investigation of the plans and books of reference of the DGJR. Whilst notice was given that the Bill would be again submitted in the 1885 Session, it was in fact withdrawn in April. Also in April, the Dublin Chamber of Commerce wrote to the company urging it to, 'use vigorous action for constructing the CofDJR' now that the rival scheme was gone. The withdrawal of the GS&WR and the MGWR brought about a financial crisis for the scheme however and the DW&WR chairman, on the occasion of the half yearly meeting of shareholders in August, said the DW&WR were not inclined to proceed without the co-operation of the other two companies. An approach was made to the Treasury in September seeking Government assistance with the project but this came to nothing. Another rival had now appeared on the scene in the shape of the Kingstown & Kingsbridge Junction Railway. Smith, reporting on this scheme in December 1885, gave details of railway No 1 which was to run from Booterstown to Inchicore, a distance of about seven miles of which an aggregate length of more than one mile was on a gradient of 1 in 70 with two curves of ten chains. If made, the result to the Kingstown line would be simply to abstract traffic from the portion between Booterstown and Westland Row. A triangular junction was to be formed with the Harcourt Street line near Milltown. Smith commented that: 'since this company (the DW&WR) obtained their Act for the Waterford extension, the GS company have shown a determination to obstruct the development of the Wicklow system. This, as far as I have means of judging, appears to arise from their belief that the result of that development would be to

Left: **The new bridge for the Loop Line over Westland Row, to the north of the station, under construction in 1890. The ornate ironwork of the bridge, a mandatory requirement allowing for its construction, is clearly visible.** Sean Kennedy collection

Above: **Kingstown station in 1902 with the single through, down side, platform, behind which is the ex-D&KR bay with overall roof. Typical of the period are the various enamelled advertising signs.** IRRS collection

divert a large amount of business from their lines to those of the Wicklow company and also to interfere with their probable intention of conveying traffic and ultimately mails from North Wall to Enniscorthy and Wexford over their rails. This view, if correct, invests the projected railway with great importance as affecting the interests of this company'.

Having considered the matter, the DW&WR solicitor, Keogh, was authorised to petition against the Bill but incurring as little expense as possible. It is worth mentioning that the Midland also considered railway No 4 of the K&KJR to be objectionable in that it would have a curve of ten chains radius and a gradient of 1 in 75. Railway No 4 was to connect the GS&WR's North Wall branch with the Midland at Fassaugh Bridge near Liffey Junction. Little happened during the year 1886, the only item of note being a further approach from the Chamber of Commerce urging construction of the CofDJR or the Loop Line as it came to be known.

Some prospect of further moves towards construction came in February 1887 when a question was asked of the Postmaster General in the House of Commons regarding the Loop Line and the postal contract. He replied to the effect that the Government was not in a position to give any pledge but would say that the non-performance of this undertaking by the various companies had operated very strongly to counterbalance the advantages of the Queenstown mail route and if the Loop Line was not constructed without delay, it must tend to prejudice that line whenever future contracts were under consideration. A further Act was passed into law in August 1887, the main provision of which was to re-arrange the securing of the guarantees. The guarantee from the CofDSP was increased to £4,000 and power was also given to that company to subscribe towards the capital of the CofDJR.

In the previous month the decision had been taken to proceed at once with railway No 1, but it was not until the following March that tenders were ready to go out to prospective contractors. Contract No 1 from Westland Row to George's Quay was awarded to Messrs Meade for £16,000 on 28th March. Two months later, Smith was directed to advertise for tenders for the construction of the Liffey bridge, this being awarded to Messrs Arroll Bros. of Glasgow on 21st June in an amount of £14,369.

June also brought objections from Dublin Corporation in respect of Beresford Place viaduct. On being informed that though the company could not consent to reconsider the entire design, they were prepared however to submit designs of some ornamentation. In reply, the Corporation stated that the proposed ornamentation was wholly unsuitable and that the design of the bridge was not at all in accordance with the requirements of the Act of 1884. Having submitted the matter to Mr Walker QC the company offered to refer the matter to B B Stoney CE, the Corporation preferring a Mr Strype. Neither party was acceptable to the other and the BoT was then proposed and accepted. Major Marindin duly attended and inspected the plans, suggesting that stone be substituted for iron in the abutments. The revised plans were finally approved by the Corporation on 23rd October. While this matter was being resolved, Messrs Meade had been awarded the contract for works north of the river and plans were prepared for bridges over various streets. Messrs D & W Grant of Belfast were given the contract for the bridges over Park View, Great Brunswick Street, Shaw Street and Townsend Street, which were to cost £10,805.15s.0d.

The tender of Messrs Arroll Bros. was accepted for the ironwork of the Beresford Place viaduct in November, on the understanding that the work would be completed by 1st July 1889. It was now however the turn of the BoW to complain about the design for this bridge. They were told that the design had been agreed by the Corporation in accordance with plans approved by the DP&DB. The time for reconsideration of the design had now passed.

We now move to the northern end of railway No 1 where discussions had been taking place with the GNR(I) regarding the proposed junction and station at Amiens Street. Correspondence had also been entered into with the BoT to have the gradient on railway

No 2 altered from 1 in 75 to 1 in 60, which was approved. Plans of Westland Row station were submitted to the board in August 1889 where it was proposed to raise the platforms as a means of carrying out the junction arrangements here. £20,453.16s.0d compensation was submitted by the DW&WR for the value of the portion of the station taken over by the Loop Line. The actual works were estimated at £12,467.

Smith reported to the board in January 1890 as to progress to that time. The work was basically divided into three classes – masonry, iron bridges and general work including stations, permanent way and signalling. Apart from the contracts already mentioned above, the contract for the remaining seven street bridges had gone to Messrs Andrew Handyside of Derby for £23,000 in March 1889. The works had slowed down considerably in the second half of 1888, and it was necessary to go back to Parliament in 1889 for an extension of time.

Difficulties emerged in April 1890 in regard to the proposed junction at Newcomen Bridge. The DW&WR had submitted altered plans to the BoT which had approved them, but when Kelly, the Midland's Engineer, attended the site he said he could only approve the plans originally drawn up by him and this was affirmed by the Midland board. The C of DJR wrote to the Midland in June to the effect that, 'the Joint Committee feel it would be useless to further discuss a subject upon which the MGWR have finally made up their minds adversely, but the action of the Committee in abstaining from further discussion is not to be taken as any indication that they at all assent to the contention put forward'. The DW&WR now applied to the BoT for the appointment of a referee under Section 9 of the Railway Clauses Act of 1863. The Midland approached the GS&WR asking that their engineer attend the hearing and to be prepared to state their views on the proposed junction. The GS&WR declined to become involved as they said that it was of no concern to them as they had no intention of ever using the junction for their traffic.

Meanwhile, the GS&WR had been in correspondence with the DW&WR enquiring as to what arrangements were in contemplation for working the Loop Line. The DW&WR suggested that the American and south of Ireland mails should be worked through to Amiens Street in GS&WR vans and carriages on the mail train, at which point they would be detached and brought forward by a DW&WR engine for interchange at Inchicore. Bayley advised against changing engines at Inchicore due to the adverse gradient and suggested Kingsbridge. As the GS&WR would not agree to the use of the Newcomen connection, they insisted that their rolling stock should operate via East Wall Junction and the L&NWR station in the North Wall. In due course, it was agreed that the DW&WR would work the train through to Kingsbridge. While this correspondence was being exchanged, Sir Douglas Galton had been sent over by the BoT and having inspected the plans and the site of the proposed junction, announced in favour of the Wicklow scheme. When the latter wrote to the MGWR requesting a meeting to carry the eminent gentleman's award into effect, to their surprise, the MGWR said they would not accept it.

It was now mid-September and works on railway No 1 were in a forward state and correspondence was passing between the DW&WR and the GNR(I) as regards Amiens Street. W H Mills, the GNR(I) Engineer, suggested the removal of their carriage shed to an alternative location and the conversion of what was then a siding into a dock line for the Howth line, that siding to be pulled nearer to the down main line. A platform wall was to be built on the east side of the DW&WR local platform (to create what later became known as the Howth bay) and proper connections were to be made to the GNR(I) main lines. These alterations would enable through passengers simply to walk across the platform for their connections. The GNR(I) expressed their willingness to incur the expense of removing the carriage shed, building the platform wall and making the necessary connections with signalling and interlocking if the DW&WR would construct the platform roof. The DW&WR however felt that the GNR(I) should pay for half the cost of the roof and this they did eventually agree. On 29th September, a meeting was held between the two companies to discuss some matters relating to the service to be provided. Payne advised that the mail trains from Kingstown to Amiens Street would take 18 minutes. The formation of these trains would be that the GS&WR vehicles would be in front, followed by the GNR(I) and MGWR stock. The running of local trains was discussed and it was agreed that Payne would draw up a timetable. Through services would not operate initially, but a five minute connection would be provided between the DW&WR and Howth line services. Instructions were issued that all through trains would be equipped with Smith's simple vacuum brake.

The tender of the Railway Signal Company of Fazakerley was accepted on 8th October for the necessary works at Amiens Street at a cost of £1,748, including the provision of one signal cabin. At a further meeting in November, it was agreed that the GNR(I) vehicles on the mail should consist of a Travelling Post Office van and a composite coach with a large locker. It was at this meeting that the GNR(I) agreed to pay half the cost of the platform roof, subject to them having the use of the subways for their passengers. The DW&WR now wrote to the Post Office stating that they should be in a position to open the Loop Line for the night mails as from 28th November. In fact it was 12th December before an experimental service was run from Carlisle Pier to Amiens Street with the northern mails, but at least one portion of the Loop Line was now open, albeit single tracked. Instructions were issued to the effect that no engine or train was to work over the line without a pilot porter.

While these arrangements were being completed, railway No 2 was providing considerable interest and amusement for the citizens of Dublin. The DW&WR, despite the setback of the MGWR refusal to accept the BoT award in the matter of Newcomen Junction, were determined to proceed and having taken legal advice, decided to take the matter into their own hands. So having completed this section of railway as far as the boundary of MGWR property, the DW&WR workmen breached the wall and commenced work on the far side. Returning from a lunch break, they found the breach filled up with old rails and other material. What was described as the 'War Correspondent' of *The Irish Times* in its 29th October edition as 'the Battle of Newcomen' took place between the opposing sides, as they built up and tore down barricades. The whole thing was farcical and of course it was inevitable that the entire question would end up being sorted out in the courts. However by the time it reached the Master of the Rolls in March 1891, the MGWR had advised that they had decided not to proceed with litigation, 'although this does not mean a change of opinion or approval of the awarded mode of junction nor will we make any use of it unless satisfied of its safety'.

In due course, the line was completed, but not before the DW&WR had cause to complain to the MGWR regarding the number of trains being passed over the line while works were being carried out. On one particular Sunday in August, no less than 22 up and 18 down trains passed the site of the junction, many of these empty wagon trains. The MGWR responded by saying they could not undertake to change or discontinue the running of trains required for the traffic of their railway. A number of derailments occurred at the junction and on each occasion the DW&WR were deemed responsible. The line was duly inspected by Lieutenant-Colonel Hutchinson on behalf of the BoT on 10th December 1891 and he found everything to his satisfaction. He did however impose a 5mph speed restriction through the junction. Notice was given to the GS&WR of the proposed opening of the line as from 23rd January 1892, but once again they declined to use it, arranging for the DW&WR to work through to Kingsbridge. This brought about a necessity for additional motive power, leading to the order for the three 4-4-2 tanks, Nos 52 to 54. Once again the MGWR refused to accept the BoT ruling and it was necessary for the DW&WR to resort to the Railway & Canal Commissioners to force them to allow the use of the junction. Eventually, the line was opened for through traffic as from 2nd June 1892.

As mentioned, the line from Westland Row to Amiens Street was initially single, nor was the station at Tara Street constructed. Plans for this station were only submitted to the Committee late in March, when it was decided that there should be no entrance from Tara Street itself, but from George's Quay. It was also at one stage intended to have a station at Beresford Place, but plans for this were shelved. April saw final plans for the opening of the line for passenger traffic and it was agreed that this should commence as from 1st May. Agreement was obtained from the BoT for the extended use of the line under the same arrangements as existed for the mail trains, namely pilot working. As facilities at Amiens Street were not completed at this time, the GNR(I) kindly offered the use of engine turning and watering facilities as well as booking office, waiting rooms and toilet accommodation. The second line was duly inspected by the BoT and opened for traffic at the end of 1891.

Below: **A later scene at Carlisle Pier showing the improved facilities.**
From a postcard in the IRRS collection

The Link Line

Despite the opening of Railway No 2 of the Loop Line, there can be no doubt that the GS&WR could never have considered the Kingsbridge to Amiens Street connection as more than a temporary expedient. They had been paying a substantial rent for the privilege of running over the MGWR line since 1877 and they had of course been the principal opponents of the junction at Newcomen Bridge. One might have thought therefore that they would have shown some enthusiasm when approached in September 1891 by an influential group interested in promoting a high-level railway to serve the Drumcondra district and which would have given them the connection they so obviously desired. It is interesting to record a total lack of interest, although it has to be said however that the GS&WR directors were quite expert at biding their time and buying up smaller concerns at a bargain price.

Notwithstanding this rebuff, the Drumcondra & North Dublin Link Railway obtained its Act of Incorporation in August 1894 for a line joining the GS&WR's North Wall line near Glasnevin and rejoining it at Church Road Junction. There was to be a direct line to the DW&WR at Amiens Street. The GS&WR now began to show some interest and by an Act of 1896, the powers of the D&NDLR were transferred to them in return for a consideration of £6,000. An examination of the smaller company's plans showed a number of serious flaws and it became necessary for the GS&WR Engineer to re-examine these. Consideration was briefly

given in February 1897 to the provision of a connection enabling trains from either North Wall or Kingstown to run direct into Kingsbridge, but this was discounted on grounds of cost. The GS&WR plans deviated somewhat from those contained in the original Act, particularly as regards the exact position of the junction with the DW&WR at Amiens Street and the taking of certain lands belonging to the latter on which sidings had been laid. The Government arbitrator in due course made a draft award providing for the acquisition of these lands, to which the DW&WR objected and the matter remained in abeyance until the GS&WR requested the BoT in October 1900 to appoint a referee to determine the issue.

The BoT duly appointed Charles Langridge Morgan, Engineer of the London, Brighton & South Coast Railway, in February 1901. It should be mentioned that the DW&WR had been far from idle in the intervening period prior to Morgan's appointment. In January 1899, they had approached William Moffatt, General Manager of the Great North of Scotland Railway, seeking his advice on the matter. Having come to Dublin and inspected the site of the proposed works, Moffatt made the following suggestions. In the first instance, the company should make no proposals but should call upon the GS&WR to state what traffic they proposed to bring over the line. They should, if at all possible, prevent the GS&WR from executing any of the works on the company's property but should themselves carry out the works. The DW&WR should insist on

an additional line and platform as the minimum required, the GS&WR to reimburse the DW&WR for their outlay and they should also make an adequate payment for the use of the station, any such payment to be subject to revision as traffic increased. These suggestions formed the basis of negotiations between Shannon and Bayley, Engineers of the DW&WR and the GS&WR respectively. During these negotiations, the GS&WR hinted that they intended constructing a station at Inchicore, at which all main line trains would stop and provide connections to the local services to Amiens Street. The GS&WR were in fact seeking through connections with GNR(I) and DW&WR trains, as well as an hourly service in connection with either Bray or Kingstown local services. If these trains could be run through between either Kingstown or Bray and Inchicore without a change of engine, then this could probably render unnecessary any material alterations at Amiens Street.

The DW&WR responded, seeking sidings, some covered for sheltering carriages, a locomotive shed, watering facilities, use of a turntable and other facilities at Inchicore along with power to appoint whatever staff they felt necessary. There the matter rested until Morgan's appointment in February 1901. This appointment was strenuously opposed by the Wicklow company on the basis that as the GS&WR's plans proposed a deviation from the original Parliamentary plans of 1894, it was not competent for them to apply to the BoT. The GS&WR response was to the effect that the DW&WR had gone ahead with the filling up of waste land and the construction of sidings thereon in the full knowledge of the GS&WR plans. Despite the protestations from Westland Row the referee completed his investigations and made his award in April 1901.

Basically the award gave authority to the GS&WR to take up the two existing DW&WR sidings at Amiens Street and appropriate the site for the formation of the junction. Before

proceeding with this work however, they were obliged at their own expense to construct a replacement siding which was to become the property of the DW&WR. The latter company maintained its hard-line position, continuing to dispute the validity of Morgan's appointment and refusing to be bound by any award. They did however agree to a meeting to discuss the matter further. It should be pointed out at this juncture that the line between Glasnevin and Church Road Junctions was opened for traffic on 1st April 1901, leaving the direct connection from North Strand to Amiens Street uncompleted. Hardly can there have been a clearer instance of procrastination and sheer bloody-mindedness displayed on the part of any railway management than that now shown by the DW&WR directors with the connection remaining uncompleted for a further 5½ years. Various meetings ensued and in November 1902 some measure of agreement appeared to have been reached. This agreement allowed for works to be carried out by the DW&WR at the expense of the GS&WR and also set out the service of trains to be run by the latter, facilities to be provided at Amiens Street and the rent thereof and fares to be charged.

The DW&WR now proceeded to compulsorily purchase the necessary lands, appoint a resident Engineer, and carry out other works required. When the GS&WR submitted a draft of the proposed agreement to the DW&WR in February 1903, it was clear that it deviated in a number of respects, requiring further meetings. Then on 29th August, the GS&WR wrote expressing some concern that the proposed surrender of the D&KR lease under the terms of the DW&WR's Act of 1903 would seriously affect the agreement. The DW&WR endeavoured to allay these fears on the basis that they would have running powers over the D&KR and in any event would retain full control over the Loop Line, Amiens Street, and the mail service to and from Kingstown. Yet more nego-

tiations followed, the DW&WR offering arbitration to settle any compensation in the unlikely event of their failure to provide facilities. This suggestion proved unacceptable. By this time, the line had been completed up to the point of junction, the final piece of trackwork now awaiting only a final agreement.

The matter continued to rumble on however and it was not until May 1905 that the two companies' solicitors met and some prospect of finalising matters appeared. In fact, agreement was virtually complete, and appeared to have been resolved by July, but even now another difficulty was entered into the equation, namely the signalling at Amiens Street, the plans for which the GS&WR considered much more elaborate than anticipated or thought necessary. Finally in September 1905 this matter was put to rest but it was not until 1st December 1906 that the final piece in the jigsaw which formed the railway system of Dublin was put in place with the opening of the Link Line into Amiens Street.

One has to ask the question whether the Link Line was worth all the trouble and expense, and the answer must be no! As far back as 1897, some of the GS&WR shareholders had queried the proposed expenditure on what was clearly a duplicate route. The Chairman, J S Colvill, replied to the effect that there would be a great saving in time, of the order of 'nearly half an hour' between Kingsbridge and Kingstown. This was patently untrue as to save 25 minutes would have required an average speed just short of 60mph for the 10¼ mile journey. The commuter service, calling at Drumcondra and Glasnevin was short-lived, being gradually withdrawn from 1907 onwards.

Below: **Kingstown to Kingsbridge boat train, hauled by 4-4-2T No 54, runs through Salthill station. The small signal cabin, which survived until 1926, can be seen on the up platform.** IRRS collection

Chapter Seven

DIFFICULT YEARS

D URING the 1880s the ordinary share-holders had been receiving a steady, if not large, 2% dividend on their holdings. By 1890, this had fallen to 1½%. This was down to 1¼% in the following year and to ¾% in 1892-93. Little did they know that the days of payouts on ordinary shares were virtually at an end. In fact by 1900, only the 6% and 5% preference stocks were receiving any dividend at all, the latter only at the rate of 2½%. During 1893 a committee was formed to investigate the company's affairs. With the sanction of the board, an engineer, W C Furnivall, was called in to report accordingly. Furnivall was born in 1837 and had gained his early engineering experience with the Great Western Railway of Canada, later being appointed District Engineer of the Sind, Punjab & Delhi Railway. He went on to become involved in the construction of a number of railways in the sub-continent. He left India in 1890 and returned to England. The report was received by the directors in January 1894, their initial reaction being that they believed, 'that much benefit will be derived from it'. Basically, Furnivall dealt with the railway under five headings (i) the physical condition of the way and works, (ii) sufficiency and quality of rolling stock, (iii) traffic arrangements and how they could be improved, (iv) practicable economies and (v) organisation of establishments.

Under the heading of Way & Works, four broad parameters were considered. Apart from the section of line between Killiney and Wicklow where the sea was causing major problems, the earthworks were in good order. Some criticism was levelled at the engineer as regards bridges. Furnivall had requested designs of bridges in the Avoca valley so as to check their suitability for the heavier engines then in service and was surprised to learn that the engineer possessed no such plans. In relation to permanent way and ballast, bearing in mind the different types of rail and fittings in use, Furnivall found the line in good order and well ballasted. The design and layout of stations came in for some criticism, although this was not peculiar to the DW&WR. However, the goods arrangements, centred as they were on Harcourt Street, were described as being, 'really bad', even with the light goods

traffic being handled. It was suggested that consideration might be given to moving this facility to Grand Canal Street and finding an alternative location for the locomotive works. This latter was an area which came in for particularly severe criticism.

His opening comments in relation to the Factory were, 'Anything worse than the Locomotive Erecting Shops of the DW&WR line I have never seen, and it appears to me extraordinary how the Locomotive Department can have done its work at all in such quarters – the cramped nature of which must entail great expense in the erection and repair of engines'. As regards a likely location for the works, Bray or Wicklow were suggested, the former at the junction of the two lines from Dublin, the latter where land would probably be cheaper and where there was a good port. Turning next to rolling stock, Furnivall had scathing remarks on the number and types of locomotives, making economical working practically impossible. There were in fact nine distinct locomotive types, which he considered a severe tax on the department to maintain. As all varied in reference to hauling power and fuel consumption, 'the confusion must be apparent'. The passenger rolling stock, he regarded in the main as being of 'an antiquated pattern, and some decidedly uncomfortable'. The goods wagons fared no better.

Furnivall next turned his attention to the extent of the traffic and the adequacy of the train service. Gross receipts indicated that the traffic potential existed, but operating expenses had increased from 43.18% of receipts in 1877 to an unacceptable 52.32% in 1893. This increase was shown under all headings and there were clear indications that the timetable and the number of carriages running were not best suited to the traffic. Cheap fares as an inducement to travel appeared to be borne out by the breakdown of passengers into the three classes available. First class represented 6.85%, second 33.76% and third class 59.39%. The report stated that it was the simple duty of a Traffic Manager to study market values of commodities and adopt rates accordingly. This was not the case on the DW&WR and it was suggested that an investigating committee might be necessary to consider the position over an extended period of time.

In relation to possible economies, the expenses of the Traffic Department were undoubtedly excessive. For example, the shunting mileage of 31,536 was regarded as quite extraordinary on so short a line, equivalent to 61 hours per week. The arrangement of passenger trains was excessive for the traffic demands and one suggestion was the replacement of certain trains by mixed trains which could also therefore cater for goods. The latter came in for particular comment as already stated. It was however in the area of the Locomotive Department that Furnivall had many adverse remarks to make and one wonders whether Wakefield and Furnivall had crossed swords at some time in the past. In particular, the question of fuel consumption was singled out, as this had increased considerably since 1877. At this latter date, the annual consumption was 10,841 tons at a cost of 14s.10d per ton, equivalent to 26 pounds per traffic mile. By 1893 the comparative figures were 17,523 tons at 14s.11d per ton with a consumption of 34.5 pounds per mile. This latter was excessive in the extreme. It had been admitted by Wakefield that a long time had elapsed since there had been a stocktaking of fuel, a situation which left the company open to pilfering. This did no justice to the Locomotive Department and the directors should immediately call for an explanation.

Under the final heading – Organisation of Establishments – the line was costing 34⅓% more to manage in 1893 than it had in 1877, a fact which the shareholders might with much reason call for an explanation. Directors' fees were too high for such a small company, the Secretary and his office were costing far too much, the former's salary being £770 per annum. The appointment of a General Manager in recent years should have lightened the Secretary's administrative duties, 'if he ever performed any'. In regard to the Locomotive Department, the message was quite clear – 'it is questionable whether the present head officer is competent to continue in chief charge' and it would probably be as well if the board accepted the responsibility of building a new locomotive works and securing the services of a man qualified in the design of such shops. Finally, as regards the Chief Engineer, the appointment of an Assistant

Engineer had become necessary owing to the most unfortunate failure of the former's eyesight. In this situation, the directors were, 'incurring a very serious responsibility in maintaining him in his position'.

All in all, this was a damning report and one which could not be ignored and resignations and retirements followed in February 1894. Edward Maunsell, who had been Secretary since 1862 was replaced by E M Cowan and W L Payne, the Traffic Manager since 1863 was replaced by David Stewart from the Clogher Valley Railway. It is hardly surprising therefore to find that Wakefield handed in his resignation at the board meeting on 12th August and was granted a pension of £150 per annum. The Civil Engineer, John C Smith was replaced by T B Grierson, his assistant, who in addition was given charge of mechanical engineering matters. The combining of civil and mechanical duties had been singularly unsuccessful on other railways. Grierson in fact did not appear to have a grasp of locomotive matters as two locomotives ordered by him in 1896 proved to be too heavy and caused problems for some time after delivery until rebuilt. This weakness may have led to the resolution at the board meeting on 17th December 1896 that a Locomotive Superintendent should be appointed, following which Grierson should devote all his time to the Permanent Way Department. Other changes were made at board level, including a new Chairman, Lieutenant Colonel J S Tighe,

being replaced in December 1896 by Frederick Pim. The period from 1896 was a difficult one for the DW&WR, facing as it did the ever-advancing challenge of tramway competition, which in turn was to lead to a long running dispute with the D&KR over the rent payable for that section of line.

Tramways and the 1903 Act

The Company's Act of 1903 was in some respects the most important piece of legislation passed in reference to the DW&WR. It dealt on the one hand with the leasing arrangements with the D&KR and on the other made provision for large scale diversions of the line where it was suffering from the ravages of the sea. We must first take a look at the growth of the tramway competition in Dublin and how this affected the fortunes of the company. In the year 1878 an Act was obtained by certain English capitalists for the incorporation of the Dublin Southern Districts Tramway Company, a concern connected with the Imperial Tramway Company in England. Two lines specifically affecting the railway were sanctioned, from Haddington Road to Blackrock (5ft 3in gauge) and from Kingstown station to Dalkey (4ft 8½ins). The first of these lines was to connect at the Dublin end with a line of the Dublin Tramway Company from Nelson's Pillar (Sackville Street, now O'Connell Street) to Sandymount via Bath Avenue. This latter had been sanctioned by an Act of 1871 and opened in the following year.

The DW&WR petitioned against the DSDT Bill but were unsuccessful although haulage was restricted to animal power. The Blackrock to Kingstown section between the two authorised tramway lines was operated by a wagonette service. Powers were successfully obtained in 1883 for doubling the Haddington Road to Blackrock line, again unsuccessfully opposed by the railway company.

Also in 1883, Messrs Robert Gardiner and Robert Worthington promoted a Bill for the Blackrock & Kingstown Tramways Company to join the two sections of the DSDT. The DW&WR were unsuccessful in their petition against the Bill. With the completion of this line it was now possible to travel from Dublin to Dalkey by horse tram although the journey occupied two hours with three changes of car *en route*, and cost 8d, whereas the train took only 30 minutes with the same fare. It was at the time suggested that the DW&WR should have availed of the opportunity of purchasing the tramway but it is highly unlikely that Parliament would have approved of this. In 1893, the DSDT promoted an Order in Council under the

Tramways (Ireland) Act of 1860 to authorise the alteration, reconstruction and enlargement of tramways between Haddington Road and Dalkey, that is including the Blackrock & Kingstown. A separate Act was obtained in 1893 for the purchase of that tramway for £7,500, which included rolling stock, machinery, horses and stables. More importantly, powers were obtained to electrify the system throughout. The gauge of the Kingstown to Dalkey section was altered to 5ft 3ins to allow through running. The new electrified line was ready for traffic in 1896, in the same year that it was sold to the DUTC. Despite determined petitions against these various pieces of parliamentary legislation, they all passed into law.

There is no doubt that the electrification of the tramway system had a disastrous effect so far as the DW&WR's traffic receipts were concerned. During the years 1890 to 1895 the line produced an operating surplus after paying the Kingstown rent of £36,000. The electrified tramway opened on 16th May 1896 and the D&KR section returned a deficit of about £7,000 for the year ending 31st December 1896. Every year thereafter there was a deficit varying from £15,828.11s.10d to £21,708.12s.2d and the dividends had ceased to be paid on all but two classes of stock. It was in the context of this downturn in revenue that the DW&WR Secretary wrote to his opposite number in the D&KR on 19th April 1901 with a request for a revision of the fixed rent. The position regarding the rent was briefly as follows. It will be recalled that the first agreement between the two companies dated 23rd March 1846, allowed for the leasing of the D&KR subject to the 3Ws completing its line within a specified time. In consideration of the lease, there was to be a fixed rent of £34,000 per annum, to which was added a figure of 50% of gross income in excess of £55,000 per annum.

Over the next 20 years a series of further agreements was made, culminating in the Dublin & Kingstown Railway (Lease) Act of 1866. This Act altered the leasing arrangements from three separate rents to one fixed amount of £36,000 per annum with a term of 980 years (999 from 1847) substituted for the previous 35 year period. Perhaps more importantly, Section 6 of the Act contained the provision that if any railway or tramway capable of competing with the D&KR was opened for public traffic and if the Bill for that competing line was in good faith opposed by the DW&WR, the modification of the lease effected by the Act should absolutely cease and revert to the three previous rents.

The DW&WR were to give notice of the reversion within three months of the opening of the opposing line.

In the initial correspondence with the D&KR, reference was made to the DW&WR's efforts to promote traffic by reductions in fares and the provision of a more frequent service of trains in an attempt to meet and counter the tramway competition. The Wicklow shareholders had put up money for improvements to the Kingstown undertaking and as a reward for this they were being deprived of dividends, whereas the D&KR shareholders were enjoying a dividend at the rate of 9½%. The D&KR replied to the effect that they could see no reason to alter the agreement as the Wicklow directors could have availed of the option to amend the lease in 1886 but they had not done so. The DW&WR responded that there was virtually no tramway competition in the year 1886. It was only following the electrification of the tramway in 1896 that the company had suffered.

Protracted correspondence ensued to no avail and consequently the DW&WR incorporated clauses in a Bill promoted in the 1902 session of Parliament to have the lease amended.

The Bill came before a select committee of the House of Commons at the end of April. First to give evidence was Frederick Pim, Chairman of the DW&WR board, who outlined the relations between the two companies up to and including the passing of the 1866 Act.

Right: A notice produced by the Traffic Manager's Office showing the arrangements made for the commencement of goods traffic on the Waterford extension.

Dublin, Wicklow, & Wexford Railway.

TRAFFIC MANAGER'S OFFICE,
50, WESTLAND-ROW,
10th *February*, 1904.

Opening of New Ross and Waterford Extension Line for Goods Traffic, February, 1904.

ON AND AFTER FEBRUARY 15th, 1904,

the following Time Table will come into force on the Macmine, New Ross, and Waterford Section :—**a. m.**

		Goods	a. m.	a. m.	a. m. a. m.	p. m.	p. m.	p. m.	p. m.
Wexford	... a.	5 20							
Killurin	... a.	5 35							
Do.	... d.	5 37							
Macmine	... a.	5 45		Mail	Mixed Mixed	Mixed	Goods	Mixed	
Do.	... a.	6 0	7 30	9 5	11 0	1 32	2 50	6 40	8 50
Chapel	... a.	6 15	7 44	9 14	11 14	1 46	2 59	6 49	8 59
Do.	... d.	6 25	7 45	9 15	11 15	1 47	3 0	6 50	9 0
Palace E.	... a.	6 40	7 55	9 25	11 25	1 57	3 10	7 0	9 10
Do	... d.	6 55	8 15	9 26 10 25	11 26	1 58	3 15	7 10	9 15
Rathgarogue	... d.	Sig.	Sig.	Sig. Sig.	Sig.	Sig.	Sig.	Sig. Sig.	
New Ross	... a.	7 25	8 30	9 45 10 45	11 45	2 15	3 35	7 31	9 30
Do.	... d.	7 40			4 30 **p. m.**				
Aylwardstown	... d.	Sig.			Sig.				
Waterford	...arr.	8 30			5 30				

		Mixed	Mixed	Mixed	Mail	Mixed	Goods
Waterford	... d.		11 0				6 30
Aylwardstown	... d.		Sig.	p. m.	p. m.	p. m.	Sig.
New Ross	... a. a. m.	a. m.	a. m. a. m.	11 45	Mail		7 20
Do.	... d.	6 30	7 45	9 0 10 0 12 30	d. 20	3 45	5 30 7 40
Rathgarogue	... d.	Sig.	Sig.	Sig. Sig.	Sig.	Sig.	Sig. Sig.
Palace East	... a.	6 49	8 5	9 20 10 15	12 50 1 40	4 5	5 50 8 0
Do.	... d.	6 50	8 25	10 20 12 55	2 5	4 6	6 5 8 5
Chapel	... a.	6 59	8 34	10 29	1 4 2 19	4 15	6 14 8 20
Do.	... d.	7 0	8 35	10 30	1 5 2 20	4 16	6 15 8 25
Macmine Jn.	... a.	7 15	8 50	10 45	1 20 2 35	4 32	6 25 8 40
Do.	... d.				4 40		
Killurin	... a.				4 49		
Do.	... d.				4 50		
Wexford	... a.				5 5		

Wagons for Waterford, etc., off Up Day Goods to be forwarded per 1.32 p.m. *ex* Macmine.

The 5.20 a.m. Goods Train from Wexford will pick up at Macmine all Wagons for Waterford and intermediate Stations, left off by Up and Down Night, and Down Day Main Line Goods Trains.

Wagons for Wexford per 6.30 p.m. Goods *ex* Waterford, to be brought on by Down Day Goods (Main Line).

In connection with the opening of the Waterford Line, Mr. Hickey's duties will extend to and include Arklow and Shillelagh, and all Reports *re* Wagons, Report Sheets, &c., from intermediate Stations, are to be addressed to him here.

Mr. Delany's duties will extend from Inch to Waterford and Wexford. All communications to be addressed to him at Wexford.

JOHN COGHLAN.

Mr Balfour Browne KC for the company then proceeded to set out the reasons behind the clauses in the Bill dealing with the rent revision, in support of which he quoted figures for receipts from 1890 onwards. Reference was also made to the fact that dividends to shareholders were being progressively reduced. Apart from the severe competition, the company were faced with expenditure calculated at up to £300,000 for the relaying of sections of line damaged by the continuing ravages of the sea between Killiney and Wicklow. There was considerable legal argument as to why the DW&WR had not exercised their option under the 1866 Act, Pim being recalled to give evidence regarding the dividends paid after 1890. Attention was then concentrated on the improvements which had been carried out to the D&KR section after it had been taken over in 1856 – the relaying and subsequent doubling of the Atmospheric section, the rebuilding of stations, including the major reconstruction of Westland Row, and of course the opening of the Loop Line, which it was pointed out was of most benefit to the Kingstown line, as without it Kingstown would most likely no longer exist as the mail packet port. There was now a continuing annual liability of £4,000 by way of guarantee on the CofDJR stock.

The next item to be discussed was the urgent necessity for the diversion of the line at several points between Killiney and Wicklow, estimated to cost upwards of £200,000. It was argued that if the line were to disappear into the sea, the wherewithal to provide the annual rent would vanish with it and it just simply could not be paid. As against this, the D&KR shareholders were

enjoying their 9½% dividend without any input or worry on their part. It was extremely unlikely that the line would have been allowed to close beyond Bray as the L&NWR had a vested interest in it by way of opposition to the GWR scheme for a shipping service from either Fishguard or Milford Haven to Rosslare. The L&NWR were in fact preparing to advance a sum of £100,000 towards the completion of the line from New Ross into Waterford.

A number of other witnesses were called to give evidence, including Michael Keogh, the Company Secretary, W F Cotton, a member of Dublin Corporation and a director of both the Alliance & Dublin Consumers Gas Company and the DUTC, Maurice Dockrell and Sir Henry Cochrane, eminent businessmen in the city. Cotton referred to the serious inconvenience caused to the public by the altering of trains and by the closing of stations, the latter a reference to the closure of Sandymount and Merrion stations as from 1st October 1901. At the resumed hearing on 1st May, the chairman of the committee, Sir Samuel Hoare, Bt, stated that in his opinion this particular application was of a very exceptional character in that Parliament was being asked to intervene in a leasing arrangement between two private commercial undertakings. At the close of the hearing, the verdict was that Parliament could not accept the DW&WR's proposals in relation to the leasing agreement. The Bill in its modified form passed into law on 23rd June 1902, giving the company revised powers in relation to compulsory purchase of lands originally obtained under the Shillelagh Extension Act of 1897 and the Waterford Extension Act of the same year.

Despite this rejection, a similar application was made to Parliament in 1903 and although much the same ground was covered at the parliamentary hearing, success was achieved. Section 5 of this Act made provision for the yearly rent of £36,000 to, 'be reduced to such a yearly rent as may be agreed upon in writing between the company and the Kingstown company'. Section 7 went further in making provision for a surrender of the lease within a year of the passing of the Act. In the event of no agreement the matter was to be referred to arbitration. The DW&WR duly wrote to the D&KR on 30th January 1904 suggesting a meeting to discuss the action to be taken under section 7 of the 1903 Act. The Kingstown board was not enamoured with the idea of a meeting and requested that the matter be put in writing. Very general proposals put by the Wicklow board in February were met with a request for an inspection of the accounts of the D&KR section by a firm of London railway accountants. This was reluctantly agreed to but it soon transpired that all of the necessary figures were not being made available and the entire matter was becoming bogged down in needless correspondence. The DW&WR wrote at length in November to the BoT requesting the appointment of an arbitrator. Lord Balfour of Burleigh was in due course appointed to act in this capacity, the proceedings taking place in April 1905.

Below: **0-4-2 No 20 shunts a permanent way train in Dalkey sidings while 2-4-0T No 44 passes with an up suburban train.**
Sean Kennedy collection

Above: **From Killiney & Ballybrack to Bray the Westland Row line was single prior to 1915. Here one of the 1893 Kitson 4-4-2Ts heads south from Killiney & Ballybrack towards the site of the old Ballybrack station.** H Fayle - IRRS collection

Much the same ground was covered as at the hearings before the 1902 and 1903 Acts. The agreement arising from this arbitration dated 2nd May 1905 stipulated that the rent was reduced to an annual figure of £30,000 with a contingent rent of 30% of gross income in excess of £75,000, subject to a maximum in any one year of £36,000. This revised rent was to take effect as from 1st January 1906. Separate accounts were to be maintained in respect of the Kingstown section and these were to be available for inspection at all reasonable times. The Wicklow company was to spend an amount of £30,000 on various improvements between Westland Row and Bray, including both of these stations and in addition the Wicklow company was to obtain at its own expense any statutory powers to carry out the provisions of the agreement. Both companies were to pay the costs of the arbitration in equal proportions. So came to an end a dispute which had been rumbling on for some considerable time. The Act giving effect to the agreement was granted Royal Assent on 20th July 1906, the agreement being incorporated as a schedule. The Act authorised the company to borrow an amount of £350,000, part of which represented the £30,000 already referred to under the agreement. Amongst other items, this was to be expended on improved accommodation at

Kingstown, Bray and Harcourt Street, the construction and equipment of a new locomotive, carriage and wagon works, the provision of new rolling stock as well as various alterations at outlying stations. A complete revision was made in the stockholding of the company, which in addition changed its name as from 1st January 1907 to the Dublin & South Eastern Railway.

Major Diversions
Reference has already been made to the fact that difficulties were constantly being encountered with coastal erosion between Killiney and Wicklow, a distance of almost 20 miles. Seventeen months after the opening of the line around Bray Head, a heavy rock fall occurred in March 1857, a similar fall occurring seven months later and even at that early stage it was necessary to shift the line inland by about 8 to 10 feet. Following on the derailment of a train at Bray Head in August 1867, all trackwork in the area was renewed and in addition plans were drawn up to ease the line's curvature at Brabazon tunnel. Powers were obtained under an Act of 1870 to undertake a diversion 7 furlongs and 25 yards long between the first timber viaduct south of Bray and a point 330 yards from the Bray end of the third tunnel. Additionally, powers were obtained to provide a third line from Shanganagh Junction to Bray.

It was not however possible to raise the necessary capital for the completion of the full deviation at Bray Head and the company had to be content with the boring of two short tunnels bypassing Brabazon tunnel. This section was opened in 1876.

In 1879, two short bridges between Brandy Hole and Cable Rock tunnels were replaced by a single arch of stone and two shorter arches to support the rock above. Further to the south, Morris's Bank, the steep hillside of clay in the barony of Rathdown Lower, was also causing concern, so much so that an Act was obtained in 1882 for another diversion. The powers so obtained were renewed in 1886 and the work was carried out in 1888-89. It involved a 7 furlongs and 200 yards long deviation with a new stone underbridge built at Redford. The year 1897 saw plans for yet another deviation, 1¼ miles in length on the south side of Bray Head which would have moved the line well away from trouble. However by now the company was finding itself in extreme financial difficulties, largely the result of the tramway competition already referred to in this chapter.

On the night of 12th/13th November 1901, the east coast was rocked by a violent storm with hurricane force winds from a north-easterly direction and this, combined with a spring tide, caused considerable damage. At Corbawn Lane to the south of Killiney about 36 yards of the sea wall was undercut and fell down, while at Bray Head, the toe of the bank at Brandy Hole was cut away, causing the side of the bank to slip leaving the railway in a precarious state. Further south, between Morris's Bank and Ennis Lane Bridge, piling and groynes were disrupted. Between Greystones and Kilcool, just past milepost 17½, the railway bank was practically all washed away to a depth of between five and eight feet below rail level. Similar damage occurred at Ballygannon between mileposts 18 and 18¾.

Above: **One of Naylor Brothers' 4ft 8½in gauge locomotives, 0-4-0T *Percy* (Manning Wardle No 1399 of 1898), and a steam crane, both of which were used during the construction of the long tunnel at Bray Head between 1913 and 1917.**
D Paine collection

Largely as a result of this damage, plans and estimates were prepared by Shannon for a major diversion of the worst affected portion of the line from near to milepost 15 to a point 250 yards south of milepost 26, that is ¾ mile beyond Killoughter. The new line would have passed well to the west of Greystones, necessitating a new station alongside the main Bray to Greystones road close to its junction with Ennis Lane. Another idea was for a station in the neighbourhood of Church Road and the north end of the golf links. From Greystones it would have passed close to Killencarrig Mill and by-passing Kilcool about 500 yards to the east and Newcastle 350 yards to the east, new stations would have been provided to serve these villages, with two platforms and facilities for crossing passenger trains. The line would have been single to Newcastle and double from there as it was at the time. The works were estimated to cost in the region of £100,000. To enforce their views, the directors requested Sir John Wolfe Barry & Company to carry out an inspection and report. Their Mr Brereton visited and inspected the line in October 1902, his views coinciding with those of Shannon, except for a recommendation to double the new line southwards from Greystones rather than from Newcastle.

Plans were prepared and clauses inserted in the Bill for the 1903 session of Parliament. As early as May 1902 a Mr Wynne wrote on behalf of the Burnaby Estate stating they would strenuously oppose the scheme as proposed. For one thing it bisected the golf links at Greystones and also was to take in grounds belonging to the lawn tennis club. In December 1902, the provision of two stations for Greystones was suggested, one about 300 yards north of Church Lane, the other near the old mill at Killencarrig. The latter request was reinforced in January with a memorial from a total of 194 signatories,

the company agreeing to consider the matter. A deputation met with the directors on 5th February and let it be known that there was a large body of opinion in favour of moving the line even further inland to pass through Newtownmountkennedy and Ashford. It was reported that the deputation's ardour was somewhat dampened by the news that the company simply did not have the financial resources for such a course. Apart from the Greystones diversion, powers were also sought to divert a similarly affected stretch of line between the old Ballybrack station and the Bray River bridge. As a part of this deviation a physical junction would once again be created between the main line and the Westland Row line at Shanganagh. The relevant Act became law on 11th August 1903 but it is to be regretted that once again it was not possible to raise the necessary capital to carry out these works. It was a great pity that this was not possible as such diversions would undoubtedly have saved the company and its successors considerable sums of money.

Moving ahead to July 1910, Shannon reported to the board that a length of upwards of two miles of foreshore between Killiney and Bray was devoid of protecting walls. A slip occurred on Bray Head on the morning of 14th November 1911. Luckily it was possible to pull the rails over, leaving them some eight feet from the edge of the cliff. Co-incidental with this slip, the BoT wrote to the company enclosing correspondence from a Mr Edward Archer of

Greystones referring to the 'frightfully dangerous condition of the railway between Bray and Greystones', so bad that, 'a fair south-easterly breeze may be the cause of hurling hundreds over the embankment'. Archer suggested that if the BoT could not insist on the line being moved, then it should be compulsorily closed down. The directors carried out an inspection of the offending line on 23rd November and then drafted a reply to the BoT. The problem was due to the exceptionally heavy rains following on a particularly dry summer. They had every confidence in their Engineer who pronounced their line safe for traffic. With respect to Mr Archer, he was alarmist and was not an expert on such matters. Powers were once again sought to carry out deviation works and correspondence entered into both with the BoW and the Treasury seeking financial assistance. It was suggested that the BoT might like to send someone to inspect the line. This they did early in December.

Lieutenant Colonel von Donop carried out a thorough inspection and reported back to the BoT. He did not regard the line as being unsafe for traffic but did concede that further slips would occur and the line would in time become unsafe. The speed limit of 12mph imposed by the company around Bray Head should be permanently adhered to so as to reduce vibration as far as possible. A third diversion was undertaken in 1912, namely a stretch of line about a mile in length at Ballygannon, the line being moved inland by about 15ft to 18ft. The 1912 Act which received Royal Assent on 7th August, empowered a diversion from a point just south of No 3 tunnel to a point 1,070 yards north of Greystones station, a distance of 1 mile 6 furlongs and 3 chains. No financial assistance was forthcoming from the Government, hence the restricted works. The powers for the Killiney diversion obtained under the 1903 Act had been renewed in the interim and so instructions were given in January 1913 for the obtaining of tenders for the two diversion railways. It was reported in March that the tenders of Naylor Brothers of Huddersfield had been accepted.

A start was made almost immediately on the works at Killiney followed shortly afterwards by those at Bray Head. At the latter point, instructions were issued in June that the siding at Bray Head should be connected with the Bray and Greystones signal cabins for the purpose of warning approaching trains when blasting operations were about to take place. Two temporary sidings were installed, at milepost 14¾ facing to down trains and at milepost 16¼ to up trains, both being worked by keys on the section staff. Work on the Killiney diversion progressed sufficiently for estimates to be sought in February 1914 for a new frame for the signal cabin at Killiney, that of McKenzie & Holland being accepted in June. Here also, temporary connections were provided for the use of the contractor. The up diversion line between Bray and Shankill was brought into use on 27th March 1915. Instructions were issued at the end of September 1915 to the effect that the Killiney diversion would be opened for traffic on Sunday 10th October, the new signal cabin at Shanganagh Junction having been brought into use on the previous Friday. The new works were inspected by Lt-Col von Donop on 17th November and pronounced satisfactory apart from a couple of minor points. It is interesting to note that the BoT report incorrectly refers to the gauge of the new line as being 5ft 6in. Rails were 45ft in length, 85 pounds to the yard with 17 sleepers per length. Two new platforms were provided to replace the old Woodbrook halt and provide a service for Sir Stanley Cochrane's cricket ground.

With the Killiney contract approaching completion, a notice appeared in *The Irish Times* on 10th July 1915 advertising the sale of the contractor's plant on Friday 30th July at their yard near Shankill station. The sale was to include two 6-wheeled saddle tanks of 4ft 8½ins gauge with 12in cylinders, one by Manning Wardle, the other by Hudswell Clarke, a 12-ton Ruston steam navvy, 42 five cubic yard side tipping wagons, 3,000 sleepers and 30 tons of 60 pound rail. Two days later, Shannon wrote to the contractors informing them that they were obliged under their contract to obtain the company's permission to remove plant. In May 1916, Shannon reported that the navvy and two locomotives had been sold to a Mr Wake of Darlington, the navvy for £450 and the two engines for £450 and £400. These were most likely Hudswell Clarke No 672 and Manning Wardle No 1399. A second Manning Wardle 0-6-0T of 5ft 3in gauge (their No 1099 and named *Blackburn*) was taken over by the company in 1916 in connection with the Bray Head contract.

In the interim, work had been proceeding on the Bray Head contract, although not without problems. Early in January 1915 it was reported that a great deal of water was coming through the roof of the new tunnel along with subsidence in the surface over the excavations. By this time, 1,142ft of tunnel had been excavated from the Bray end, an average of 12ft per week. Shortage of miners and labourers was being blamed for the slow progress in June, while by November 371 yards of the 1,084 yard long tunnel required to be completed. Another severe storm on the night of 12th November led to

damage over a four mile stretch between mileposts 17½ and 21¾, while at milepost 13½, a 30ft breach was made in the sea wall. It was fortunate that the company had on hand old girders recently removed from Adelaide Road Bridge at Harcourt Street and these were used to span the breach. Side tipping wagons were borrowed from the GNR(I) and Naylor agreed to supply ten wagons of stone per day from the tunnel excavations at 10s per wagon.

All was not well however as far as Naylor Brothers were concerned and on 19th April 1916, Griffith, who had become Secretary in the previous November following Reid's resignation, reported to the board that he had served formal notice under clause 7 of the contract dismissing Naylor's. Furthermore, the plant and machinery was being taken over. William Henn Hinde, who had been appointed resident engineer to the company in charge of the diversion works, had

agreed to take over the construction works. He was to resign his position as engineer and the contract would be transferred to him. In passing, it should be mentioned that Shannon resigned his position as Civil Engineer in November 1916 and was replaced by C E Moore, his assistant, at a salary of £450 per annum.

Work on the diversion was completed towards the end of 1917 and was opened for traffic on 17th December following provisional BoT approval. The official inspection was carried out on 5th February 1918 by Lieutenant Colonel Druitt.

So came to an end the diversion works in D&SER days. The final cost of construction was £127,510.4s.6d, the Bray Head diversion costing £66,821.9s.5d and Killiney £60,688.12s.8d. The two figures, although similar in total, differ considerably in make-up, illustrating the diverse nature of the work in each case.

Right: **Construction of one of the portals of the new 1,084 yard long No 4 tunnel at Bray Head in 1917.** D Paine collection

Chapter Eight

THE D&SER ERA AND BEYOND

THE YEARS from 1907 up until 1920 were largely uneventful as far as the D&SER was concerned apart from the diversions carried out between 1913 and 1917, which were dealt with in the previous chapter. There are however a few events which must be chronicled at this point. A siding and loading bank were requested at Ferns in January 1907 by a Mr John Bolger and it was agreed that the company would pay for the necessary work on their lands, Bolger to provide additional land and pay for any work required on it. Correspondence was entered into with the GWR in regard to the service to be provided in connection with the Rosslare boat via the GS&WR. Letters were also exchanged with the GS&WR regarding the use of Wexford station, agreement on this matter being reached in 1908.

The siding on the Trader's or Mineral Wharf at Kingstown had been constructed by and at the expense of the company on land belonging to the Harbour Commissioners, subject to an agreement whereby they would remove it on one month's notice from the Commissioners. Rent was payable at the rate of £75, later increased to £100 per annum, the agreement to be renewed annually. Complaints were made in April 1911 by the BoW in relation to a considerable accumulation of permanent way materials on the Wharf, thus blocking the Quay as regards ships berthing there. The matter was referred to Shannon who pointed out that the stockpile of materials resulted from the recent import of a large supply of permanent way materials, including 200 tons of rails and 2,000 sleepers. The BoW had also complained in 1907 regarding the practice of loading and unloading wagons on a plot of ground near the Irish Lights Depot at Kingstown and also that the company's staff were in the habit of sweeping out wagons and leaving straw, coal and the like there. It was agreed that the company would remove such materials.

In September 1908, Shannon reported regarding the provision of a creosoting plant at an estimated cost of £3,000 which was briefly considered but deferred. The matter was brought to light again in September 1917 when correspondence passed between Moore and Messrs Alex Bruce & Company of Glasgow. Later in the same month, the Irish Railways Executive Committee reported that the GS&WR were prepared to undertake the creosoting of sleepers for the D&SER provided the latter were able to obtain and store the necessary supply of creosote. Once again nothing transpired but in March 1918, Coghlan reported that Moore had been making enquiries from a Mr Abercrombie as to the purchase of a creosoting plant which had been constructed for a Chinese railway. It was ordered that the plant be purchased for the asking price of £2,000 and a suitable site suggested by the General Manager for its installation. In the following month, it was arranged that the plant should be installed at a spot adjoining Ennis's Lane, near milepost 16. The BoT were approached for sanction and they agreed subject to the working of traffic at the (Jubilee) siding with an engine at the lower (Greystones) end of

the train. The use of the creosoting plant was short-lived as with an improvement in the supply situation, the decision was taken in November 1921 to dispose of the plant. The Jubilee siding remained into recent times, being used in its latter years for the storage of redundant 6-wheeled stock awaiting scrapping.

In July 1909, Sir Stanley Cochrane wrote requesting the company to seriously consider the erection of a platform on a piece of ground near to the cricket ground at Woodbrook and of stopping two or three trains there on the occasion of English matches. Cochrane agreed to provide the cost of the platform's erection if the company would undertake the work. It was agreed that Cochrane would be happy if the company tapped the Westland Row line only for down passengers and possibly put a platform on the up side of the Harcourt Street line. An existing underline bridge just north of the proposed platforms would suffice for passengers to cross the line. Total estimated cost was £450, which included two platforms and the necessary signalling. Cochrane came back in August to advise that in his opinion a platform on the Kingstown line only would suffice and requested that the work proceed urgently, instructions to this effect being given to Shannon. The platform was opened for traffic on 3rd February 1910. With the diversion of the railway in this area, a new halt was opened on the diversion line on 10th October 1915, this time with two platforms.

Electrification proposals.
The first reference to a possible electrification of the Kingstown line came in the Notice for a Bill, details of which were published in the press in November 1896. A brief report stated that it was the intention of the directors to make application in the next parliamentary session for powers to equip their line between Dublin and Kingstown as an electric railway. The Notice sought powers to work railways of the company and of the CofDJR by electricity, to erect generating stations, enter into agreements for supplying electricity and to acquire patent rights. Nothing came of this and the two Acts of 1897 make no reference to it. Four years later, Messrs Bennett & Ward-Thomas, consulting electrical engineers of Manchester, offered to draw up a scheme for electrifying a part of the company's system.

In 1904, Cronin visited some of the electric railways operating in England, including the recently converted Liverpool and Southport line of the Lancashire & Yorkshire Railway. This latter appears to have impressed Cronin most as it approximated 'more nearly to our own line and conditions than any other line I saw'. His report comprised brief details of the power sources, trains, receipts and expenditure for the various lines and then moved on to estimate the cost of electrifying the line from Westland Row to Dalkey. One of the necessities would be the running of a more frequent service, say every ten minutes, which would require six train sets running at any one time. A generating station would be provided at Grand Canal Street, the only point with an adequate supply of water. Two substations would be required, at Booterstown and Kingstown. Provision would be by third rail; no mention is made of the proposed voltage, but as all the English lines operated at either 500 or 600 volts, it is reasonable to assume this would have been the ideal. Total cost of electrification from Amiens Street to Dalkey was estimated at £127,453, including £32,000 for the provision of rolling stock in the form of multiple units. Once again, nothing further ensued.

Six years later, Pim and Reid paid a similar visit to various lines in Britain, not all of which were electrified. Opinions were divided as to the merits of electrification, the North Eastern Railway officials being very positive about the benefits from converting their Tynemouth line. On the other hand, neither the GWR or the London & South Western Railway saw any benefits to be obtained from the huge capital costs involved. Both of these companies had successfully introduced rail motors to combat tramway competition, whereas the latter's neighbour, the London, Brighton & South Coast Railway found electric units had considerably increased their traffic. A file under the heading of 'Parliamentary Powers' dated 1910 includes a long memorandum from Reid on the subject of financial and other matters relating to the D&KR which suggests that the latter company might be approached to see if they would, 'share equally the cost of obtaining expert advice on the subject (of electrification) with a view to a joint scheme'. There is no evidence that the D&KR directors were ever approached.

It was to be another ten years before Wild again produced figures, this time for electrifying the line from Amiens Street to Bray. Based on a half-hourly service for ten hours per day with two coach sets (140 seats) and a 20 minute service for three hours with four coach sets (280 seats), capital expenditure would be in the region of £220,000. This figure included eleven power cars at £5,000 each and fourteen trailers at £2,500 each. From the overall figure could be deducted £40,000 from the sale of redundant locomotives and carriages. Overall journey time from Amiens Street to Bray for an all-stops train would come down from 53 to 40 minutes.

This was the last mention of electrification and during the remaining few years of the company's independent existence, attentions were turned to the idea of petrol railcars. In October 1921, Wild produced general specifications for such a vehicle, which would be capable of carrying 50 passengers and of doing a six mile run on the level in 20 minutes with eight intermediate stops of 20 seconds each. Two months later, the L&NWR offered a petrol-electric railcar which Wild inspected at Croxley Green in December. Whilst in good condition, Wild considered it unsuitable for use on the D&SER. It had worked for some time on the Penygroes to Nantyle branch in North Wales, being withdrawn when it proved inadequate to carry the traffic on that line.

Opposite page, left: **The Royal train of July 1911 with chief officers. The group includes J Coghlan, Traffic Manager; R Cronin, Locomotive Superintendent, and F W Pim, Chairman On the extreme right is A G Reid, General Manager.** IRRS collection

This page, right: **A pass issued in connection with the 1907 Royal visit.** IRRS collection

No. 4

ROYAL VISIT.

ADMIT BEARER

to Special Enclosure at Kingstown Railway Station on Wednesday, 10th July, 1907.

By Order of the Directors,

M. F. KEOGH,

Secretary.

THIS CARD TO BE PRODUCED.

Quotations were obtained from Messrs Claytons in February 1922 for four petrol-electric railcars but there the matter rested. Further correspondence ensued with various companies, including the Great Central and North Eastern Railways in England and the MGWR. As late as March 1924, the J G Brill Company offered to supply the 'Model 55 Gasoline Rail Car'.

In the event, we had to wait another 30 years for diesel railcars to appear on the South Eastern and 60 years for electrification of the suburban section, apart that is from the Drumm Battery train experiments of the 1930s, referred to later.

War, Rebellion & Civil War.

The outbreak of the First World War in August 1914 had little immediate impact on the D&SER. Unlike Britain, where railways were put under Government control immediately on the outbreak of war, this was found unnecessary in Ireland. It was not until December 1916 that all the Irish railways would be placed under Government control under the Regulation of Forces Act of 1871. It was agreed that compensation would in due course be paid on the basis of net receipts for the year 1913.

The Irish Railways Executive Committee was set up to take control of railways as from 1st January 1917, the committee consisting of six members, including the Under-Secretary of State for Ireland and one representative from each of the five larger companies, including the D&SER. This situation lasted until August 1919, when the Government set up the Ministry of Transport, H G Burgess being appointed to the position of Director-General of Transport in Ireland. Government control finally came to an end on 15th August 1921.

While the war was raging in Europe, difficulties were being encountered nearer to home. The Easter Rising of 1916 had as one of its objectives the isolation of Dublin from the rest of the country. The D&SER were particularly unfortunate in that both ends of the system were affected and traffic was almost entirely suspended except for military purposes. The line between Westland Row and Kingstown was placed under military control and under partial control between the latter point and Ferns. The stations at Westland Row and Harcourt Street were seized by the rebels on Easter Monday, the 24th April, and held respectively until 3rd May and 25th April. The Works at Grand Canal Street also fell into rebel hands, remaining so for the duration of the rebellion. A workmen's train was held up at Enniscorthy and the occupants forced to walk back the 15 miles to Wexford. The Loop Line Bridge was damaged by shell fire from the gunboat SS *Helga* which was moored in the river. All in all, the D&SER estimated property damage at £2,000 and lost receipts

at £14,000. In due course, compensation of £3,000 was awarded. Claims from the travelling public for refunds on unused portions of season tickets were declined, the standard reply being to the effect that the military authorities were responsible for the stoppage. Following an enquiry to the Great Northern, it was decided to extend season tickets by the period of interruption. In due course, the directors expressed their high appreciation of the manner in which the staff and officers carried out their duties despite considerable danger to themselves. A number of staff received bonuses in this regard.

The leaders of the 1916 Rebellion were duly court-martialled and sentenced to death. One of their number however, Eamon DeValera, escaped the firing squad. In December 1918 elections were held, with the Sinn Fein party securing 73 of the 105 Irish constituencies. They refused to take their seats in the Westminster Parliament and set up their own Parliament in Dublin, with DeValera as Taoiseach (Prime Minister). He was in due course arrested and held in Lincoln Jail from which he escaped to the USA, where he set about raising funds to further the Irish struggle. The period from 1919 onwards was one of much civil strife in Ireland. DeValera returned to the country in 1921 and in December a Peace Treaty was signed, whereby most of Ireland was to have its own Parliament although remaining in the Commonwealth; the six north-eastern counties were to remain as part of the United Kingdom. Despite apparent independence, there were dissenting voices with almost half the members of the Irish Parliament voting against the Treaty, causing a split which was to lead to the outbreak of civil war in May 1922.

Following the deployment of the Black & Tans, a volunteer force recruited to quell unrest arising from the War of Independence, a group of L&NWR employees at the North Wall refused in May 1920 to unload a shipment of munitions and were duly suspended. Their action was widely supported by railwaymen throughout the country, who refused to work trains carrying British forces or munitions. Within days, D&SER men refused to move military stores from the Victoria Wharf at Kingstown for Fermoy and were duly suspended. On the morning of 26th June, when the up Wexford train arrived in Greystones, a party consisting of a Sergeant and six men of the King's Own Regiment from the nearby Kilpedder camp boarded the train. The driver and guard declined to work the train forward when the soldiers refused to leave. The stalemate continued for some 30 hours when the soldiers left. In October, the 09.30 from Wexford was held up at Rathdrum in similar circumstances, although the military left after about twenty minutes. However, their actions

were repeated on almost a daily basis until they eventually tired of the exercise after two weeks.

Services on the D&SER were not so badly disrupted as those on other lines. The railwaymen met at the end of December and reluctantly called off their ban. The company's General Manager, Frank Brooke, was murdered in his office in Westland Row on 30th July 1920, for allegedly being involved in undercover activities for the Viceroy. During 1921, there were a number of isolated incidents, none of which caused major damage or disruption to the railway, including the ambushing of the up day mail near Killurin and an armed raid on Milltown station.

In March 1923 the General Manager reported that at the request of the military an armoured train was being fitted up at the Factory. Immediately on completion in April it was commandeered by the military for use on the Killarney branch of the GS&WR. The train consisted of 2-4-2T No 64, fitted with armour plating, together with ten other vehicles converted from passenger and goods stock. The name *Faugh-a-Ballagh* was painted on the side of the locomotive. After nearly two months away the train was returned on the 20th June, but without the engine which was undergoing some light repairs at Tralee, the necessary spares being forwarded the next week. However, it was 16th August before the locomotive returned and it was not until October that Wild was given authority to dismantle and refit the whole of the armoured train.

As far as the D&SER were concerned, the twelve months of civil war ending in May 1923 represented the most destructive period and was to lead to a very severe shortage of locomotives and rolling stock, a problem which had to be urgently addressed by the Great Southern Railways in 1925. The major disruptions occurred in the south-eastern corner from Macmine to Wexford and Waterford. Having said that, a number of attacks were made on the system further north. It would not be possible within the confines of this history to detail more than a few of the more serious or spectacular incidents which occurred. Appendix J lists all the major attacks. An excellent two-part article in Volume 3 of the *Journal of the Irish Railway Record Society* by Dr George Hadden gives a detailed account of 'The War on the Railways in Wexford, 1922-23'.

Killurin was to be the scene of a number of ambushes and derailments. From the raiders' point of view it was an ideal location, isolated, with a good cover of fences and trees and a network of laneways and byroads providing escape routes. In addition, the railway ran alongside and above the River Slaney, this fact leading to a number of trains finding their way into the river. On 15th August 1922, two lengths of rail were removed from the Wexford end of Killurin

Enniscorthy station in Edwardian days, showing the original signal cabin which was destroyed in 1922. The warehouse seen behind the station belonged to Messrs Donohoe's who provided considerable traffic to the company. Courtesy A Kendrick

tunnel. The down night mail came upon the gap without any warning. Locomotive No 14 turned over, pinning Driver George Turner of Bray who was badly scalded and was off work for a year. Twenty-two wagons were also derailed, the road being restored 17 hours later. In November, No 18 ended up in the Slaney while working the down night goods. She was removed to Grand Canal Street in late December along with No 32 which had suffered a similar fate.

On the night of 10th December 1922, both the D&SER and the GS&WR goods sheds in Waterford were destroyed by fire. In the former, nine D&SER wagons were destroyed. The civil war took on a new intensity in January 1923 and a number of serious incidents occurred. On the night of 18th January, the down 18.05 passenger from Harcourt Street was ambushed at Scarawalsh, no warning being given. Hauled by 4-4-0 No 68, the six bogie train was doing about 60mph when it came upon the broken road in the pitch dark. As the train derailed, machine gun fire was opened up, the raiders having expected a large contingent of troops. Miraculously there were no serious injuries amongst the passengers who were removed from the train by the raiders, who then set it on fire.

Another spectacular event occurred two days later when a collision was staged between two trains at Palace East. The up 06.30 goods from Waterford, hauled by 0-6-0 No 51, running very late due to an earlier disruption, was standing in the station at Palace East at about 10.00. No 68, which had been involved at Scarawalsh only 36 hours earlier, was working an empty passenger train and was shunting when the raiders arrived. They took No 68 and ran her back down the steep gradient towards Chapel. There, they set her in motion back towards Palace East. In the meantime, No 51 with part of her train, had been sent off down the grade to meet No.68. Although the combined meeting speed was quite low, considerable damage was done to both engines, which remained on the rails with the wagons piled up around them. The two engines were later scrapped.

A week later an even more spectacular occurrence was enacted at Macmine Junction. In all, some 35 to 40 raiders descended on the station and once again it was believed, erroneously, that the mail was carrying a number of armed troops. The first move was the stopping of the mail at Killurin at about 16.30, but finding no soldiers aboard the train was allowed to proceed to Macmine. By the time of its arrival, there were four trains already at Macmine, an empty cattle special and a ballast train in the sidings, the 16.15 from Enniscorthy on the down road and the Waterford connection out of the mail in the branch platform. The mail having been brought in to the up platform between the two passenger trains,

No 67 was sent off to de-rail herself at a point about half a mile from the station where the road had been broken. This job had not been fully completed and No 67 stayed on the rails eventually stopping short of steam some 18 miles away beyond Camolin. The Enniscorthy train was sent out about a mile along the Wexford line so as to bring her back to collide with the Waterford train which followed. Then the cattle and ballast trains were heaped up on the pile, the whole lot being set on fire. One amusing part of the whole exercise was that 0-4-2 No 22 struck an isolated van at speed. The latter was demolished with its roof coming to rest in one piece beyond the engine. Total damage was estimated at £50,000. It was reported that nothing of the carriages remained apart from the wheel sets. The last incident of note was the destruction of Amiens Street central signal cabin on 26th April 1923. The significance of this destruction was that pilot working had to be established, resulting in engine No 47 being derailed at the turntable, ending up in the postal sorting office below.

In all, 14 engines, 29 carriages and 65 wagons were either destroyed or seriously damaged, a further six engines and 33 carriages being described as slightly damaged. This represented a sizeable proportion of the total stock of the company. It has to be said that in the main, railwaymen remained loyal, some going beyond the call of duty. One such was Permanent Way Inspector Michael Forde, who was responsible for the repairing of all the Wexford area disruptions. It should be mentioned that in an attempt to

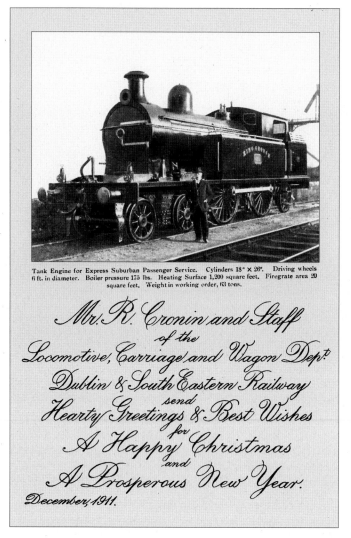

Tank Engine for Express Suburban Passenger Service. Cylinders 18" × 26". Driving wheels 6 ft. in diameter. Boiler pressure 175 lbs. Heating Surface 1,200 square feet. Firegrate area 20 square feet. Weight in working order, 63 tons.

Mr. R. Cronin and Staff
of the
Locomotive, Carriage and Wagon Dept.
Dublin & South Eastern Railway
send
Hearty Greetings & Best Wishes
for
A Happy Christmas
and
A Prosperous New Year.
December, 1911.

2

MAIN LINE—WEEK-DAYS.

Distance from Harcourt-st.	DUBLIN to WEXFORD		1 Pass	2 6.55 am Mail ex Westland Row.	3 Shillelagh Goods	4 Day Goods	5	6 Pass	7 Mineral	8 Mixed	9 Pass	10 Pass	11	12 Goods and Mail	13	14
Miles			A.M.	A.M.	A.M.	A.M.		A.M	P.M.	P.M.	P.M.	P.M.		P.M.	..	..
—	Harcourt Street ..	dep.	..	..	7 20	..	..	10 10	2 40	..	..	5 10	..	9 50	..	..
12½	Bray ..	arr.	..	7 28	8 5	..	..	10 37	3 20	..	..	5 37	..	1040	..	..
		dep.	6 45	7 32	8 20	9 30	..	10 45	3 40	..	..	5 45	..	1055	..	..
17	Greystones ..	arr.	6 57	7 43	8 40	9 50	..	10 57	..	..	..	5 57	..	11 15	..	..
		dep.	6 58	7 46	8 55	10 10	..	10 59	..	..	..	6 0	..	11 16	..	..
19¾	Kilcool ..	arr.	7 4	..	..	10 20	..	11 4	..	..	..	6 5	..	..	..	..
		dep.	7 5	..	..	10 30	..	11 5	..	..	..	6 6	..	..	..	..
22½	Newcastle ..	arr.	7 11	..	9 15	10 40	..	11 10	..	..	..	6 11	..	..	..	..
		dep.	7 12	..	9 25	10 50	..	11 11	..	..	..	6 12	..	..	..	..
27¾	Wicklow ..	arr.	7 22	8 4	9 45	11 10		11 21	..	..	..	6 23		11 47	..	..
		dep.	STOP	8 6	1035	12 10		11 23	..	..	..	6 26	..	11 48	..	..
29¾	Rathnew ..	arr.	..	8 11	..	12 25	..	11 28	..		..	6 31	..	..	..	..
		dep.	..	8 12	..	12 35	..	11 29	..	..	..	6 32	..	..	..	..
33¼	Glenealy ..	arr.	..	8 21	11 10	..	..	11 38	4 50	..	..	6 41	..	..	..	..
		dep.	..	8 22	11 15	..	..	11 39	5 30	..	..	6 42	..	..	..	..
37¼	Rathdrum ..	arr.	..	8 33	11 35	1 15	..	11 50	5 50	..	..	6 52	..	1 0	..	..
		dep.	..	8 36	12 15	1 30	..	11 56	5 55	..	..	6 57	..	1 5	..	..
38¼	Balleece Siding ..	arr.	..	..	..	..	..	..	6 5	..	..	..	..	..	..	..
		dep.	..	..	..	..	..	..	STOP	..	..	..	..	..	..	..
41½	Cronebane Siding	arr.	..	..	..	..	..	..	..	..	..	..	..	..	..	..
		dep.	..	..	..	..	..	..	..	..	..	..	..	..	..	..
42¾	Avoca ..	arr.	..	..	12 35	1 50	..	12 7	..	..	..	7 8	..	1 25	..	..
		dep.	..	..	12 45	2 0	..	12 8	..	..	..	7 9	..	1 26	..	..
44¾	Woodenbridge Jun.	arr.	..	8 49	12 55	2 10	..	12 12	..	..	..	7 13	..	1 35	..	..
		dep.	..	8 51	1 10	2 25	..	12 17	..	..	..	7 17	..	1 40	..	..
49	Arklow ..	arr.	..	8 58	..	2 40	..	12 25	..	..	..	7 25	..	1 55	..	..
		dep.	..	9 0	..	2 55	..	12 27	..	..	..	7 27	..	2 10	..	..
51	Kish Siding ..	arr.	..	..		3 10	..	..	..	..	..	..	..	..	..	..
		dep.	..	..		3 20	..	..	..	..	..	..	..	..	..	..
53½	Inch ..	arr.	..	..		3 35	..	12 36	..	..		7 36	..	..	..	..
		dep.	..	..		3 45	..	12 38	..	..		7 38	..	..	..	..
59½	Gorey ..	arr.	..	9 15		4 5	..	12 48	..	..		7 48	..	2 45	..	..
		dep.	..	9 17		4 40	..	12 51	..	..		7 51	..	3 0	..	..
67	Camolin ..	arr.	..	..	To Shillelagh	5 0	..	1 4	..	..	From Waterford	8 4	..	..	..	..
		dep.	..	..		5 10	..	1 5	..	..		8 5	..	..	..	..
69¾	Ferns ..	arr.	..	9 32		5 20	..	1 10	..	..		8 10	..	3 25	..	..
		dep.	..	9 33		5 50	..	1 12	..	..		8 12	..	3 35	..	..
77½	Enniscorthy ..	arr.	..	9 44		6 10	..	1 25	..	..		8 25	..	3 55	..	..
		dep.	..	9 46		STOP	..	1 30	..	3 25		8 30	..	4 15	..	..
78½	St. John's Siding ..	arr.	..	..		..	..	..	..	..		..	..	..	..	..
		dep.	..	..		..	..	..	..	..		..	..	..	..	..
81	Edermine Ferry ..	arr.	..	..		..	..	1 37	..	3 33		8 37	..	..	..	..
		dep.	..	..		..	..	1 38	..	3 34		8 38	..	..	..	..
83¼	Macmine Junction	arr.	..	9 55		..	..	1 43	..	3 40	..	8 43		4 30	..	..
		dep.	..	9 58	..	..	..	1 47	..	4 5	3 55	8 47	..	4 45	..	..
86	Killurin ..	arr.	..	..	..	..	..	1 52	..	4 12	4 0	8 52	..	..	..	..
		dep.	..	..	..	..	..	1 55	..	4 15	4 3	8 55	..	..	..	..
92¾	Wexford ..	arr.	..	10 15	..	..	..	2 10	..	4 30	4 15	9 10	..	5 15	..	..

No. 7 will run only when there is sufficient traffic for it.
No. 6 will pass No. 4 at Wicklow, and No. 3 at Rathdrum.

Above: **The DSER Locomotive Department's Christmas card of 1911, with Cronin posing in front of his latest creation, 4-4-2T No 20 *King George* – also a page from a Working Timetable which came into force on 13th October 1919.** W E Shepherd collection

isolate Waterford, the viaduct at Taylorstown on the Rosslare to Waterford line, was blown up in July 1922 putting the South Wexford line out of action for the duration of the civil war. As a result, the GS&WR Rosslare to Cork boat trains worked via Wexford and Macmine Junction until December 1923.

Economies and a Resignation

Under the provisions of the Irish Railways (Settlement of Claims) Act of 1921, compensation totalling £3 million was paid to the Irish railway companies arising from the period of Government control. Of this figure, the D&SER received a sum of £163,282. In April 1923, the Chairman, Sir Thomas Esmonde, prepared a lengthy memorandum on the company's financial position. At the time of payment of the first installment of the compensation, the general account was in debt to an amount of about £30,000; it was therefore absolutely essential that a brake be put on all further expenditure. A number of suggestions were put forward to bring this about: improving traffic receipts, withholding all expenditure on works which could be delayed (this would include the cancellation of works already approved), sale of old materials, a reduction of expenditure by substituting cheaper alternatives and the early collection of debts due to the company.

Traffic receipts for the first quarter of 1923 showed a reduction of £6,800 as against the corresponding period in 1922 and a close examination of the Summer train service was suggested to bring about economies and increase receipts. Since the beginning of the year, works to the extent of £50,359 had been authorised, much of it on relaying. Sir Thomas felt that it might be possible to dispose of surplus materials. Some savings might be possible in the Head Office and clerical work at stations. Particular attention was directed to the company's motor car and motor cycle combination purchased in June 1921. The principal reason for the purchase of the former was to ensure the safe movement of the company's cash. Unlike the GS&WR and the MGWR, which respectively hired a horse cab and a taxi daily, the D&SER had the additional difficulty of having two Dublin termini. The motor cycle had been intended to expedite the work of traffic officials south of Bray.

Reports from the various company officials in response to this report were discussed at the board meeting on 30th April. Reference was made to the run-down state of the rolling stock resulting from the war period and subsequently the effects of the civil war. In addition, many of the undamaged engines and carriages were very old and under ideal conditions should have been scrapped many years previously. No new carriages had been purchased since 1914 and some 32% of the stock had been maliciously damaged or destroyed during the previous ten months. The Factory at Grand Canal Street was sorely stretched in its efforts to keep up with day to day maintenance. The works were old fashioned and totally unsuited for building and repairing vehicles - it will be recalled that Furnivall had reported unfavourably in 1894 and nothing had happened since that time.

The General Manager reported that further savings had been effected in the Traffic Department, resulting in staff being reduced to the borderline between comparative safety and positive danger in working. A number of stations had effectively been reduced to halts with a consequent reduction in the number of Stationmasters. In relation to permanent way, an average of £100,000 per annum had been expended on arrears of relaying. Moore, the Civil Engineer, went on to point out that reductions had been made in 1916 in the number of milesmen employed, with further drastic reductions in June 1921. Numbers had been reduced by 10% and lengths increased by 20%. The latter were longer than on any of the other principal companies. The purchase of a ballast pit at Scarawalsh (milepost 73¼) and its proposed extension would provide a good alternative to the Balleece Quarry.

The General Manager, Michael Maguire, submitted a lengthy report. In his view, the current situation had been brought about principally by two factors – the present stagnant position of trade generally resulting from the activity of Irregular Forces and the interference by the Government in the issue of wages and the eight-hour day. Every possible effort had been made to reduce expenditure in the Traffic Department, including re-organisation of services to reduce overtime working; the abolition of the post of Assistant Stationmaster; abolition of some signal cabins and the switching out of others, with a consequent reduction in the number of signalmen; the replacement of Stationmasters by junior clerks; the introduction of an 'omnibus' train service on the Harcourt Street line on Sundays and the abolition of the Balleece and other special trains where possible. A further report was requested from Maguire in August 1923. Included in this report were details of staff employed in his and the traffic departments. In 1923, there were 14 male and ten female clerks employed at £5,064.17s.0d per annum, the corresponding figures for 1916 being thirteen, one and £1,082.10s.0d. The reasons for the increase were the introduction of the eight-hour day, national wage agreements and a requirement for more detailed statistics. Nevertheless, Maguire now considered he could dispense with three staff. The board pointed out that he should be able to dispense with more than three and he was ordered to report yet again. His attention was also drawn to the inefficient state of discipline as proved by two recent accidents. The matter had to be put right immediately or drastic action would be taken.

Adverse comments were also made regarding the slackness of the workmen in the Permanent Way Department.

Yet another report was submitted in October when Maguire noted that, 'in deference to the opinion of the board . . . further reductions should be made', the proposal being to let another eight go. The directors strongly disapproved of the suggested reductions being made, 'in deference to the board' and the last straw came when it was suggested that the General Manager's staff actually be increased and the reductions be made elsewhere. It was pointed out that duties and responsibilities of the Engineering and Locomotive Departments had been transferred to the respective Superintendents and the Audit Department had been placed under the control of the Secretary. At a board meeting on 17th October, it was agreed that the substitution of Stationmasters by junior clerks was false economy and it was ordered that they revert to the old system.

While these matters were being considered, another matter came to light, namely a report from R D Griffith, the Company Secretary, regarding the Rathdrum Hotel following a number of complaints from the hotel manageress, Miss McGuinness, of active obstruction from the Rathdrum Stationmaster. On one occasion, he had burst into the bar at 20.30, ordering all the customers out amidst scenes of abusive shouting. Delph which had been loaned by the hotel was not returned and Miss McGuinness was informed that it had been accidentally broken at Westland Row. Chickens sent from Rathdrum to Westland Row were not accepted there and ended up being disposed of when they rotted. The ordinary station staff were most apologetic but advised that they were carrying out orders. Further investigation revealed that obvious attempts were being made to obstruct Miss McGuinness in the discharge of her duties. On being questioned, Maguire confirmed he knew of

the affair and had endeavoured to put a stop to it. After full consideration of the problems, the decision was taken to recommend that the position of Maguire be altered to that of Traffic Manager at a salary of £1,500 per annum. It is hardly surprising to find that Maguire resigned his position shortly after this meeting.

Amalgamation

The new Government appointed a commission in 1922 to consider the future of the railways in Ireland. There was talk of either grouping or nationalisation of the railways operating in the State. As regards the latter, the D&SER considered, rightly, that the political situation in Ireland was unfavourable to the taking over by the fledgling Government of such an important and highly technical business as the railways. On the question of a grouping, it was felt that this would have the effect of eliminating immediately and absolutely all competition. Considerable emphasis was put on the company's difficulties, including the payment of a nil or very low dividend compared with companies such as the Belfast & County Down and the GNR(I) returning 5½% to 6½% and the GS&WR's 3½% to 5%. The difficulties of coping with coastal erosion were brought to the commission's attention, the conclusion being that the line south of Bray would, some day, have to be moved further inland.

At the end of the commission's deliberations, two separate sets of conclusions were put forward. The majority view was that the Government should purchase the railways, but that their management should not be directly under a Minister of the State. Instead a national railways board should be constituted which would have absolute powers of management. The minority report felt, like the D&SER, that the time was inappropriate to ask the newly formed Government to undertake such a heavy financial burden. Instead, it was recommended that

Right: **2-4-2T No 29, formerly *St Mantan*, waits to depart from Bray with an up local to Amiens Street circa 1924.**
J M Robbins - IRRS collection

the railways within the Irish Free State be unified and placed under Government control for a three year period. The Government's preferred option was that of voluntary grouping, but without direct Government control. A meeting was held on 6th February 1923 between the boards of the D&SER and the GS&WR to see if any terms could be agreed. The South Eastern people recommended two groupings, one between the GNR(I), the MGWR and the D&SER, incorporating all railways connected with them. The other group would comprise the GS&WR and all the light railways. It should be pointed out that the GS&WR and the Cork Bandon & South Coast Railway had already held discussions in April 1922 and come to an agreement for their amalgamation, but this had been put on hold pending the outcome of the commission's investigations.

It is clear from correspondence files that any proposed groupings, as far as the D&SER were concerned, were being orchestrated from the London Midland & Scottish Railway boardroom in Euston. At a meeting of the directors of the GS&WR and the MGWR held on 23rd April 1923, Sir William Goulding, Chairman of the former company, expressed the view that the prospects for a complete amalgamation in the south were good. As far as the D&SER was concerned, everything had been arranged except for the relative values of the Ordinary stock to be exchanged. On this, arbitration had been offered but was turned down. Goulding had been to see Mr Cosgrave, President of the Executive Council of the Irish Free State, to explain the position and seek more time for negotiations. Cosgrave emphasised the desirability of the formulation of an agreed scheme by the companies. Failing this, the Government would proceed with their own scheme. The GS&WR and the Midland duly drew up a preliminary agreement, but the D&SER now withdrew from the negotiations and sought copies of the correspondence between the Government and the GS&WR, the LMSR advising them, 'not to meet anyone, individual or committee on any subject until we send our own case to the Government'.

The D&SER files include a further proposed amalgamation, that of the D&SER with the MGWR. They would jointly take over the GNR(I) line as far as Dundalk. Running powers were to be sought over the Irish North to Derry so as to tap the Donegal traffic. The D&SER's existing running powers to Waterford and Limerick would be exercised and extended to include Cork. Under this proposal the GS&WR would take over the CB&SCR and 'other small railways in the south'. If the Government was already committed to a GS&WR/MGWR merger, then these two would form one group, the other being the D&SER and the GNR(I) routes in

the Free State and the Donegal railways, together with a new line from Sligo to Bundoran. Once again, the D&SER would exercise their Cork and Limerick running powers. This scheme was put to the President in June 1923 and he in turn sent a copy to the GNR(I) for their views, so that when the D&SER wrote to the latter company suggesting a meeting, they were informed that such a meeting would serve no useful purpose 'as the scheme is one which does not in any way commend itself to this company'. In reply to this rebuff, the D&SER wrote almost in desperation seeking to know if there was any scheme which would appeal to the Northern company. In fact, the Government favoured unification of all the railways in the State, excluding the GNR(I), due to its cross-border operations.

The main problem in relation to the D&SER was financial. It will be recalled that the L&NWR, as predecessor to the LMSR, had subscribed a loan of £100,000 towards the construction of the Waterford extension, also purchasing £87,000 of the Guaranteed Stock of that undertaking. This loan automatically set in motion clause 29 of the 1870 Act under which the L&NWR were empowered to appoint a director to the DW&WR board. This was the Rt Hon Henry Givens Burgess and he remained a director until he was appointed Director General of Transport in Ireland in August 1919. When Government control ended in August 1921, Burgess returned to the board, serving as Deputy Chairman. He had in fact commenced his railway career as a junior clerk with the DW&WR in 1873 at the age of fourteen, leaving to join the L&NWR five years later. He served in various posts with that company, eventually becoming General Manager of the LMSR, then the largest railway company in the world with some 300,000 employees. Returning to 1902, the terms of the loan provided for the payment of interest at 3½%. In addition to the loan, the D&SER were in receipt of what were described as, 'voluntary advantages' to the tune of more than £20,000 per annum. This figure included a payment by the LMSR in respect of the 'whole expense of cross-channel staff at Westland Row', and a preferential percentage on all cross-channel traffic. It was these two items which created most of the problems in resolving the D&SER position as the LMSR would not guarantee continuation of these payments to the new company.

A further meeting between the Government and representatives of the South Eastern was held in November 1923, when the company's favourable position with the LMSR was discussed at some length. The Government line was that the amalgamations should not be held up because of such arrangements. If an agreement should be reached on the price to be paid for the com-

pany's ordinary shares, the LMSR issue could be separately resolved. Failure to come to an agreement would force the Government to refer the entire matter to an arbitration tribunal. At a meeting of the Irish Railways Joint Committee in January 1924, it was announced that the D&SER had refused to meet the committee as a whole but had offered to meet with the GS&WR alone. The whole matter continued to drag on in a most unsatisfactory manner and in due course it was agreed in July that the other companies should proceed with the amalgamation under the title of the Great Southern Railway, the Railways Act of 1924 giving authority to this.

The LMSR continued to press either for repayment of the loan of £100,000 or a seat on the board of the new company. Failing an agreement, the LMSR would not guarantee a continuance of the rebates to the South Eastern. Eventually the D&SER question was referred in November 1924 to the Arbitration Tribunal, agreement being reached in the following month. An amount of £47.10s.0d was to be paid for each £100 of D&SER stock, representing a considerable increase on the initial offer of £20 made by the GS&WR on behalf of the amalgamating companies, later increased to £30 by the Great Southern Railway after its formation under the Railway Act of 1924. As far as Euston were concerned, it was agreed that Burgess should become a director of the Great Southern Railways which officially came into being on 1st January 1925. In celebration of their achievements, the D&SER directors awarded the office staff a sum of £5,000 much to the annoyance of their shareholders and the National Union of Railwaymen. The issue of the D&KR had perforce to be held over until the larger company's future had been settled. They were awarded £100 of 4% Debenture stock and £60 in Guaranteed Preference stock for each £100 of their ordinary stock. So came to an end the company which had been incorporated almost 80 years previously and had only finally realised its ambitions of reaching Waterford 20 years prior to its demise.

Post D&SE Era

One of the first acts of the new company was the rationalisation of goods services in Dublin, Harcourt Street Goods Depot being closed at the beginning of March 1925. Reference has already been made to the inadequate facilities at Kingstown and Bray. The latter was resolved in September 1927 with the provision of a second platform on the down side, thus allowing greater flexibility in operation there. Land had been purchased with the Royal Marine Hotel in 1900 for the purpose of providing a second platform. The opportunity was also taken to rationalise the signalling, the north and south cabins being replaced by a single box on the down side just inside the level crossing gates. The situation at Dun Laoghaire was more complex due to the restricted space available. The line was situated at low level in cutting beside Crofton Road and it was not until June 1957 that a new platform was put in on the up side. In addition, the overbridge at the south end of the existing platform was not of sufficient width to cater for two trains. Coincidental with the provision of the second platform, alterations were made to the signalling arrangements, the cabin at Dunleary crossing had its block instruments removed and the section now was from Dun Laoghaire to Merrion. The new platform was actually brought into use on 23rd June 1957.

In an attempt to effect further savings, Clayton steam railcars operated for a short period in 1929 between Harcourt Street and Foxrock. They were very unpopular with the crews due to poor steaming and high coal consumption.

A much more interesting innovation was reported in September 1931 when Drewry railcar No 386 was converted to operate on batteries perfected by a Dr Drumm. The experiments were sufficiently successful for two 2-car sets to be put into service in 1932, initially between Amiens Street and Bray. In 1939 they were transferred to the Harcourt Street line to join two newly constructed sets, lasting there until 1949, after which the batteries were removed, enabling them to be used as normal coaches.

During the period between October 1934 and November 1937, various alterations were made to the suburban section signalling and these are detailed in Chapter Fourteen. Other track alterations included the singling of the Newcastle to Wicklow section in August 1927, 50 years after it had been doubled. This was part of a cost-cutting exercise carried out by the GSR. Most of the Midland main line was singled at the same time. The short section from Amiens Street to Newcomen Bridge Junction was also singled, in 1929. Various stations were reduced to halts, these and others being subsequently closed – closure dates can be found in Appendix F. In contrast, Sandymount and Merrion stations were re-opened on 5th March 1928 after a lapse of 27 years. The latter was short-lived as it was again closed, permanently, in 1934. As part of a further economy drive, Sandymount must have been the most opened and closed station in Ireland. As part of a further economy drive, it, along with Sydney Parade, Booterstown and Salthill were closed on 13th June 1960.

However, insufficient public notice had been given and they were re-opened a week later before closing again on 10th September 1960. The various private sidings, including the Wicklow Quay tramway, were also closed. The last to survive was the RDS siding at Ballsbridge, closed in October 1971. As against this, new sidings were opened in 1964, at Shelton Abbey in the Vale of Avoca and at Stafford's Wharf in New Ross in 1927. The former was built to serve the fertiliser factory of Nitrigin Éireann Teoranta (now Irish Fertiliser Industries) and produces a good traffic in ammonia and fertilisers.

War time cutbacks saw many branch lines closed, including that from Woodenbridge to Shillelagh as from 24th April 1944. In April 1945 it was announced that the Aughrim to Shillelagh section would not re-open. Between 1947 and 1952 the up Enniscorthy goods went to Aughrim to serve Fogarty's Mills. However in December 1952, application was made to the Transport Tribunal for permission to close the branch, this being granted in the following year despite strong objections; the last working occurred in June 1953, lifting of the branch being completed by the end of the Autumn. Woodenbridge itself was closed from 30th March 1964.

In the intervening period, a much more contentious closure occurred, that of the main line section between Harcourt Street and Shanganagh Junction as from 31st December 1958. It is difficult to understand the short-sightedness of the closure of a 10½ mile stretch of suburban railway. It was replaced by a bus service intended to call at all the stations on the closed line, but Route 86 was soon cut back to a new terminus at Cabinteely. Bearing in mind the considerably longer journey time, very few people would have used it as a replacement for the train service.

There has been talk down the years of the

route of the old line being utilised either as a dedicated busway or for a Light Rail Transport system, so it is interesting to record the announcement in December 1995 giving the go-ahead for such an LRT, though currently only as far as the old Stillorgan station near Sandyford. The only remaining South Eastern branch, from Macmine to Waterford, was closed throughout to passenger traffic on 1st April 1963 and to goods traffic from Macmine to New Ross on the same date.

Under the Transport Act of 1944, the GSR was amalgamated with the Dublin United Transport Company to form a new company, Córas Iompair Éireann, which was nationalised in 1950, when it also took over the Grand Canal. Shortly after the nationalisation, attention was turned to the dieselisation of the system. In the period 1953-54, a total of 60 diesel mechanical railcars were delivered from England, some of these being fitted out for suburban working. Following this, 94 diesel electric locomotives in two classes came from Metropolitan Vickers of Manchester. It was not long before the South Eastern services were operated by diesel traction. By the 1970s, despite very run-down equipment in the form of the railcars, de-engined and fitted for push-pull working, suburban traffic was buoyant. Sydney Parade was re-opened on 6th June 1972, Booterstown on 3rd March 1975, and a new station was opened at Corbawn Lane in Shankill on 10th June 1977. This was followed on 9th June 1980 by the re-opening of Kilcool, closed since 1964.

The mid-1980s were to see a major development in the suburban services, under the brand name of Dublin Area Rapid Transport with the introduction of electric traction at 1,500 volts DC on the Howth to Bray line on 23rd July 1984, the same day seeing the re-opening of Sandymount and Salthill stations.

Right: 4-4-0 No 56, *Rathmines*, departs from Bray with the 15.00 Dublin to Wexford train on the 21st July 1914.
Ken Nunn collection - LCGB

Forty 2-car sets were constructed in Germany by Linke Hoffman Busch. They are generally operated in 6- and 4-car sets at peak hours and 2-cars off-peak. It was announced in 1995 that the DART is to be extended to Greystones. Passenger carryings increase annually and an additional five 2-car units have been ordered. These will also allow a mid-life overhaul of the existing fleet, many of which have now clocked up close to one million miles in service.

One regrettable development during the electrification of the line in preparation for the DART services was the closure in October 1980 of the connection from Dun Laoghaire to Carlisle Pier. However, the new terminal for Stena Line's high speed service to Holyhead is only a few minutes walk from Dun Laoghaire station. The inconvenience caused to passengers transferring from rail to ship which resulted from the closure of the line out to the pier has, to a large extent, been overcome by the recent developments.

Top: **The signal cabin at Enniscorthy following its destruction on the 16th September 1922.** Enniscorthy Museum

Centre left: **A pigeon special crosses the 210ft Slaney Bridge south of Enniscorthy in CIE days.** L A Dench

Below: **The armoured train at Grand Canal Street in April 1923 with, in the middle, locomotive No 64, as fitted with armour plating in the D&SER works.** Sean Kennedy collection

Chapter Nine

SERVICES AND TRAFFIC

FOR THE opening of the line between Harcourt Road and Bray on 10th July 1854, down trains departed Dublin at 08.00, 10.00, 13.00, 15.00, 17.00 and 20.00, calling at Dundrum, Stillorgan, Carrick-mines and Shankill. There were corresponding up trains and on Sundays there were five trains in each direction. On the Dalkey to Bray section which opened on the same day, all trains called at Killiney, leaving Dalkey at 09.30, 11.00, 13.00, 16.00, 18.00, 19.30 and 21.00, with five trains each way on Sundays. On weekdays, in addition there was a train from Killiney to Dalkey only at 08.54, return-ing from the latter at 17.30. The board gave some consideration to the timetable at their meeting on 12th November 1856 and as a consequence advised the Traffic Manager that the 08.48, 09.40 and 11.00 up and the 15.30, 16.30 and 17.30 down trains were to be regarded as, 'permanently fixed'. Trains from each end of the suburban section were not to exceed eight in number, the remain-ing five in each direction to be started at hours which would suit both Wicklow and local traffic. *The Financial Journal* for 30th May 1859 announced that third class weekly tickets would be issued for workmen by the 06.30 down on Mondays, returning at 19.25 from Bray. Fares were quoted as being 3s to Kingstown and Sandycove, 3s.6d to Dalkey and 4s to Killiney and Ballybrack stations. These privileges were subsequently extended to Bray at 4s.6d.

By June 1859, the Harcourt Street line had eleven down trains between 06.00 and 23.00, four of which ran on to Wicklow; two further trains ran only as far as Dundrum - these latter were referred to as short trains. The Bray trains took 45 minutes with the exception of the 23.00 down which stopped only at Dundrum and consequently required only 30 minutes. On the Westland Row line, there were thirteen down trains, five run-ning only to Ballybrack in 48 minutes, two to Dalkey in 42 minutes and the remainder to Bray. The Kingstown section appeared sepa-rately with trains every half hour on week-days from 06.00 to 23.30, calling at Booterstown, Blackrock and Salthill. Cer-tain trains also called at Merrion. First and second class tickets carried the privilege of bathing at the company's baths on weekdays on payment of 2d each per person for towels

and attendance. About this time, the Traffic Manager was ordered to make arrange-ments for the running of an early morning train, about 06.00, for workmen from Har-court Street to stations down to Bray. It would appear that such a train, known as a Parliamentary train, was running on the coast line as the Secretary reported in July 1860 that he had written to the BoT request-ing their sanction to an alteration of the up Parliamentary train from Kingstown from 06.30 to 07.30 in order to avoid clashing with the new postal and passenger service, a request which was approved. Parliamentary trains were introduced to railways in Britain and Ireland under the Regulation of Rail-ways Act of 1844, 'to secure to the poorer class of travellers the means of travelling by railway at moderate fares, and in carriages in which they were protected from the weather'. An interesting point regarding the July 1861 timetable is a reference to two trains leaving Bray for Greystones at 08.45 and 08.55, arriving at 09.00 and 09.10, clearly indicat-ing that trains were being operated at that period on the time interval system.

Following on the extension of the line to Rathdrum (Kilcommon) in August 1861, four trains ran through from Harcourt Street, the journey time being two hours in each direction for the 36¼ mile trip. There were two trains each way on Sundays. No extra trains ran beyond Bray. It is of interest to note at this time that there was a short working from Harcourt Street to Carrick-mines at 09.20, arriving 09.44 and with only a four minute turnaround, arrived back in Harcourt Street at 10.20. There were also two trains to Ballybrack only, while on Sun-days these trains ran to Dalkey. On the Har-court Street line, a 19.00 ran to Dundrum in ten minutes. Through fares from Dublin to Kilcommon were 6s, 4s.6d and 3s, first, sec-ond and third class single, with return fares of 9s, 6s.9d and 4s.6d.

It should also be mentioned that with the opening of the extension, engines were detached at Wicklow Junction and the train brought into and out of Wicklow by horse power. This situation lasted until April 1867 when the board ordered that trains to and from the south of Wicklow were to be driven into Wicklow station and not shunted by horses as formerly.

With the opening to Ovoca (Newbridge) in July 1863, a total of five trains were pro-vided each way daily on weekdays, four of which accommodated all three classes, the remaining one being first and second class only. There were three trains each way on Sundays. Journey times varied from 2 hours and 20 minutes to 2¾ hours. Four months later, the line reached Enniscorthy and the service was reduced to four trains each way, at 08.15, 13.15, 17.15 and 20.30 down, the latter being the mail train. The mail, far from being the fastest of the four, took 5 hours for the journey, the fastest being the 13.15 and 17.15 in 3¾ hours. The up mail left Enniscor-thy at 01.15, the remaining up trains were at 08.15, 12.15 and 17.15. There were two trains each way on Sundays. The opening to Wexford on 17th August 1872 produced a notice in *Freeman's Journal* indicating three trains from Dublin at 09.00 (arriving at 13.20), 13.00 (17.15) and 17.05 (21.25). There were four up trains from Wexford, the 15.00 running to Ovoca only.

The timetable for December 1879 is still extant, a table inserted inside the front cover referring to the Ballywilliam line as the Bally-william (New Ross branch). Connections were provided out of the 09.00 and 14.00 from Harcourt Street, the former right through to Kilkenny, the latter only to Bally-william. In addition, there was an 08.30 from Enniscorthy to Kilkenny. Up trains left Kilkenny at 07.15 and 14.30 and connected into Dublin trains at Macmine Junction, while the 19.00 from Ballywilliam ran to Wexford. As regards main line services, there were three through trains from Dublin at 09.00, 14.00 and 17.10; in addition, there was an 06.00 from Ovoca to Wexford and an 09.00 Woodenbridge to Arklow. Two down trains ran on Sundays, at 09.00 and 20.00, the latter arriving in Wexford at 01.00 the next morning. In relation to the suburban services, on the Harcourt Street line there were nine local trains to Bray, the first leav-ing the city at 06.30, for third class passen-gers only. The morning mail stopped at Milltown, Dundrum and Stillorgan, while the evening mail made all stops to Bray. The 17.10 from Harcourt Street stopped only at Shankill and reached Bray in 30 minutes. There were in addition an 09.30 limited stop to Shankill and 12.30 and 14.30 to Dundrum

Above: **The imposing terminus at Harcourt Street, designed by George Wilkinson for the Dublin & Wicklow Railway and opened on 7th February 1859.** IRRS collection

only. The Shankill train returned at 10.00 and made all stops to Dublin. In all there were fifteen trains each way on Sundays, three of which only ran to and from Dundrum.

The 1879 timetable states that the service on the Kingstown line commenced at 06.00 and finished at 23.30, leaving each terminus every half hour. In addition, 17 express trains not stopping at intermediate stations between Dublin and Kingstown, were run to Bray. It may be of interest to make reference to some of the fares at this time. Dublin to Wexford single fares were 15s.6d, 11s.7d and 7s.8d, return 25s.10d, 19s.4d and 12s.10d. Harcourt Street to Dundrum fares were 6d, 5d and 3d, and to Bray 2s, 1s.6d and 1s, the same as from Westland Row. On Sundays, return tickets were issued from Westland Row, Harcourt Street, Bray and intermediate stations to stations south of Bray at single fare for the double journey. Return tickets for all three classes for any distance exceeding 15 miles were available for return on the following day, for distances exceeding 25 miles for two days and for journeys in excess of 50 miles for three days from the date of the ticket. Subscription or Season tickets were issued for periods of one, three, six or 12 months on the coastal line as far as Delgany (Greystones) and on the Harcourt Street line to Wicklow, the annual rates for the latter being £25 and £22, first and second class gentlemen, £16.13s.6d and £14.13s.6d for ladies and tutors and £12.10s.0d and £11 for children under 19 years of age and governesses. Tutors and governesses were required to produce a certificate from a family in which they were engaged in order to avail of the reduced rates. A reduction of 15% was allowed for three or more members of a family subscribing at full rates (ladies or gentlemen). This reduction did not apply to tutors or governesses. Subscribers on the Kingstown line were entitled to cold sea bathing at the company's bathing places free of charge (except 1d for attendance, towels and dresses) on weekdays during the times

the baths were open between 1st May and 1st November.

The Daily Express for 5th May 1882 announced an improved service on the Westland Row to Bray line. Journey times were reduced to 35 minutes each way, trains running non stop from Kingstown to Westland Row. The revised service resulted from the doubling of the line between Kingstown and Dalkey and the opening of one new station at Killiney to replace Killiney and Ballybrack stations. The main line service basically remained at three trains each way daily on weekdays. In January 1886, there was in addition an 07.30 from Bray to Wicklow Old station and a 10.00 Dublin to Gorey, the latter returning at 13.15. The Wicklow train had been put on in response to considerable agitation from residents of Wicklow with the opening of the new station at Brickfields. The short workings to Dundrum had gone by 1881, the Shankill service lasted a bit longer, but it had also ceased by January 1886. At this date, six trains ran each way from Dublin to Greystones. The Dundrum working appears to have been reinstated as the board decided in July 1888 that it should be extended to Foxrock, being shown in the timetable as leaving Harcourt Street at 10.35 and returning from Foxrock at 11.00.

With the New Ross line open for traffic, there were three trains from Macmine Junction to New Ross plus two through to Ballywilliam and Bagenalstown. There was also a short working from Palace East to New Ross. On the main line, there was now a 10.00 to Gorey and a 10.30 Wexford to Gorey. One train returned to Dublin at 13.15 and as there is no mention of a return working to Wexford, we must assume that it was an empty carriage working. The opening of the Loop Line in May 1891 introduced for the first time through services from Bray to

Howth in a time of 1 hour 5 minutes, five minutes longer than the electrified DART services in 1995, the latter albeit with many more stops. Initially there were 12 trains each way from Bray to Howth on weekdays and ten on Sundays. The through service ceased in January 1907 when the GNR(I) introduced a rail motor coach on the Amiens Street to Howth service. The opening of the Drumcondra Link line in December 1906 saw a through local service from Kingsbridge to Amiens Street. This consisted of seven trains each way on weekdays, there being no Sunday service. The service was however short-lived, the DW&WR minutes for 16th January 1909 referring to the discontinuance of the one remaining local train a fortnight earlier.

An interesting concept was put forward in August 1892 when Payne was called upon to report as to how the train services on the Westland Row and Harcourt Street lines might be made interchangeable so that passengers could proceed in either direction without delay. One suggestion from the Board was that trains might run round from Harcourt Street to Westland Row and vice versa, but this might affect the Greystones trains. Having listened to Payne's views on the matter, the directors decided that there should be a 'continuous train service' in both directions, the various officers being instructed to prepare a scheme for its implementation. The proposed service quickly became known as the 'circular' train service. Following further consideration of the matter, Payne was instructed in January 1893 to alter the times of the ordinary trains from Harcourt Street to Bray so as in as many cases as possible to secure a connection at Bray with up Westland Row line trains. There is little doubt that this alteration led to the installation at Bray of the scissors crossing, enabling two trains to use the single platform simultaneously.

On 23rd April 1897, the company announced that as from 1st May the 07.00 express mail from Harcourt Street would be altered to leave from Westland Row at 06.20, calling at Kingstown, Dalkey, Killiney, Bray and all stations south as in the previous timetable, arriving in Wexford at 09.20. The up mail was to stop at Killiney and Kingstown and arrive in Westland Row at 19.30. Co-incidental with the opening of the halt at Bray Head and the introduction of the railmotor service between Bray and Greystones, an improved service was provided as from 1st October 1906, with 15 trains each way, including main line services. Down trains called at Bray Head Halt four minutes after departing Bray and occupied 13 minutes between Bray and Greystones, one minute longer than the non-stopping trains in the section. The railmotor service lasted only a year, yet in October 1910 Greystones enjoyed a service of 13 trains each way on weekdays.

Following the outbreak of war in Europe in 1914, a number of trains were discontinued or altered. From 12th August the 09.25 Harcourt Street to Wexford was discontinued as were two trains on the Shillelagh and Macmine branches. As the War of Independence intensified, some local services were curtailed in November 1920. Further changes were made in March and April 1921 to fit in with curfew regulations in Dublin. As from Monday 21st March the last down trains from Harcourt Street and Westland Row departed at 19.30 with corresponding up departures from Bray at 18.45 and 18.50. The 20.00 curfew was altered in April to 22.00, enabling the last down trains to leave at 21.00. Resulting from the coal miners' strike in Britain, further curtailments took place from 11th April 1921. The withdrawal of curfew regulations in July resulted in a resumption of late evening services. An interesting item in the timetable at this time was a 07.00 mixed from Harcourt Street to Bray, withdrawn on 3rd October 1921 and replaced by a 07.15 passenger. The outbreak of the Civil War early in 1922 resulted in the issue of timetables on virtually a bi-monthly basis for the next twelve months as services were altered to suit circumstances.

As from 3rd April 1923, stopping trains between Harcourt Street and Bray were accelerated from 35 to 30 minutes, this being achieved by the weight of trains being reduced and the discontinuance of the checking of tickets on up trains at Ranelagh. In August 1922, it was ordered that the goods train services be altered to run during the hours of daylight, 'as a measure of safety in the present unsettled state of the country'. Details of the composition of main line passenger trains were listed. Restaurant cars were withdrawn from the day mails, which in future were to be comprised only of 6-wheeled stock. As an example, the 16.20 up mail was to be made up of one first, two thirds, three vans (including a milk van for Harcourt Street) and the Travelling Post Office, with another third attached at Wicklow. This latter had been worked down on the 13.00 from Harcourt Street. In the event of heavy traffic offering, the agent at Wexford was authorised to add an extra third. The up day goods was authorised to stop additionally at Avoca, Rathdrum, Newcastle and Greystones to pick up wagons left behind by the 11.15 Woodenbridge goods. With the ending of civil war, the June 1923 timetable saw a resumption of full services throughout the system. Bogie coaches were re-introduced on main line trains south of Greystones and the up and down night goods trains were reinstated.

Reporting to the board in November 1921, Maguire stated that the number of suburban passengers carried in 1909 amounted to 3,096,754, whereas the projected figure for 1921 was only 972,000 odd. Proposals were submitted for an experimental Sunday train service between Dublin and Bray, but more particularly between Westland Row and Dun Laoghaire, where he proposed a half-hourly service in each direction. The trains would consist of an engine, bogie coach and a small van with tickets being issued by a conductor/guard, thereby reducing the number of staff on Sunday duty on the Kingstown line. Authorisation was given for an experimental service and for the alteration of the necessary coaches. In the following June, the Chairman gave particulars of trial trips conducted with the first of these coaches, (the conversion of which cost £2,040), stating it was hoped to have another five ready for traffic in August. The September 1922 Sunday timetable shows a 15 minute frequency operating between Westland Row and Dalkey, with trains hourly between Westland Row and Bray.

A note in the working timetable stated that a light engine would leave Bray for Harcourt Street at 08.30, stopping at all stations. A train conductor was to travel on this engine for the purpose of opening each station, the engine then working the 09.30 to Wexford. There was an hourly service from 10.15 to 21.15 and then at 22.30. The last train of the day left Harcourt Street empty at 23.15 and called at all stations to enable the train conductor to close all stations and extinguish all station lights.

Below: **2-4-2T No 46 Princess Mary drifts into Shankill with a down local, comprised of ten 6-wheelers and a brake van, circa 1914.** H H Coghlan - Real Photographs

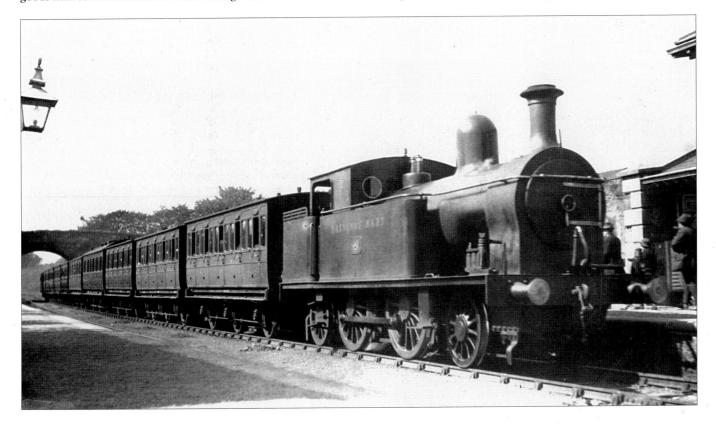

Above: **2-4-2T No 27, formerly *St Aidan*, waits to depart from the down platform with a Dalkey-Amiens Street working. The locomotive displays the GNR(I) style of lettering, applied during its overhaul at Dundalk in 1923.** Sean Kennedy collection

Below: **Foxrock looking north, showing the new and enlarged signal cabin of 1924 on the right and the island platform on the up side, behind which is the track** for racecourse traffic and the race platform. Leopardstown Race Course can be seen in the upper left background, and former Drumm Battery train 'D', converted for locomotive hauled working, stands in the race siding. Sean Kennedy

Shillelagh branch

With the opening of the Shillelagh branch, in May 1865, two through trains were provided in each direction; from Harcourt Street at 09.10 and 17.00 (arrivals respectively at 12.25 and 20.10), with up trains at 09.45 and 17.30. Within three months of the opening, the Traffic Committee recommended that trains on the branch be stopped on 15th August at a temporary platform near Aughrim for the convenience of persons wishing to attend the consecration of a new church at Annacurragh. It was also recommended that for the future, main line trains should wait half an hour for branch trains at the Ovoca Junction in case of the latter running late. This would suggest that the through service from Harcourt Street had been replaced by a branch connection. By December 1879, there were three trains in each direction and this remained the pattern until May 1895, when there were four trains each way, at 09.30, 12.00, 17.00 and 20.05 down, and 08.45, 11.10, 16.10 and 19.10 up. These times show that the branch was worked from the Shillelagh end. For the first time, one train is shown each way on Sundays, 12.16 down and 18.30 up. Four trains remained the norm for the remainder of the company's independent existence, except during the war years, one train each way being taken off in August 1914.

The timetable for September 1924 shows down trains at 08.50, 12.00, 17.55 and 20.15, the first two being mixed, the former running every day except Wednesdays, when there was an 08.25, also mixed. The Sunday service had ceased entirely by 1920. Between October 1910 and November 1920, the Sunday passenger trains only ran on the first Sunday of each month. Goods traffic was catered for by the provision of one train each way, generally leaving Shillelagh in the morning and returning in the middle of the day. In October 1908, the company persuaded the BoT to assent to the running of a mixed train on the branch. Following correspondence with the BoT early in 1923, Electric Train Staff working was suspended as from 5th February 1923 with the intention of working with one engine in steam. This was estimated to effect a saving of £10.6s.9d per week to the Traffic Department, but it was short-lived, the line reverting to ETS working within a week. It was finally dispensed with in April 1945.

Goods traffic

Working timetables prior to the last decade of the company's existence are no longer available, making it difficult to catalogue the goods trains prior to about 1910. However we can glean some useful information from the board and traffic minutes as well as BoT accident reports. As an example, in November 1863 the Finance and Traffic Committee recommended that the goods train be discontinued between Arklow and Enniscorthy for the present, and that the goods traffic from the, 'lower end of the road' be conveyed by the night mail trains. In September 1872 it was agreed to run the day goods to Shillelagh instead of to Arklow, returning at 12.45 and bringing passengers, the same as the 13.00 from Arklow, in other words a mixed train. The night goods was to leave Wexford at 20.00. In May 1880, on Payne's recommendation, it was ordered that an additional goods be put on between Harcourt Street and Ovoca, possibly in the hope of reviving the mineral traffic which was in decline at this period. Ten months later, the goods was altered to leave Shillelagh in the morning instead of in the evening time.

Brief reference has been made to the mineral traffic carried by the railway, but some additional information will give the reader a better understanding of the extent of this traffic. The opening of the Mineral or Trader's Wharf at Kingstown in 1863 brought about a change in attitude to the railway as a means of moving ore from Ovoca to a suitable port for export to Swansea. The first mineral train to use the new wharf ran from Ovoca on 12th January 1864, carrying 130 tons of ore. With the railway now having a virtual monopoly, various complaints were made in 1865 regarding the excessive charges made for the carriage of ore. In reply to these criticisms, the DW&WR stated that ore from Ballymurtagh was brought by horse-drawn wagons over the tramway to Ovoca, where it was loaded on to special 5ft 3in gauge wagons and then taken the 38 miles to Kingstown Mineral Wharf. The DW&WR also completed the shipping documents as well as shipping the ore, all for 4s.3d per ton, the company's profit being only ¾d per ton per mile. An agreement was finally reached in November 1866, whereby the mining company was to be responsible for delivering all ore to Ovoca station. The new rates agreed were 3s.9d per ton for pyrite and 3s.6d for iron ore to Kingstown, 1s.6d to Arklow and 4s to Harcourt Street. At one point in 1865, the Wicklow Copper Mine Company reverted to the use of road carriage rather than pay the high rates of carriage, but with the new agreement they returned to the railway. A short branch was installed at Sroughmore for the use of the Connorree Mining Company in 1865, being removed four years later due to non-payment of carriage charges.

Prior to 1872, the company's rolling stock returns do not distinguish between open goods and mineral wagons. In that year however, mineral wagons appear to have reached their peak with 271 such vehicles, a figure reduced to 148 by December 1880, 99 by 1888, and their complete disappearance from stock in 1900. These reductions coincided with a decline in the quantity of ore being extracted from the Ovoca mines. The second half of 1875 saw production down by 10,400 tons on the corresponding period of the previous year. This reduction resulted from increasing supplies of ores becoming available from Norway, Spain and Portugal at competitive prices. In 1878, total imports into Britain amounted to 679,312 tons, of which Spain contributed 419,000 tons and Portugal 136,000 tons. In comparison, Ballymurtagh produced 13,542 tons

Ever mindful of the necessity for effecting economies wherever possible, the Chairman reported to the Board in November 1895 that unnecessary wagons and engine power were being used. As a consequence, Grierson and Coghlan were ordered to consider the recasting of the timetable in respect of, 'the whole goods and cattle traffic', to see what trains they could dispense with. When the company decided to use their running powers between Waterford and Limerick Junction early in 1904, it was arranged to run one train each way, from Waterford at 07.55 and from Limerick Junction at 15.25, with arrivals respectively at 13.15 and 19.35. The times of departure were altered somewhat in the 1906 and 1907 timetables and as mentioned in Chapter Four, these trains were withdrawn in 1908.

The working timetable for October 1919 shows a Shillelagh goods leaving Harcourt Street at 07.20, the day goods for Enniscorthy from Bray at 09.30, arriving Enniscorthy at 18.10 and a combined goods and mail train for Wexford at 21.50 from Harcourt Street. There was also a mineral train leaving Harcourt Street for Balleece Siding, arriving at 18.05. This train and its return working at 18.35 were to run only when sufficient traffic was on offer. Later, as part of the company's economy drive, the separate mineral train was dispensed with and this traffic was handled by the down day goods. The day goods worked the Kish Siding south of Arklow as required. As regards St John's Siding for Davis's Mill south of Enniscorthy, wagons were propelled out from Enniscorthy by the station pilot engine.

Postal services.

The postal authorities approached the Board in February 1855 enquiring whether the company would undertake the carriage of mailbags between Dublin and Bray. This was agreed to at a charge of £60 per annum, with an additional £10 for every additional station at which bags might be delivered. During the period when the D&KR section was being re-gauged, complaints were received from the postal authorities regarding delays to the mails between Kingstown and Dublin. The Secretary was directed to reply to the effect that the company were doing all they could to maintain the service, but the Post Office should remember that single line working was causing difficulties. In connection with an improved postal service a new contract was entered into for the conveyance of mails.

One element of the new service was the completion and opening for traffic of the extension from Kingstown to the pier. Under the agreement, dated 9th October 1858, the company were obliged to run two express mail trains daily in each direction between Dublin and Kingstown Pier, starting at certain fixed hours as laid down by the Postmaster General and running non-stop in 15 minutes. Mail vans were to be provided by and at the expense of the company. In return for this service, the company was to receive the sum of £2,000 per annum. The revised service was to have commenced on 1st August 1860, but was delayed for a month due to the non availability of the new steamers.

A new contract was concluded in May 1867 for a rail service from Harcourt Street to Enniscorthy with a coach connection onwards to Wexford. Trains were to leave Harcourt Street at 09.10 and 19.30, with coaches departing Wexford at 07.30 and 20.15 to connect with up trains from Enniscorthy. The company were obliged to carry the mails between Enniscorthy and Wexford in coaches, 'suitably fitted up, painted and furnished with lamps', the drivers of which were to be, 'steady and sober ... not less than 18 years of age'. Payment was £6,000 per annum. In July 1869, the company wrote seeking to discontinue the contract and in due course it was replaced by a new five year agreement providing for an annual payment of £6,500. At the board meeting on 27th October 1874, some consideration was given to the subject of a new agreement. It was agreed that the company would ask for £10,000 per annum, but were prepared to accept £8,000 rather than let the matter go to arbitration. In due course, a figure of £8,500 was agreed for a ten year period, subject to an undertaking that the day mail service to Wexford be not altered so as to be less convenient than the existing service.

Mr Allen, the Inspector of Mails, attended the Board on 15th April 1875 and a long discussion ensued as regards the times of the up and down day mails. It was in due course agreed that the down train should leave Harcourt Street no later than 09.00 daily, Sundays excepted, and arrive in Wexford no later than 13.30. The up mail was to leave Wexford not earlier than midday with an arrival not later than 17.40. With the completion of the new arrival platform at Westland Row, permission was sought from the BoT in September 1880 for its use by the mail trains, subject also to the agreement of the postal authorities. Yet another agreement was concluded in July 1884, payment now being £12,000 per annum and to take effect from 1st January 1885. Some changes were made. The up day mail was now to arrive at 18.00, the 06.30 down from Westland Row was due at Kingstown at 06.52. Ordinary morning trains from Kingstown

could be held back for 10 or 15 minutes, if by so doing the English mails could be dispatched so as to catch the Cork and Belfast trains.

With the opening of the Loop Line, the Secretary of the Post Office wrote to the company in July 1891 inviting an offer for the conveyance of mails. It was agreed that a figure of £4,000 per annum be requested for the entire service, but pending arrangements for the carriage of the southern and western mails, a figure of £2,500 would be accepted. In the following October, Payne was instructed to arrange with the Post Office for the running of a special train every Thursday morning between Carlisle Pier and Westland Row in connection with the Canadian mail service.

Excursion traffic

As early as July 1858, excursionists were considered by the board, when special trains were advertised for Wicklow Races to be held over a two day period. Special fares were quoted, only valid for travel on the special trains. Similar excursion trains were run for regattas at Bray and Wicklow, and Easter 1859 saw return journeys being provided at single fare for return on the day of issue only. In April 1870, Payne was instructed to make such arrangements as he might see fit in connection with the approaching Spring Cattle Show of the Royal Dublin Society. The RDS traffic was to be important to the company, with sidings later being installed at the RDS grounds at Ballsbridge. The Wicklow Steeplechase was held in Rathdrum each year and so important was this event, that all passenger traffic south of Bray was suspended on the day of the races, with the exception of the day mail trains. Special trains operated from Harcourt Street, Wicklow, Arklow, Shillelagh and Wexford. These races were held at Rathdrum until 1876, when they were transferred to Redcross, the nearest station being Ovoca. To cater for the heavy traffic to this event, it was normal to borrow up to 15 carriages from the GS&WR. On one such occasion, it was reported that seats had been stolen from some of these carriages. Similar races were held at Wexford. Mention was made in August 1871 of private excursions being available for groups of eight persons to Rathdrum. A wagonette service was provided to Glendalough, the Devil's Glen and Newrath along with a five course dinner, all for 12s.6d per person.

Amongst other interesting excursions was a Cook's excursion to London, Paris and Brussels advertised in July 1875. Validity of return tickets from stations south of Bray was to be extended for 16 days without extra charge. In May 1879, a Great Temperance excursion was run from Wexford as well as a special from Dublin to Gorey for Courtown Harbour, while for a football match between Wicklow and Wexford in December 1887, trains ran from Bray and Shillelagh to Wex-

ford. In later years, circular cycling tours were offered in conjunction with the Dublin & Blessington Steam Tramway. Participants travelled by train from stations south of Bray to either Harcourt Street or Westland Row, thence by road to either Poulaphouca or Blessington, and returning to Dublin by tram. Examples of fares quoted were 3s.6d first class rail and tram from Bray, from Wicklow 4s.9d first class and 3s third class. These fares were applicable in 1897.

In March 1888, the company received a request from a Captain Quinn for accommodation at Foxrock for passengers to and from the contemplated racecourse at Leopardstown adjoining the station. Smith was requested to submit plans and estimates for an additional platform and sidings. These were approved in May at an estimated cost of £1,040 for earthworks, platform and signalling. Later, an amount of £480 was included for a third departure platform. In November 1888, Smith was ordered to carefully inspect the old girders of Dundrum Bridge to see if these could be utilised in a new footbridge at Foxrock. This idea appears to have been rejected as Messrs Hill & Smith's tender for a new footbridge costing £522.10s.0d was accepted in February 1889, the old one at Foxrock being moved to Shillelagh. When plans were being prepared for the extended works at Foxrock, consideration was given to seeking permission to close Leopardstown level crossing and divert traffic by the overbridge at Stillorgan station, but this was opposed by the Grand Jury and was not pursued. Later, it was proposed to replace the crossing by an overbridge but this idea was also shelved.

A special shuttle service was operated from Harcourt Street to Foxrock on race days from early morning. (These trains continued to run on race days into the CIE era. A delightful sequence made on Boxing Day 1952, showing such specials arriving at Foxrock features in the Midland Publishing video Irish Railways volume 8, *From Baltimore to Belfast*). Initially in July 1888, it was agreed to issue tickets from Harcourt Street, including admission to the course at an all-in charge. This appears to have worked until 1896 when the company sought to revoke the agreement. In return, they offered £100 for a 'Railway Plate' each year. Specials carrying horses worked through for many years from the Curragh. The directors were approached in June 1910 by the committee of the Aero Club of Ireland seeking a guarantee in connection with a proposed aviation meeting at Leopardstown. The company offered a guarantee of up to £200. The meeting was held on the Monday and Tuesday of the week following Horse Show week in August and was adjudged to be a success. The company enlisted the assistance of the police in maintaining order at Foxrock station in view of the large numbers expected to attend.

Above: **The Mail train, headed by 2-4-0 No 25 *Glenart*, stands outside the carriage sheds at Westland Row. The three bogie carriages behind the TPO are first No 12, second No 41, and kitchen van No 11 respectively.** IRRS collection

In the event, screens were erected alongside the railway to prevent patrons gaining free access. So well handled were the arrangements that the staff concerned in the Locomotive and Traffic Departments were granted an extra day's pay. A further 30 guineas (£31.10s.0d) was later paid to help clear the Aero Club's debt. The Club organised an air race for 7th September 1912 starting from Leopardstown. On this occasion, the company agreed to the payment of a bonus or percentage in the event that they gained substantial advantage from the fixture. The outbreak of war two years later put an end to these events, although it should be mentioned that a series of flights occurred from Woodbrook in July 1914, the company laying on special trains.

The company published a booklet of excursion arrangements, that for the 1915 season running to 20 pages. It included such items as special cheap evening fares from Dublin to Bray and Greystones, coach tours from Bray to beauty spots in north County Wicklow, combined travel and hotel tickets, Sunday seaside excursions and a number of different tours to Glendalough, the Vale of Avoca and Woodenbridge, the latter referred to as the Balmoral of Ireland.

By this time, eight day contract tickets were available for unlimited travel through Wicklow and the eastern counties to passengers booked from any station in England, Scotland or Wales. Fares were 20s first, 15s second and 10s third class.

Road services

It was agreed in August 1856 to make a loan to Messrs Critchley and Sherman for keeping a four-horse coach on the road between Wicklow and Wexford, with an extension to Enniscorthy. In July 1859, a Mr Darlington approached the board with a proposal to run an omnibus service between Bray and Enniskerry. It was agreed to give him an amount of £3 per month towards the cost of running the service, which was seen as being advantageous to the company. An advertisement in the *Wicklow Newsletter* for 13th October 1860 in connection with the timetable of trains, includes a list of vehicles operating every weekday and meeting trains at Wicklow station. Two cars met the 09.35 down train – a four-horse coach for Wexford, serving Arklow, Gorey, Ballycanew and Enniscorthy, operated by a Mr J Sherman, and a two-horse car for Tinahely via Rathdrum and Aughrim (proprietor J Cowley). Two vehicles also met the 13.35, a four-horse van for Gorey via Arklow (Hudson & Bates) and a three-horse coach for Shillelagh via Rathdrum and Aughrim (Cowley & Kenny). Finally, there was a three-horse van for Arklow, operated by Mr Bradford and connecting with the 18.05 from Harcourt Street.

With the joint purchase of the Ballywilliam branch, a car was put on between Ballywilliam and New Ross by Mr John Wallis. The DW&WR and the GS&WR jointly agreed to guarantee Wallis' receipts of £18 per week for running a three-horse car on the route. Fares were quoted as 1s.6d inside and 1s outside. Losses, if any, were to be borne in the proportion of two-thirds by the GS&WR and one-third by the DW&WR. The 1879 timetable listed the various vehicles running to and from stations on weekdays. These ran from Bray to Enniskerry, Delgany to Newtownmountkennedy, Ferns to Newtownbarry and Shillelagh to Tullow. As regards the latter, a Mr Kennedy had been appointed an

agent of the company at Tullow, it being agreed in October 1878 to allow him £35 per annum, plus 1s per ton for all goods traffic. The Enniskerry bus was in the news again in May 1882, when the proprietor sought a subscription of £30 towards the expenses of making four extra journeys daily during the summer season – a request declined.

In September 1903, it was ordered that the Engineer, Locomotive Superintendent and Traffic Manager confer as to the requirements of a motor service with Newtownbarry. It is not clear when the service was introduced but in October 1904, Shannon reported to the board on the condition of the road between Ferns and Newtownbarry, and it was decided to put a steam lorry to work between these two points instead of Shillelagh as hitherto. This resulted in correspondence being received from Wicklow County Council alleging damage to the Shillelagh road and requesting that it be repaired. The lorry service was withdrawn in 1908, and in December of that year it was agreed to accept a Mr Rob Mosely's offer of £80 for the lorry.

Private Sidings

Over the years, a number of private sidings existed, some of which provided the company with a good revenue. We will deal with these on a geographical basis from Dublin to Wexford, returning to look at the branches. At Bray Head, a siding was provided for the contractor, Robert Worthington, in 1873 in connection with the provision of stone to Dublin Corporation. A siding for handling this stone was also provided at Harcourt Street. Moving south, a request was received in August 1861 for a siding into the premises of the Hibernian Brick, Tile & Drain Pipe Works at Wicklow. Le Fanu was ordered to have the necessary work carried out at a cost of about £50. In April 1868, Messrs McMullan Shaw & Company approached the board

Above: **Shankill, looking towards Bray in 1902. The siding on the left was originally constructed for lead ore traffic to the nearby smelting plant at Ballycorus. A standard cattle wagon, two covered vans and an open centre covered wagon stand on it.** H Fayle - IRRS collection

asking to be allowed to use surplus water from Wicklow station in connection with their chemical works about to be erected at the Murrough. Within a few weeks this request was followed by one for a siding, Smith estimating the cost at £135. Initially, Shaw McMullan were requested to pay for the works, their reply being an offer of £50 towards the siding which appears to have been accepted. In May 1895, the Dublin & Wicklow Manure Company, as successors to Shaw McMullan, requested additional siding accommodation, this being provided in the following year.

An approach was made in December 1858 by the Wicklow Harbour Commissioners requesting a tramway from the railway terminus to the Quay, which would enable ores from Ovoca to be more readily exported through the port of Wicklow, but this request was declined. Early in February 1861, with the company's line under construction towards the mining district of Ovoca, a meeting was held to once again consider the construction of a tramway, which would, the promoters believed, increase the prosperity of the company's line between Bray and Wicklow. The Town Commissioners agreed to grant the necessary ground at a rent of 1s per annum. It was announced that Mr Markham Browne, proprietor of the Connorree Mining Company, heartily approved of such a connection being made. A prospectus for the Wicklow Tramway Company Limited appeared in the *Wicklow Newsletter* of 23rd March. The capital required was £2,000 and included among the provisional directors were John Hayden, the Chairman of the Town Commissioners,

Francis Wakefield and Markham Browne. Apart from the construction of the tramway, it was planned to raise the walls on the north side of the river so that loaded wagons could be tipped direct into vessels.

Sporadic references appear in the local press, but it would appear that there was little activity during the next five years or so. Writing to the paper in March 1865, Wakefield pointed out that the DW&WR should be taking more of an interest in the harbour at Wicklow as the GWR were about to complete a line to, 'some place exactly opposite Wicklow', Port Dynllaen on the Llyn Peninsula on the south side of Caernarfon Bay. A board minute of 1st November 1866 refers to a deputation from the tramway company offering to transfer all the latter's rights to the DW&WR, which was to construct the tramway and pay 1d per ton on all goods carried over it. The board promised to consider the matter but did not accept the offer. Traffic through the port of Wicklow in 1867 amounted to imports of 21,016 tons. of which coal made up 12,054 tons, and exports of 30,537 tons, which included 25,001 tons of sulphur ore from Ovoca.

Once finally started work proceeded rapidly and the tramway was in use by 25th November 1868. A further board minute of 1st January 1870 refers to the tramway as being 'inconvenient and dangerous', although at the same meeting it was recommended that a wagon turntable be provided so as to give accommodation to the various yards. The tramway was offered for sale to the DW&WR in January 1874, but the company declined the offer. It may be that it was already out of use.

At a meeting of the Town Commissioners in March 1879, attention was drawn to the state of the tramway in Strand Street, where houses were being flooded. As the rails were never used, it was suggested they be removed. The only remaining reference to this tramway is in the board minutes in 1890 when it was again offered to the company, this offer also being declined.

A letter was received from the Earl of Fitzwilliam's solicitors in April 1904, advising that His Lordship intended to apply to the Lord Lieutenant for an Order in Council authorising the construction of a tramway by way of an extension from the company's goods station to the North Quay at Wicklow. It was intimated that a large quantity of timber from the Fitzwilliam estate would be sent by rail from Rathdrum for export through the port. The company agreed to a connection being made, subject to rails being laid and maintained by them, but at the Earl's expense, all traffic passing over the tramway to be worked by the railway. In the following March, Shannon reported that a total of 658 yards of rails plus a wagon turntable would be required to complete the tramway at a cost of about £800. By this time, a charge of 1s per loaded wagon had been agreed, empties to be moved free.

The tramway was opened for traffic on 2nd July 1906 and was initially operated by horse. This soon proved inadequate, as did a doubling up of the horse power. It was then decided to utilise the travelling crane which had been provided by the Earl, but this in turn was reported in September 1907 to have suffered damage. Receipts for the year ended September 1907 totalled just £97.

It was now arranged that the company should provide one of its smallest engines, which in addition to working the tramway, could be used for shunting at Wicklow goods yard. It commenced work on 7th September 1907, but soon proved uneconomic. His Lordship now made an agreement, whereby in return for a payment of £30 per annum, the company took over complete control of the tramway. There are only brief references to the tramway after this, and it is likely that it had a short working life. Reid, reporting in July 1912, stated that the working for the year just ended showed a deficit of £16.9s.11d. It remained *in situ* until about 1931, being shown on a GSR plan dated 1927. Leaving the goods yard, it ran along Strand Street to a head shunt near the outer end of the North Quay, from which point another line trailed back along the quay itself. Engines were not permitted to work on the quay.

A little beyond Rathnew station was the location for a siding in connection with a local brickworks. Enquiries were directed to the company in November 1892 when it was agreed to provide the facility subject to the company being paid the cost of its construction and maintenance. Carriage of materials was offered at a rate of 16s.6d per wagon, this being declined, but following further approaches in April 1893, it was agreed to charge 2s per ton provided at least 120 tons per week were offered. The necessary works were not carried out until late in 1895, being inspected by Colonel Addison on behalf of the BoT in July of the following year. The siding faced to up trains and was worked by a key on the section staff. Messrs Thompson, who also owned an extensive brickworks at Kingscourt on the MGWR, appear to have ceased work at Rathnew at the end of 1902 as the company were approached in the following April by solicitors acting on behalf of clients who expressed an interest in forming a new company to take over the works. It was agreed to extend the siding at a cost of £29, although the new owners considered the provision of a tramway from the works to Rathnew station. The siding was out of use by 1930 and was lifted in the following year.

The first indication of a siding at Balleece, situated between Rathdrum and Avoca was in June 1900, when the question of requiring a guarantee of traffic from the new siding being provided there was considered. It was decided that no guarantee would be required for the first three months after opening. By the following February, agreement had been reached and when the Balleece Wood Whinstone Quarry Company Limited paid £300 into the Hibernian Bank at Wicklow to cover a proportion of the cost of the new siding, it was ordered that work should proceed, BoT sanction being given in December 1901.

Correspondence was received from the quarry company in April 1902 seeking a reduction in the rates for carriage of stone. Coghlan however gave his opinion that the existing rates were low enough – it had been 1s.9d per ton but had been temporarily increased by 3d to cover additional costs incurred by the railway company, the siding having cost £150 more than originally estimated. Unconvinced, the quarry company responded by stating that some 12,552 tons of stone had been carried by the railway, entitling them to a reduction of the 3d and a refund for alleged overpayment. A dispute arose as to the correctness of the figure quoted by the quarry company, which included almost 4,000 tons carried on behalf of the DW&WR and on which no charges were payable. In December 1909, it was reported that the quarry company were in arrears with their account, and it was ordered that the supply of wagons be suspended. This matter was apparently quickly resolved as in the following month instructions were given for another siding to be laid, subject to suitable arrangements being concluded as to payment. Agreement on this matter was reached in July 1911 with the quarry company contributing £100 in six half-yearly installments towards the estimated cost of £250.

Complaints were received from time to time regarding a shortage of wagons for the carriage of traffic from the quarry. Cronin was ordered in March 1911 to put in hand eighteen 12-ton mineral wagons for the quarry's use. A further complaint in October 1911 led to a suggestion from Reid that a special man be appointed to look after the supply of wagons. A further request was received in December 1912 for additional wagons, a request which was declined by the D&SER as being unnecessary. The company fell into arrears with their account again in 1915 and a letter was sent on 4th March threatening to close the account. This matter dragged on for some considerable time. In January 1916, the Chairman and Deputy-Chairman met with the Managing Director of the quarry company and it was agreed that the D&SER would accept £200 in discharge of a sum of £300 due for a disallowed rebate, subject to the rebate not being deducted for the future. This rebate was however subsequently deducted and the law agent was ordered to serve a writ for the full amount due. The quarry company defaulted on their payments again in March, resulting in the closing of their account and the necessity to pay freight charges on delivery.

Despite these problems, the quarry company continued to complain about the shortage of wagons, and perhaps this was in part the reason for their defaulting on their payments. In September 1916, the Managing Director wrote to the D&SER stating, 'You are still taking up your usual attitude of endeavouring to harass us in every conceivable way, today we have no wagons at all at Balleece, and yesterday we had only eight'. Again in June 1920, Dublin Corporation were moved to write to the D&SER complaining that they were being left short of stone due to shortage of wagons. The company replied to the effect that due to the unusual times, with, 'the whole countryside stocking coal', there was a shortage of wagons. However, if the quarry company would load and unload more energetically, the effect would be, 'almost unfelt by them'. The siding was closed sometime after 1941, although the quarry is still operational and in fact stone was moved out by rail during 1994, being loaded on the main line.

Reference has already been made to the mining activities in the Avoca valley. Two sidings were provided in the Rathdrum to Avoca section to serve this traffic, at Connorree and at Cronebane or Tigroney. The former was short-lived, being installed in 1865 and removed four years later due to debts owing to the railway. A request for its reinstatement in September 1881 was declined on the grounds 'that it would be dangerous'. Early in January 1873, Smith was ordered to provide storage room for Messrs Williams' minerals at Cronebane platform. A siding was apparently provided during the year as a collision occurred there on 25th November between a down passenger train and a mineral train. As the result of the accident, the guard and fireman of the latter were charged with criminal neglect. The BoT subsequently ordered the provision of distant signals and interlocking. The site of the siding can still be traced on the down side of the line.

In February 1885 the *Wicklow Newsletter* announced that a number of men had been employed at Arklow Rock, south of the town, quarrying and dressing paving setts, the quarry having been leased from the Earl of Carysfort by an associate of C S Parnell. Apparently Parnell and Lord Carysfort, who were cousins, had fallen out some years previously due to the former's politics. The quarry was opened in 1885 and was connected to the South Quay by a tramway worked by horse power. Shortly after the quarry's opening, expenditure of £310 was approved for putting in a siding at Kish for loading setts, subject to Parnell agreeing to send 10,000 tons over the following two years at 2s.6d per ton. If less than this tonnage was transported, Parnell was to pay the full cost of the siding. In May 1886, Smith stated that the siding had been working for

Left: **A notice concerning the working of Balleece Siding dating from 1923.**
W E Shepherd collection

Dublin and South Eastern Railway.

GENERAL MANAGER'S OFFICE,

WESTLAND ROW STATION,

10*th October*, 1923.

WORKING OF BALLEECE SIDING.

With reference to the above and instructions contained in the Appendix to the Working Time Table, page 117, please note that on and from the 1st November, 1923, these instructions will be cancelled, and the following, which have been sanctioned by the Ministry of Industry and Commerce, Transport Department, substituted, namely :—

An engine with or without empty wagons in rear may proceed from Rathdrum Station to the Siding, lift a number of laden wagons, not exceeding 10, and propel them to Rathdrum Station.

In cases where there are more than 10 wagons to be attached at Balleece Siding, the train is to be left in Rathdrum Yard, and the engine and van with any empty wagons are to proceed to the Siding. The van is to be placed behind loaded wagons on Siding, the engine to go round the wagons and van inside the catch points, back out on Main Line, and bring all the wagons for Up or Down the Line to Rathdrum.

In the case of Down trains having empty wagons to detach at Balleece Siding, the empty wagons may be marshalled at Rathdrum Station in the rear of train outside the brake van, and backed into Balleece Siding when the train reaches it.

Under no circumstances must any shunting be done on the Main Line at Balleece.

Please advise all concerned and acknowledge receipt.

M. J. MAGUIRE,

General Manager.

[To be inserted at page 117 of the Appendix to the Working Time Table.]

some time and enquired regarding the provision of a cottage there, this being approved. The siding was lengthened in April 1890. Parnell's brother, John, took over the working of the quarry in 1895 but sold out to the contractor T H Falkiner, the Parnell title being retained.

Parnell Quarries Limited wrote to the company in June 1904 complaining of a shortage of wagons, a complaint which appears to have remained unresolved for some time as it was raised again in March of the following year. Dublin Corporation wrote in October 1906 to the effect that they were unable to obtain a steady supply of whinstone from Arklow due they were told to a shortage of wagons. The Rathdrum and Arklow quarries were by this time in the ownership of Messrs Thompsons. It would appear that they had offered to invest £2,000

in the provision of their own wagons, the company declining to even consider this proposal. An Ordnance Survey map of the area in the possession of the IRRS shows a proposed siding pencilled in from the quarry, joining the main line nearer Arklow, beside which is a note, 'curves too sharp'. Plans also existed for an aerial ropeway to the station.

A Board minute of 24th January 1907 refers to a proposed siding and loading bank at Ferns station for the use of Mr John Bolger, who was to provide the land and pay the cost of any work. This is apparently the siding and goods bank on the up side at the Wexford end of the station. Later, in September 1920, another siding was provided at the Dublin end for O'Connor of Ferns. It was approved by the Ministry of Transport in October 1920.

Enniscorthy had three private sidings in the vicinity of the station, with another a mile south of it. The oldest was Roche's, first requested in April 1879, at which point it was refused. The siding was ordered to be installed three months later at a cost of £150, exclusive of a turntable. In June 1886 the board considered a letter from a Mr Donoghue requesting that a turntable and additional rails be put in at his siding. There is no information as to when the original siding was installed, but as regards the extension, the company offered to supply him with rails if he would carry out the work himself. This he appears to have done, compensating the Stationmaster for a crop of potatoes which had to be removed. The last of the station sidings was that for Messrs Buttle Bros who produced a large traffic in bacon products. In September 1893, they offered a sum of £50 if the company would undertake the work, subsequently agreeing to pay half the cost. The siding was ready for use in June 1894. Signals were later provided at the behest of the BoT at a cost of £157.10s.0d. A mile south of Enniscorthy, a siding was provided in 1873 into the cornmill of Messrs Davis. Also known as St John's Mills siding, it was first requested in 1869 and was worked from Enniscorthy, wagons being hauled out and then propelled into the mill siding which faced to up trains. Sometimes as many as three trips per day were required involving the movement of up to 50 wagons. A loading bank was also provided at the headshunt of this siding beside the main line to cater for tile, cement and general merchandise traffic for Mr Kavanagh. The siding finally closed in 1965.

Even before the Shillelagh branch was opened, the company were approached by Messrs Fogarty & Company, flour millers of Aughrim, requesting a siding, this being approved in April 1865. Once again, these mills produced a fair amount of traffic. Because of coal shortages in the Free State during the Second World War, rail services were withdrawn from the branch in April 1944, the intention being to re-open it when fuel supplies improved. This was not to be, although the up Enniscorthy goods engine was sent as far as Aughrim to serve the mill siding between 1947 and 1952.

At Kingstown, the Mineral Wharf siding was installed in 1863 to allow export of the mineral products from Ovoca. Constructed by and at the expense of the company on land belonging to the Harbour Commissioners, a rent of £75 per annum was initially paid, later increasing to £100 when a second line of rails was laid in April 1887. It later became known as the Traders' Wharf siding and was used for general goods, remaining in existence until swept away by the alterations for the introduction of the DART services. Between the Mineral Wharf and Carlisle Pier, another siding was installed to serve Victoria Wharf (later known as St Michael's Wharf) at the expense of the War Office, again on lands belonging to the Harbour Commissioners. Intended to facilitate the conveyance of troops and other purposes of the War Department, the total cost of its construction was £1,174.10s.0d.

A siding was requested in February 1877 by Robert Worthington Junior at Williamstown. He offered to pay two-thirds of the cost, but the company declined the offer. In 1909, Shannon produced plans for a 350ft long siding there to accommodate six wagons. It would have trailed off the up line near to the Martello Tower. The probable cost was estimated at £700 to £800, which it was hoped would be defrayed by Blackrock Urban District Council. Nothing came of this, nor of a similar scheme in January 1922.

Finally, we come to the Royal Dublin Society sidings at Ballsbridge, first suggested in September 1888, but it was not until February 1893 that the company agreed to sell 950 sleepers at cost to the RDS. The latter obtained rails which came available when the construction of the Bray & Enniskerry Tramway, for which they had been originally acquired, was abandoned. During 1893, the bridge over the River Dodder at Lansdowne Road station was widened to provide a footpath for passengers to the show grounds.

Permission was given in May 1895 for passenger trains to operate into the sidings, these workings continuing until about 1924. Shortly after the arrival of the two railmotors in 1906, they were tested on a Lansdowne Road to Ballsbridge shuttle service along this siding.

The company approached the Society in May 1899 suggesting additional siding accommodation due to the increased number of exhibits at shows – 246 wagons had been into the sidings during the 1899 Spring Show as against 182 the previous year, while the Horse Show later in the year produced 341 wagons. The RDS declined to agree to increased accommodation on the grounds of cost, eventually conceding the point in

1902 after the company had offered to provide rails, points and buffer stops. The additional accommodation came into use in the following year. Plans for a further extension were put forward in the 1920s but came to nought.

Below: **The opening of the Royal Dublin Society sidings at Ballsbridge in May 1893.** Sean Kennedy collection

Bottom: **Aughrim, looking towards Woodenbridge in the 1930s with a down mixed train at the platform. Fogarty's Mills are in the background behind the goods store.** Sean Kennedy collection

Chapter Ten

ACCIDENTS

A LOOK at a list of accidents in relation to the D&SER and its predecessors might give the impression that the company suffered more than many of its contemporaries. However if one considers the very intensive suburban service operated, in particular over the Kingstown to Bray section which was single for so many years, the company was no worse or better than others. One must also remember that the section south of Bray was single throughout, apart from the short Newcastle to Wicklow stretch.

One of the earliest recorded accidents occurred on 9th February 1858 between Sandycove and Dalkey when a down passenger train ran into two wagons of granite reported to be, 'running wild'. The wagons in question were in course of being moved out of a siding at Dalkey by hand when they ran away. Colonel Wynne, on behalf of the BoT, commented on the unsuitability of the siding, constructed as it was on an incline.

On 26th March 1858, a potentially serious collision occurred at Harcourt Road station.

The line was at that time in course of being extended across Adelaide Road into a new terminus at Harcourt Street. The Harcourt Road station had only one platform which was used not only for passenger trains but also as a goods siding and storage road for passenger coaches. At the time of the accident there were three wagons standing at the inner end of the platform used as a goods store, and on the Bray side of these, two carriages ready to go out on the 14.00 to Carrickmines. The 11.55 from Wicklow, which consisted of a tank engine, five loaded goods wagons, brake van and two carriages, apparently approached the station at too high a speed and collided with the standing vehicles almost propelling one of the wagons out into the street. Captain Tyler came to the conclusion that there was an error of judgement on the part of the driver and guard of the train. However, he also commented on the inadequate brake power on the company's trains. There was no brake van at the rear of the train, a practice which arose from the difficulties of shunting at

Harcourt Road. Tyler also suggested that all trains approaching Harcourt Road should stop for ticket collection or other purposes at least 100 yards outside the station. Instructions were issued for a second brake van to be provided at the rear of trains, and for stopping them before entering Harcourt Road. However after mature consideration of the Inspecting Officer's report, it was decided to discontinue the stopping of trains outside the station and to only provide one brake van at the rear.

A minor collision occurred at Greystones on the morning of 10th August 1861. Greystones was at that time a single platform station with a through (loop) siding. A short train consisting of engine, third brake and a

Below: **Blackrock station during an easterly storm showing how badly the railway could be affected by such weather. Despite this kind of flooding it was, in many instances, possible to maintain services.**
Sean Kennedy collection

composite, left Bray at 08.00 to pick up the few passengers, 'who might be desirous of travelling by the 8.40 a.m. train from Bray to Dublin'. When the train reached Greystones, the fireman uncoupled the engine in order to run round the train. However the guard had neglected to apply his brake and the train rolled forward, coming into collision with the engine and injuring one passenger who had jumped out of the carriage in a state of alarm. Captain Tyler inspected on behalf of the BoT. Whilst one person had been injured as the result of the collision with the engine, had it not been there, the train would have run away a considerable distance towards Wicklow. It transpired that a porter had been sent from Bray to act as guard and had fallen asleep in his van. Had he applied the brake, as was his duty, the accident would not have occurred. The gentleman in question had been at a wake in a friend's house and had not slept for two nights and was only aroused by the collision. The BoT recommended that in future guards should uncouple engines from their trains and that the carriages should be taken from the platform until the locomotive was recoupled to them, thus preventing passengers gaining access to them.

The Locomotive Superintendent reported briefly on a collision on the evening of 15th July 1863 between the 17.45 down and the 18.00 up which was just departing from Kingstown. So far as Haughton was aware, no person had been hurt. However the Finance & Traffic Minutes for 30th July indicate that ten passengers were injured. Five of these claims had been settled by the end of July, one of the remainder being estimated at £1,000.

As recorded elsewhere, the extension of the line to Enniscorthy was opened on 17th November 1863. The opening was characterised by two derailments. When leaving Enniscorthy, the up night mail was inadvertently diverted into a siding and derailed. A substitute train left Enniscorthy at 01.15 but was derailed at Inch when it ran into a slip.

The section of line around Bray Head was the scene of a number of accidents. The first of note occurred on 23rd April 1865 when a carriage was derailed on the 09.00 down train just as it emerged from the second tunnel. The driver stated that he was running at a normal pace, a statement contradicted by at least one passenger, and on looking back saw the second carriage off the road. In the driver's judgement it was better to slow the train gradually to prevent a more serious derailment. The accident was investigated by Colonel Rich who commented adversely on the curves at this point. It was later ordered that a guard rail be laid around the curves on Bray Head as recommended by Rich, and also that a pilot porter should travel on all trains to check speeds on this section of line.

A little over two years later, on 9th August 1867, a more serious derailment took place. On this occasion the 06.30 from Enniscorthy became derailed as it crossed the Ram's Scalp bridge. The engine and tender broke through the hand rail on the land side of the viaduct and fell down the ravine a height of about 33ft, followed by the rest of the train with the exception of the last carriage. The engine and tender turned over completely, the third class carriage next to the engine had its body separated from the frame and broken to pieces. The second carriage also had its body smashed to bits but the frame stood on end and protected the third carriage which was left hanging over the platform of the viaduct. A Mr Murphy died at the scene, another passenger, a Mrs Hackman, died subsequently of her injuries. Twenty-three other passengers were injured. The driver suffered a broken leg and the fireman had severe internal injuries. There was little doubt as to the cause of the derailment. Colonel Yolland stated in his report that there were no less than four different types of permanent way in the immediate area, 80lb bridge rail, 69lb bridge rail, 80lb flat bottomed rail and an old 56lb bridge rail much worn. By the time of the BoT inspection, four lengths of rail had been replaced. It transpired that work was being carried out in the area on the day prior to the derailment. Yolland commented that the inspector and the ganger were, 'not proper men to be entrusted with the looking after and relaying of permanent way'.

On 17th February 1868 the 17.00 down train to Enniscorthy was diverted into a siding at Bray resulting in a collision with some ballast wagons, resulting in minor injuries to some third class passengers. As a consequence of this accident, it was resolved that, 'the services of Mr Murphy, the Resident Engineer, be no longer retained'. He was replaced by John Challoner Smith. In addition, the Bray Stationmaster, John Tozier, was informed that he also would have been dismissed but for his long service.

Improvements in boilermaking techniques and in hydraulic testing coupled with the invention of the tamper-proof Ramsbottom safety valve brought about a decline in the number of boiler explosions after 1870. Though rare enough on Irish railways, the DW&WR were unfortunate to experience such a catastrophe on the morning of 16th September 1872. On that morning, engine No 4 had already completed one round trip from Bray to Westland Row and was standing at Bray at the head of the 09.00 up train when without warning the boiler exploded throwing Driver Patrick Dowling and Fireman Patrick Smith off the engine. Both died shortly afterwards. Initial investigation revealed that the engine had been in shops only two months previously when no defects were observed. It soon became clear that Dowling had screwed down the safety valve in order to improve the engine's performance. Colonel Rich and the company's Engineer suggested that the boiler had given way at the bottom end next to the firebox where the plate was grooved by corrosion. An expert was called in from the Manchester Steam Users' Association along with Mr Bailey of Messrs Courtney & Stephens. They believed the manhole had first given way due to the excess pressure but Rich still believed that the weakest part was the lap joint between the barrel and the firebox shell at the right hand side near the bottom of the barrel in a seam patched in 1865. The destruction of the crank axle and framing all tended to show that the force of the explosion was downwards. If the manhole had first given way, the roof of the station would have been destroyed. Rich now recommended the fitting of Ramsbottom safety valves and the periodic testing of boilers to double their normal working pressures.

A rather unusual accident which might have had serious consequences occurred at Rathdrum station on the evening of 26th April 1873. Rathdrum was at that time the venue for the County Wicklow steeplechase, and such was the number of specials operating from all over the system that the normal practice was to cancel all main line trains apart from the up and down day mails. For the 1873 races, three specials left Harcourt Street, two from Wexford and one each from Wicklow, Arklow and Shillelagh. The *Wicklow Newsletter* in its issue of 3rd May, reported that a mass of spectators beat their way to the station after the last race where, 'the regulations were as lax as in the preceding years'. It was reported that the footbridge was thronged with about 300 persons when it gave up the unequal struggle and the girders on the up side gave way. Luckily for all concerned, there was a train at the platform, the driver of which saved the situation by raising the bridge by means of the screw jack carried by all engines at this time. The bridge was in due course replaced in 1876 and remains in use today.

A serious collision, luckily without any injuries took place at Cronebane siding on 24th November 1873 when the 14.00 down passenger collided with a mineral train which was standing on the main line about 200 yards on the Dublin side of the signal. As a result of this accident, the driver and guard of the mineral train were dismissed, while the driver of the passenger train was reprimanded for not keeping a proper lookout and for having the guard on his engine.

On Friday 8th May 1874, the 19.00 down mail train was derailed as it ran through Blackrock station. The train consisted of engine No 28, a second class carriage No 23 and luggage van No 17. The carriage and van were derailed and dragged quite a distance along the down platform, the carriage going

Above: **The ravaging effects of the sea south of Greystones, near Ballygannon. This photograph clearly shows the kind of problems the company suffered with coastal erosion throughout the years.**
S E Beggs

over on its side and being so badly damaged that it was reported to have been removed in small pieces in the van of the breakdown train. The cause of the accident was the breaking of a tyre under the carriage. The mail guard was injured in the accident and in due course claimed compensation.

Smith reported to the board on 5th July 1877 on an accident which had occurred on the previous day at Dalkey station, resulting in the death of one man and injuries to seven. As the 07.55 up train from Bray was passing through the loop facing points at the Bray end of Dalkey station the tank engine left the rails, stopping 90 yards further on and across the up road. Next to the engine was an open third and it mounted the rear framing of the engine, the next carriage, another third, in turn mounting the rear of the leading carriage. The two end compartments of the latter were badly crushed. The remainder of the train stayed on the rails. Seven sleepers and 32 broken chairs were reported. Major General Hutchinson concluded that the facing points were not properly closed. The points in question had been moved out 50 yards some eight weeks previously and awaited the fitting of a new compensation bar to the point rods as that provided was not central. Hutchinson commented that such a serious alteration should have been referred to the BoT. He also commented that the engine could not be weighed as the company did not possess an engine weighing table. This latter was to remain the situation during the remainder of the company's existence.

On 27th February 1878, another collision occurred at Glenageary when a passenger train collided with part of a mineral train which ran away from Dalkey when the coupling of a wagon broke. On this occasion one passenger unfortunately died, 16 others and one railway employee were injured.

The stone siding on Bray Head was the scene of a collision on 19th April 1878 when the 14.00 down passenger train ran into the siding, colliding with some wagons. The quarry siding was under the control of a watchman who also patrolled the line. There were no injuries and the train continued its journey after some time. The watchman admitted that he had forgotten to reset the points after an engine from Bray had taken a stone train out of the siding at about 14.00. The driver stated that neither he nor the fireman saw the watchman. This siding had formed part of the single line but when diverted in September 1876, a portion of the abandoned line was retained as a stone or quarry siding entered by facing points at the Bray end. When inspecting the deviation works on 26th September 1876, the inspecting officer stated that the junction required to be controlled by means of interlocking with the signal and the distant signal. In the course of a further inspection in June 1877, it was stated that, 'the home and distant signals at the junction of the deviation line with the old line are completely out of order and cannot be used'. Shortly afterwards, they were put in working order but they were always allowed to stand at danger, no instructions having been issued for their use and they were consequently disregarded by drivers.

An amusing incident occurred on 17th June 1881 at the Mineral Quay at Kingstown. A ballast train had arrived at about 17.30 and was shunted into the up sidings to await the passing of the up mail. Following the latter's departure, the brake van was left in the siding and the engine pushed the 14 empty wagons across the running roads with the intention of allowing them to descend by gravity and under the control of a brakesman to the Mineral Wharf where they were to be loaded with sleepers. However gravity took over and the brakesman, who was travelling on the leading wagon, had to jump for his life, all but one of the wagons ending up in the harbour. In evidence the brakesman stated that he had pinned down what he thought were sufficient brakes. Colonel Rich commented on the dangers of fly shunting across two running roads as well as a public road. Some comment was also passed in relation to the poor state of the buffer stop at the end of the siding – it was however better than that on the adjoining siding as this latter had been moved but the stopblock was left in its original position!

Kingstown was the scene of a minor derailment on 19th July 1883 when an engine, van and a second class carriage got off the road due to points not being properly closed. One passenger, a Mr D T Arnott claimed for injuries and was in due course awarded compensation. In the following April, Arnott wrote to the company enclosing a cheque for £600 in refund of part of the compensation as he had recovered more quickly than expected. So impressed were the directors by this display of Victorian integrity that they provided Arnott with a free pass for the year and instructed the Secretary to write to the press acknowledging his honourable conduct in the matter.

A serious collision occurred at Blackrock station on the morning of 9th April 1884, when a light engine en route to Kingstown to bring up the mail ran into the rear of the preceding 06.00 passenger train. Thirty-five passengers were reported as having suffered injuries. The accident was investigated by Colonel Rich on behalf of the BoT. The morning in question was quite foggy with visibility down to 150 yards. It was reported that the driver of the light engine was travelling at excessive speed and passed the Booterstown signal at danger. This the driver and fireman denied, going on to say that the Blackrock signal was at caution as they approached, being thrown to danger at the moment of the collision. Rich suggested that to avoid accidents of this kind in the future, the light engine should leave Dublin before the passenger train, that the block telegraph should be adopted, and that fog signals should be used in foggy weather.

A collision occurred at Enniscorthy on 21st February 1888, a fair day in the town. Just before 17.00 with the light fading, a number of laden cattle wagons were in the course of being shunted from a siding into the loop to clear the station for the down passenger train which was due. The station staff felt however that they had sufficient time to complete the manoeuvre before the latter's arrival. The movement required the cattle train to pass through the station on the main line prior to reversing into the loop. The crew were amazed to see the passenger train approaching at speed, the two trains coming into violent collision. The two locomotives were derailed along with two livestock wagons. Three horses were killed and a cow had to be subsequently put down. A number of passengers and the driver of the passenger train were injured. The BoT inspector stated that the passenger train ran through the signals but was also travelling at excessive speed. He was critical of the decision to shunt the cattle train along the main line so close to the expected arrival time of the passenger train. He finally pointed out that the accident could have been prevented had block signalling and interlocking been in force.

Shankill was the location for the next occurrence on 27th November 1890 when a main line train collided with the Bray goods, the result of which was that consideration was given to the dismissal of the guard of the Wexford train and the driver of the goods. However bearing in mind their good character, it was decided to reduce their grades respectively to porter and fireman. After protracted correspondence, Mr Robert Smith, a passenger on the Wexford train, received compensation of £400 and costs together with a free pass for three years.

On Wednesday 6th August 1895, a collision occurred near milepost 39¾ in the Rathdrum to Ovoca section. The previous Monday had been a Bank Holiday and as a result a special worked down from Harcourt Street, arriving in Arklow at about 23.50 on the Tuesday night. It was immediately turned around and dispatched back to Dublin as an empty stock train. On arrival in Ovoca at 00.40, the driver was requested to take three empty carriages from the mineral siding on the up side. To do this, he had to pull his train forward into the Rathdrum section to gain access to the siding and then reverse the manoeuvre. It appears that when the train was back on the main line, the guard without checking the position of the starting signal, gave the driver the right-away and it was only when they had travelled nearly three miles that the driver realised that he did not have the section staff. The driver immediately shut off steam and was in course of setting back to Ovoca when the down 20.00 goods on the falling 1 in 90 gradient came into violent collision with the empty stock train. The driver of the goods lost three fingers of his right hand, the fireman of the up train suffered broken ribs.

There were conflicting versions of what had happened that night. The Ovoca signalman, when he realised what had occurred, immediately telephoned Rathdrum to have the goods stopped, having already approved the removal of a staff for the down train. However by this time the goods had already left and the ensuing collision was inevitable. The up train should have been given a staff at Ovoca as it had to enter the section to Rathdrum to carry out the shunting manoeuvre according to the company's Rule Book. Had the regulations been properly carried out, the down train could not have received a staff at Rathdrum and left for Ovoca. The signalman stated categorically that he had not lowered the starting signal after the engine had brought out the extra carriages, although he did admit that little regard was paid to the rule stating that an engine or train should not be shunted outside the starting signal without being in possession of the staff. He did also state that he thought the driver and the guard were intoxicated, a fact which appeared to be disproved by others.

The driver said the signal had been lowered after the shunting, a view shared by Colonel Marindin of the BoT. Marindin had some adverse comments to make regarding the hours worked by the men on the special. The driver, who it was stated was, 'a good driver and a very steady man' had been on duty since 08.00, while the guard had been on duty for nineteen hours at the time of the accident. Marindin said, 'I am informed that these long hours were exceptional, owing to some special traffic; but the running of trains with men worn out by long hours is a distinct danger to the public, as well as an injustice to the men, and should under no circumstances, be countenanced'. Marindin also pointed out that interlocking would have prevented the accident. The driver of the special and the Ovoca signalman were dismissed, a harsh action as far as the former was concerned in view of Marindin's com-

ments in relation to long working hours.

Railways are recognised to be by their nature dangerous, and this is borne out by the number of railway employees who have been killed or seriously injured as the result of a temporary lapse of memory or concentration. On Tuesday 27th December 1898, Head Inspector (PW) Lynch was tragically killed at Bray. He had stepped back to allow the 10.00 up train to pass him, not realising that an empty carriage was being shunted on the adjoining road. The weather was very bad with a strong wind blowing at the time and Lynch obviously never heard the second train. Two milesmen were killed in similar circumstances at Shanganagh on 28th March 1914. At the time the men were engaged in loosening fishbolts in the up road and moved out of the way to allow the up Wexford train to pass. They stepped back into the 6-foot and were struck and killed by the 10.15 down from Harcourt Street. One of the victims left a wife and seven children.

On the morning of 3rd November 1899 a minor derailment occurred at Kingstown station, sufficient however to require the calling out of a breakdown train from Grand Canal Street. In the meantime, single line working had been introduced between Kingstown and Blackrock over the down line. Engine No 54 was quickly dispatched from Grand Canal Street with a brake van to act as the breakdown train. Ahead of it was the 08.00 down mail followed by a local train. At Blackrock, the mail train was sent off with a ticket as the pilotman intended to travel to Kingstown on the following local train When the breakdown train reached Blackrock No 54 and the engine of the local were exchanged, No 30 taking over the breakdown train which was dispatched immediately although the starting signal had not been lowered.

On arrival at Kingstown, the pilotman transferred to the 08.00 up from Bray and being unaware that the breakdown train was approaching from Blackrock departed for

Right: **A contemporary print of the boiler explosion which destroyed locomotive No 4 at Bray on the 4th August 1872.**
G R Mahon collection

Above: **Not the most serious, but probably the best known of the DW&WR accidents was that at Harcourt Street on St Valentine's Day, 1900, when a cattle special from Enniscorthy failed to stop and ran through the end wall of the station into Hatch Street. Locomotive No 17 *Wicklow*, is seen suspended on the remains of the stop block. On the hoarding in the background is a poster relative to news of the Boer War.** W E Shepherd collection

Below: **The Ovoca collision of the 6th August 1895 showing 0-4-2 No 48 and one of the wrecked third class carriages, either No 10 or No 12 of 1892.** K A Murray - IRRS collection

the latter station on the down line. The stage was now set for a disaster which took place at Seapoint. The impact was severe as the up train met the breakdown train head-on, the two engines and the two leading vehicles of the passenger train suffering damage, 28 passengers and 8 staff being more or less seriously injured. In due course, compensation totalling almost £8,500 was paid out. Colonel Marindin had some scathing remarks to make in regard to the company's operations, in particular as regards non-observance of rules. It was clear that the breakdown crew were unaware that single line working had been introduced; apart from this however, the driver had entered two sections against the signals. This accident indicates that little had changed since Marindin had investigated the Ovoca accident. One interesting claim arising out of this accident was in respect of a lost connection with the GNR(I) at Amiens Street, the claimant being paid 19s.

The collision at Harcourt Road in March 1858 has already been alluded to, but a much better known incident at Harcourt Street was the crash on St Valentine's Day 1900 when an up cattle special failed to stop. At about 16.35 on the afternoon of 14th February, the cattle special from Enniscorthy, made up of 29 cattle wagons and brake van, hauled by 0-6-0 No 17 *Wicklow*, ran through the station and hit the buffer stops at the end of the line, which gave way, resulting in No 17 going through the end wall of the station and hanging suspended over Hatch Street. Fireman Peter Jackson jumped off as the train ran along the platform at little more than walking pace. Driver William Hyland however remained at his post, receiving severe injuries to his right arm necessitating its amputation before he could be removed to hospital. Following on the accident, a Mr Grimshaw wrote to the BoT on the subject of the condition and working of the line.

Colonel von Donop carried out an inquiry on behalf of the BoT. Whilst it was clear that the driver had miscalculated his speed on the approach to the station, the inadequate arrangements there whereby a train could not run direct into the goods yard also came in for criticism. Von Donop recommended the provision of direct access, pending which all goods trains should be made to come to a stand at the home signal or at the previous station, Ranelagh. The Harcourt Street accident left its legacy right up to the closure of the line in that all up trains, passenger and goods, were required to stop at Ranelagh. The BoT wrote in the following September expressing regret that the directors were not prepared to provide the direct access to the goods yard, a situation which was never rectified.

At Glenealy on the evening of St Patrick's Day 1900 another collision occurred when the 18.10 down passenger train collided

Above: **Another view of the Ovoca collision showing 0-6-0 No 50 *Arklow* amid the debris.**
K A Murray - IRRS collection

with an up empty wagon special, injuring two passengers. This accident, which was to be the last accidental collision for 21½ years, led to the dismissal of the Glenealy signalman, the driver of the passenger train and an order that the Stationmaster, 'be moved to a station where his responsibilities will be less'. It was later reported that he had refused to accept a transfer to Edermine and had forwarded his resignation along with a request for a pension. The former was accepted and the latter declined! These various collisions show a poor state of management at this period in the company's history, and which appear to have improved little despite the purge following the Furnivall report.

Another unusual accident occurred at Harcourt Street on the night of 30th August 1917, luckily without injury, when 0-6-0 No 18 *Wexford* ran through the end of the engine shed and fell into the garden of No 9 Peter Place. As the result of this accident, the night cleaner, who had interfered with the regulator, was dismissed. The decision was also taken to appoint a competent man, qualified to move engines in steam at all locomotive sheds.

The derailment of three wagons of the down night goods near milepost 39¾ on 4th December 1914 would not normally warrant a mention in this chapter but for the unusual circumstances surrounding the incident. The remains of the wagons concerned were found for a distance of more than half a mile to the south of the initial derailment, and it was only when the train arrived in Avoca more than two miles away that the driver realised he was missing 13

wagons and the brake van. A total of 235 chairs and 50 sleepers were damaged as well as minor damage to three bridges. Subsequently, two leaves of a wagon spring were found half a mile north of the derailment point. The interesting aspect of this accident was that one of the wagons involved (No 96) had been labelled 'Not to Go' some days earlier. The checker who had loaded the wagon was suspended for a week and an instruction issued that any person who in future loaded such a wagon would be dismissed.

Another accident involving staff occurred at Edermine on 7th December 1918, when the Stationmaster there was struck by the engine of a down cattle special while he was opening the crossing gates. The driver was arrested on a charge of manslaughter, having apparently gone through a signal, but the charges were later dropped. Following this accident, the BoT drew attention to the unsafe arrangements at the crossing and in due course the gates in question were interlocked with the signals.

The one remaining collision occurred on 5th August 1921 and involved a light engine and a permanent way trolley, as the latter was emerging from the north end of Enniscorthy tunnel. Regrettably one employee was killed and five others injured, all on the trolley. The cause of the accident was that the ganger in charge of the permanent way men had made no official arrangements to have flagmen on duty.

Arising out of the political disturbances during the civil war detailed elsewhere, the central signal cabin at Amiens Street was destroyed on 26th April 1923, as the result of which pilot working was in force. Only a week later, an accident occurred there on 1st May when engine No 47 overran the turntable and broke through the wall of the cloakroom of the postal sorting office injuring two officials.

Chapter Eleven

LOCOMOTIVES

Locomotive Superintendents

Following the agreement in 1856 for the lease of the D&KR, S. Wilfred Haughton, the Locomotive Superintendent of the D&KR, continued in his post at Grand Canal Street. Frederick Pemberton, first Locomotive Superintendent of the D&W, resigned on 24th September 1856 to take up a post with the St Petersburg & Moscow Railway.

Haughton was appointed to succeed him line. He remained with the company until he retired on 26th February 1864 and was replaced by William Meikle who came from the Whitehaven Junction & Furness Junction Joint Railways. Meikle resigned on 13th May 1865, on the grounds of ill health, and he was replaced as Locomotive Superintendent by John Wakefield who came from the GS&WR at Inchicore, and who had actually been passed over in favour of Meikle just over a year previously.

Following the death of John Wakefield, his nephew (and adopted son) was appointed Locomotive Superintendent from 1st June 1882. William Wakefield had served under his father and had risen to the position of foreman at 'the Factory' when he succeeded in obtaining an appointment as Locomotive Superintendent of the WD&LR in March 1878.

It was no doubt this family connection that led to the arrangement between the two companies for the loan of Nos 20 and 22 for six months from 28th July 1878.

However William Wakefield's stay on the WD&LR was short lived, he being relieved of his post in August 1879. He was subsequently appointed Principal Assistant to the Locomotive Superintendent by the DW&WR in May 1880, and with the older Wakefield's health failing, he had, to all intents and purposes, taken control of the department some time before his father's death.

Despite the resignation of Smith, Payne and Foot, his long standing colleagues, in February 1894, following the presentation of the Furnivall report, Wakefield struggled on. T B Grierson was appointed Chief Engineer at the same time, and the board decided to grant him general control and supervision over Mr Wakefield and the locomotive department. This arrangement was destined not to work and Wakefield resigned six months later on 12th August, just three days after the appointment of Charles Calverley as Locomotive Assistant.

There is no doubt that Grierson's failure in locomotive matters, as manifest in his decisions regarding the proportions of the '55' class and the selection of the goods tanks, resulted in the board deciding in December 1896, 'to provide in future for the administration of the Locomotive and Carriage Department separately from the Permanent Way Department and therefore that immediate steps be taken to find a suitable person to act as Superintendent thereof'.

After a full and careful consideration of candidates it was decided to appoint Mr Richard Cronin, Principal Foreman at the Inchicore Works of the GS&WR, to the post of Locomotive Superintendent with effect from 1st May 1897. Calverley continued as assistant until pensioned in May 1909, at which time George Ridgeway was appointed to succeed him. Ridgeway resigned in March 1911, the position then being held by Cronin's son John until October 1915.

On 13th April 1916 it was agreed to appoint George Henry Wild, at that time District Superintendent of the GNR(I) at Londonderry, as assistant to the Locomotive Superintendent in succession to John Cronin, and then just over a year later, after 20 years in office, Richard Cronin retired at the end of April 1917. Wild succeeded him, remaining in office until the amalgamation. William Powell, who had been appointed Draughtsman in 1915, carried out the functions of assistant to Wild although not officially given the title until April 1921.

Locomotive Livery

Details of the earliest locomotive liveries are unknown, but by the early 1870s a shade of green, different to that of any other Irish railway, was being applied. This was the colour of light fresh ivy leaves, and may have been applied as early as 1864 on the Sharp Stewart engines delivered that year. Lagging bands were black with yellow pencil lines on the edges and lining on side tanks, cab sheets and tenders was the same, the overall width of the black band with yellow pencil lines on each edge being 2in. As delivered, the Neilson tanks of 1865 for the D&KR section were painted plain dark green with claret frames and bright red buffer beams, but in their later days they were painted brick red instead of the standard green.

In 1907 the locomotive livery was changed from the standard green to black. The lining was changed to 1 inch red bands with yellow ⅛in pencil lines spaced approximately ⅜in away from each side of the red band. It was with the introduction of this change in livery that the names, which had been applied by Cronin to new and rebuilt engines from 1898 onwards, began to be removed. By the time of the amalgamation only the four Beyer Peacock locomotives of 1905, together with *Glenageary*, *Kilcoole* and *Glendalough*, still carried names.

Workshops

In the 1830s, at the point on the up side where the D&KR line crossed over the Grand Canal, there was the disused premises of the Dock Distillery of Messrs Coffey & Company. The other Dublin distillers did not wish it to re-open and, as some of them were also on the D&KR board, they persuaded the company to purchase the buildings, they themselves contributing £1,000 towards the asking price of £5,500. After the installation of the necessary machinery by Messrs Courtney & Stephens and Messrs J & R Mallet, it opened in July 1837 as the locomotive workshops of the D&KR at Grand Canal Street and was generally known as 'the Factory'.

The D&WR constructed its own workshops at Bray, and it was not until the signing of the long term lease of the D&KR in 1866 that attention was turned to consolidating activities at Grand Canal Street.

In October 1856, when Haughton took over as Locomotive Superintendent of the whole line, Jonathan Pim was placed in charge of the Locomotive and other Works at Bray. However, he was in the post for hardly four months when he was appointed Locomotive Superintendent of the Waterford & Limerick Railway on 1st February 1857.

The works at Bray continued in use until October 1868 when the board requested Wakefield to reduce the hands employed there, and one week later he reported that he had transferred the foreman, a blacksmith, a helper, two fitters and a labourer/cleaner to Grand Canal Street. One fitter was retained at Bray to do the jobbing repairs.

At the time of the 1856 lease, the workshops at Grand Canal Street were shown as consisting of a foundry, boiler shed, smithy, engine room, fan room, punching and sawing shop, yard, copper shop, fitting shop, pattern room, offices and two houses for the use of the Locomotive Superintendent and Factory Foreman.

The main block of 'the Factory' faced, but was not parallel to, the running lines. The most unusual aspect was that the locomotive section, which although at rail level, was situated on the first floor, which must have created doubts as to the safety of the building. There were eight repair bays on this floor and, in later years, as locomotives increased in length they were accommodated by the simple expedient of demolishing the front wall and supporting the roof with new pillars. To enable engines to be lifted, Meikle installed an hydraulic lift consisting of a framework of timber to span the two roads at the front of the building, on top of which was a vertical piston actuated by water pressure. It had a lifting capacity of 30 tons. In later years some heavy repairs and modifications to locomotives were also carried out in the running shed opposite the works.

Along Barrow Street there ran a two-storey building with the machine and fitting shops on the upper floor and what was known as the boiler shop below at ground level. Although not actually used for locomotive boilers this shop was where tanks, footplates, cabs, smokeboxes and the like were fabricated. On the northern side of the site, beside the Canal Dock, there was another two-storey building which housed the sawmill on the lower level and the carriage shop at rail level above. This, like the engine shop, was entered from turntables on the adjacent siding. In early days, carriage bodies were lowered to the basement through a large opening in the floor.

In March 1878 the company purchased an adjoining site from the Boston Lime Works which enabled an extension of the carriage shop to be erected, a hay shed previously at Shillelagh being used for this purpose. This enlarged shop enabled Wakefield to undertake the building of new carriages to meet the company's needs, and in later years it was where Cronin had bogie carriages built. Work on goods wagons was carried out in two places. Repairs were undertaken in a long shed on the siding adjacent to the Dock, its side doors leading directly out onto the up main line. New wagon construction took place in a small building on the far side of the line known as the 'Red Shed'.

Although the D&KR had built eleven locomotives at Grand Canal Street between 1840 and 1851, it was not until 1869 that the DW&WR undertook any new locomotive building there, all early locomotives being supplied by recognised manufacturers.

Top: **No 8, seen here following its rebuilding in 1880, was one of the original Vulcan Foundry 2-4-0STs with Dodd's Wedge motion dating from 1855.** IRRS collection

Centre: **Fairbairn 2-4-0 No 13 of 1860, photographed at Bray.** Sean Kennedy collection

Above: **Neilson 2-2-2WT *Kate Kearney* in its original condition.** IRRS collection

Fairbairns and Vulcans

For the opening of the line from Dublin to Bray the D&WR ordered two 2-2-2WTs from William Fairbairn and Sons in 1853. Nos 1 and 2 appear to have been delivered in May 1854, and cost £3,662 for the pair. The delivery was supervised by Purdon, the Resident Engineer, but on 6th June 1854 the board of the D&WR appointed Frederick Pemberton as their first Locomotive & Carriage Superintendent.

At the board meeting on 8th August 1854 it was reported that the company had five locomotives for the opening of the line, but available evidence indicates that only Nos 1 and 2 had been delivered by that date. It is not likely that this figure included engines on order as the same report did not do so for the carriage stock. It must therefore be assumed that Dargan had made three of his locomotives available pending delivery of additional engines.

Three more locomotives from Fairbairn, No 3 a 2-4-0 tender engine delivered in late 1854 and two larger 2-2-2WTs, Nos 4 and 5, which were added during the first half of 1855, cost a total of £7,043. It was decided to convert No 3 into a tank engine in August 1884, when its tender required rebuilding, as by that time the engine was too light for the goods trains then being operated. No 4 was the locomotive whose boiler blew up at Bray in 1872 and was never repaired, but No 5 had already got a new boiler in 1870 and back sheets were added to the cab in 1882.

The board originally intended to purchase two tank engines and two tender engines for the extension of the line to Wicklow, but the locomotives ordered from the Vulcan Foundry on 6th October 1854 were two 2-2-2STs, Nos 6 and 7 and two 2-4-0 STs, Nos 8 and 9. Just over a month later, on 9th November, an order for a further two 2-2-2STs, for the re-opening of the Dalkey to Kingstown section, was placed with the same builder. All had domeless boilers with very shallow saddle tanks and Dodd's wedge motion. Following the derailment of a train hauled by one of these locomotives as it approached Wicklow station on 10th March 1859, it was recommended that one of the engines, 'which in their present condition are injurious to

the line' be altered by the Locomotive Superintendent. Haughton consulted with George Miller and Joseph Cabry, his counterparts respectively on the GS&WR and the MGWR as to the best means of remedying the defects and by November the proposed alterations were authorised for three of the locomotives. It is also possible that the saddle tanks were removed and replaced by well and trough tanks at this time, and not during later rebuilding, as well as the replacement of the Dodd's wedge motion by link motion.

Five locomotives were ordered on 9th March 1860 for the extension to Rathdrum, three of them being 2-4-0 passenger engines, Nos 12 to 14, supplied by Fairbairn at £2,180 each. All got new boilers and were fitted with cabs in 1880-81. No 14 was reconstructed at Grand Canal Street in 1907 with new frames, cylinders and boiler, emerging as No 31 *Glen of the Downs*. As rebuilt, 'it was a wonderful, speedy little engine, whose performance was far greater than its proportions would suggest'.

The Sharp Engines

As well as the Fairbairn passenger engines, two 0-4-2 goods engines, Nos 15 and 16, were ordered from Messrs Sharp Stewart for the Rathdrum extension, at £2,320 each. A further addition to this class was made in 1877 with the arrival of No 37 which for many years was the spare engine at Wexford. Nos 15 and 16 were the engines generally used on the pig specials through to Kilkenny via the Bagenalstown line. No 16 was rebuilt with a new boiler as an 0-4-2T in 1901, and was thereafter stationed at Grand Canal Street shed.

In 1863 ten more locomotives were ordered from Sharp Stewart to handle the traffic on the Enniscorthy extension and the Shillelagh branch. Three goods engines Nos 17 to 19 and three passenger engines, Nos 24 to 26, were ordered on 2nd July and shortly afterwards, on 27th August an order was placed for a further four goods engines, Nos 20 to 23. The contract price was £2,295 each for the goods engines and £2,235 for the passenger engines. Later additions to both classes included passenger engines Nos 32 and 33 in 1873, and goods engines Nos 38 and 39 in 1876. One more goods engine of the '17' class, No 48, was built at the Factory in 1889.

Of the goods engines No 21 was rebuilt as an 0-4-2T in 1905, and Nos 38 and 39 were given larger boilers in 1908 and 1905 respectively. No 20 ran for a while after 1911 as No 20A before becoming No 22, though it was wrecked beyond economic repair at Macmine on 27th January 1923. In relation to the passenger engines, Nos 32 and 33 were specifically rebuilt in 1898-99 for use on the Mail train due to the poor performance of the Vulcan 4-4-0s. No 26 was

rebuilt as a 2-4-0T in 1900 and No 24 was reconstructed with new frames, a large boiler and new cab in 1908, No 25 having received a similar boiler and new cab in 1903.

The Kingstown Engines

Although the Kingstown locomotives were worked by the company from June 1856, they were considered as separate stock until the signing of the long term lease in 1866. Because of the small size and power of the D&KR locomotives it was decided on 9th September 1864 to accept Messrs Neilson's tender for the supply of six 2-2-2WTs as replacements. On 17th November Neilson notified the company that they would build another locomotive of this type for the Dublin Exhibition of 1865 and offered to sell it to the company at the close of the exhibition at the price agreed for the other six, namely £1,564.

These locomotives, like the other D&KR engines, carried names only, but it appears that after an audit of stock in 1884 they were nominally allocated numbers in the series 45 to 51. The names are shown in Appendix C under Type XI. There is no evidence that any of them ever carried a number, however, new locomotives bearing these numbers replaced the small tanks between 1888 and 1891 without any change in the locomotive stock totals.

Kate Kearney was taken out of service in 1886 for re-construction as described below, the drawings actually showing the No 46 altered to 27. *Ariel* was replaced in 1888 and *Kelpie* and *Titania* the following year, all three of these redundant locomotives being sold to Worthington in April 1889. *Banshee*, *Oberon* and *Elfin* were replaced in 1891, Murphy purchasing *Oberon* in March of that year and *Elfin* in April 1892. The last one to be disposed of was *Banshee* which was sold to Fisher and Le Fanu in June 1894.

In July 1865, following the delivery of the Neilsons, the Traffic and Finance Committee, acting on a special report by Wakefield, recommended that five of the old D&KR engines, 'be repaired at a cost not exceeding £3,680 and that the remaining six be sold for whatever they would fetch', a Mr Connolly purchasing four of them in November 1866. In 1866 the number series 27 to 31 was allocated to the five locomotives that were to be kept, but it is very unlikely that any of them ever carried these numbers in addition to the names which they retained. However, their respective replacements built at the Works did take up the numbers in the allocated series.

Two of the 'Burgoyne' class, *Cyclops* and *Vulcan*, were reconstructed at Grand Canal Street in 1869 and 1870 respectively and re-entered service as Nos 27 and 28. However, this reconstruction proved too costly relative to the results achieved and it was decided

Photographs on the opposite page:

Top: **No 27, the 1887 reconstruction of *Kate Kearney*, seen at Bray in 1906. Some of the original details, especially the brass edged splasher, are clearly identifiable when compared with the previous photograph on page 81.** H Fayle – IRRS collection

Bottom: **Neilson 2-2-2WT No 35 of 1873, stands at Salthill with a down train in 1907.** H Fayle – IRRS collection

to replace the other three Kingstown locomotives with a new design of 2-2-2T. Nos 27 and 28 survived until 1887, when replaced by new coupled tanks Nos 46 and 28.

The late E L Ahrons referred to a County Dublin correspondent whose earliest recollections of the DW&WR dated back to 1872-23 and who remembered two very old locomotives *Jupiter* and *Juno*. The DW&WR never possessed a locomotive named *Juno*, and so this account has always been dismissed as inaccurate. Evidence now reveals that this could have been possible as *Jupiter* spent its last years in the Wexford area, probably working Wexford to Enniscorthy local trains, prior to its sale to Mr Hamilton of Wexford in June 1876. *The People* (Wexford) of 5th August 1876 confirms that *Jupiter* had been transferred to the W&WR and had made a trial run from Ballygeary on Saturday 29th July. At the same time a locomotive named *Juno*, which had been purchased from the MGWR, was working on the Bagenalstown and Wexford line, and it is quite probable that Ahrons' informant saw these two locomotives at Macmine.

2-2-2WTs

This is an appropriate point to deal with the 2-2-2WTs which were built by the company from 1871 onwards. The first three were Nos 29 to 31, replacements for *Comet*, *Burgoyne* and *Jupiter*. Three others were a replacement for No 4 and two additions to stock, Nos 36 and 40. There has always been a question surrounding the building of the 2-2-2WT No 27 as late as 1887, some six years after the decision to build coupled tanks for the local services. It has also been suggested that No 27 was in fact to be a coupled tank, but evidence now points towards No 27 being a reconstruction of *Kate Kearney*, and this would account for its marked difference to the other 2-2-2WTs. This was probably a last ditch effort to see if something useful could be made of these engines at a reasonable cost. Although No 27 gave good service for 19 years it was decided that the cost of reconstruction was such that to proceed with the rest of the class was not as effective as building new coupled tanks.

More New Engines

The increase in traffic occasioned by the opening of the Wexford extension prompted an order for four locomotives in late 1872. Two, Nos 32 and 33, were identical 2-4-0 passenger engines of the '24' class and were ordered from Sharp Stewart at a cost of £2,818 each. Nos 34 and 35, ordered from Neilson at £1,885 each, were 2-2-2WTs, basically similar to the design being built by Wakefield at Grand Canal Street. Whether or not these tank engines were intended to release larger locomotives then working the Shillelagh branch is not known, but they cer-

tainly spent the greater part of their lives working the branch. On 11th May 1876 Wakefield wrote to the board indicating that three more locomotives were required in consequence of the acquisition of the Bagenalstown branch. This resulted in an order being placed with Sharp Stewart for one '15' class small goods engine at £2,365 and two '17' class goods engines at £2,410 each. These locomotives, delivered in early 1877, became Nos 37, 38 and 39 respectively.

No 41

It is generally assumed that the change to four-coupled tanks was initiated by William Wakefield. Whether his father had a hand in the design or not, it was certainly recorded in the press that it was William Wakefield who was in charge of a new locomotive, for the heavy traffic between Harcourt Street and Bray, when it arrived at the latter station from the Works on 3rd January 1883. As originally built No 41 had 15in x 22in cylinders and very short side tanks in addition to well tanks. It was rebuilt in 1903 with 16in x 22in cylinders, a new steel boiler from the Vulcan Foundry, full side tanks instead of well tanks and at the same time received its name *Delgany*. Although not officially listed as ready for scrap until 1924 it appears to have been laid up, out of use, around 1913.

Beyer Peacock 2-4-0Ts

In February 1882 tenders were invited from Sharp Stewart and Beyer Peacock for three locomotives in accordance with Wakefield's 2-4-0T specification. Sharp's tender was generally in accordance with specification but Beyer Peacock offered a design of 4-4-0T which they were building for the Victoria Railways. However, Wakefield preferred his design and an order was eventually placed with Beyer Peacock on 23rd March for three 2-4-0Ts at £2,100 each. These locomotives were required for the improved suburban service, incorporating the new stations at Sandymount and Merrion, which had opened on the day they were ordered. It is therefore understandable that the company complained bitterly when the new engines had not been delivered by April 1883. Nos 42, 43 and 44 were eventually delivered by the end of June.

Water tank capacity of the '42' class was 900 gallons, and the 66 cu ft bunkers could carry 1½ tons of coal. New boilers were ordered from the Vulcan Foundry in November 1899 for their rebuilding in 1901 (43), 1902 (44) and 1903 (42). These engines gave the best performance and cost the least in upkeep of any engines on the line, the workmanship in their building being of a very high standard.

'2' Class

Following the success of the Beyer Peacock tanks Wakefield decided to continue the

replacement of suburban tanks with his coupled design. The '2' class eventually comprised twelve engines constructed at Grand Canal Street between 1885 and 1897, one being built in each year with the exception of 1892. These locomotives were a development of the '42' class with the cylinder stroke increased to 24in and driving wheel diameter enlarged to 5ft 6in. Tank capacity was 800 gallons and the bunkers could hold 1½ tons of coal. The earlier engines had round cabs, similar to the Grand Canal Street built 2-2-2WTs, and bell mouthed domes with lock up safety valves. Cylinder diameter was increased to 17in for the last six built, and these locomotives were sometimes referred to as the '49' class. Nos 6, 7, 10 and 11 had square cabs, round top domes and larger water tanks.

Five of these locomotives were rebuilt as 2-4-2Ts of the 'St Patrick' class. Being newer engines the work on Nos 10 and 11, which were converted in 1903 and 1900 respectively, only involved the lengthening of frames and bunker and the provision of trailing wheels. However Nos 28, 45 and 46 were reconstructed respectively in 1909, 1910 and 1911 with new frames, boilers and 1,430 gallon tanks, and as such were virtually new locomotives.

'50' Class

In April 1890, Wakefield was ordered to prepare drawings and specifications for two new six-coupled goods engines. The order for these, the first 0-6-0s on the system, was placed with the Vulcan Foundry in May 1890 and they were delivered one year later. Nos 50 and 51 were reconstructed with new frames, cylinders and Belpaire boilers in 1912 and 1915 respectively, their weight increasing by 1½ tons as a result. Both were stationed at Bray and were used mainly on the Shillelagh goods.

'52' Class

At the beginning of September 1892, Wakefield set about preparing drawings and specifications for new engines which were required for the Loop Line service, and six weeks later he submitted photographs of bogie engines he considered suitable for the Mail service between Kingstown and Kingsbridge. By mid-November, tenders had been received for the supply of the new locomotives and the contract was awarded to Sharp Stewart & Company, the engines costing £2,275 each. The three 4-4-2Ts delivered in 1893 had Adams type leading bogies, 1,400 gallon tanks and 2½ ton coal bunkers. In 1901 they were equipped with steam heating apparatus to enable them to work the GS&WR Mail Train, the requisite fittings being supplied by Inchicore. No 54 was reconstructed at the Factory in 1913 with a larger diameter boiler and 1,530 gallon tanks.

Right: **One of the Wakefield 2-2-2WTs built at Grand Canal Street, No 36, dating from 1877 was a genuine addition to stock rather than a replacement for an old D&KR engine.** IRRS collection

Below, centre: **One of the Sharp Stewart small 0-4-2 goods engines, No 37 of 1877, complete with its 4-wheel tender, was recorded at Bray around the turn of the century.** IRRS collection

Bottom: **The solitary example of the large 0-4-2 goods class built by the company at Grand Canal Street, No 48 of 1889 was photographed outside Harcourt Street engine shed.** IRRS collection

'55' Class

Grierson was ordered to obtain tenders for two new 4-4-0 engines in October 1894, showing the relative merits of 17in x 24in cylinders with 6ft 0in driving wheels and 18in x 26in cylinders with 6ft 6in driving wheels. However, the two locomotives ordered from the Vulcan Foundry at £2,500 each on 21st February 1895 were to Grierson's hybrid proposal using the larger cylinders and smaller driving wheels. Within a week of their delivery on 10th October the company ordered two more similar engines, Nos 57 and 58. These differed from the first two in having larger cabs, no steam sanding apparatus, regulator handles opening towards instead of away from the driver, and slightly different shaped front footsteps.

These engines all suffered from broken frames due to badly positioned horn plate bolts on the driving wheel horns. They were notoriously bad steamers and, even when steaming reasonably well, were bad pullers and would labour on Dundrum bank on a load that a 2-4-0 would walk away with. They were improved by the fitting of Belpaire boilers; this job requiring a modification of the spectacles in the front cab plate. In a desperate effort to make something of this class, No 58 was reconstructed at Grand Canal Street in 1915 with new frames adopting the wheelbase of the '68' class. A larger Belpaire boiler, pitched almost 6in higher, and a new leading bogie were also fitted, and in its new guise named *Rathdrum* No 58 was practically a new engine. Following reconstruction it was based at Bray and shared the Mail workings with Nos 67 and 68.

Grierson's Folly

In March 1896 a need for more goods and tank engines arose, and bearing in mind the construction of the Waterford extension with the requirement to haul heavy goods trains up the long incline from New Ross to Palace East, the solution adopted by Grierson was to purchase two 0-6-2T goods locomotives. These were ordered from Messrs Kitson the following month at £2,575 each and were delivered in the month before Cronin's appointment as Locomotive Superintendent from 1st May 1897.

Top: **One of three Beyer Peacock 2-4-0Ts of 1883, No 43, formerly *Shanganagh*, at Bray shed.** IRRS collection

Centre: **No 28 of 1887, an early example of William Wakefield's standard 2-4-0T design, with round top cab and cab front plate with square spectacles.** IRRS collection

Bottom: **The first 0-6-0s for the line were supplied by the Vulcan Foundry in 1891. One of them, No 51, is seen here at Bray sometime before receiving its name, *New Ross*.** R N Clements – IRRS collection

They were to the same design as engines built for the Lancashire, Derbyshire and East Coast Railway and the Rhondda & Swansea Bay Railway. The 4ft 8½in gauge versions of these engines weighed only 58t 4cwt, and the DW&WR specification called for a maximum of 60t 13cwt; Kitson's gave the weight of the Irish versions as 62t 4cwt.

Most of the additional weight was on the trailing driving wheels and as a result these engines were prone to derailments. Following one such incident in the GS&WR yard at North Wall on 4th June 1897 they were both sent to Inchicore for weighing, No 4 turning the scales at 64t 8cwt and No 5 at 64t 0cwt, even heavier than the manufacturer admitted. Thereafter, they appear to have been based at Harcourt Street prior to rebuilding as 0-6-0 goods engines in 1908, the new tenders required having been obtained from the Vulcan Foundry. After rebuilding, these engines were stationed at Bray and, although they sometimes worked the Shillelagh goods, they were mostly used on cattle specials. Three new boilers ordered from the Yorkshire Engine Company in April 1920 were the last to be obtained by the D&SER. One of these Belpaire boilers was fitted to No 55 of the previous class in 1923, and the others went to Nos 4 and 5 in 1924 and 1925 respectively.

'St Patrick' Class

Cronin's first new locomotive was No 3, turned out from Grand Canal Street in 1898. It was a development of the '2' class with trailing wheels, cylinder diameter enlarged to 17in, tank capacity increased to 1,500 gallons and a coal bunker with a capacity of 2½ tons. Shortly after its introduction Cronin adopted the idea of naming locomotives, No 3 becoming *St Patrick*. Further locomotives of this class were added in 1900 and 1903 by the modification of Nos 10 and 11 of the '2' class. As mentioned above, this was achieved simply by lengthening the frames to accommodate the trailing wheels and the larger coal bunker. However, three further additions made in each of the years 1909-11 involved the reconstruction of Nos 28, 45 and 46 with new frames, boilers and enlarged water tanks. No 46 was pilot to the Royal Train in 1911 just after it was turned out from Grand Canal Street in its rebuilt form. Its name, *Princess Mary*, was originally painted in the form of an arc on the side tanks. The six locomotives of this class were all stationed at Bray and used on the Harcourt Street line.

17 and 36

In October 1897 the board decided that, 'as according as goods engines require new boilers that they be adapted as 6-wheeled coupled engines instead of 4-wheeled as at present'. The first to be so treated was No17 which emerged from Grand Canal Street in May 1899, by which time a second, No 36 was being, 'pushed forward as rapidly as possible'. Very little other than the motion and some fittings of the old engines were used, even the tenders were heavily reconstructed to increase their coal and water capacity.

No 17 was the engine involved in the notorious crash through the end wall of Harcourt Street station on 14th February 1900. It was rebuilt with new cylinders and a new larger boiler in 1920. No 36 was fitted with a Phoenix superheater in 1911 which required an extended smokebox and a 1ft 6in increase in front frame length. In this form the engine was run alternately with No 17 on goods trains and showed a 15.7% saving in coal consumption. The superheater was removed in 1915 but the extended smokebox was retained until the locomotive was reconstructed in 1919 with new frames, boiler, cylinders and crank axle.

'40' Class

In 1901 construction commenced on a series of six 2-4-2Ts whose coupled wheelbase was increased by 3in over that of the 'St Patrick' class, though in all other respects they were similar to the earlier locomotives. The first three had round top boilers but the others completed in 1906-09, were fitted with Belpaire boilers from the outset. All six members of the class were shedded at Bray.

The L&NWR Tanks

In November 1901, following correspondence between Cronin and Francis Webb, Locomotive Engineer of the L&NWR, the offer of the latter company to supply six 2-4-2 tank engines altered to the Irish gauge, and put into thorough repair at £1,500 each, was accepted. As delivered to the DW&WR they had all the well-known L&NWR features, Ramsbottom safety valves, Webb chimney, Allan straight-link motion, regulator in the smokebox and cylinders cast in one piece with slide valves in 'V'-formation on top. The visible outer sideplates of the tanks were dummies, the real tanks, having a capacity of 860 gallons, being self-contained units behind them. These engines were not appreciated by the drivers, some of whom swore that the old single tanks could do better.

Named after Earls, they were originally stationed at Bray and used mostly on the Harcourt Street line, but by 1913 only No 59 was in regular use, the others being laid up at Bray. No 64 was taken into the Works for reconstruction and turned out in 1914 with new '40' class frames, a larger boiler and 1,430 gallon water tanks with a resultant increase in weight of 5t 9cwt. Thereafter it was stationed at Grand Canal Street and used on the second pier train.

In December 1916 the Secretary reported that he had been negotiating for the sale of five of the L&NWR engines and that at a meeting with Captain Cairns of the War Office he and Cronin had accepted the offer of £700 per engine for four of them on condition that repairs could be arranged in England. Following examination by the Inspector of Iron Structures the sale of Nos 60, 62 and 63 was agreed and they were sent to Crewe for repair and re-gauging. Nos 60 and 62 became Inland Waterways and Docks Nos 42 and 43 and were used at Richborough Port before being sold by auction for scrap in October 1919. No 63 went to the War Department Shoeburyness Garrison as their No 12 and as WD4190 still retained its D&SER name, *Earl of Carysfort*, when observed at Shoeburyness in May 1921. Nos 59 and 61 were sold to J F Wake of Darlington, for £400 each in July 1917. They were converted from Irish gauge at Wake's works, being overhauled and fitted with steel fireboxes at the same time. In December 1919 they were advertised for sale in the Glasgow Herald at £2,850 each and were purchased by the Cramlington Coal Company becoming their Nos 13 and 14, eventually being scrapped in 1923 and 1929 respectively.

Heavy Goods Engines

In 1904 it was decided to replace old 0-4-2 goods engines Nos 13 and 14 by new 0-6-0 locomotives. No 13, completed at Grand Canal Street in the same year, had 18in cylinders though this was increased to 18½in for No 14 which was completed the following year. Two more engines to this design were ordered from Beyer Peacock in late 1904 at £3,200 each. These had 18¼in cylinders and boiler pressure increased from 160 to 175 psi. Nos 65 *Cork* and 66 *Dublin* were delivered in May 1905 and had brass nameplates which they retained until the amalgamation. All of these locomotives had large side window cabs.

A further locomotive of this type was constructed at the Factory in 1910. This had 18½in cylinders and a 175 psi boiler, but 4ft 11½in driving wheels, recovered from the old 0-4-2s, were used instead of the normal 5ft 1in wheels on this class. No 18 also differed in having a smaller cab, originally with triangular windows. It was the first locomotive in Ireland to be equipped with Ross Pop safety valves and was coupled to one of the three tenders purchased from the Vulcan Foundry at the time of the conversion of the 0-6-2Ts.

New Mail Engines

At the same time as the two Beyer Peacock goods engines of the previous type were ordered, on 27th October 1904, the company placed an order for two new main line bogie passenger engines. Contracted for £3,250 each, they were based on the design of the GNR(I) 'Q' class locomotives and delivered during the first week of June 1905. Both of these fine engines were stationed at

Bray and used on the Mail. No 68 *Rathcoole* was the favourite and No 67 *Rathmore* the stand-by engine, their brass nameplates being retained until the amalgamation.

The Railmotors

These vehicles were the result of one of the railway crazes which appeared at the beginning of the twentieth century. In January 1906 Cronin prepared drawings and specifications for a Railmotor, and a contract was placed with the Leeds firm of Manning Wardle in March of the same year, it being stipulated that one of the Motors was to be fitted with Marshall's Valve Gear, at a royalty of £65, in place of the Walschaert's Valve Gear. The first unit went into service during the last week of August between Lansdowne Road and the Ballsbridge sidings, in connection with a show at the RDS grounds, and was transferred the following week to take up the working of the Bray to Greystones service. The Railmotors made ten return trips daily doing the one-way journey in 13 minutes including a stop at Bray Head Halt.

The carriage section catered for all three classes of passengers in open saloons. Communication between the control compartment of the coach and the footplate was by means of a ship's telegraph, the driver, however, having direct control of the brake from that end of the unit. In service, Railmotors Nos 1 and 2 proved very uncomfortable. It was reported that it was impossible to read a newspaper when travelling, and that their oscillating motion made children seasick!

The engines and carriages were separated in 1907-08, the resultant 0-4-0Ts being renumbered 69 and 70. They were amongst the first locomotives on the system with Belpaire boilers and the only ones with outside cylinders and valve gear.

At first they were painted chocolate, lined in yellow, but when the colour of the carriage stock was changed to Midland red they were painted in that colour.

No 69 received a leading pony truck in 1914, but this was subsequently removed by the GSR at Broadstone in 1925. No 70 was put up for sale and, in August 1918, the IREC requested that it should be sold to the Dublin & Blessington Steam Tram Company, adjacent to whose line a new aerodrome was being built at Tallaght. Payment of £800 for the engine was received in September, but it proved unsuitable for the D&BST and was exchanged in that same year for GS&WR 0-4-0T *Cambria*. The former D&SER tank was not re-numbered by the GS&WR but was given the name *Imp* instead. Similarly, No 69 became *Elf* when it was absorbed into the GSR stock in 1925.

'20' Class Tank Engines

No 20 was the outcome of a fashion which was started by the London Brighton and South Coast Railway with their 6ft 7in wheeled tank engines built for working the 'Southern Belle' express trains over the 51 miles between London Victoria and Brighton in the even hour. The desire to build tank versions of the largest passenger engines was followed by the D&SER, but there was really no job that justified the large driving wheel diameter and for many years No 20 operated only 90 miles per day. It was intended that No 20 *King George* should work the Royal Train in July 1911, but as it was not ready, No 56 was used instead. The boiler for No 20 was purchased from Kitson and the frameplates from the North British Locomotive Company.

In January 1924 Wild submitted designs for two new tank engines similar to No 20 but with Belpaire boilers pressed to 175 psi and other detail improvements. On the 29th of the same month, Beyer Peacock's tender at £5,376 each, delivered to Grand Canal Street was accepted. Nos 34 and 35 weighed 63t 14cwt, an increase of 2t 4cwt over that of No 20. It was intended to use these locomotives on main line trains, but they were all stationed at Grand Canal Street and used on suburban traffic.

Blackburn

Following the termination by the D&SER in April 1916 of the contract with Naylor Bros for the Greystones diversion, the plant and machinery was taken over by the company's Engineer. Included amongst the effects was an 0-6-0T which had originally been built by Manning Wardle in 1888 for use on the Manchester Ship Canal contract by T A Walker. It was subsequently purchased by Fisher and Le Fanu and, having been altered to the 5ft 3in gauge, was used on the construction of the Claremorris to Collooney line. It was advertised for sale in 1906 following the completion of the Newcastle to Ballyroney contract, but its whereabouts, until appearing with Naylor on the D&SER diversion work, is unknown.

After the completion of the works at Bray Head it was used by the D&SER as a departmental locomotive for tunnel and permanent way work, retaining its name until taken over by the GSR. With only 600 gallon tanks and 1½ ton coal capacity its relatively small size made it difficult to find a use for this engine on the new owner's system. The GSR offered it to the Electricity Supply Board and the Carlow Sugar Beet Factory, but both declined. It was eventually sold as scrap in March 1925 to Messrs Deby Barrett & Company of London for £77, being cut up and loaded into wagons.

The Beyer Peacock Moguls

On 11th January 1921 the purchase of two new locomotives was authorised by the General Manager and within two weeks five tenders had been received, that of Beyer Peacock at £13,500 for the two, delivered at Dublin, being accepted. However, the actual cost as delivered was £19,326 due to price escalation of materials. These magnificent engines were a new departure for the D&SER, incorporating the most up-to-date steam locomotive practice, being equipped with Belpaire boilers, 18 element superheaters and 8in piston valves. Their overall length was limited by the clearance to the buffer stops behind Harcourt Street turntable.

Due to the disruption and destruction being suffered by the company as a result of the Civil War the new locomotives were sent to Belfast following delivery on 14th December 1922 and stored in the GNR(I) running shed at Adelaide. At the end of May 1923 they were returned from Belfast and brought into use discreetly. Having been used for three months on the day goods trains Wild was given authority to use them on the night goods from the end of August. No 15 was retained by CIE for preservation and has been restored to working order by the Railway Preservation Society of Ireland, albeit with the GSR 'N' type boiler, which was fitted at Inchicore in 1944.

Proposed 4-4-0 of 1923

In January 1923 the General Manager was authorised to obtain quotations for the supply of two new engines suitable for main line passenger trains. On 12th June Wild submitted a design for them, but the subject was deferred. It was raised again at the board meeting of 16th October 1923 but was once more deferred and, regrettably, the idea was never proceeded with. The design was essentially a 4-4-0 version of the Beyer Peacock Moguls with an estimated weight of 49tons 16cwt. The same superheated Belpaire boiler as used on the Moguls, working at 175 psi and centred at 9ft 0in above rail height, was to be fitted. The wheelbase and wheel diameters as employed in the 1905 engines of the '68' class were to be adopted, and the 18½in x 26in cylinders with 8in piston valves were to be inclined at 1 in 8.5. The tenders were to be the same 2,600 gallon type with 5 tons coal capacity, as coupled to the Moguls.

Declining availability

Over the years locomotive availability generally kept up with the demands of traffic, but in the financial climate affecting railways after the First World War the situation began to deteriorate rapidly, to the extent that by October 1921 only 35 of the 64 engines were in full working order. Six others were working at reduced pressure due to the age or condition of their boilers and another one was only allowed to work occasionally. There were twelve engines awaiting attention, of which tank engines Nos 3, 10, 24, 41, 44, 45, 46 and 53, together with goods engine No 65 were in need of urgent repairs.

Above: **Sharp Stewart 4-4-2T No 54, one of three built in 1893
especially for the Kingstown to Kingsbridge mail trains, stands at
Carlisle Pier, sometime before being named** *Duke of Leinster*.
H Fayle – IRRS collection

Below: **Vulcan Foundry 4-4-0, No 56** *Rathmines* **of 1895,
photographed outside Harcourt Street shed in February 1908 in
original condition.** H Fayle – IRRS collection

Top left: **No 4, one of the two Kitson 0-6-2T goods engines of 1897 which in their original form proved too heavy for the line and were subsequently converted to 0-6-0 tender engines in 1908, photographed outside Harcourt Street shed in February 1907.** H Fayle - IRRS collection

Top right: **D&SER 0-6-0 No 5, rebuilt from one of the 0-6-2T goods engines, is seen as GSR No 449 at Grand Canal Street in October 1933. This photograph shows the former tank engine as it was after its second rebuilding. The fitting of Belpaire boilers to the pair in 1924-5 made them the most powerful 0-6-0s on the GSR.** L&GRP

Centre: **The second 0-6-0 to be built by the company, No 36 *Wexford*, photographed outside Grand Canal Street when new in 1901.** IRRS collection

Left: **A 2-4-2T, No 40 *St Selskar* of 1902, stands outside Harcourt Street shed in February 1908.** H Fayle - IRRS collection

Three other engines were confined to working light trains only. In addition to the foregoing there were seven engines stopped and had not worked for some time.

On 8th November the board approved the Locomotive Engineer's recommendation to scrap six of the stopped engines (Nos 16, 23, 31, 34, 35 and 37) and agreed that the nine requiring urgent repairs should be sent to Beyer Peacock, one or two at a time. In regard to the former recommendation, the six locomotives were sold as scrap in April 1923 to Thomas Ward Ltd of Sheffield for a total of £625. The company removed the copper, brass and other valuable parts and retained the boilers of all but Nos 34 and 35. The latter recommendation was not proceeded with but four tank engines, Nos 3, 10, 27 and 44, did go to the GNR(I) Works at Dundalk for overhaul, returning with numbers and lettering applied in the GNR(I) style.

The position became worse when the expenditure estimates for 1922, which included a provision of £18,000 for the complete renewal of nine locomotives as well as £19,000 for the two new goods engines, were drastically cut at a board meeting on 14th February, the engine renewal programme being suspended. However Wild was requested to submit a close estimate for the cost of renewing No 45, though this work was not undertaken. Fourteen locomotives suffered serious damage as a result of the Civil War, three of them, Nos 22, 51 and 68, being wrecked beyond economic repair.

By December 1924, the end of the D&SER era, the fleet consisted of 54 locomotives, plus the departmental engine *Blackburn*. In addition there existed four engines ready for scrap (Nos 19, 21, 41 and 48), and the three engines maliciously damaged beyond economical repair. The numbers 23, 31, 37, 59 to 63 and 70 were vacant at that time. The 54 working engines were originally to have been re-numbered by the GSR in the series 410 to 462 plus *Elf*. Forty-four of the D&SER engines were transferred to Inchicore on the night of 28-29th January 1925 for examination and it was decided to withdraw 12 of the fleet. The locomotives concerned (Nos 1, 2, 6, 25, 26, 32, 33, 38, 39, 42, 43 and 44) were nominally replaced by the 12 Woolwich Moguls then under erection in the former MGWR Works at Broadstone, as a result of which the GSR number series for ex-DSER locomotives was revised to commence at 422.

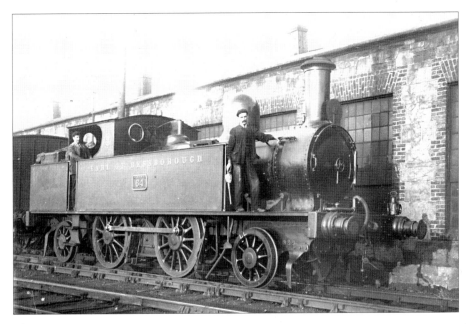

Top: **A former L&NWR 2-4-2T , No 64 *Earl of Bessborough*, clearly showing her ancestry, stands outside Bray shed circa 1908. This was the only one of the class to be retained by the D&SER, having been reconstructed with 'Saint' frames in 1914.** IRRS collection

Centre: **Former D&SER 2-4-2T No 61 as Cramlington Coal Company No 14.** R N Clements collection

Bottom: **A 1908 view of No 21 *Kilcoole*, the 1905 rebuild as a tank of the Sharp large goods engine of the same number.** H Fayle - IRRS collection

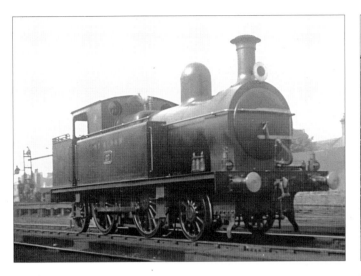

Photographs on this page

Above left: One of the three 2-4-2Ts built with Belpaire boilers, No 27 *St Aidan* of 1907, is seen at Bray in July 1914. The locomotive coaling stage and coal crane are just visible behind the bunker of the locomotive. Ken Nunn - LCGB collection

Above right: Railmotor No 2 photographed when new at Bray in 1906. This loco was supplied with Marshall valve gear instead of the Walschaerts valve gear as fitted to Railmotor No 1. The carriage portions were separated from the engines in 1908 as they proved too uncomfortable for passengers. H Fayle - IRRS collection

Below: Cronin's express tank engine of 1911, No 20 *King George* at Grand Canal Street when new. IRRS collection

Photographs on the opposite page

Top: Two additional heavy goods engines were built by Beyer Peacock in 1905. This view shows one of them, No 65 *Cork*, outside the engine shed at Wexford. IRRS collection

Bottom: No 68 *Rathcoole*, one of the two fine 4-4-0s supplied by Beyer Peacock in 1905, photographed at Wexford in May 1908. This locomotive was wrecked in a maliciously staged head on collision with No 51 at Palace East on 20th January 1923. H Fayle - IRRS collection

Top: **The official builder's photograph of No 15, one of the two Beyer Peacock 2-6-0s of 1922. As their arrival coincided with the Civil War, they were sent to Belfast for safe keeping in the GNR(I) shed at Adelaide. These were the only engines with Robinson superheaters on the D&SER. No 15 is preserved as CIE No 461 and is operated by the Railway Preservation Society of Ireland.** Beyer Peacock

Above, centre: **The official photograph of No 35, one of the two 4-4-2Ts built in 1924 by Beyer Peacock to the same design as No 20, but with Belpaire boilers.** Beyer Peacock

Left: **The interior of the fitting shop at Grand Canal Street Works.** IRRS collection

Chapter Twelve

ROLLING STOCK

I N 1895 THE DW&WR drew up a new regis ter of its carriage stock and about 1908 this was carefully copied by the late Canon T W B Nicholson, an early Irish railway enthusiast. He added considerable data from his personal observations in the early 1900s, and this comprehensive record, supported by other contemporary documents, has enabled the preparation of an almost complete schedule of the company's carriages which is given in Appendix E. Additional details are presented in this section to give a fuller picture of the development of the passenger stock.

General Policy
Until 1879 it was generally company policy to obtain its passenger carriages from well known builders, only a handful of vehicles being built at Grand Canal Street up to this time despite the construction of many carriages at the Factory in D&KR days. Those vehicles actually built at Grand Canal Street during this period mostly tended to utilise underframes and ironwork from vehicles which had been badly damaged in accidents, as will be recounted below.

Following the enlargement of the carriage shop at the Works in 1878, and coincident with the appointment of William Wakefield as the Assistant Locomotive Superintendent in May 1880, construction of passenger carriages at Grand Canal Street became the norm for the company's requirements.

Due to an increasing demand for third class vehicles in the 1890s the company turned to outside carriage builders again, but following the appointment of Richard Cronin in 1897 all new passenger vehicles were built at the Factory.

The policy for replacing coaching stock was that first class carriages were generally in use for 40 years or more, though some gave longer service following conversion to brake vans at the end of their passenger carrying days. The earlier second class vehicles were replaced after about 20 years life. These were then reclassified as thirds and gave as much as 30 more years of service in that capacity. This method of adding to the third class fleet was common during the 1870s and 1880s.

In 1893 TPO vans were introduced on the Mail trains. The first lavatory vehicles were

introduced in 1895, bogie vehicles appearing in the same year. On-board catering and carriages with interconnecting gangways were introduced in 1904 with the opening of the extension to Waterford. The decline in second class patronage saw the conversion of many second class carriages to third class in the early 1900s.

The eventual abolition of second class travel by the D&SER in early 1922 resulted in the remaining vehicles being reclassified as firsts and thirds. At the same time 1st/2nd class composites were reclassified as 1st/3rd composites or firsts. A major attempt was made to compete with the DUTC in 1922 with the conversion of six bogie carriages to Bus Coaches, these vehicles being known as the 'Maguire Bogies'.

Early Wicklow Vehicles
In August 1854 the company reported that for the opening of the line it possessed 27 carriages: three firsts, eight seconds, 13 thirds, one composite and two passenger vans. However, these proved insufficient and the MGWR loaned a second and three thirds from June to October 1854. A further two vehicles, a second and a composite were added before the end of the year, the latter being one of the former Atmospheric vehicles taken over with that section in March 1854. The other Atmospheric vehicles in the original D&WR fleet consisted of four seconds and four thirds all of which were regauged at Grand Canal Street in 1854. Two of the thirds were converted into vans in 1859, the other vehicles were replaced between 1869 and 1875. Three firsts and three seconds were ordered from J S Dawson of Dublin in 1853, however, it appears that one of the seconds was probably delivered as a composite. The balance of 14 vehicles, three seconds, nine thirds and two passenger brake vans, were purchased from Brown Marshall of Birmingham in 1853-54.

Three further Dawson vehicles were obtained from the Waterford & Tramore Railway in late 1854 but, as they were not added to stock until later in 1855, it is possible that they received further work at Dawson's workshop before arriving on the line. In the meantime, Brown Marshall supplied 18 more carriages in 1855 - four firsts, six seconds and eight thirds, and two pas-

senger brake vans were ordered from them in November of the same year. They also manufactured nine thirds and two carriage trucks which were delivered in 1856 and supplied the first three horseboxes for the line in 1856-57.

The 26 Brown Marshall seconds and thirds of 1854-55 were five-compartment 22ft 0in 4-wheeled vehicles. Seven of the seconds, were converted into thirds Nos 53 to 59, in 1877. Most of these vehicles had long lives, all but three of them still being in service in 1895, and the last few surviving until 1906. However, the same could not be said of the thirds which came from the same builder in 1856, as all were replaced during 1884-88 by former D&KR seconds after only about 30 years of service.

A total of 14 carriages consisting of four firsts, four seconds, four thirds and two composites were supplied by Dawson in 1860-62. Most of the Dawson vehicles were extensively rebuilt by the DW&WR at Grand Canal Street between 1875 and 1886.

Another Dublin carriage builder, T&C Martin of North Wall, supplied six 25ft 3in passenger brake vans in 1863-64 built to Haughton's plans and specifications. Manufactured chiefly from teak, their frames were reported to be 'not as strong as they should be'. However, following rebuilding at the Works between 1878 and 1881, they all continued in service until 1903-06.

In December 1863 an order was placed with the Metropolitan Carriage & Wagon Company of Birmingham for the supply of four firsts and four seconds. These six-wheeled vehicles, delivered in the following year, were far superior to any other of the carriages on the line. The four-compartment firsts were 25ft 2in long and the six-compartment seconds 31ft 4in. These designs were to form the standard for construction of first and second class carriages for many years as will be recounted in the section dealing with the Wakefield era.

The Kingstown Stock
Although the D&WR worked the Kingstown line from 1856, the rolling stock was considered separate until the signing of the long term lease in 1866 and was not assimilated into the company's fleet until then. The schedule of rolling stock handed over by the

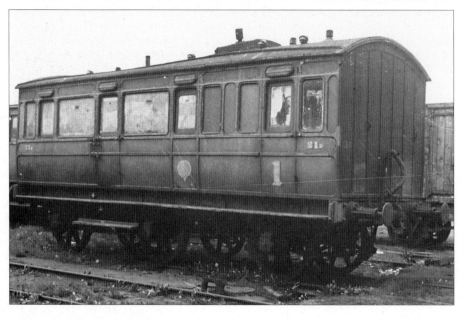

D&KR in 1856 consisted of nine firsts, 27 seconds, 12 open seconds, 20 thirds, eight parcel and mail vans and the state saloon. In each of the main classes there were three types of vehicle, classified by the railway as small, medium and large. Apart from ten of the open seconds, which had been built in 1834 by Beeston & Melling of Manchester on underframes supplied by Galloway & Bowman of Glasgow, none of the original stock built for the opening of the Kingstown line had survived. These open seconds held 28 passengers in 3½ compartments. Two similar vehicles were built at the Works in 1842.

Five three-compartment firsts, which had been built at Grand Canal Street during 1839-42, passed to the D&WR as two small firsts of 18 seats and three small seconds of 24 seats. The four-compartment small thirds, containing 32 seats, had been built at the Factory between 1837 and 1842. Two survived to be handed over, both being converted into wheel trucks during 1862-63. A further eight of these small thirds formed the total stock of parcel and mail vans, having been converted from passenger vehicles in D&KR days.

All of the medium stock, built at Grand Canal Street during 1843-45, was handed over. This type consisted of six firsts, each with 24 seats in three compartments; 14 seconds with 32 seats in four compartments; and 12 thirds of 40 seats in four compartments. Three of the thirds were converted into brake vans in 1860, 1861 and 1865 respectively.

The large vehicles, built at Grand Canal Street between 1849 and 1851, were designed for ready conversion to the 5ft 3in gauge. The 18 vehicles of this type consisted of a first with 32 seats in four compartments, ten seconds of 60 seats in six compartments, six thirds with seating for 60 in five compartments; and also the 17-seat state saloon.

Apart from the changes mentioned above the only other alteration to the D&KR fleet between 1856 and 1866 was the acquisition by the D&WR of a new first class carriage in 1860, specifically for the Kingstown line, which was built by Dawson at a cost of £400.

Top: **This was originally a 31ft 4in six-compartment second class carriage, No 11, built by Metropolitan in 1877. It was converted into third brake No 69 in 1914 and is seen here in March 1946 as Material Van 161A.** J M Robbins - IRRS collection

Centre: **Two of the 1878 Metropolitan 21ft 6in 4-wheeled third brakes photographed in use as Locomotive Department vans at Bray.** J M Robbins - IRRS collection

Left: **1880 24ft 6in First class saloon No 21 photographed in GSR livery at Inchicore in August 1946.** R N Clements - IRRS collection

It is known that this carriage became No 21 in 1866 in the DW&WR first class list and was converted to second No 55 in 1881.

Because the D&KR rolling stock was considered separate it was not re-numbered until after 1866. The precise details of the re-numbering cannot be ascertained, but it is known that the firsts became 17 to 26, the seconds (including the two 1842 open seconds) 19 to 40 and 42 to 48, the ten original open seconds 51 to 60, the thirds 34 to 48, and the vans 13 to 23 in the passenger stock list. The second class numbers, 41, 49 and 50, were taken up by three of the 1864 MCW vehicles which were nominal additions to the D&KR fleet. The state saloon appears to have never been given a running number.

The Wakefield Era

From the time that John Wakefield took over the affairs of the Locomotive Carriage and Wagon Departments, standardisation of design was evident. We have already seen that four firsts and four seconds were purchased from MCW in 1864, and Wakefield used these designs as the basis of the standard vehicles for these classes for many years. The first class carriages were built to both 24ft 6in and 25ft 2in lengths. The second class carriages were always known as 31-footers but were actually built to a length of 31ft 4in or 31ft 5in.

Firsts

In addition to the 1864 vehicles, MCW built four more firsts, two each in 1870 and 1877, this time 24ft 6in long. The two 1870 vehicles were converted into passenger brake vans in 1913, but the 1877 ones survived into GSR days. Following the 1870 MCW order, the DW&WR built three firsts at Grand Canal Street in 1871-72 one of which, No 26, was converted into kitchen van 201 in 1908. The other two became passenger brake vans as did the kitchen van following the removal of its catering equipment about 1912.

Following this short interlude of construction at the Factory the company turned to outside builders once again, Craven Brothers of Sheffield supplying three vehicles in 1876 and the Ashbury Carriage Company of Manchester four vehicles in both 1874 and 1878. The 1874 Ashbury's reverted to the 25ft 2in length, three of these carriages eventually replacing composites Nos 1 to 3 in 1910-11. Ashbury also supplied a first brake with three passenger compartments in 1878.

From 1879 the construction of firsts was undertaken at the Works. One was built there in 1879 and six more were turned out from the factory between 1882 and 1887. A first class carriage was built in 1881 as a 19-seat Directors' Saloon. Numbered 21, it included a small kitchen for the provision of sustenance to the board members as they made their inspection tours of the line. The Dawson vehicle of 1860 which it replaced was converted into second class No 55. The last two firsts built to the 24ft 6in length were turned out from Grand Canal Street in 1889 and differed from the others in having three passenger and one luggage compartment.

The final four firsts built at the Works during Wakefield's time marked a change in design. These four compartment vehicles, turned out in 1892-94, were constructed to an increased length of 28ft, the same as the standard being employed for new seconds and thirds at that time.

Seconds

The fleet of 31ft seconds eventually totalled 29 vehicles. In addition to the four MCW vehicles of 1864, the DW&WR built four in 1868 using ironwork and other parts of the vehicles wrecked in the Bray Head accident of August 1867. Two of these were rebuilt in 1882-83, and the other two were replaced in 1894, their underframes apparently being used for two new lavatory seconds turned out in the following year. Three of the 1864 MCW carriages were rebuilt at Grand Canal Street in 1899, two of them later replacing thirds Nos 10 and 12 which had been destroyed in the Ovoca collision of August 1895.

MCW supplied a total of fifteen 31ft 4in seconds in 1870, 1875 and 1877. Cravens delivered six 31ft 5in vehicles in 1876. The Craven order, which included firsts and covered wagons, was a particularly difficult contract with the DW&WR threatening to cancel the order due to late delivery by the manufacturer. In the end they only agreed to accept the carriages on the basis of a 5% reduction in price. The company never placed another order with Cravens as a result of this experience.

All of these seconds were converted into third class vehicles between 1901 and 1915, eleven of them becoming third brakes. Three of these third brakes retained five compartments with just one of the end compartments being converted into the guard's brake compartment, but the other eight had the two centre compartments converted into a guard's brake and luggage compartment.

In 1880 William Wakefield introduced the first of his standard five compartment seconds. It was 27ft 6in long, and five more were built to this length between 1881 and 1884. In 1885 the length was increased slightly to 28ft, and a total of thirty vehicles of this type were constructed during Wakefield's time. Six of these 36 seconds were converted into thirds in 1918, but the rest survived until the abolition of second class in 1922 when they were also converted into thirds, retaining their old numbers with the addition of an 'S' suffix.

Thirds

Following the delivery of the four thirds from Dawson in 1861, no new thirds were purchased or built for some ten years. However, three of the open seconds were converted to thirds in 1868. A new 26ft 3in vehicle, No 41, appeared in 1873, and three more followed in 1875. All but one of these four thirds were converted to third brakes in 1882-83.

The introduction of standard second class carriages during 1875-77 created a surplus in this category and so in 1877, ten old seconds were converted into third class Nos 53 to 62, and in the following year thirds 72 to 77 came into being with the conversion of four more seconds and a first. The first was the solitary former D&KR large first No 18 which became No 72 in the third class stock list. The cascade effect created by the introduction of the new Directors' Saloon in 1881 resulted in the displaced open second No 55 also becoming a third class vehicle.

Between 1884 and 1888 the nine Brown-Marshall thirds of 1856 were replaced by seven former D&KR seconds and the two Dawson seconds of 1854, one of the latter being rebuilt as a cattle brake in 1886.

What was to be the first of a standard class of 28ft six-compartment thirds, No 73, was built at Grand Canal Street in 1883. Others numbered 37, 44 and 80 to 83 followed in 1890-92. Twelve thirds purchased from Brown Marshall in 1892 were to the same design and were numbered from 1 to 12 in the third class list, though two of them, Nos 10 and 12, were destroyed in the Ovoca collision of August 1895. The vehicles which the Brown-Marshalls displaced were in turn re-numbered 85 to 96. The number 84 in the list had already been taken by the conversion of first No 3 to third class earlier in 1892.

Third Brakes

As a result the BoT inquiry into the Harcourt Road accident of March 1858 additional brake power was recommended for passenger trains and three third brakes were created by the conversion of existing third class carriages. Four more thirds were converted in 1866. One of these third brakes, No 24, was destroyed in the Glenageary collision of February 1878 and was replaced by a new vehicle built at the Works in the same year.

The most numerous third brake design was the cattle brake, thirteen of which were constructed at Grand Canal Street between 1875 and 1890. These vehicles had three third class compartments for cattle drovers and were ballasted for use as goods brake vans on cattle specials. All were re-classified as goods brake vans in 1913 although they retained their third class numbers until scrapped.

In 1878 the company purchased ten 21ft 6in 4-wheeled third brakes, four from MCW and six from the Midland Carriage & Wagon Company. The MCW vehicles were noticeably different having flat sides and square beading to the panels. The Midland variety had the traditional tumblehome to the lower body and round cornered beading to the panelling.

The stock of third brakes was further increased in 1882-83 by the conversion of nine more thirds, six being former Brown Marshalls vehicles of 1855. A new 30ft 0in four-compartment third brake, No 42, was introduced in 1884 and was one of the vehicles maliciously destroyed in 1923. Two more 30ft 0in third brakes were obtained in 1893 from the Lancaster Carriage & Wagon Company.

Composites
Three 30ft 0in composites with five compartments were built by the DW&WR in 1869 utilising the ironwork of three vehicles destroyed in a fire at Westland Row the previous year. One replaced the former Atmospheric composite and the other two, Nos 7 and 8, were additions to stock. Composites 1 to 3 were rebuilt during 1881-83, but no more composites were added to stock during the Wakefields' time.

Between Wakefield and Cronin
As we have already seen, the three years following Wakefield's retirement proved a turbulent time for the Locomotive, Carriage & Wagon Department. Despite the difficulties, a number of vehicles were constructed at Grand Canal Street during this period and others were purchased from the Birmingham Carriage & Wagon Company.

One of the first things Grierson did was to purchase the redundant 5ft 3in gauge stock from the Finn Valley Railway when that line was converted to 3ft gauge. This included two composites, a third and two third brakes, all 27ft 6in long, built by Brown Marshall in 1874. The composites were eventually converted to passenger brake vans and one of the third brakes, No 97, received a completely new body in 1908.

The 30ft 0in underframe that had first appeared with the two 1893 third brakes was used for eight vehicles constructed at the Factory in 1894-97. The two 1894 composites were unique in having centre luggage compartments. First class saloons Nos 45 and 46 of 1895 were built primarily for the conveyance of members of the Leopardstown Race Club from Harcourt Street to Foxrock but were also used for other special duties, including Royal Trains. Two passenger brake vans, built at Grand Canal Street in 1896, were to the same design as those built by BCW at the same time. However, the two passenger vans built in 1897 were not fitted as brake vans. No 1 was a mail van for the Pier trains, No 22 was a milk van specially constructed for the traffic from Shillelagh to

Harcourt Street.

In 1895-96 two vehicles appeared with underframes different to those normally being used at that date. Two second class carriages with lavatories were constructed in 1895 on the 31ft underframes of old seconds Nos 33 and 36 which, as we have already noted, were replaced by new vehicles in 1894. In a similar manner firsts Nos 47 and 48, constructed in 1896 for the Pier train, utilised the 28ft 0in underframes of the two thirds which had been wrecked in the Ovoca collision the previous year.

The first bogie carriages on the line, two 44ft 0in six-compartment lavatory tri-composites, were supplied by the Birmingham Carriage & Wagon Company in 1895. In the following year the same company received orders for the supply of 24 6-wheel vehicles (six seconds, 14 thirds and four passenger brake vans). The seconds and thirds were 33ft 6in long and had five and six compartments respectively. The vans were built on 30ft 0in underframes the company building two vehicles to the same design, as noted above. The design of the BCW vehicles set standards that were to apply for new construction in the years ahead.

Mahogany, High Roofs and Bogies
Richard Cronin's 20-year tenure in charge of the Locomotive Carriage & Wagon Department saw many developments in carriage design, and in order to deal satisfactorily with this period it is necessary to consider the non-bogie and bogie stock separately.

The first three passenger vehicles built by Cronin were turned out in 1898 on 30ft 0in underframes, probably utilising materials already available at the Works. Two were third brakes and the other was a second. Following these three vehicles the 33ft 6in underframe, which had been introduced with the BCW stock in 1896, was adopted as standard for 6-wheeled vehicles. The eleven vehicles built to this length between 1900 and 1903 consisted of four firsts, five seconds and two thirds. The length of the standard non-bogie vehicle was increased to 34ft 4in with the introduction of two passenger brake vans built in 1903, both of which were fitted with gangways. The twelve 34ft 4in 6-wheelers built from 1904 to 1910 had high roofs to conform to the profile of the bogie stock then being introduced. Extensive use was made of mahogany in the construction of the two firsts, two composites, four thirds, two third brakes and two passenger brake vans which resulted in the production of the heaviest 6-wheelers of these types on the system.

One other 34ft 4in vehicle was built by the D&SER in 1922. This was passenger brake van No 18 which was a replacement for the one of the same number destroyed in the Civil War. It is generally assumed that the remains of third brake No 59, which had

also suffered in the troubles, were utilised in its construction. It was a high roofed vehicle and, like vans Nos 23 and 24 of 1903, was equipped with gangways. It was the only new item of carriage stock constructed during George Wild's tenure of the department.

The first two bogie vehicles on the line, BCW composites Nos 11 and 12, have already been referred to above, but it was not until 1899 that any more bogie carriages were to appear. From the introduction of composite No 10, in that year, until 1915 a total of 30 bogie carriages were constructed at Grand Canal Street. The first four, two composites a third and a second, were built to a length of 45ft, second No 41 of 1902 being the first open centre vehicle on the line.

In 1903 the length of the bogie carriage underframe was increased to 50ft 0in and ten carriages were built to this length. Open centre first, No 12, was unique in that it was the only vehicle the company possessed which had a clerestory roof. It was rebuilt in 1918 as a composite, the large side lights being replaced by a door and two small side lights for each seating bay, though later reverted to a first. The other 50ft vehicles included a first saloon, two side corridor composites, a centre kitchen composite, three open side corridor thirds and two kitchen vans. Saloon No 13, which was displayed in the Dublin exhibition at the RDS in 1907, was used in the funeral train for John Redmond in March 1918, but when somebody refused to travel in it because it carried the 'unlucky' number 13, it hastily became No 18, which number it retained into early GSR days.

The two Manning Wardle steam railmotors have already been described in chapter eleven. In 1908 when the saloons were separated from the engines the two carriage portions became open tri-composites Nos 19 and 20. These 44ft 0in vehicles were rather odd looking as their bogies were not equidistant from the centre of the body due to the design of the underframe.

The first 54ft 0in vehicles appeared in 1908, one of these being a corridor composite restaurant car. The five other carriages built to this length were compartment stock for suburban traffic and comprised a composite, two second brakes and two third brakes. The second brakes had five compartments and a large luggage and guard's compartment whereas the third brakes had nine compartments and a small guard's compartment. The first Westland Row suburban set was formed by second brake No 14, composite No 18 and third brake No 41.

For the second Westland Row suburban set the composite provided to operate with the other two 54ft 0in brakes was No 22 of 1910. This, together with two identical vehicles built in the following year to strengthen the suburban sets, were the only 57ft 0in carriages on the system.

Top: **Third class 165D, formerly 28ft 0in second No 36 of 1894, and later 36S, photographed at Cork in 1946.**
R N Clements - IRRS collection

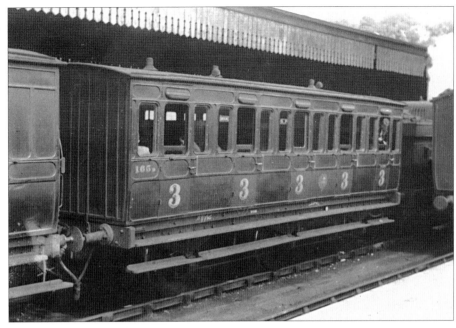

Centre, right: **30ft 0in first class saloon No 45 of 1895** K A Murray collection

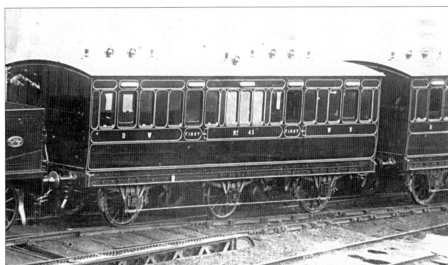

Below: **50ft 0in bogie open first No.12, the only vehicle in the carriage fleet with a clerestory roof, was photographed at Abbey Junction in 1904, whilst operating as a restaurant car. It became composite No.28 in 1918, but reverted to its former first class status in 1922.** H Fayle - IRRS collection

Above: **The interior of open first No 12, the vehicle pictured on page 99, its unique clerestory roof clearly visible in this view.** IRRS collection

Seven bogie carriages built at Grand Canal Street between 1912 and 1915 were all different types although they were all constructed on 58ft 0in underframes. The first to be built, in 1912, were two side corridor carriages for the Mail train, composite No 25 and third No 72, arguably the finest vehicles to run on the D&SER. Unfortunately the third was destroyed in the malicious burning of the Mail at Scarawalsh in 1923. In 1913 two compartment carriages, a composite and a third, were built specially for the Kingstown Boat Train. These were the only two vehicles in the carriage stock fitted with steam heating. The last three bogie carriages to be constructed, a second brake, composite and third brake, formed a third suburban set for the Harcourt Street line.

Because of the length of the 57ft and 58ft carriages it was necessary to use 10ft 0in wheelbase bogies instead of the 8ft 0in bogies used previously on the shorter carriages. This was necessary to ensure that the inner wheelbase of the vehicles did not exceed the length required to ensure that point locking bars were kept depressed whilst these carriages traversed them. These steel framed 10ft 0in bogies were supplied by MCW.

In January 1922, it was decided to introduce a 'Bus' service in an attempt to compete more effectively with the electric trams. To provide for this a fleet of twelve 'Bus Coaches' was proposed, but in February it was decided to reduce expenditure by altering six existing vehicles. Three 57ft and three 58ft suburban carriages were converted, the work involving the removal of compartments and the provision of tram type seats with throw-over backs in open saloons. Two large double door entrances were provided, one on each side of these composite vehicles which in their new guise could each seat 28 first and 50 third class passengers. The cost of re-fitting the six carriages amounted to £12,500. Although all nominally the same, there were detail differences in window spacing as well as length due to their origins which actually resulted in three variants of this type of vehicle.

In July 1922 quotations were sought from leading British carriage building firms for the construction of six bogie suburban carriages of open saloon layout with a minimum accommodation of 76 seats. The lowest tender received was £2,500 each, but nothing ever came of the scheme.

The General Manager was authorised to obtain quotations from outside contractors for two new main line trains in January 1923. Quotations were to be sought for two trains of the side corridor type and two trains of the latest saloon type. However, the subject was continually deferred at board meetings and it was not until January 1924 that the board approved the design of corridor carriages submitted by Wild. He was requested to obtain quotations and, in addition, he was to seek full particulars from the LMSR of any of their redundant stock that might be suitable. The tenders for the new carriages were examined in February, but as the carriages could not be delivered in less than six months, which would be too late for the summer traffic, it was decided to defer the subject until the autumn. By that time the amalgamation issue had come to the forefront and the new carriages were never ordered.

Catering Vehicles

In 1904, for the introduction of through services to Waterford, a restaurant car service was provided on the down and up Mail trains from Westland Row, the Waterford portion of the train being detached at Macmine Junction and worked thence to New Ross and Waterford. Initially, bogie van No 11, equipped with a kitchen at one end, was used coupled to first No 12 and second No 41, both open centre corridor bogie vehicles. In the following year provision was made for third class passengers by the addition of bogie open side corridor third No 74. Thus, the Waterford Mail became the first Irish main line train to provide and maintain, until the abolition of second class travel on the D&SER in January 1922, a catering service for all three classes of passenger.

In 1905 a second catering set was provided by composite kitchen car No 14 and another open side corridor third No 57. The composite was equipped with two end saloons, one for 12 first class passengers and the other for 16 second class passengers, and a centre kitchen. This shorter set probably provided adequate accommodation for winter services on the Mail in addition to acting as a standby in summer. The third class carriage was another of the victims of the malicious burning of the Mail train at Scarawalsh in 1923.

In the summer of 1908 a service was introduced to connect with the GWR sailings between Rosslare and Fishguard, with through working over the GS&WR from Wexford to Rosslare Harbour. Catering was provided on both the down and up trains, which departed at 08.20 from Harcourt Street and 17.20 from Rosslare respectively. This increase in catering services resulted in bogie composite No 17 and another bogie open side corridor third, No 38, being built. However, it is likely that only two vehicles ran through to Rosslare, in which case the catering on this service was probably provided by composite kitchen car No 14 coupled to one of the thirds.

Also in 1908, a spare kitchen van was provided by the conversion of six-wheeled 24ft 6in first No 26 which became 201 in the miscellaneous carriage stock list. This vehicle usually operated on the summer Sunday Tourist trains to the Vale of Avoca which ran from Harcourt Street at 13.15, returning from Woodenbridge at 17.30. This service was probably the earliest regular scheduled Sunday restaurant car train in Ireland.

In 1912 a new bogie kitchen van, No 16, was constructed. It is not clear whether the kitchen equipment used in this van came from composite No 14 or kitchen van 201. However, it is known that the kitchen had been removed from the composite before the end of 1913 and that kitchen van 201 had become brake van No 20 in 1912. It is probable that, following the withdrawal of catering services during the coal strike of 1912, a decision was made that only two sets of catering vehicles were needed; one for the Mail and the other as standby or for use on specials. In any event the through service to Rosslare had disappeared not to return until after the formation of the GSR when operation of South Eastern section trains was logically extended to connect with the steamers at Rosslare Harbour.

The two composites and three thirds were listed as restaurant cars in the stock returns from 1913 onwards, but on the formation of the GSR they were all re-classified as ordinary passenger stock and, at the same time, the kitchen equipment was removed from the bogie vans. However, this was not to be the last use of D&SER vehicles in catering services as the GSR converted first saloon No 18 into tea car 74D in 1927 and bogie First 29D was rebuilt as a kitchen car in 1938.

Other Carriage Stock

As with other railways the company possessed a variety of non passenger carriage stock. These consisted of passenger brake vans, horseboxes, a mortuary van, carriage trucks and fish vans. Although the carriage trucks and fish vans were always listed with passenger vehicles in the stock returns, they

Top: **No.46, a high roofed 34ft 4in third built at Grand Canal Street in 1906, which survived until 1956, is pictured in GSR livery at Inchicore circa 1946.**
J M Robbins - IRRS collection

Centre: **54ft 0in bogie vehicle, running as CIE third 202D in July 1946. This was formerly composite No.9, built at Grand Canal Street in 1906.**
J M Robbins - IRRS collection

Right: **One of the former Railmotor carriage portions, running as third 212D in 1946. Following separation from its engine in 1908 it became composite No.20.**
J M Robbins - IRRS collection

carried wagon fleet numbers, and because of this their introduction is more appropriately dealt with in that section

We have already noted that the first four passenger brake vans were supplied by Brown Marshall in 1854-56 these being rebuilt at the Factory in 1869-70. The two brake vans created by converting Atmospheric thirds in 1859 were soon replaced by two new vehicles in 1861 and 1863. The next additions were the six brake vans built by T & C Martin in 1863-64 which became Nos 7 to 12, and they were followed in the stock list by the eleven vans of D&KR origin which were renumbered in 1866.

Two passenger brake vans, Nos 23 and 24, which were built at the Works in 1874 lasted until replaced by two new vans with gangways in 1903. MCW supplied two 21ft 6in passenger brake vans in 1878 and two superior brake vans were constructed at the Works in 1886, another being added in 1891. The first milk van, No 2, was built in 1892 and in the following year two Travelling Post Office vans, Nos 32 and 33, were completed at Grand Canal Street. The twelve non-bogie and two bogie vans built between 1896 and 1911 have already been referred to in preceding sections.

Between 1898 and 1913, 20 of the original vans were replaced by vehicles converted from former passenger carriages. These conversions were made from the following vehicles: the two Finn Valley composites, a Dawson composite which had been rebuilt in 1882, the four Brown Marshall 22ft 0in firsts of 1855 and eight of the 24ft 6in / 25ft 2in firsts originally built between 1860 and 1872, four 22ft 0in third brakes which commenced life as Brown-Marshall seconds and thirds in 1855 and the former kitchen van No 201 which when converted to a passenger van retained its gangways. Further details are given in Appendix E.

The first horsebox for the line was ordered from Brown-Marshall on the 10th

October 1856, and two more from the same builder followed in 1857. The only vehicles built for the company by Thomas Frith of Belfast were the three horseboxes supplied in 1863. There were nine Ashbury built vehicles, three being supplied in 1872 and six in 1879 and, apart from rebuilds, no further additions to stock were made until 1894 when one horsebox was obtained in the selection of vehicles purchased from the Finn Valley Railway. This vehicle, numbered 16 by the DW&WR, had originally been built in 1872 by Brown-Marshall.

Four additions to the horsebox fleet were made between 1895 and 1904; all vehicles being built at Grand Canal Street. All of these horseboxes were 4-wheeled and certainly those built from 1872 onwards were constructed to a standard length of 15ft 3in over headstocks.

In December 1906 racehorse owner 'Boss' Croker approached the company with a view to purchasing a private horsebox. The company agreed to this with arrangements being made for the D&SER to undertake the maintenance of the vehicle. This horsebox was a unique vehicle, being built on the 30ft 6-wheeled underframe of an old third class carriage, and was painted in Croker's racing colours of dark blue. When not in use it was stored on the sidings at Foxrock. In June 1910, a special shed was erected at that station to provide shelter for this vehicle. In May 1914 Croker decided to dispose of his horsebox and a month later, he accepted the company's offer of £40, following which it became No 21 in the horsebox fleet.

In November 1907 Mr Coghlan's proposal that a mortuary van should be provided was agreed to. This vehicle, which was piped, was constructed at the Works during 1908 on the 21ft 6in underframe of four-wheeled brake van No 25 of 1878, and was numbered 200 in the miscellaneous stock list. It survived into CIE days, having been converted into a fish van by the GSR in 1935.

Liveries & Lighting

Although the early liveries of the D&KR carriages are known to have been purple lake for the firsts, yellow for the seconds, green for the open seconds and Prussian blue for the thirds, the earliest liveries of the DW&WR carriages are unknown. However, in May 1875, at the suggestion of Sir Ralph Cusack, it was decided to try as an experiment graining instead of painting one or two first class carriages. Prior to this, in August 1872, it had been ordered that 'the class of each compartment be painted on carriages in full sized letters inside as well as outside the carriages.' One of the firsts used by the Duke of Connaught in October 1876, was finished in a blue, buff and gold colour scheme and early photographs certainly show carriages in two-tone colour schemes. For many years up to about 1910 or 1911 the carriage stock was painted chocolate, lined yellow, but thereafter the shade applied until the end of the D&SER was Midland (of England) red with yellow lining.

Lighting of carriages was originally carried out by oil lamps, but in 1878 the application of Pintsch's new gas lighting system was discussed. However, no steps were taken in this direction and in August of the same year 'Imperial Roof Lamps' as in use on the MGWR were adopted. Although consideration was also given in 1878 to a proposal by the Alliance Gas Company of Dublin and to Seagrave's method of lighting carriages with petroleum, the company persisted with the Imperial, further lamps of this type being purchased in the following year. This would

Below: **Bogie 54ft 0in composite kitchen car No.14 at Abbey Junction in 1905-06. This vehicle had two first class compartments at the left hand end and two second class at the right with a kitchen in the centre, between them.**
H Fayle - IRRS collection

Right: **54ft 0in bogie third brake No 41 of 1909, in early CIE livery of dark green and eau-de-nil, at Inchicore on 17th April 1947.** R N Clements - IRRS collection

Lower right: **Bogie third No 28, was one of the two 58ft 0in vehicles specially built for the Pier train in 1913. They were the only carriages on the system fitted with steam heating apparatus. It was photographed in early CIE livery at Grand Canal Street, 9th March 1948.** R N Clements - IRRS collection

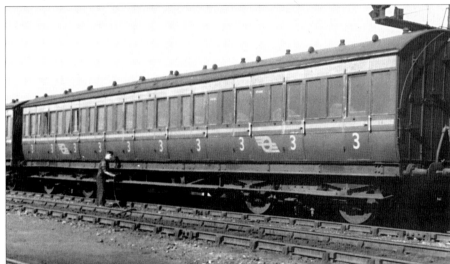

appear to have been the standard until October 1884, when Pintsch's Gas Company offered to fit up a carriage free of expense lit by their patent compressed oil gas. It was subsequently agreed to adopt this system, a gas works being erected at Bray, and the carriages fitted out as they passed through the works, all being completed by 1890.

Under the GSR and CIE

The civil war had its effects on the passenger stock with a total of 17 carriages being destroyed in seven separate incidents between the 18th January and 7th April 1923 as detailed in Chapter Eight and Appendix J. In addition 12 other carriages were seriously damaged and 33 more slightly damaged. The most serious incident was the burning of the mail train at Scarawalsh on the 18th January 1923 when three bogie carriages – side corridor first No 31, side corridor third No 72 and open side corridor third No 57 – were destroyed along with 6-wheeled third No 19.

Although the D&SER had 268 vehicles on its carriage stock register as of the 31st December 1924 this included the aforementioned 17 vehicles that had been maliciously damaged during the civil war and 42 others listed as 'out-of-service'. The GSR did not take any of these 59 vehicles into stock so the former D&SER fleet was reduced to 209 at the stroke of a pen. However, 22 of the out-of-service vehicles, together with four vehicles from the capital list, were painted in shop grey for use on excursion trains between Amiens Street and Dun Laoghaire in the summer of 1925, generally known as the Cockle Trains. These vehicles were formed into two sets officially designated 'Cockle Train No 7' and 'Cockle Train No 8' and ran again in the summer of 1926 before being withdrawn at the end of the season.

Severe withdrawals of D&SER carriage stock took place during the GSR years resulting in only 81 vehicles passing into CIE ownership on the 1st January 1945. By the end of January 1961 the only passenger vehicles left in revenue earning service were tea car 74D and kitchen car 29D. The former was withdrawn in 1962 and the latter was destined to become the last D&SER passenger vehicle in revenue service, not being withdrawn by CIE until 18th March 1964.

Goods Stock

The surviving register of D&SER wagons was drawn up by the GSR in 1929, by which time many vehicles had been scrapped and it has therefore been necessary to refer to contemporary documents to construct the early history of the wagon fleet. The reader is referred to Appendix E for a schedule showing the development of the wagon stock. However, early revenue rebuilds and subsequent replacements have proved complex to trace. The following is a brief description of the various wagon types owned by the company.

Open Box Wagons

The first non-passenger vehicles to be ordered by the company were two coke wagons which Pemberton was authorised to procure in June 1855. These vehicles, supplied by Brown-Marshall, were for the Locomotive Department. They were always listed separately in the stock returns until their demise in 1885 when they were replaced by new open wagons.

The first 12 open wagons were ordered during March 1860 from Dawson & Russell,

and the next ten vehicles of this type formed part of the company's second order with the MCW in April 1863 and were delivered during the latter half of the same year. At shareholders meetings in the years from 1855 on, references are made to the company turning away goods traffic due to a lack of facilities to handle it. As so few wagons were purchased from 1855 to 1859, it must be assumed that goods traffic did not have a very high priority for the company.

Two open wagons which were added to stock in 1864 are a mystery as no record exists of their order or for three covered wagons that appeared at the same time. They may have been part of the contract variation with T & C Martin in 1864 for additional mineral wagons but, on the other hand, they could have been second-hand vehicles. They were numbered 295 to 299.

Following the breaking of a drawbar at Foxrock on 12th April 1872, part of a goods train was derailed and it was ordered that side coupling chains were to be at once put on all wagons in use on the line.

Forty open wagons were ordered in 1872, 20 each being delivered from MCW in 1872

and the Midland Carriage & Wagon Company, Shrewsbury, in 1873. No more were added to stock until 1885 when Wakefield was authorised to build three new 8-ton open wagons at Grand Canal Street. However, a total of five open wagons were built at this time, the other two being replacements for the two old coke wagons of 1855 which were due for renewal.

Two open wagons were included in the stock purchased from the Finn Valley Railway in 1894, both having been originally built in 1872 by Brown-Marshall. Also in that year an order was placed with the BCW for 25 open box wagons of 10-ton capacity. These vehicles were delivered in 1895, and in the same year the company built three 8-ton open wagons at Grand Canal Street. A further six of the company's design were built as locomotive coal wagons later in the same year, but they were transferred to general traffic after 1898.

The bodies of the 8-ton open wagons were 15ft 1in long, 7ft 1in wide, 2ft 8in high and ran on 9ft 0in wheelbase underframes, whereas the 10-ton version were 17ft 6in long, 8ft 1in wide with 4ft 0in high bodies, the wheelbase being 6in longer. Tare weights were 5½ tons and 6¼ tons respectively.

The final version of the open wagon was the 12-ton design for the Balleece stone traffic, the first 30 of which were delivered in 1904. Nos 901 to 915 had been approved in August 1903 and were built at the Factory whereas the other 15 were built by Hurst-Nelson of Motherwell on an order placed with them in October of the same year. These 7-plank vehicles had bodies which were 15ft 7in long, 7ft 9in wide and 4ft 3in high, fitted to a 9ft 0in wheelbase underframe, their tare weight being 7½ tons.

It should be noted that the 12 open wagons built as renewals at the Factory in 1910 (Nos 54, 295, 413, 415, 416, and 418 to 424) were to the same 12-ton design as the Balleece wagons as were the 18 additional vehicles which were authorised for construction by the company in March 1911 as Nos 1047 to 1064.

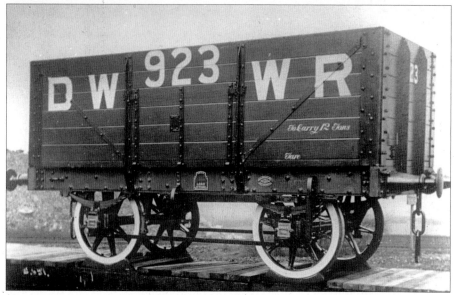

Top: **A scene at the north end of Bray showing a standard D&SER cattle wagon behind the locomotive, in the rear of which is a MGWR horsebox. A D&SER horsebox is visible in the background.** IRRS collection

Centre: **Official photograph of one of the 15 12-ton Balleece wagons by Hurst Nelson of Motherwell in 1904.** IRRS collection

Left: **No 841D was a 7-ton mineral wagon, one of 12 purchased from Parnell Quarries in 1899. These were first used on DW&W tracks in 1896 as private owner wagons, their precise origin and original builder are unknown.** Desmond Coakham

The final delivery of this type, Nos 1065 to 1089 for use in general traffic, were built by Charles Roberts of Wakefield to which company the order was given in June 1914.

Steel underframes were used for the last six open wagons built at Grand Canal Street in 1922, Nos 56, 58, 226, 286, 306 and 318 being replacements of earlier vehicles.

Covered Goods Wagons

On the 30th November 1855 an application was directed to be made to the MGWR for the loan or sale of two goods wagons. No record of a transaction supporting this has been traced in either the company's or Midland records. The following week tenders were issued for the supply of two goods wagons and on the 14th December 1855 an order was placed with Dawson & Russell of Dublin for two wagons costing £105 each. It is impossible to tell at this distance in time whether Nos 1 and 2 were in fact ex MGWR with Nos 3 & 4 being the Dawson vehicles or whether in fact all four vehicles came from Dawson, but the only payment recorded to Dawson at that time for wagons was on 14th March 1856 in the amount of £214.

In April 1856 a further eight covered wagons were ordered from Brown Marshall, followed by 12 more which came from the Ashbury Carriage and Wagon Company in 1857. Dawson & Russell were selected as the builders for 24 covered wagons which were ordered in June 1858. These three batches were followed by a further 24 which were built by Brown Marshall against an order dated 8th March 1861.

The company had already placed one order with Joseph Wright in 1862 for side tipping mineral wagons and it was to his Metropolitan Carriage & Wagon Company of Saltley Works, Birmingham, that a large order was given on the 9th April 1863 which included 40 covered wagons.

Thomas and Charles Martin, who had worked for Dawson & Russell until the demise of that company in 1862, set up their own carriage and wagon building business at North Wall, Dublin. On the 3rd July 1863 the DW&WR placed its first order with this new builder, which was for the supply of 50 covered goods wagons at the same price as the previous order with the MCW. Ten of these wagons were supplied in 1863 and the remainder during 1864.

As will be recounted below in the section on mineral wagons, there appears to have been an extension of the contract entered into on the 1st January 1864 with T & C Martin such that additional vehicles were supplied without specific board approval. It has already been noted above that two open and three covered wagons were added to stock in 1864.

In July 1870 the company placed an order with the MCW for the supply of 20 covered wagons. From the cost allocation in the GSR register it appears that 14 of these were replacements for the lead ore wagons, Nos 228 to 241, and that the other six were an increase in stock numbered 385 to 390. A further 20 vehicles were ordered from the same builder in April 1871 and delivered in 1872, and again in 1873 they were the supplier of 20 more covered wagons which were ordered in May of that year.

The company placed its one and only order with Craven Brothers of Sheffield in 1876 and, as was described in the carriage section, this proved to be a disaster in terms of delivery. As in the case of the carriages, the final settlement on this contract resulted in Cravens agreeing to a reduction of 5% in the contract price, the 50 covered wagons concerned being put on the books at £133 each.

A contract for the supply of 40 covered wagons at £130 each was awarded to Ashbury on the 11th April 1878. In fact 41 vehicles, Nos 521 to 561, were delivered before the end of the year, the reason for the supply of one additional wagon probably being compensation for late delivery which was certainly sought in the case of the first class carriages on the same order. Sixteen of these vehicles survived into GSR days without being rebuilt.

The pace of wagon fleet expansion slowed down to virtually nothing for nearly ten years following the 1878 delivery, the company concentrating on rebuilding and renewing existing stock. However, 50 covered wagons were ordered in May 1887 from the MCW and a further 30 were supplied by the same builder in 1891. These 80 vehicles were paid for on extended terms, the first order being met by 12 quarterly installments of £410.12s.6d between January 1888 and October 1890 and the second order by a similar arrangement at £327.3s.9d per quarter between October 1891 and July 1894.

All covered wagons supplied up to this time were 14ft 0in long and ran on 8ft 6in wheelbase underframes. The 4ft 4in centre section at the doors had no roof, covering against the elements being provided by tarpaulins. The standard width of the side door used for both open and covered wagons was also 4ft 4in, those on the covered wagons being 5ft 0in high. These wagons had very curved roofs of 5ft 6in radius and weighed 6 tons.

Vans with higher sides and much flatter curved continuous roofs were first introduced for perishable traffic in 1886 (see below). A batch of 40 vans for general traffic delivered in 1894, was ordered from the Midland Carriage & Wagon Company on the 4th May 1893 at a discount of 1.25% on the tendered price of £115-15s. These were part of a considerable increase in the number of covered wagons which took place in 1894-95, a total of 115 vehicles being added to stock. The vans were followed by 25 vehicles built in 1872 by Brown Marshall for the Finn Valley Railway which were part of the stock purchased from that company by the DW&WR for £1,000. An order for a further 50 standard covered wagons was placed with the BCW in November and were delivered as Nos 719 to 768 in 1895.

In 1896 the BoT required that wagons be provided with brake handles on both sides and the company agreed that all new wagons should be so fitted. In 1902 it was decided to purchase 25 more vans, this time fitted with through vacuum pipes and screw couplings so that they could be operated under the BoT regulations on passenger trains. Ashbury tendered at £118 and the company offered £110, the parties agreeing on the 24th April to a contract price of £116. In November 1898 it was decided to build 12 more piped vans at Grand Canal Street as replacements for worn out covered goods wagons, the new vehicles taking up the running numbers of the old ones they replaced. The construction of vans as replacements continued with 12 being built in 1901, 16 in 1904-06, and six in 1910-12, none of these being piped for vacuum brakes. One further replacement and seven rebuilds in 1919-21, together with Nos 96, 146, 156, 184, 410 and 890 constructed on steel underframes brought the total of general traffic vans to 125.

The last covered wagons to be built as additions to the capital stock were 40 standard open centre vehicles built by the company in 1906. Also in 1906, a total of 35 covered wagons on the duplicate list were re-numbered in the series 976 to 1010. By 1912 the quantity of these vehicles on the stock list had dropped to 18 and in the following year to 16. A further six disappeared in 1919 leaving only Nos 1000 to 1010 extant by 31st December 1924. The earliest instances of covered wagon rebuilds from the 1870s on were generally occasioned by accident or other damage Later renewals of covered wagons built before 1878 were in reality new vehicles the cost of which was charged to the revenue account.

As of the 31st December 1924, 12 vehicles in the covered wagon fleet were allocated for specific traffics. There were the six yeast wagons, Nos 24, 140, 157, 590, 1000 and 1006. Four vehicles, Nos 507, 880, 889 and 892 were classed as meat wagons and there were two gunpowder vans, Nos 402 and 1010, built specifically for the traffic from Kynoch's cordite works at Arklow.

Cattle Wagons

Until 1896 cattle, sheep and pigs had been conveyed in covered wagons which were used for all types of goods traffic. Towards the end of the 19th century both the Board of Trade and Veterinary Department issued regulations which dictated the introduction of wagons designed specifically for the conveyance of livestock.

The company commenced the construction of such purpose-built vehicles in 1896, many of them being replacements for old stock. The first 20 built between 1896 and 1899 were replacements for five covered wagons, one open wagon, two mineral wagons and twelve side tipping wagons. None of these were fitted with falling doors, and all but two, Nos 202 and 206, were of standard size. The latter were identified as large cattle wagons and both were converted to covered wagons in 1903.

Cattle wagons built from 1900 on were fitted with falling doors, and all cattle wagons in the fleet were equipped with screw couplings and vacuum pipes to enable them to run with passenger trains. The 143 cattle wagons introduced between 1900 and 1915 consisted of 58 replacements for covered wagons which were all built at Grand Canal Street and 85 new vehicles. The latter were purchased as genuine increases to the wagon stock the first order being on the 13th March 1902 when the board authorised the construction at the Works of 25 new 8-ton cattle wagons. The next delivery of new vehicles of this type was made in 1906 when Hurst-Nelson supplied 35 in fulfilment of an order placed on the 15th March of that year. On the 9th April 1914 the company authorised the construction of 25 cattle wagons at Grand Canal Street which were in fact to be the last additions ever made to the D&SER wagon stock.

Mineral Wagons
The mineral traffic from the Vale of Ovoca provoked the introduction of a large fleet of purpose built vehicles during the early 1860s. The first 20 vehicles were side tipping wagons built specifically for the traffic from Ovoca to the Mineral Wharf at Kingstown, to a design very similar to some used on the Furness Railway. They were supplied in 1862 by the MCW and it appears that at first they were numbered in a series of their own as it was not until 1864 that they were allocated the numbers series 196 to 215. These vehicles had a very short 5ft 0in wheelbase, and dumb buffers at one end. MCW also supplied twelve 3-plank mineral wagons as part of the order for wagons placed with them in April 1863.

On the 1st January 1864 an order was placed with T & C Martin for the supply of 30 mineral wagons at £84.10s each, and on the 10th March the company accepted the builder's quotation to fit four of these vehicles with double brakes, including a seat for the brakesman, at an additional cost £19.0s each. The 26 mineral wagons were delivered during the first half of 1864 and the mineral brakes followed later in the year. A further 48 mineral wagons, in two batches of 23 and 25 respectively, were supplied by the same builder in 1864 in what appears to have been an extension of this contract. They may

also have supplied the 11 side tipping wagons, 325 to 335, ten of which were delivered in late 1864 and the other in early 1865. In June 1866 another order was placed with T&C Martin for 20 more mineral wagons, and in April of the following year for a further 30, all 50 being delivered during 1867.

On the 24th September 1868 Wakefield reported as follows: '53 Mineral Wagons, delivered by Messrs T & C Martin in 1863, are built too light for their work and not sufficient iron work to keep the frames together. Some of the side soles are split, but the timber is hard and strong and free from decay. These wagons were too low on the rails; when new and in the working they have bent down at the ends more or less varying 3 to 5 inches below the proper height of the buffers. Also through these weaknesses the middle of the wagon has gone down so much I am putting an iron rod across from side to side to keep up the centre. These wagons were a great deal used in carrying long rails, the weight resting on the ends of the wagons, one end of the rails projecting 9 feet beyond the end, which tended very much to bend the ends down with the overhanging weight. I have raised some of the wagons up by putting a piece of wood between the frame and spring so as the buffers will stand proper height from the rail. I recommend the remaining be done with as little delay as possible. 25 Mineral Wagons were delivered in 1864; they are built with strong timber frames but not sufficient iron work to keep them together. They also stand too low on the rails. I recommend them to be raised up and additional iron knees put on to put them in good order. 50 Mineral Wagons were delivered in 1867; they are built with strong timber frames and ironwork to hold them together which are in good working order. I beg to remark there is no safety side coupling chains on the goods or mineral wagons, therefore when a drawbar cotter pin breaks there is no protection for the latter part of the train but the guard's brake. Therefore, I recommend that side chains should be put onto the wagons.'

Due to the decline in ore traffic the fleet of 170 mineral wagons soon exceeded the demand of the business, and as early as June 1870 Wakefield was ordered to raise the sides of such mineral wagons as were not required for ore traffic and make them suitable for general traffic. Nothing much seems to have happened until February 1876 when Wakefield was requested to raise the sides of 20 mineral wagons to enable them to carry 8 tons of coal, lime and other general traffic. This caused some confusion in regard to the stock returns as they were incorrectly shown as additions to the covered wagon fleet in that year without a corresponding reduction in the quantity of mineral wagons. This error was not corrected until an audit of rolling stock was undertaken in 1884.

In April 1877 Wakefield was directed 'at once to put in repair 5 mineral wagons to be given to Smith to be used as ballast wagons'. This was the beginning of the decline in the mineral wagon fleet, the other 165 being replaced between 1879 and 1900 by 132 open wagons, 18 timber trucks, 12 cattle wagons, one covered wagon, one carriage truck and one gas tank wagon, all built at Grand Canal Street.

Special Purpose Vehicles
In June 1856 the company obtained its first two carriage trucks from Brown Marshall, and in February 1860 two more were ordered from Dawson. These four vehicles were probably numbered in their own series with the timber trucks until 1864 when they received the Nos 191, 192, 194 and 195 in the wagon stock list; all being subsequently rebuilt or replaced. A further carriage truck was added to stock in 1888 as a replacement for mineral wagon 338, and in 1894 another one, built by Brown Marshall in 1874, was obtained with the stock purchased from the Finn Valley Railway. This latter vehicle, No 718, was rebuilt by the DW&WR in 1902, the same year as No 847 was built new at Grand Canal Street. All seven of the carriage trucks passed into GSR ownership in 1925.

The first two timber trucks were ordered in May 1859. Four more followed from Dawson, two in late 1861 and two in early 1862. As mentioned above, these six vehicles were probably numbered in a series of their own until 1864 when they received the numbers 186 to 190 and 193 in the wagon stock list. The fleet was doubled in 1879 by the conversion of six mineral wagons to timber trucks, but after that no more additions were made until 1891 when No 321 appeared as a replacement for a mineral wagon. Two more mineral wagons were replaced by timber trucks Nos 345 and 346 in 1894 and No 335 was a similar replacement in 1895. Also in 1895 four new timber trucks, Nos 797 to 800, were added to stock. Yet again it was replacements of mineral wagons that took place when six more were added to the fleet in 1899, though the four vehicles that brought the total number of timber trucks up to 30 in 1904, were built new at the Factory.

The company possessed six vans for the conveyance of fish. Nos 43 and 47 had been built in 1886 as renewals of 1858 covered wagons and Nos 647 to 650 were built at Grand Canal Street as new additions to stock in 1892-93, two in each year. All were fitted with through pipes for vacuum brakes and screw couplings so that they could run in passenger trains. All six, together with the mortuary van, were classified as miscellaneous coaching stock vehicles from 1913 onwards.

At a board meeting in March 1895 the subject of running all Wexford shed's coal requirements by train from Dublin, where it was to be loaded direct from the steamers, for which wagons for locomotive coal would be necessary, was deferred. However, by early April the authority was given for the construction of six 8-ton wagons for this traffic. These wagons were released to general traffic following the delivery of 25 vehicles in 1898, specially built for the Locomotive Department. Two further locomotive coal wagons were built at the Works, one each in 1900 and 1907, and three general traffic wagons were assigned to this duty by 1913, bringing the total of this type to 30 vehicles.

Co-incident with the introduction of Pintsch's gas lighting on the carriage fleet in 1885 a need arose for two trucks to carry large gas tanks. As the loaded tanks only weighed 3 tons, Wakefield utilised the iron-work and wheels of two old wagons in the construction of Nos 131 and 242. No 131 carried tank No 2 and No 242 tank No 1. Two new 18ft 6in long gas tank trucks, Nos 832 and 833 were built at Grand Canal Street in 1898, to carry tanks Nos 3 and 4 respectively. The tank from No 131 was fitted to an ex-GS&WR underframe in November 1959, and that from No 242 was also put on a GS&WR frame in 1955.

In 1904 the need for a special vehicle for the conveyance of boilers was recognised. Such a vehicle, No 935, was constructed by conversion of a 30ft 6-wheel carriage underframe with suitable strengthening applied, and cost £106.18s.1d. It survived until 1942 when it was destroyed in a fire at Athlone .

Top: **The three D&SER wagons pictured on this page all survived into the CIE era. No 889D was one of an order for 25 vehicles built by Ashbury in 1902. They were equipped with through vacuum brake pipes and screw couplings in order to comply with BoT regulations for the working of such vehicles in the formation of passenger trains. This explains the apparent unusual marshalling of the wagon in the picture between two passenger coaches.** Desmond Coakham

Centre: **No 412D was originally part of a batch of 40 such vehicles ordered in 1872 from two suppliers, this wagon was one of the 20 built by the Metropolitan Carriage & Wagon Company. It was rebuilt by the D&SER at Grand Canal Street Works in 1907.** Desmond Coakham

Bottom: **No 601D, built by the Metropolitan Carriage & Wagon Company in 1887, was rebuilt by the D&SER in 1920. This type of covered wagon with solid roof sections at each end and a canvas centre section which could be rolled back to assist in loading or unloading, was a design favoured by many Irish railways in the 19th century. Although wagons of this kind survived well into the 1950s, sadly no example of this archetypal Irish wagon has been preserved.** Desmond Coakham

In May 1923 it was agreed to fit one of the company's wagons with a tank for the purpose of conveying tar between Dublin and Balleece Quarry, the expense being borne by the quarry company. Unfortunately, the precise running number and subsequent history of this vehicle is unknown.

Goods Brake Vans

Until 1875 it appears to have been the practice to use passenger brake vans or third brakes on goods trains, but in that year 'two superior third class goods brakes' were constructed at Grand Canal Street. These were the first members of a fleet of 13 vehicles which were more commonly known as Cattle Brakes. These have already been referred to in the section dealing with third class brakes amongst which they were numbered.

The first three purpose-built goods brake vans were built at the Works in 1892 and carried the numbers 29 to 31 in the passenger brake van list. Two more vans of this type, Nos 34 and 35, were built in 1894. All other goods brake vans also carried numbers in this series throughout their days despite the separate classification of this type of vehicle from 1913 onwards.

In 1902 the first two of six 15-ton brake vans, numbered 42 to 47, were turned out from the Works, the second pair entering service in 1905. The last two, constructed in 1912, were subsequently upgraded to 20-ton brakes in CIE days.

Ballast Wagons

In April 1856 the board ordered that tenders be obtained for six 'stone' wagons. The company also inherited three ballast wagons from the D&KR in 1856 and two more vehicles resulted from the conversion of small D&KR third class carriages in 1862-63. In the meantime the D&WR had obtained a further eight ballast wagons in 1860.

In March 1863 Haughton advised that he was 'preparing four trucks, hitherto in use on the Kingstown line, for the purpose of carrying metal water pipes. These will be additional to the Ballast Trucks (14) from the Wicklow line'. By 1864 the 14 ballast wagons were classified as lead ore wagons and given the numbers 228 to 241. They, and the life-expired D&KR vehicles, may have been replaced by 20 ballast wagons offered for sale by the contractor J J Bagnall in June 1864, on completion of his work on the Nenagh branch. The board agreed to purchase them at £42 each delivered on the rails at Harcourt Street provided they were approved of by Meikle who was instructed to go to Nenagh and examine them. As no record of payment has been traced some doubt must surround their purchase.

In January 1877 Wakefield was ordered to put into working order the 15 ballast wagons belonging to the company and Smith was directed to enquire when and on what terms 15 additional spring ballast wagons could be procured. Smith's enquiries must have proved inconclusive as Wakefield was requested in April of the same year to put five of the mineral wagons in repair at once, to be used as ballast wagons.

Mention has already been made in Chapter Ten of the 13 ballast wagons which were pushed into the harbour at Kingstown on 17th June 1881. Whether they were all recovered or not, the stock totals did not change and it could be that any shortfall was made up by further mineral wagons which were being replaced by new wagons. Also, on 7th May 1894, nine ballast wagons filled with new sleepers were accidentally burnt to ashes near Chapel station by a spark from the engine.

Three large ballast wagons were put in hand towards the end of 1899, and two more were started in March 1901. Each of these five vehicles replaced two of the older small ones. The ten surviving small wagons carried on until 1918-19 by which time they had got into such a dreadful state that they had to be withdrawn. This resulted in a difficult state of affairs for the Permanent Way Department which was not resolved until 1922 when 15 hopper wagons and a ballast plough van were obtained from the MGWR for £4,131.16s.6d.

Private Owner Wagons

In November 1890 Cooper & Company of the Drinagh Cement Works, requested to run their private wagons over the DW&WR. The factory, which operated from 1882 to 1918, was served by a siding on the Rosslare line, 2½ miles south of Wexford.

In January 1896 Mr Coghlan submitted correspondence from the Parnell Quarry Company seeking to run their private wagons on the company's lines. The board agreed, 'subject to the rules as to the use of private wagons being strictly adhered to'. This arrangement was only to operate for three years as the Quarry decided to dispose of the 12 wagons in January 1899, the DW&WR purchasing them for £32 each.

Civil War Losses and Liveries

The Civil War had its effects on the goods stock with a total of 24 wagons being destroyed in three separate incidents between the 7th November 1922 and 27th January 1923, as detailed in Chapter Eight and Appendix J. In addition 41 other wagons were seriously damaged and 4 more slightly damaged. Although the precise details of which vehicles were destroyed at North Wall, Waterford and Macmine is not documented, the numbers of 23 of the 24 wagons which were lost are known. These were covered wagons Nos 8, 23, 83, 95, 151, 467, 588, 608, 619, 654, 665, 722, 735, 953 and 1009, open wagons 132, 223 and 287, cattle wagons 509 and 849, and brake vans 16, 30 and 35.

The wagons supplied by MCW in 1863 had lettering and figuring painted in white, but it would appear that the bodywork of the wagon stock may not have been painted at first. It was not until November 1869 that the board ordered 'that the wagon stock be gradually painted as opportunity offers, the work to be done as much as possible at Harcourt Street and Bray'. Three years later instruction was given to have the carrying weight of each wagon painted upon it 'to prevent overloading'. In later days wagons were painted slate grey with the company initials applied in large white letters.

Third class brake van No. 18 was blown up on 7th April 1923 on the siding overlooking Grand Canal Quay. First class carriages Nos 38 and 68 and third class carriage No 1S were also damaged. The wrecked vehicles are belatedly being guarded by a Free State soldier. IRRS collection

Chapter Thirteen

THE LINE DESCRIBED

Harcourt Street station, with its imposing facade and high central arch with colonnade each side, (see the photograph on page 64) gave an impression of great strength and permanence. A terrace of five steps ran the length of the colonnade, from which entrance was gained to the main hall through doors under the central arch. The booking office was to the right hand side of the hall while to the left was the restaurant and bar. The railway lines were above street level being carried on arches which were leased as bonded stores to W & A Gilbey & Sons. Access to the single 597 ft platform on the up side of the line was from a landing at the back of the main hall; third class passengers turning left and ascending by a straight staircase towards the inner end of the station. First and second class passengers turned right at the back of the hall and ascended a winding stairway entering the platform between the General Waiting Room and the Stationmaster's Office. In later years this was the only entrance used for regular passenger traffic.

Inside the end wall of the station, through which the cattle special from Enniscorthy had crashed on St Valentine's Day 1900, was the 45ft 9in turntable, located immediately beyond the north end of the platform, with hydraulic buffer stops behind it. As well as the platform road, the turntable gave access to two parallel release roads and a short spur which ran to a carriage dock in the goods yard. The Left Luggage Office was also at this end of the platform, between the third class entrance and the turntable. Opposite the Left Luggage Office, between the second release road and the outer station wall, was a building constructed in 1939 to house the mercury arc rectifiers and transformers for controlling the charging current for the Drumm Battery trains.

The platform and three adjacent tracks were spanned by an overall roof for 300 ft southwards from the turntable. Beyond the roof, the platform continued towards Harcourt Road and just before crossing the bridge there stood the 12,750 gallon water tank which was a familiar sight to pedestrians passing in the street below. Harcourt Road station, of which all traces disappeared many years earlier, was situated immediately across the bridge approximately on the

site of the release roads. Near the end of the passenger platform, on the south side of Harcourt Road bridge, was a building which housed an office, workshop and stores for the Carriage & Wagon Examiners. During the period of Drumm train operations a plant was installed in these premises to produce the distilled water required for topping up the batteries of these trains.

Harcourt Street was also the main goods station in Dublin for the D&SER. There were two goods platforms; the one nearest the station having the main goods shed on it at the northern end, opposite the main station building. This goods shed was gutted by fire on the evening of 30th June 1947, but following the construction of a new roof in 1953 it became a tyre depot for the Irish Dunlop Company, who occupy it to this day. The other goods platform, known as the cattle bank, was primarily for livestock traffic, the sidings beyond it being used for stone traffic, initially from Bray Head and later from Balleece Quarry, much of the stone being used for road-making by Dublin Corporation. The goods yard was originally entered by a ramp from Hatch Street, but in 1904, following complaints from the Dublin carriers who were finding it difficult to haul ever increasing loads up the old ramp, a new entrance on a gentler grade was provided from Adelaide Road. At the same time an additional goods store was built in the north eastern corner of the yard. With the amalgamation in 1925, goods services in Dublin were concentrated at the MGWR's North Wall depot and Harcourt Street became basically a passenger station. However, the goods facilities were temporarily re-opened at the end of January 1933 for the duration of the 9½ week GNR(I) strike.

Just opposite the Bray end of the passenger platform, on the southern end of the goods platform, was the electro-mechanical signal cabin built by the GSR in 1938 in conjunction with the installation of colour light signalling at the station. It replaced the original 1878 signal cabin which had been located beyond the end of the cattle bank on the south side of Albert Place bridge. Passenger trains departing from Harcourt Street, crossed Albert Place Bridge before traversing a facing crossover to join the track from the west side of the goods platform which

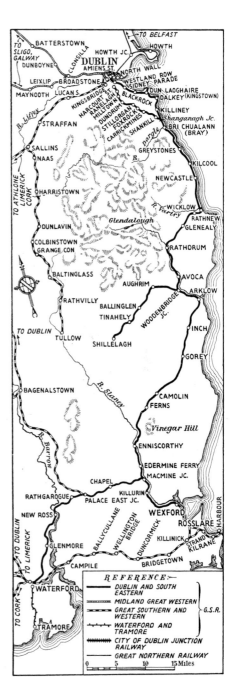

Map showing the Dublin & South Eastern and other lines of the Great Southern Railways system. Reproduced courtesy of *The Railway Magazine*: Special Irish Railway Number, Volume LXXXII, No 491, May 1938.

Railway Station, Dundrum.

Top left: **Harcourt Street from the signal cabin footsteps showing the passenger platform, girders of the bridge across Harcourt Road, the water tank and the goods platform. On the right are the walls of the goods shed which was gutted by fire on the night of 30th June 1947.** K A Murray

Centre left: **Dundrum station looking north with the signal cabin and waiting sheds on the up platform. The main station building on the down platform was more ornate than the other intermediate stations between Harcourt Street and Bray as it was originally intended to be the terminus of the D&WR.** From a postcard in the John Kennedy collection

Bottom left: **The Bride's Glen viaduct between Carrickmines and Shankill.** H Fayle - IRRS collection

then formed the down main line. The two road engine shed was adjacent to this crossover on the down side.

The sidings from the goods yard and engine shed trailed in just before the line crossed over the Grand Canal and two parallel public roads, by a three-span plate girder bridge and proceeded on a stone-faced embankment, crossing four more streets by plate girder bridges within the next half mile. After crossing Ranelagh Road the line began climbing at 1 in 169 to Rathmines & Ranelagh station. Opened on the 15th July 1896, and always known simply as Ranelagh, this station originally had all timber platforms, but the majority of the up platform was renewed in concrete in 1943. Typical DW&WR curved roof buildings of timber and corrugated iron construction were situated on each platform, the signal cabin being an integral part of the Dublin end of the down building. Access to the station was gained from Dunville Avenue, the Booking Office and Stationmaster's Office being to the right of the entrance at street level on the up side. A white tiled subway provided access to the down side and wooden stairs led up to both platforms which were above street level.

After a further ¾ mile climbing at 1 in 169 the line reached Milltown, a quiet station in an equally quiet suburb of the city. Opened on 1st May 1860 it became a halt under Dundrum as from 1st October 1938. There were up and down platforms, with the station house at the Dublin end of the up platform and a small waiting shelter opposite on the down one. To the north of the platforms a level crossing gave access to private residences and just before this crossing, on the down side, there was a substantial signal cabin which survived until 1936 although Milltown ceased to be a block post in 1906. Immediately after leaving this station, the line crossed over the River Dodder by a magnificent nine-arch stone viaduct and began climbing, first at 1 in 100, then at 1 in 80, on the 1¼ mile run to Dundrum.

Originally intended as the end-on junction point between the D&WR and the D&BR, Dundrum possessed an imposing station building on the down platform. The busiest intermediate station on the line to Bray, it was also a block post with the signal cabin on the Bray end of the up platform. For many years a large enamelled sign on the front of the signal cabin proclaimed that this was the station for St Columba's College, situated about two miles away. A small open-fronted waiting shed, to the Dublin side of the signal cabin, was the subject of complaints to the company in 1870 due to its inadequacy. A much larger enclosed shed was subsequently constructed to the Dublin side of it, which in later years housed a small shop at one end, the small shelter later being reserved for use by staff and pupils from St Columba's. The goods siding and loading bank were at the Bray end on the up side, and a headshunt from this siding, which ran behind the signal cabin, was used for milk traffic from Shillelagh which was processed at the nearby O'Connor's Farm Dairy.

Leaving Dundrum, the climb resumed at 1 in 96, steepening to 1 in 75 as the line entered the deep Dundrum cutting, scene of an accident on 23rd December 1957 when two diesel railcar sets collided, fatally injuring the driver of one of them. The summit was reached 1½ miles beyond Dundrum after which the line ran gently downhill for ¾ mile into Stillorgan station. The station building was on the down platform and access to the up one was via a footbridge located at the Bray end. The signal cabin on the down platform was not dispensed with until January 1942, Stillorgan having previously become a halt under Foxrock in November 1931. A ¼ mile further on the line passed Leopardstown crossing, the first of two public road level crossings on the journey to Bray. It was a busy crossing and suggestions were made on more than one occasion that it should be replaced by a bridge. On the occasion of the visit of King Edward VII to the Leopardstown Races in 1907, the crossing was decorated with a triumphal arch by local residents.

A sweeping right hand curve of half a mile brought the line to Foxrock station. A temporary station was opened in 1859, the permanent one followed on 1st June 1861. This station had an extensive layout which was developed in connection with horse racing at the adjoining Leopardstown Race Course which opened on 27th August 1888. It also served as the terminus for short distance suburban train workings from Harcourt Street.

Approaching the station the main line was paralleled on the down side by a 334 yard long siding with a narrow wooden wagon washing platform, this being the location to which all cattle wagons were brought for a lime wash following unloading at Harcourt Street. This siding joined the main line by a trailing crossover just before the down platform, an extension of the siding running behind the down platform to serve the goods store located in the Bray end of a stone building halfway along the platform.

The same building also housed the waiting rooms and between it and the main station house, which was at the Bray end of the down platform, was the site of the original signal cabin. This cabin, which was destroyed during the Civil War, together with an interlocking ground frame just beyond the Dublin end of the up platform, controlled the layout until replaced in 1924 by a new enlarged cabin at the Dublin end of the down platform.

Facing crossovers at the Dublin end provided access to the race platform and, following the derailment of a race special in 1912, a permanent speed limit of 10 mph was imposed on all down trains using these crossovers. A siding at the Dublin end on the up side, known as the 'Race Siding', was used in later years together with the wagon wash siding for the storage of redundant carriages, including some of the Drumm Battery train sets.

Below: **Approaching Shanganagh Junction from Bray with the home signal 'off' for the main line to Harcourt Street. This junction was constructed as part of the 1915 Killiney diversion, the signalling and cabin being provided by McKenzie & Holland.**
Desmond Coakham

The up platform was an island with a timber and corrugated iron waiting shed near the Bray end. The track at the back of the island platform also served the race platform, all three platforms being connected by a double span standard D&SER footbridge. In 1893 the two sidings on the up side at the Bray end were modified, the one nearest the main line being extended and the outer one connected to it to form a loop. A timber platform was constructed on the racecourse side of this loop. Known as the 'Members Platform' it was used exclusively by the special trains which conveyed the members of the Leopardstown Club and their guests to the race meetings, but it appears to have fallen out of use about 1914.

The level stretch through Foxrock station continued to just beyond the end of the members sidings before the line curved to the left and began its descent towards Carrickmines, approaching the station on a falling grade of 1 in 100. Carrickmines possessed the usual up and down platforms with the station house at the Dublin end of the up one. It was the only station between Harcourt Street and Bray to have watering facilities for locomotives, these being supplied from a 6,800 gallon tank on the up platform and via a water column at the Bray

end of the down platform. In December 1951, this station became a halt under Foxrock.

The line continued its descent down the 1 in 90 Carrickmines bank, passing Tulla crossing, and still on a falling gradient, crossed the Bride's Glen on a five-arch granite viaduct before reaching Shankill, the last station on the now closed section. The station buildings at Shankill were on the down side with a short siding at the Dublin end entered by a facing connection. At one time this was used in connection with lead-ore traffic for the nearby Ballycorus lead works. In D&SER days this siding trailed off the up line. There were crossovers at each end of the station to enable engines to run round trains terminating here, a signal cabin being provided at the Bray end of the up platform.

The later Shanganagh Junction came into being in October 1915 with the opening of the Killiney diversion line. It was located 10 miles 42 chains from Harcourt Street and 11 miles 77 chains from Westland Row. The 'branch' from Amiens Street and Westland Row trailed in on the down side, and the signal cabin was on the down side just on the Bray side of the junction. Prior to the 1915 diversion, the track layout between Shanganagh and Bray consisted of the up

and down main lines from Harcourt Street and a single track from Killiney running parallel on the down side, with no physical connection between the lines at Shanganagh. This arrangement had come into use in May 1877 replacing the junction and platform that had existed at Shanganagh since August 1861.

The original Woodbrook Halt was opened in February 1910 to serve a cricket ground adjacent to the line on the estate of Sir Stanley Cochrane of the well known Dublin soft drinks firm of Cantrell & Cochrane. Initially, it was planned to have a second platform on the up main line, but in the event only one platform was provided to serve up and down trains on the Westland Row line. Harcourt Street line passengers would have had to travel to Bray and double back to Woodbrook by car or on a Westland Row line train.

Below: **Bray station, photographed from the adjoining hotel, showing a connecting Bray to Enniskerry omnibus preparing to depart. Behind the station building is the old carriage shed and the south signal cabin. The line to Greystones swings to the left to sweep around Bray Head, which can be seen in the background.**
IRRS - K A Murray collection.

When the diversion railway was constructed in 1915, up and down platforms were provided on the new line. Cricket did not resume after the First World War, but on 11th November 1920 the Woodbrook Golf Club was instituted and, until the closure of the halt in September 1960, the railway provided a handy means of reaching the golf course.

Approaching Bray, the line crosses the Bray River beside the harbour where a dock was provided by the company at the request of the Admiralty. Here, on the down side before the level crossing, was the Tower siding. Equipped with inspection pits, it was used during the 1930s and 40s for maintenance of the Drumm Battery trains which could also be charged while standing there. Opposite, on the up side of the line, was the cattle dock and siding, an additional siding being created between it and the up line in 1915 by the abandonment of the third line from Shanganagh.

The D&SER station was very different from that existing today with but one long platform and fine station buildings on the up side. This platform was capable of being used by two trains simultaneously by the provision in 1895 of a scissors crossing midway along its length. The down platform with its extensive glass roofed canopy, referred to by railwaymen as the 'Crystal Palace', was added in 1927 as was a new signal cabin at the Dublin end of this platform beside the level crossing. Originally there were two signal cabins, North and South, the former just to the Dublin side of the level crossing on the up side and the south cabin at the Wexford end of the station on the down side.

Many changes occurred to the arrangements at Bray over the years. Originally, the goods store was situated on the up side at the Wexford end on a site occupied in later years by the southwards extension of the up platform. The old locomotive shed south of Albert Avenue became the new goods store in 1877. The railmotor service to Greystones operated from a bay to the back of the up platform extension, and behind this bay was the turntable and water tank. This area was cleared in May 1980 to provide additional car parking. Beyond this there were sidings on the up side, at the south end of which a shed was provided in 1906 for stabling the railmotors. Opposite this, on the down side, was the two road engine shed built in 1878 which remained in operation until the withdrawal of steam from Bray in 1957. It is now used for stabling DART units while they are being valeted.

From Bray to Wexford the line is single, and on leaving Bray it immediately begins climbing at 1 in 90 over the surrounding roads passing the three Bray Head sidings which are at a lower level on the up side. The two nearest of these sidings marked the end of the original 1854 line from Harcourt Road. Swinging to the left, the line passes

the site of Bray Head Halt opened in March 1906 in connection with the adjoining swimming baths at Naylor's Cove. This halt, with its short sleeper and rubble platform on the down side, was served for just over a year by the railmotor service between Bray and Greystones until it closed in September 1907. It was to have been re-opened in August 1929 in connection with a summer camp on Bray Head but, although some work was carried out to put the platform into repair, this did not in fact happen.

Passing around Bray Head, the line climbs high above sea level and a little beyond milepost 13½ diverges from the original route of 1855. The old alignment and the abandoned Brabazon tunnel can be seen on the seaward side, part of the original line at the Dublin end having been retained after the 1876 diversion as a siding for Worthington to load stone from a rock crushing plant installed here. The line then passes into the 307 yard Bray Head No 1 tunnel, constructed as part of the 1876 diversion, and emerging from this picks up the original alignment at milepost 14, passing the site of the Stone siding on the up side before entering the first of the two original tunnels still used on this section. Brandy Hole (Bray Head No 2) tunnel is 143 yards long and the section of line between it and the 210 yard No 3 tunnel (the original Cable Rock tunnel) is that of the 1879 diversion. In the early D&WR days, the line at Bray Head crossed ravines by means of wooden bridges designed by Brunel, one of which was the scene of the August 1867 derailment.

The major diversion work completed in 1917, including the 1,084 yard long No 4 tunnel with its airshaft, commences almost immediately after leaving No 3 tunnel. The original alignment through the townland of Rathdown was to the seaward side of the No 4 tunnel along Morris's Bank, a notorious spot for coastal erosion. Considerable slewing of the line inland was undertaken in 1880, but continued erosion required a diversion of nearly a mile in length at the same spot in 1888-89, and yet again in 1911-12 slewing was required. Before leaving No 4 tunnel, the line commences a 1 in 82 fall towards Greystones, easing to 1 in 112 past Ennis Lane accommodation crossing and ¼ mile further on, the site of Jubilee Siding on the down side. This siding was constructed in 1918 in conjunction with the erection of a sleeper creosoting plant, but the plant was removed in 1921 after the availability of ready creosoted sleepers improved. The siding, however, was retained and in early CIE days it was used for the storage of 6-wheeled carriages awaiting scrapping.

Greystones, variously known as Delgany, Delgany & Greystones, and Greystones & Delgany, was opened in 1855 and initially had a single platform on the up side with a passing loop. The main station building is

on the up side as was the goods shed, the latter at the Dublin end. The down platform was added about 1867-68 upon which the signal cabin was later located near the Dublin end. Behind the down platform were sidings and a turntable, the first turntable of 24ft diameter being provided in June 1891 and located adjacent to where the present footbridge now stands. In 1914 this was replaced by a 32ft turntable on a new siding to the seaward side. In December 1939 a new 42ft table was installed and finally in 1953 this turntable was in turn replaced by a 45ft one nearer the inner end of the new siding. The present location of the footbridge dates from August 1900, when it was moved from the Dublin end. It should also be mentioned that the footbridge just beyond the platforms at the Dublin end of the station replaced a level crossing at this point in 1897. Finally, there is a long siding on the up side at the south end of the station, at one time used for accommodating the D&SER ballast train.

The line now falls to sea level, passing another noted coastal erosion trouble spot at Ballygannon, where diversions of the line inland for almost a mile were carried out in 1912 and 1971. The 9½ miles from milepost 18¾ form the longest stretch of level track in Ireland. At Kilcool the platform is on the up side, the original one having been washed away in a severe storm in February 1890. A siding, cattle bank and goods store existed at the Wexford end on the up side, and there was a double arm station signal, situated in the centre of the platform, which was removed by the GSR in August 1931. The station was reduced to a halt under Greystones in November 1930 and was closed on 31st March 1964, but re-opened on 9th June 1980 for suburban traffic.

Newcastle, opened in August 1856, had its original platform and station building on the up side. A crossing keeper's cottage, which dated from the opening of the line, was also situated on the up side. An island platform was added on the down side in September 1867 with a goods loop on the seaward side, from which a long siding trailed back on the down side at the Dublin end. A portion of the down loop and the goods siding were washed away in July 1962. The line from Newcastle to Wicklow Junction was doubled in 1877 at which time the two 'signal huts' at Newcastle were retained pending the doubling north to Greystones. However, this was never done and a new cabin was built on the up side at the Dublin end in 1888. As part of the economy measures adopted by the GSR, the section to Wicklow was singled again on 21st July 1927, the up line being retained. Newcastle was reduced to a halt under Wicklow in November 1930. The station was closed on 31st March 1964, but the signal cabin was occasionally switched in for crossing trains and permanent way work,

being finally taken out of use on 21st April 1968.

Three miles beyond Newcastle was Killoughter, one of the original stations opened in October 1855, with its station building on the up side. In 1864, a cargo vessel en route to Wicklow was wrecked on the shore close to the station after her captain had mistaken the station lights for those of Wicklow Head. A similar event occurred in 1885 when two Italian vessels ran aground on the same night, one at Five Mile Point just south of Newcastle, the second at Killoughter. In August 1866, with the anticipated opening of the new Rathnew station as from 1st September, the decision was taken to close Killoughter. A deputation to the board against the closure led to it being retained in use until 1st April 1867.

Wicklow Junction dated from the extension of the line to Kilcommon in August 1861, and became a block post in July 1877 when a signal cabin was opened in conjunction with the doubling from Newcastle. The line into the old Wicklow station diverged from the main line by a facing junction on the down side, a trailing crossover providing the connection to the up main line during double track days. From the up main line, a trailing connection gave access to sidings serving the chemical works adjoining the line on this side, company land having been leased to the Wicklow Chemical Company in 1870. A water tank situated beside these sidings served locomotives shunting in the chemical works yard or at Wicklow goods. The cabin, which controlled all movements to and from the old station as well as to the chemical works sidings, remained in operation until August 1927 when it was replaced by a ground frame following the singling of the line from Newcastle.

The old station handled passenger traffic for Wicklow until the new station on the main line was opened on 6th August 1885,

Top: **Beyer Peacock-built 4-4-0 No 67**
***Rathmore* heads a down train away from Bray.** R N Clements collection - IRRS

Centre: **4-4-0 No 57, *Rathnew*, arrives at Bray with the 15.20 Shillelagh-Dublin train on the 21st July 1914. The Bray Head sidings are on the right.**
Ken Nunn collection - LCGB

Left: **Bray Head looking south towards the 210 yard No 3 Tunnel (the original Cable Rock Tunnel). The photograph dates from the period 1879-85, as the line in the foreground is that of the 1879 diversion, but the Earl of Meath's footbridge, giving access across the line to a private strand, is the original wooden structure which was replaced by a metal bridge in 1885. The lower of the two paths above the railway line was maintained by the company as a tourist attraction.** W E Shepherd collection

following which it remained in use as the goods station for the town. There was a single platform on the up side with several long sidings, a cattle dock, goods bank and goods store opposite the platform on the down side. Originally the layout included engine and carriage sheds and a turntable, the latter being removed to Wexford in 1872. Following the extension of the main line, carriages for the Wicklow terminus were detached at the junction and brought in by horse. In March 1867 however, the board instructed, no doubt at the instigation of the BoT, that these movements were in future to be made by a locomotive. A short siding off the goods line was provided for Veha Limited in 1965.

At the southern end of the yard a line extended from the station to the quay. Details of the two separate tramways constructed are given in Chapter Nine. The second of these tramways was operated at first by horses, and latterly, by the company's engines, although the latter were not allowed on to the quay itself. Wicklow Goods was re-opened for suburban passenger traffic as Wicklow Murrough station on 16th March 1969, closed to goods traffic on 6th September 1976 and to all traffic on 1st November of that year.

The parliamentary plans prepared in 1854 in connection with the intended extension to Woodenbridge at that time clearly show a triangular junction at Wicklow, the proposed southern line from the station rejoining the main line just before it crossed the Broadlough. In the event it was only the main line from Wicklow Junction which was constructed and, from 1885 until 1927, it was a double track which curved to the right across the Broadlough Bridge to enter the new Wicklow station. Here there are two platforms with the station buildings on the down side, as is the signal cabin which is situated by the corner of the footbridge, a cabin which is reputed to have its own ghost. There is a short siding on the down side adjoining a loading bank at the Wexford end, a similar siding on the up side at the Dublin end having been lifted in 1969/70.

Leaving Wicklow the line begins climbing and, apart from a brief respite just after Glenealy, this continues to Kilcommon, just short of Rathdrum, some eight miles away. After an initial ¼ mile at 1 in 500 the next 3¾ miles is at 1 in 100 interspersed with short level sections. Rathnew was situated on one of these, 1½ miles from Wicklow. The station building was on the up side; it had a single platform, but no other facilities. A double arm station signal stood on the centre of the platform until removed by the GSR in August 1929. Rathnew Brickfields Siding, ¾ of a mile beyond the station, trailed in on the up side. The siding crossed the public road to serve the brickworks owned by Thompsons. The siding was opened for traffic in June 1896, being closed in 1931.

The grade stiffens to 1 in 90 through Ballymanus level crossing, the site of the original Glenealy station, and past the repositioned Glenealy station ½ mile further on. Glenealy, which was reduced to a halt under Rathdrum in 1931, had a single passenger platform and station building on the up side with a signal cabin at the Wexford end of the platform. There was a down side loop for passing goods trains opposite the platform, and a siding which led to a goods loading bank was located on the up side at the Wexford end. Due to the difficulties encountered in breaking through the steep rock cutting on the last mile approaching Rathdrum, a temporary station was provided at Kilcommon where the station building can still be seen on the down side. A mile before Rathdrum the line commences falling at 1 in 90, a gradient which continues for more than three miles, across the five arch Rathdrum viaduct and through the station.

Rathdrum opened on 18th July 1863, on which date Kilcommon was closed. There are two platforms with the station building on the up side as is the signal cabin, once again at the corner of the footbridge. Immediately behind the up platform is the hotel built by the company in the hope of attracting custom from the tourist traffic to Glendalough, some seven miles away, combined rail and hotel tickets being issued. The goods yard was situated behind the down platform and could be entered only from the north end. Facilities consisted of cattle and goods banks, coal yard, carriage dock and a goods shed. A turntable was installed in the yard in 1861, but removed seven years later. At the Wexford end, on the up side, the Wood siding trails back towards the tunnel and was a useful refuge for long goods trains wishing to take water. The goods yard was closed in March 1964 and is now in private ownership, only the goods shed still remaining. There were water columns at both sides of the station, with a tank of 5,360 gallon capacity on the down side.

Leaving Rathdrum, the line enters the 190 yard long Rathdrum tunnel and on emerging from this begins its descent through perhaps the most beautiful part of what overall is a most scenic line, the run down the valley of the Avonmore River and into the Vale of Avoca. On the down side, a mile beyond Rathdrum, sidings were installed in 1901 to cater for traffic from the Balleece Quarry Company which produced whinstone of a very high quality. Much of this stone was transported to Harcourt Street in special trains for use on Dublin city road works, and such was the intensity of traffic that complaints were constantly made by the management of the quarry as to shortage of wagons. As the sidings joined the main line on the 1 in 90 gradient, special instructions were issued for the operation of trains at this location. Two miles further on, there was a

siding at Connorree which was in operation between 1864 and 1869 in connection with adjoining mines. Cronebane or Tigroney siding, a little over a mile beyond Connorree, had a somewhat longer and more successful existence. This siding was on the down side and included a loading bank where copper, iron ore and sulphur were handled.

Avoca, known until 1912 as Ovoca, had two platforms with the station building on the down side, behind which was the goods yard. A signal cabin existed on the up platform from 1891 until January 1931. There was also a horse box siding on the up side at the Dublin end, both it and the loop being lifted in 1982. Also on the up side at the Dublin end there was evidence of the mineral tramway in the shape of a tunnel under the road. There was a loading bank enabling ore from the tramway wagons to be transferred to the main line wagons. South of the road bridge was a locomotive shed for main line engines. A further two miles down the Vale of Avoca the line reaches the site of its third junction, at Woodenbridge, where the Shillelagh branch diverged on the up side by a connection facing down trains. The 3 ft 6 in gauge mineral tramway crossed the branch here and to avoid accidents, the junction was equipped with Anderson's patent locking apparatus. A description of this junction can be found in *Transactions of the Institution of Civil Engineers in Ireland* for 1868. There were up and down platforms with the station building and signal cabin on the up one, the back face of which served the branch line trains. The connection to the branch remained *in situ* until August 1965, the station, which had been a halt under Arklow since June 1947, having closed in the previous year. At the Dublin end of the station, on the up side, there were goods sidings, a cattle bank and a 45ft turntable.

From Woodenbridge the line falls gently towards Arklow passing Shelton Abbey sidings which date from 1964. These were constructed on the down side in connection with the adjacent Nitrigin Éireann Teoranta factory (now Irish Fertiliser Industries). Both inbound ammonia, which is used in the fertiliser manufacturing process, and outbound finished products are moved by rail, the former in special tank wagons. The line passes the site of Glenart, a private platform on the up side provided for the use of the Earl of Carysfort opposite to the IFI marshalling sidings; all traces of this halt have long since disappeared. The last ½ mile into Arklow sees the line climb again at 1 in 100 as it approaches the station. This is an important town with a busy port, which in the mid-19th century handled a considerable volume of mineral ores for export to Swansea and Neath. The station has two platforms, with the station building on the down side, as is the signal cabin which is located at the corner of the footbridge. The

Above: **Greystones station looking north from the Wexford end with Bray Head in the background. The line diverging to the right fans out into sidings with a turntable at the inner end. The original 24ft turntable was situated to the right of the footbridge. Bathing boxes may be observed, on the right. The rocky promontory to the shoreline gave the town its name.** K A Murray - IRRS collection

Centre left: **The loneliness of Rathnew is evident in this shot of the single platform station.** T Cott - IRRS collection

Below: **Arklow station looking north with the signal cabin at the corner of the footbridge on the right.** W E Shepherd

goods yard, originally consisting of three roads but now reduced to one, is behind the down platform at the Wexford end.

Leaving Arklow, the gradient steepens to 1 in 80 before a short descent to the site of Kish siding. Located 1¾ miles from Arklow on the up side, it was opened in 1886 to serve the Parnell Whinstone quarries. The next station was Inch, latterly a halt under Arklow. It had a single platform with timber and corrugated iron station buildings on the up side and a siding serving the local creamery. Six miles beyond Inch the line reaches Gorey. This two platform station is still open, the main buildings being on the up side and the typical D&SER signal cabin on the corner of the footbridge on the down side. The up platform has a water column still extant at the Dublin end. Messrs Bolger had a siding on the down side at the Dublin end. The goods yard on the up side at the Dublin end was once more extensive than now, including an oil depot for Shell Mex & BP Ltd. As many as 60 cattle wagons were shipped out on fair days, but now the only freight traffic is bagged cement. Camolin, 7½ miles further on, was a halt under Gorey and had a single platform on the up side along with a siding and goods store.

Approaching Ferns, just before the station, a siding protected by an Annett's Lock was installed in 1921 on the up side on D&SER land at the expense of Mr D W Dunne, trading as E O'Connor & Company, and subsequently sold to Messrs Bolger. Ferns station had both up and down platforms, the station buildings being on the up platform with the signal cabin at the corner of the footbridge on the same side. There was a long goods yard on the up side at the Wexford end, including a private siding for Bolgers. There were both Anglo-American and BP oil depots at Ferns. Leaving Ferns the line falls gradually towards Enniscorthy, and on the up side at milepost 73¼ passes the site of Scarawalsh ballast pit, which from 1918 was a source of good ballast for the company's use.

From Scarawalsh, the line runs alongside the River Slaney to Enniscorthy, an important station, with both up and down platforms. The signal cabin, rebuilt on the remains of the base of the one destroyed in 1923, is at the Dublin end of the down platform whilst the main station building is at the Wexford end of the same platform. On the up side at the Dublin end there was a locomotive shed, coal bank and 40ft turntable, and opposite on the down side, a large

goods shed and cattle loading bank. A line which ran behind the station building served the private sidings in Donohoe's yard, and at the Wexford end of the down platform a facing connection provided access to Messrs Buttles' private siding. Always a busy station for both passenger and goods traffic, it handled a heavy trade in cattle, sheep and pigs, as well as agricultural machinery.

On leaving Enniscorthy, the line crosses the River Slaney on a 210ft long seven-span bridge and, immediately on the up side, passes the site of the connection to Roche's private siding, which was opened in 1879, before entering the 405 yard long tunnel under the town. A mile from Enniscorthy the private siding to the St John's Mill of S & A G Davis trailed in by a crossover from the up side. A ground frame, released by a key on the section staff, not only operated the connecting points to St John's siding but also controlled up and down signals interlocked with the points. Wagons were hauled from Enniscorthy station to the siding turnout and propelled into the Mill yard. There were often three trips a day with up to 50 wagon loads of flour. In GSR days, the headshunt of the siding, beside the main line, was used by Messrs Kavanagh for loading cement, tiles and general traffic.

Edermine Ferry, 3½ miles beyond Enniscorthy, had a single platform on the up side with a trailing siding, loading bank, goods store and a level crossing at the Macmine end beside the signal cabin. A level stretch of just over two miles brings the line to the site of Macmine Junction, the station for connections to the Waterford branch. There were two platforms, that on the up side being an island, serving up main and branch services. The 45ft turntable, sidings and cattle pens were all located on this side behind the branch platform. The down platform had the signal cabin on it. The station had three water columns. For many years after it was opened, Macmine Junction had no road

access, being purely a railway interchange.

Killurin, the last station before Wexford, was a former block post and originally had both up and down platforms. The station building was on the up platform, the signal cabin being on the same side at the Dublin end of the platform. The goods siding with loading bank, cattle pen and store was located on the up side also at the Dublin end of the station. Half a mile beyond the station the line runs through the 89 yard long Killurin tunnel and on emerging from this passes the site of Killurin ballast pit at milepost 87. A further 3½ miles brings the line to the 296 yard long Ferrycarrig tunnel. Just before milepost 91¾ the site of Park siding, which served an early ballast pit, is passed on the down side. The original terminus at Wexford was at Carcur, the present station, 42 chains further on, opening in 1874. The station buildings are on the single 542 ft platform which is on the up side. The signal cabin is also on the up side just beyond the Dublin end of the platform. At one time, extensive facilities existed on the down side opposite the station, including a locomotive shed, 50ft turntable, cattle bank and a large goods shed. Wexford North, 92 miles and 54 chains from Harcourt Street, was the southern terminus of the D&SER main line, although a tramway was laid along the Quays in the 1870s. The present line to Rosslare leaves the station and runs along the Quay.

Waterford Branch

As stated above, the Waterford trains used the back of the island platform at Macmine Junction, crossovers allowing main line trains in either direction to gain access to this side of the platform and thence to the branch. Departing from Macmine the first mile was relatively easily graded, but the line then climbed steeply for some 1¾ miles to Sparrowsland siding. Located on the down side, at the site of a station closed in 1876 (although the local papers indicate that it

Right: **Gorey station looking north towards Arklow in 1906. The DW&WR-style signal cabin is at the corner of the footbridge, a feature to be found at a number of stations on the line. The goods shed is at the Dublin end of the up platform, partly obscured by the footbridge.** From a hand-tinted original in the Lawrence collection - courtesy NLI

remained as a flag station in the down direction only until the end of 1879), the siding was used extensively for sugar beet traffic in the years prior to its closure. An undulating section of just over three miles brought the line to Chapel with its single platform on the up side, opposite which was a loop giving access to the goods store and cattle pens.

Steep gradients were a feature of the line to Waterford and the four miles from Chapel to Palace East were no exception. At 480ft above sea level Palace East was the highest station on the system, and was the junction with the line from Bagenalstown worked by the GS&WR. Palace East had an unusual layout with the through side of the single platform serving D&SER trains and a dead end bay at the back of the platform for GS&WR branch trains. A headshunt at the end of the bay gave access to a run-round loop and the turntable road. The goods siding with loading bank, small store and cattle pens ran parallel to the D&SER main line but did not

form a loop, and therefore it was not possible to cross trains here without some complicated shunting. The signal cabin and water tank were at the Waterford end of the platform opposite to which was the cross-over giving access to the goods siding.

On leaving Palace East, the D&SER line ran parallel to the Bagenalstown branch for almost a mile, initially on a short rising grade of 1 in 85 before commencing a downhill stretch, eventually falling at 1 in 60, as both lines crossed the Enniscorthy to New Ross road on separate adjoining bridges. Following the divergence of the two lines at milepost 95 the line continued falling for a further ½ mile before commencing the 1¼ mile climb to Rathgarogue with its single platform on the up side. Leaving this station, the headlong descent continued on the 5½ miles to New Ross, including three miles at 1 in 60 through deep cuttings and over the high Ballyanne embankment, until the line levelled out to pass into the 745 yard long

Mount Elliott tunnel, from which it emerged to cross the River Barrow by a 590ft long, five-span, opening bridge. This bridge had been opened little in the last years of the line's existence due to diminishing river traffic north of New Ross.

New Ross station served a town of some 5,000 people and was unusual in that the station was situated on the west bank of the River Barrow whereas most of the town was on the opposite side. Being the terminus of the line for some 20-odd years, extensive goods facilities had developed, all of them on the up side behind the platform. The station buildings were on the down platform with the signal cabin at the Dublin end, a standard D&SER footbridge providing passenger access to the up platform. A siding was provided for traffic to Messrs Stafford's wharf by the GSR in 1927. Following closure of the signal cabin in 1966, the Waterford to New Ross section has been worked on the single engine in steam principle.

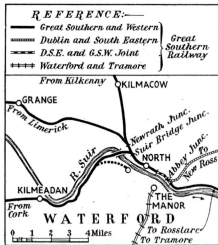

Reproduced courtesy of *The Railway Magazine*: Volume LXXXII, No 491, May 1938.

Photographs on this page:

Right: **Glenmore, the only intermediate station on the Waterford extension.**
T Cott - IRRS collection

Centre, below: **The mail train at Waterford, Abbey Junction, in 1905. 0-4-2 No 39, later named** *Suir*, **leads kitchen van No 11, bogie open first No 12 and bogie open second No 42.** H Fayle - IRRS collection

Bottom: **One of the Vulcan Foundry 2-2-2WTs of 1855-56 at Woodenbridge, with a Shillelagh branch train, at the turn of the century.** G Beesley collection

Photographs on the opposite page:

Top: **On occasions floods came to New Ross. This photograph shows 0-4-2 No 21, which was later rebuilt as a tank engine in 1905, coupled to a horsebox. A covered wagon with open centre roof stands forlornly on the hidden tracks.**
W Cavanagh - James FitzGibbon collection

Bottom: **The Barrow Bridge, just outside New Ross. One of the largest civil engineering features on the line, each of the main spans was 110ft in length. The opening span provided two lanes for shipping of 40ft each. The small control cabin for the opening and closing of the bridge can be seen on the left hand side. The bridge itself was controlled by a key on the Palace East to New Ross section staff.**
Lawrence collection - courtesy NLI

Left: **Amiens Street Junction looking south in 1933 showing the south cabin on the right and newly commissioned electric colour light signals.** K A Murray

Lower left: **A notice dating from 1892 on the working of the interlocking between the signal boxes at Amiens Street and Newcomen Bridge Junction.** W E Shepherd collection

NOTICE.

Description of Sykes' Electric Interlocking between Amiens Street and Newcomen Bridge Junction.

TO SEND TRAIN FROM AMIENS STREET TO NEWCOMEN BRIDGE JUNCTION.

Signal-man at Amiens Street (Central Cabin) to send advice of train to Newcomen Junction Cabin on ordinary block instrument, in the usual way. If road is clear for train, Signal-man at Newcomen Bridge pulls No. 4 lever partly over, then raises rod under Sykes' Electric Locking Instrument until it shows **LOCKED**, then to push in the Plunger of the instrument; this releases either No. 3 or No 7 starting signal levers in Amiens Street (Central Cabin); either can then be lowered for train to approach Newcomen Bridge Junction. When train passes over the "Lift Bridge," and over the *Electric Treadle*, it releases either No. 3 or No. 7 levers in Amiens Street (Central Cabin), so that they can be replaced back in normal position. Signal-man at Amiens Street (Central Cabin) must then push in the Plunger of the instrument, which releases No. 4 lever at Newcomen Junction.

TO CANCEL A TRAIN.

To Cancel a train from Amiens Street, Signal-man at Amiens Street (Central Cabin) places the Cancelling key in keyhole at *back* of the instrument, turns it in the direction indicated by arrow, until instrument reads **LOCKED**, then to place same key into keyhole in *front* of instrument, and turn in direction indicated, until lower slot reads **PLUNGE**, then to push in the Plunger, which releases No. 4 lever at Newcomen Bridge Junction Cabin.

When train from Amiens Street is Cancelled, and when No. 4 lever is placed back in normal position, the Signal-man at Newcomen Cabin to place the Cancelling key in keyhole in front of instrument, and turn in direction indicated by arrow, until it reads blank again in lower slot of instrument.

Should instrument from any cause get out of order, the small key that is sealed up in the Cabin to be unsealed, and the padlock on instrument unlocked, and outer case taken off, the instrument then put out of contact by pressing inwards the small plate, which will allow the signal levers to be worked in the ordinary way. Signal-man to report at once to the Manager that the instrument is out of order and key unsealed.

Irish Printing Works, Moore Lane.

The six miles from New Ross to Glenmore are predominantly uphill with the exception of a descent of just over a mile at 1 in 75. Glenmore (also at times known as Glenmore & Aylwardstown and Aylwardstown) originally had two platforms, but the down one was taken out of use in 1929 as were the signal cabin and crossing loop. The station buildings were on the up platform, and there was a goods siding on the up side at the New Ross end.

Two miles beyond Glenmore the line reaches another summit at milepost 110 and commences an almost unbroken fall of 5½ miles, including a final mile of 1 in 60, all the way to Abbey Junction. This gradient caused many a problem for goods trains on wet nights, special attention being drawn to it in an appendix to the D&SER Working Timetable. Abbey Junction was the point at which the D&SER line and the Rosslare to Mallow line of the F&RR&H converged and, prior to the 1925 amalgamation, the D&SER had a locomotive depot, turntable, and carriage sheds at this location. The last ¼ mile of double line into Waterford station was jointly owned by the D&SER and the F&RR&H. For just over two years, prior to the opening of the new Waterford station in 1906, D&SER trains had to run past the old ex WL&WR station and reverse into the west facing bays.

Shillelagh Branch

Leaving Woodenbridge, the line curved sharply to the right and crossed the Aughrim River before commencing a 4¼ mile climb up the valley. In 1897 a siding was installed ¾ mile from Woodenbridge to serve a quarry which the company purchased from a Mr Troy. The line then crossed the river two more times on its way to Aughrim station; the final 1¼ miles before the station, at 1 in 95, being the steepest gradient on the branch. At Aughrim the single platform, had the station buildings and signal cabin on the up side as was a short goods siding at the Woodenbridge end. There was a loop on the down side with the main goods accommodation on the up side. At the Dublin end there was a long private siding, crossing the Aughrim River and serving Fogarty's Mills, an important source of traffic for the branch. Just beyond the station, the river divides into the *Ow* and the *Derry Water*, the railway following the latter and crossing it in places on the 4¼ miles to Ballinglen. This was a little used halt opened ten years after the branch, although many requests had been made ever since 1865 for a station here. The platform was on the up side with a short goods siding at the Shillelagh end.

After Ballinglen, the Derry Water was left behind and the summit was reached near milepost 55¼, the line having climbed almost continuously for the 10½ miles from Woodenbridge. It then began a continuous descent for the final six miles to the terminus, passing through Tinahely where both the platform, with signal cabin and station building, and the goods accommodation were located on the up side, the latter being at the Woodenbridge end.

A run of 4½ miles from Tinahely brought the line to Shillelagh, the terminus of the branch, with its single platform, together with station building and signal cabin, on the up side. There was a two road locomotive shed on the down side opposite the Woodenbridge end of the platform, but the 42ft turntable was located at the inner end of the station yard. The original locomotive shed was in fact also situated at the inner end, having been moved in 1870. The goods accommodation was on the up side behind the platform. This may not have been the original terminus as powers were taken in the Company's Act of 1868 for the taking of lands, 'for the Purpose of their Station', while a board minute of 14th March 1872 refers to a new station at Shillelagh.

The Coast Line

As the line from Westland Row to Shanganagh Junction was measured from the former point, the line will be described from north to south. When the section from Bray to Dublin was electrified in 1984, the signalling was modernised, and so all references to signal cabins relate to the pre-electrification period.

Starting our journey at Newcomen Bridge Junction, the northern extremity of D&SER territory and the junction with the MGWR Liffey branch, the first point to note is that the lines of the CofDJR did not have mileposts. The branch is sharply curved and climbs for ¼ mile at 1 in 60 to Amiens Street Junction, a station which was used only for passenger traffic. Originally double, the line was singled as far as Amiens Street in 1929. The entrance to the junction station was separate to that of the GNR(I) station and, after nearly 26 years out of use, it was re-opened in 1984 following re-development, as the entrance to the present DART station. A subway and two ramps provided access to the three CofDJR platforms, No 1, adjoining the Howth bay of the GNR(I), and the island Nos 2 and 3. The present subway connecting the island platform was constructed during the development for the DART service, the lower part of the old ramp being abandoned. The original entrance was closed and the platforms re-numbered 5, 6 and 7 following the dissolution of the GNR Board in 1958. Prior to electrification, access from the Loop Line platforms to the GNR (I) platforms was provided by means of a footbridge.

The layout was originally under the control of two signal cabins, the old south cabin being on the down side (the line from Amiens Street to Westland Row was referred to as the up direction), opposite the south end of the island platform, and the original joint D&SER and GNR(I) central cabin just beyond the north end of the Howth Bay platform. It was the latter which was destroyed in 1923, the subsequent flag working resulting in No 47 over-running the turntable and falling into the post office cloakroom below. This 45ft turntable is still extant beyond the release road opposite platform No 7. The new central cabin was constructed further north and the D&SER levers in it were dispensed with when the new electro-mechanical signal cabin, at the north end of the island platform, was brought into use by the GSR in 1934.

Leaving Amiens Street five streets are traversed by plate girder bridges before the line crosses Beresford Place and then Custom House Quay, the River Liffey and George's Quay, on the magnificent braced girder Liffey Bridge constructed by Arroll Bros – the largest engineering structure of its kind on the system, to enter Tara Street station. For many years known as Tara Street & George's Quay, the station is located just after the line crosses the River Liffey and for a time boasted a signal cabin on the up platform which had been made a block post in 1901. Passenger access is from an entrance on George's Quay, the booking office being under the tracks at street level. Access to each platform is by flights of stairs.

In D&SER days another entrance existed from Poolbeg Street. Curving sharply to the left, and crossing Townsend Street and Pearse Street (formerly Great Brunswick Street) by plate girder bridges the line runs into Westland Row, the northern end of the D&KR line. Immediately before entering the station across the bridge over Westland Row there is a trailing crossover which was installed with the new signalling in 1936 to provide for the departure of Midland main line trains from both platforms 3 and 4 following their transfer from Broadstone in January 1937.

Westland Row (Pearse) station has remained little altered from its appearance in 1891 following the opening of the Loop Line. There are two through roads, platforms 3 and 4. On the up side (Bray to Westland Row direction), were two south facing bay platforms, Nos 1 and 2, while on the down side was the corresponding No 5 bay used by the Boat Trains and the Wexford Mail Train. On the down side a long siding was used for carriage storage as was an open sided shed. The electric signal cabin erected in 1936 straddled this siding immediately beyond the station. Still above street level on the up side the line passes the Boston sidings, still extant but now little used. The Works, or 'Factory' as it was called, was located on the up side, just before the Grand Canal, and this has already been described in Chapter Eleven. Following the 1925 amalgamation, the GSR decided to concentrate their major workshop activities at Inchicore and so the Grand Canal Street Works was closed. Just beyond the Works on the down side was the D&SER running shed at Grand Canal Street. Until 1936 there was a signal cabin at the Wexford end of the shed at roof level, access to which was from a footbridge which spanned the running roads and gave staff a safe walking route between the shed and Grand Canal Street Works.

A view taken in 1952 of the single-track section just south of Dun Laoghaire station with the junction for the line to Carlisle Pier in the middle distance, immediately beyond which was the 'Hole in the Wall' signal cabin. K A Murray - IRRS collection

Above: **A rare photograph of the old Ballybrack station looking south. In this pre-1882 view the signal cabin and siding are clearly visible as is the original route of the line to Shanganagh and Bray along the coastline.** K A Murray - IRRS collection

Below: **No 52 *Duke of Connaught* hauls the mail train from Carlisle Pier through Kingstown station in the 1890s. The gate across the line to Victoria (later St Michael's) Wharf is visible on the left.** K A Murray collection

Right: **A GSR era view of Blackrock station showing the adjacent salt-water baths, of the sort so much loved by the Victorians.** IRRS collection

Bottom right: **The Royal Dublin Society's sidings at Ballsbridge. Although taken in CIE days, this photograph clearly shows the importance to the railway of the RDS traffic.** H Richards

Approaching Lansdowne Road, the line passes under one of the rugby ground's stands and over a level crossing into Lansdowne Road station. The platforms here straddle the River Dodder and the station buildings are on the up platform. In addition to commuter traffic this station enjoys considerable activity on days when rugby and soccer international matches are held at the adjoining Irish Rugby Football Union ground. The signal cabin at the Dublin end of the down platform is switched in on these occasions purely for local control of the adjacent level crossing. For a time the station sported nameboards for Lansdowne & Ballsbridge. Leaving Lansdowne Road, with the line now at street level the connection to the Royal Dublin Society sidings trailed in on the up side, a facing crossover providing access from the down road. There were extensive facilities within the RDS grounds for blood-stock and other show traffic. The line now runs through suburban housing areas served by stations at Sandymount and Sydney Parade, both closed in 1960 and re-opened in 1984 and 1972 respectively.

Just before Sandymount, was Serpentine Avenue crossing. The 1937 signal cabin at Sandymount, which replaced an earlier one, was located at the south end of the down platform beside the level crossing, but it was demolished during the building of the new DART station. The original station buildings were on the up platform, but these were demolished some time after the station closed in 1901. A few years after re-opening in 1928, some buildings recovered from one of the Cork narrow gauge lines were utilised to provide a booking office and waiting room. The signal cabin at Sydney Parade is still extant, although unused, at the Dublin end of the down platform beside the level crossing. Merrion had a signal cabin at the Dublin end of the up platform beside what is probably the busiest level crossing in the Dublin suburban area. After Merrion the line runs alongside the sea as far as Salthill.

Booterstown was another of the stations to close in 1960 only to re-open in 1975 with the growth of local traffic, particularly that generated by nearby schools and colleges. A ¼ mile beyond is the site of Williamstown station, situated beside a Martello tower and closed in 1841. There is still a footbridge at this location.

Blackrock was the principal intermediate station between Westland Row and Dun Laoghaire and was the terminus for some lunch time services operated by Drumm trains from 1933. There was a signal cabin on the up side which closed in 1937. A crossover from Blackrock was moved to Merrion in May 1936 in connection with the automatic electric colour light signalling between Merrion and Dunleary crossing which was commissioned in November 1937. Seapoint has its main buildings on the up side as are all other station buildings from Sydney Parade. Following protests after the closure of Salthill in 1960, it was renamed Seapoint-Monkstown until the latter re-opened. Salthill & Monkstown, which was the station for the adjacent Salthill Hotel, originally had imposing station buildings on the up side, but these were demolished after the station closed in 1960 and a rather more utilitarian affair was provided when the station re-opened for DART services in 1984.

Approaching Dun Laoghaire, the line passes the site of Dunleary signal cabin, which was on the up side and controlled a level crossing giving access to the west pier. It then crosses a stone-walled embankment dating from the extension of the D&KR in 1837 from its original terminus near the west pier, and swings right through a short cutting and tunnel. The original D&KR terminus of 1837 was behind the down platform where a bay platform still exists. Storage sidings at the Dublin end of the down platform were used for holding extra boat trains during peak seasons. Off the down side, sidings ran across the public road into St Michael's Wharf and to the Coal Quay, also known as the Mineral or Traders' Wharf, the former name adopted in connection with its use for the export of mineral ores from Ovoca. These facilities also disappeared when the electrification works were carried out. There was a round water tank at the Wexford end of the through platform and a rectangular one at the Dublin end which also served

engines in the bay. The 1926 signal cabin was also located at the Dublin end of this platform.

The layout at Dun Laoghaire station today is quite different to the arrangement prior to 1957. Although plans had been drawn up in D&SER days to provide a second platform here, and even a double junction to the pier, it fell to CIE to undertake major remodelling.

The track from Carlisle Pier junction into Dun Laoghaire station was originally single and there was only a single through platform to serve both up and down trains, which severely restricted movements. An up side platform was provided in 1957. Leaving Dun Laoghaire, we pass the site of Carlisle Pier junction on the down side, the pier line having been closed in connection with electrification works.

A doorway in the cutting wall at this point was the location of the 'Hole-in-the-Wall' signal cabin which controlled the junction. Single from the point of junction, this short branch opened out into two roads on the pier and ended in a turntable at the outer end which enabled engines to run around their trains.

The line is now in a deep cutting leaving Dun Laoghaire and curves to the right to Sandycove station. The station building at Sandycove is at road level, access to the platforms being by means of ramps. A signal cabin, closed in March 1926, survived for many years at the Wexford end of the up platform. The name of the station was for a time Sandycove & Glasthule. Curving to the left the line climbs at 1 in 163 to Glenageary station which has its buildings on the up side and has always only handled suburban traffic. The gradient steepens to 1 in 138 as the line passes the site of the former Atmospheric terminus on the down side where, in CIE days, a set of catch points marked the location of the former Glenageary siding which used the old Atmospheric trackbed. Dalkey station is on a falling gradient towards Dublin, the main buildings being located on the down side. The later signal cabin was on the down side just beyond the Bray end of the down platform. This had replaced an earlier cabin situated on the footbridge. Limited siding accommodation existed on the down side behind the signal cabin, and was generally used in D&SER days for permanent way trains.

Leaving Dalkey the line curves right and passes through the 160yd long Dalkey tunnel to emerge with magnificent views across Killiney Bay, sometimes referred to as the Naples of Ireland. The gradient begins falling with the line high above the sea, passing White Rock and the site of the old Killiney station into the present Killiney & Ballybrack station which dates from May 1882. The station building is on the up side, and the signal cabin was also on this side at the Bray end. A number of stations existed in the Killiney-Ballybrack area and the reader is referred to Appendix F for a list of these and their locations. The line south of Killiney was single until 1915, at which time it was also diverted inland. In places the site of the old line can be traced. From milepost 10½ the line climbs virtually all the way to Shanganagh Junction on a gradient of 1 in 151, passing through the new Shankill station opened at Corbawn Lane in 1977.

Dublin, Wicklow, and Wexford Railway.

OPENING

OF THE

City of Dublin Junction Railways (Loop Line)

IN CONNECTION WITH

THE GREAT NORTHERN RAILWAY,

On and after FRIDAY, 1st MAY, 1891.

Week Day Train Service—Bray to Howth.

		A.M.	A.M.	A.M.	A.M.	NOON	P.M.	P.M.	P.M.	P.M.	P.M.	P.M.	P.M.	P.M.	
Bray	departure	8 0	9 0	10 0	11 0	12 0	1 0	2 0	3 0	4 0	5 0	5 30	6 30	—	—
Kingstown	"	8 21	9 21	10 21	11 21	12 21	1 21	2 21	3 21	4 21	5 21	5 51	6 51	—	—
Blackrock	"	8 25	9 25	10 25	11 25	12 25	1 25	2 25	3 25	4 25	5 25	5 55	6 55	—	—
Westland-row	arrival	8 35	9 35	10 35	11 35	12 35	1 35	2 35	3 35	4 35	5 35	6 5	7 5	—	—
Do.	departure	8 39	9 39	10 39	11 39	12 39	1 39	2 39	3 39	4 39	5 39	6 9	7 9	—	—
Amiens-street (Loop Line)	arrival	8 42 (For North)	9 42	10 42	11 42	12 42	1 42	2 42	3 42	4 42	5 42	6 12	7 12	—	—
Do. (Gt. Northern)	departure	9 0	9 45	10 45	11 45	12 45	1 45	2 45	3 45	4 45	5 45	6 15	7 15	—	—
Howth	do. arrival	—	10 5	11 5	12 5	1 5	2 5	3 5	4 5	5 5	6 5	6 35	7 35	—	—

Mails and Passengers on arrival of Steamer at Carlisle Pier (Kingstown), due at 6·10 a.m., leave by Through Carriages in connection with Limited Mail for Belfast and the North.

Week Day Train Service—Howth to Bray.

		A.M.	A.M.	A.M.	P.M.	P.M.	P.M.	P.M.	P.M.		MAIL P.M.	P.M.	P.M.	P.M.	
Howth (Great Northern)	departure	—	10 10	11 10	12 10	1 10	2 10	3 10	4 10	—	5 35	6 15	7 15	—	—
Amiens-street	do. arrival	—	10 32	11 32	12 32	1 32	2 32	3 32	4 32	—	5 57	6 35	7 35	—	—
Do. (Loop Line)	departure	9 34	10 34	11 34	12 34	1 34	2 34	3 34	4 34	5 5	6 0	6 40	7 37	—	—
Westland-row	arrival	9 37	10 37	11 37	12 37	1 37	2 37	3 37	4 37	5 8	6 3	6 43	7 40	—	—
Do.	departure	9 45	10 45	11 45	12 45	1 45	2 45	3 45	4 45	5 15	6 15	6 45	7 45	—	—
Blackrock	"	9 53	10 53	11 53	12 53	1 53	2 53	3 53	4 53	5 23	6 23	6 53	7 53	—	—
Kingstown	arrival	9 58	10 58	11 58	12 58	1 58	2 58	3 58	4 58	5 28	6 28	6 58	7 55	—	—
Do.	departure	9 59	10 59	11 59	12 59	1 59	2 59	3 59	4 59	5 29	6 29	6 59	7 59	—	—
Bray	arrival	10 20	11 20	12 20	1 20	2 20	3 20	4 20	5 20	5 50	6 50	7 20	8 20	—	—

Through Carriages by Limited Mail leaving Belfast at 3·30 p.m., direct for Mail Steamer leaving Carlisle Pier (Kingstown) about 7·25 p.m.

Sunday Train Service—Bray to Howth.

		A.M.	A.M.	A.M.	A.M.	P.M.	P.M.	P.M.	P.M.	P.M.		
Bray	departure	9 0	10 0	11 0	12 0	1 0	2 0	3 0	4 0	5 0	6 0	—
Kingstown	"	9 21	10 21	11 21	12 21	1 21	2 21	3 21	4 21	5 21	6 21	—
Blackrock	"	9 25	10 25	11 25	12 25	1 25	2 25	3 25	4 25	5 25	6 25	—
Westland-row	arrival	9 35	10 35	11 35	12 35	1 35	2 35	3 35	4 35	5 35	6 35	—
Do.	departure	9 39	10 39	11 39	12 39	1 39	2 39	3 39	4 39	5 39	6 40	—
Amiens-street (Loop Line)	arrival	9 42	10 42	11 42	12 42	1 42	2 42	3 42	4 42	5 42	6 43	—
Do. (Gt. Northern)	departure	9 45	10 45	11 45	12 45	1 45	2 45	3 45	4 45	5 45	6 45	—
Howth	do. arrival	10 5	11 5	12 5	1 5	2 5	3 5	4 5	5 5	6 5	7 5	—

Sunday Train Service—Howth to Bray.

		A.M.	A.M.	P.M.	P.M.	P.M.	P.M.	P.M.	P.M.	P.M.		
Howth (Great Northern)	departure	10 10	11 10	12 10	1 10	2 10	3 10	4 10	5 10	6 12	7 10	—
Amiens-street	do. arrival	10 32	11 32	12 32	1 32	2 32	3 32	4 32	5 32	6 35	7 32	—
Do. (Loop Line)	departure	10 34	11 34	12 34	1 34	2 34	3 34	4 34	5 34	6 37	7 34	—
Westland-row	arrival	10 37	11 37	12 37	1 37	2 37	3 37	4 37	5 37	6 40	7 37	—
Do.	departure	10 45	11 45	12 45	1 45	2 45	3 45	4 45	5 45	6 45	7 45	—
Blackrock	"	10 53	11 53	12 53	1 53	2 53	3 53	4 53	5 53	6 53	7 53	—
Kingstown	arrival	10 58	11 58	12 58	1 58	2 58	3 58	4 58	5 58	6 58	7 58	—
Do.	departure	10 59	11 59	12 59	1 59	2 59	3 59	4 59	5 59	6 59	7 59	—
Bray	arrival	11 20	12 20	1 20	2 20	3 20	4 20	5 20	6 20	7 20	8 20	—

FARES

		1st Class	2nd Class	3rd Class		1st Class	2nd Class	3rd Class
		s. d.	s. d.	s. d.		s. d.	s. d.	s. d.
Between Westland-row and Amiens-street	Singles	0 4	0 3	0 2	Return	0 6	0 4	0 3
Between Westland-row and Howth	"	1 8	1 3	0 10	"	2 6	1 10	1 3
Between Bray and Amiens-street	"	2 4	1 9	1 2	"	3 4	2 6	1 9
Between Bray and Howth	"	3 8	2 9	1 10	"	5 4	4 0	2 9

ON SUNDAYS

Return Tickets at Single Fares in both directions, between Bray and Howth, available for the day of issue only.
Through Bookings also between principal Stations on the Dublin, Wicklow, and Wexford, and Great Northern Railways.

Harcourt-street Terminus, 20th April, 1891.

WILLIAM L. PAYNE,
Traffic Manager.

Left: A 26¼" x 17⅜" poster produced to advertise the commencement of services on the Loop Line. It was issued at Harcourt Street and is dated 20th April 1891.
W E Shepherd collection

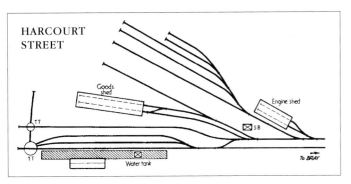

HARCOURT STREET

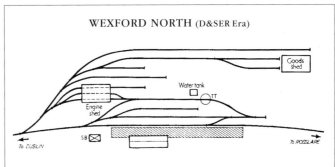

WEXFORD NORTH (D&SER Era)

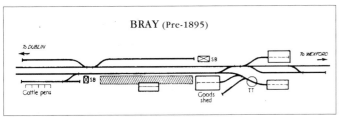

BRAY (Pre-1895)

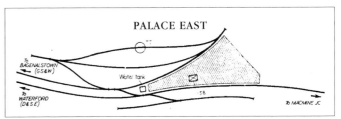

PALACE EAST

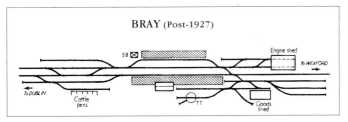

BRAY (Post-1927)

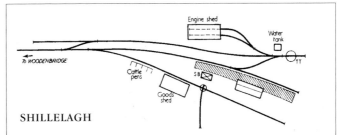

SHILLELAGH

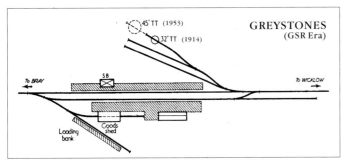

GREYSTONES (GSR Era)

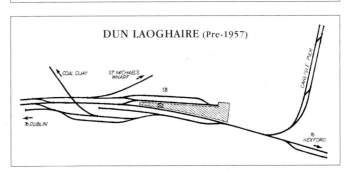

DUN LAOGHAIRE (Pre-1957)

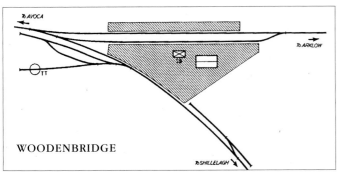

WOODENBRIDGE

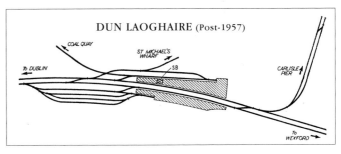

DUN LAOGHAIRE (Post-1957)

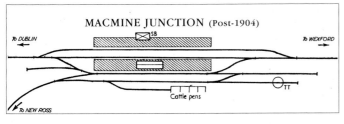

MACMINE JUNCTION (Post-1904)

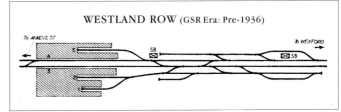

WESTLAND ROW (GSR Era: Pre-1936)

Track layouts at many stations and junctions often changed over the years. These sketch maps of some of the main locations on the system, which are not drawn to scale, are intended to be indicative of the general layout, rather than definitive.

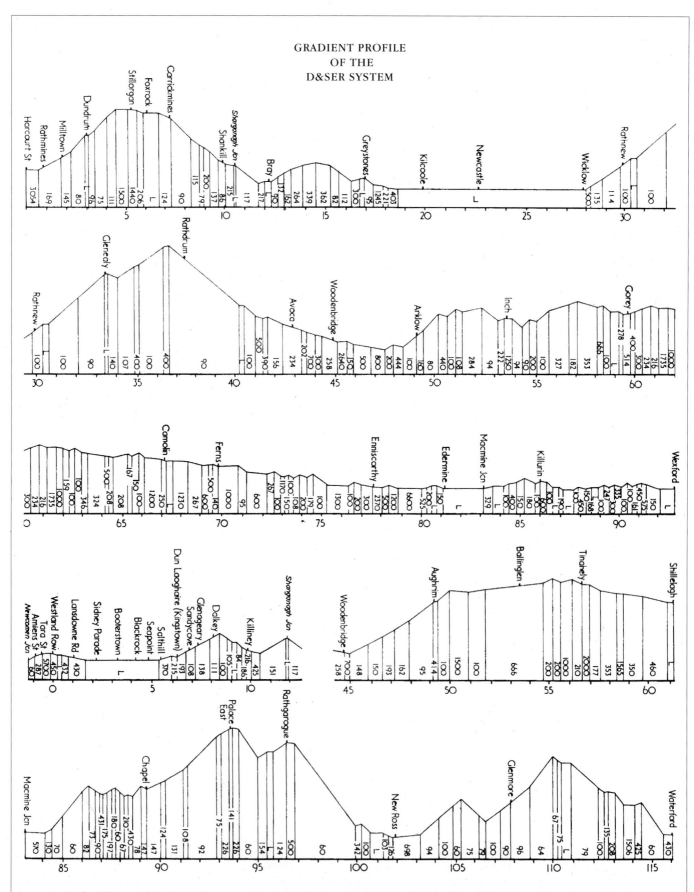

GRADIENT PROFILE
OF THE
D&SER SYSTEM

It should be noted that due to the compression of the horizontal scale, many of the smaller gradient changes have been omitted and others have been averaged. However, the general profile of the line is clearly shown.

Chapter Fourteen

SIGNALLING

IN THE early days of the line signals were provided at Harcourt Street, Shanganagh Junction and Bray and points were operated by ground levers. The signal posts were provided by John Reilly of Dublin, and he also supplied the signal posts for the line to the Carlisle Pier in 1859. Here the BoT required a communicating bell and connecting rods for the points; a pointsman's box was also provided by the company.

Courtney & Stephens, later Courtney, Stephens & Bailey, of Dublin provided signals and interlocking for the line until 1879, their first supply being for the stations between Harcourt Street and Shanganagh Junction in 1860. The signals for the Kingstown line and for the double line from Shanganagh Junction to Bray came later in the same year, a spare pointsman's box at Bray being moved to the junction. A double cottage was built at Shanganagh in 1861 for the men in charge of the points and signals there. Although the junction was dispensed with in May 1877, when the third line between Shanganagh and Bray was opened, it is interesting to note that in 1893 a pension was provided to John Walker, 'late pointsman at Shanganagh Junction'.

The original signals on the Enniscorthy extension and the Shillelagh branch were also supplied by Courtney & Stephens, the signalling arrangements installed by them at Woodenbridge Junction in 1865 being operated by an Anderson's patent interlocking frame, the first interlocking on the DW&WR. In 1868, following the derailment of the down Mail on 25th September at Sydney Parade level crossing, they provided the required signals for Haig's Lane, Serpentine Avenue and Sandymount level crossings.

Following receipt of a letter from the BoT in August 1869 it was resolved that the Block Telegraph System be introduced on the Kingstown line, between Westland Row and Blackrock, the offer of Tyers to supply and erect the necessary apparatus being accepted at £250. At the same time £100 was provided for the construction of signal cabins at the various stations. An agreement was entered into with the Post Office for the working and maintenance of the telegraphs in September 1870, but it was not until July 1871 that the system became operational. In fact the arrangements between the company and the Post Office for telegraphic services were the source of many disputes regarding payment over the years.

In June 1870 tenders were sought for the erection of patent locking signals at Westland Row and Kingstown, the offer of Courtney & Stephens being accepted at £170 for the former and £300 for the latter. In the following year the same contractor also supplied a footbridge with signal cabin and locking apparatus for points and signals at Dalkey station, the signal cabin being mounted centrally on the footbridge.

Courtney & Stephens were awarded the tender for the signalling on the Wexford extension in April 1872 and in the following year they installed point and signal interlocking apparatus to Anderson's Patent at Grand Canal Street. They also provided interlocking for the points and signals at Carlisle Pier junction in 1874, the signal cabin at this location being constructed in the 'V' of the tunnel wall between the Pier and Bray lines (see the previous chapter) and known to railwaymen as 'The Hole in the Wall'.

The practise of distinguishing distant signals by cutting a 'V' or 'fishtail' on the end of signal arms is generally attributed to John Saxby on the London Brighton & South Coast Railway in 1874-76, but early in 1874 Smith had already introduced this feature to distinguish distant signals from stop signals on the DW&WR lines.

The last major signalling installations provided for the line by Courtney & Stephens were at Bray, the interlocking and the North cabin being completed in 1876 and the South cabin in 1879. Meanwhile, in June 1878, tenders were sought for interlocking at Harcourt Street. In this case, Stevens & Sons of London were awarded the contract for £350, it being one of only two signalling installations supplied by them to the company, the other probably being at Wicklow Junction in 1877.

The first recorded installation of Annett's Patent Locking Apparatus for siding points on the main line was for the Stone Siding at Bray Head as a result of Major General Hutchinson's inquiry into the accident on 19th April 1878 at that location. Following the closure of the siding this particular Annett's lock was moved to Ballinglen in 1882 for the new siding there.

In 1881 the company decided to install interlocking signals at Westland Row, Carlisle Pier, Glenageary, Sandycove, Enniscorthy and Arklow. Having ceased to deal with Courtney & Stephens for major new installations, they sought tenders from Saxby & Farmer, Stevens & Sons, McKenzie & Holland and the Gloucester Wagon Company. In March of that year McKenzie & Holland were awarded a contract for Westland Row only.

This was to be the beginning of a long standing relationship between the railway and the Worcester company for the supply of signals, interlocking lever frames and sympathetic level crossing gates. These were gates which were operated by a wheel in the signal cabin, the four sections opening and closing in sympathy with each other, and which were interlocked with the signals. In regard to level crossings the first sympathetic gates were installed at Merrion in 1881, and later in the same year at Lansdowne Road.

Following the derailment of a locomotive and train at Kingstown on 19th July 1883, interlocking was extended to cover the No 2 points there. As the result of a serious collision at Blackrock on 9th April 1884 the main signal standing in the centre of the platform was replaced by one signal at each end of the platform. This latter accident also led the board to consider extending the block system from Blackrock to Kingstown, but it was not until 1888 that it was introduced when the necessary levers and cabins were provided at Blackrock and Salthill.

Meanwhile, in September 1886, a contract for signalling on the New Ross extension, including the Barrow viaduct, was awarded to McKenzie & Holland. This also involved improvements in the signalling arrangements at Macmine Junction. In the same year a signal cabin was erected at Dundrum and in 1888 they provided the interlocking at Foxrock, Greystones, Newcastle, Rathdrum and Enniscorthy and they completely replaced the Courtney & Stephens equipment at Woodenbridge Junction.

Following the BoT inquiry into the Armagh accident, the Regulation of Railways Act, 1889 called for the use of continuous automatic brakes, block working and interlocking.

Considerable debate took place between the railway companies and the BoT because of the cost involved in implementing such measures. Having agreed on what was necessary to meet the BoT requirements the DW&WR decided to raise £21,000 capital by the issue of debenture stock, for the purpose of carrying out the work.

In November 1890, 28 Harper's Block Instruments were ordered for the 17 signal cabins on the double line sections – one instrument each for the six cabins at the ends of double line sections and two instruments for each of the eleven intermediate cabins. This replaced the Tyer equipment in use between Westland Row and Kingstown, and with its installation absolute block working was introduced.

In February 1891 arrangements were ordered to be made at once with McKenzie & Holland for interlocking at Gorey and Carlisle Pier and in the following month their tender was approved for these two stations together with Shankill, Ovoca, Arklow, Ferns, Killurin, Aughrim, Tinahely, and Shillelagh. The installation at Gorey appears to have been the first to be completed in 1891, although not approved by the BoT until later. Carlisle Pier was inspected by the BoT in March 1892, the nine other installations listed along with Glenealy being approved in April of the following year. The signal cabins at Arklow, Gorey and Ferns were mounted at the top of the footbridge steps in the same manner as those at Wicklow and Rathdrum.

A tender for interlocking at Tara Street was sought in June 1891, and ground was obtained from Mr Henshaw for the cabin at Milltown. Following the BoT inquiry into an accident at Leopardstown level crossing on the 3rd August 1891, and considerable correspondence with the BoT as to whether the level crossing should be replaced by an overbridge, it was agreed that the gates should be interlocked with the signals. In July 1892 the company ordered the same arrangements for Tulla, Serpentine Avenue and Dunleary level crossings. A new signal box was provided in conjunction with the interlocking arrangements at Dunleary in 1893, but it was not until 1910, when 'sympathetic' interlocking gates and signals were provided, that a proper signal box was built at Serpentine Avenue.

In November 1891 a contract was entered into with the Railway Signal Company of Fazakerley, Liverpool, for the supply of Webb & Thompson Electric Train Staff instruments for Bray South and Greystones and for the main line to Wexford and the Shillelagh branch, a total of 32 instruments being provided at a cost of £1,258.10s for the 18 signal cabins concerned. However, it was not until 1894 that the Bray and Killiney section was equipped with Webb & Thompson ETS instruments and 1895 that the four instruments required for the New Ross line were obtained.

Telephone communication between the signal cabins from Greystones to Wooden-

bridge was completed in 1895 and approval was given for the extension of this to Wexford and New Ross. In the meantime a new signal cabin and frame had been provided by McKenzie & Holland at Grand Canal Street in 1894 and they completed a new cabin at Kingstown North in the following year. They also provided the replacement signal cabin and frame for Dalkey in 1896 and a new 15-lever frame for the existing Greystones cabin in 1898.

The signal cabin at Foxrock was blown down in a storm on the 22nd December 1894 and the signalman who was in it at the time was injured. The cabin had to be replaced at a cost of £200. On 17th January 1897 the signal cabin at Shillelagh was burnt to the ground. The signalman, John Ward, who went on duty at 20.00 on the 16th apparently left the cabin at 03.00, five hours early, after which the fire started. The signalman was dismissed, and the rebuilt cabin brought into use on the 20th February.

Following the Harcourt Street accident of 1900 the white lights which signals had shown for 'All Clear' at night, were changed to green. Also in 1900, a signal cabin with block instruments was provided at Sandycove while Tara Street was made a block station in 1901. With the extension of the New Ross branch to Waterford, the signalling at Macmine Junction was extended and McKenzie & Holland's tender for adding 11 new levers to the existing 20 lever frame was accepted in September 1904.

Above left: **A southbound local train, hauled by a 2-2-2WT, passes the engine shed at Grand Canal Street. Access to the McKenzie & Holland signal cabin was gained from the footbridge, which provided a safe walking route between the engine shed and the workshops on the opposite side of the line.** H Fayle - IRRS collection

Above right: **Ballymanus level crossing, showing the early style of hand-operated gates with semaphores attached. This crossing was located at the site of Glenealy's first station, which was open from 1861-66, when it was replaced by a new station, ¾ mile nearer to Rathdrum.** IRRS collection

Left: **Dalkey station with the original 1871 signal cabin on the footbridge. This cabin with its Courtney & Stephens lever frame was replaced in 1896 by a new McKenzie & Holland cabin which was in turn rebuilt following extensive damage in 1922.** IRRS collection

Right: **2-4-2T No 46 *Princess Mary*, is just out of works following reconstruction from a 2-4-0T. In pristine condition it is standing in front of the McKenzie & Holland Kingstown North signal cabin in preparation to act as pilot for the Royal train of the 4th July 1911.** Sean Kennedy collection

The construction of the D&NDLR required modifications to the signalling arrangements at Amiens Street. A new cabin with a 40-lever McKenzie & Holland frame was commissioned in June 1906 and additional levers were installed at Amiens Street (Central). The block instruments were moved from Milltown to Ranelagh in November 1906, but the cabin at Milltown remained operational, albeit not as a block post, for some years. In fact it was not until 1936 that the building itself was demolished.

The semaphore station signals at Carrickmines, Seapoint and Glenageary, worked from ground frames, were removed with BoT approval in 1913, the 4-lever frame from Carrickmines being moved to Edermine in 1919. This addition to the existing 3-lever ground frame was rendered necessary by the need to interlock the level crossing gates and signals at that location following a fatal accident to the Stationmaster there on 7th December 1918.

Considerable signalling alterations were required for the Killiney diversion in 1915. In addition to a new 20-lever signal cabin at Shanganagh Junction a new frame was installed at Killiney signal cabin and alterations were made in the arrangements at Bray North, all work being entrusted to McKenzie & Holland. The new cabin at the junction was brought into use on 10th October 1915, and three cottages at Shanganagh were rented from Sir Stanley Cochrane for the signalmen required to work this new cabin.

Although additional levers had been installed in the Bray North cabin in 1915, the report of Colonel von Donop's inspection carried out in November of that year directed the company to provide additional signalling and interlocking. Shannon's report on 24th February 1916 of the need for an extra signal arm on the north down home signal, and a slight collision between engines 31 and 58 at the north end of the station on 21st February 1916 highlighting the need for the alteration of disc signals, all pointed to the fact that the work had not been carried out. In November 1917 the General Manager again requested that the work at Bray required by the BoT be undertaken, but it was not until September 1919 that the five new levers required were added to the frame.

The signal cabins at Glenealy, Enniscorthy, Macmine Junction, Sandycove, Dalkey,

Killiney, and Serpentine Avenue had to be rebuilt as a result of damage suffered during the Civil War and those damaged at Foxrock, Newcastle, Palace East and Blackrock were replaced by new enlarged cabins in 1923-24. At Foxrock and Palace East lever frames were supplied by Westinghouse Brake and Saxby Signal Company which had been formed by the amalgamation of Saxby & Farmer and McKenzie & Holland with Westinghouse in 1920.

Two other signal cabins require mention, both being jointly worked with other companies. At Amiens Street Central the GNR(I) signal cabin was enlarged in 1906 to control the modified layout at the north end of the junction station resulting from the connection with the D&NDLR line. The cabin contained 96 levers, of which 63 were for the south-eastern side. This cabin was maliciously destroyed on 26th April 1923 and had to be replaced; the new cabin containing 122 levers of which 48 controlled D&SER tracks. A similar arrangement existed at Abbey Junction, Waterford, where the D&SER quota was 4 of the 32 levers in the GS&WR cabin. This cabin was also destroyed in 1923 and the D&SER and GS&WR lines were worked as two single tracks into Waterford until the construction of a new cabin in 1931.

Following the formation of the GSR many changes took places with the signalling on the South Eastern section. In 1926 a new 48-lever cabin was constructed at Dun Laoghaire to replace the old North and South cabins, and at Greystones an 18-lever Railway Signal Company frame was installed in another new cabin. The major reconstruction of Bray in 1927 included the provision of a new 62-lever cabin to replace the two former cabins, and in August of the same

year the singling of the Newcastle to Wicklow section saw the closure of Wicklow Junction cabin and the installation of a 22-lever frame in the cabin at the main line station. Track and signalling alterations were carried out at Foxrock in 1928 and at Shankill in 1934, in both cases allowing for the departure of up trains from the down platforms.

Electric colour light signals of the searchlight type were installed at Amiens Street (1934) and Westland Row (1936), new cabins with electro-mechanical frames being provided at the same time. The line from Lansdowne Road to Dunleary crossing was equipped with three aspect colour light signals in 1937, new signal cabins being constructed at Sandymount and Dunleary crossing at the same time. The section from Merrion to Dunleary was track circuited throughout and worked as an automatic block section. In February 1938 the old Stevens cabin at Harcourt Street was replaced by a new one with an electro-mechanical frame and at the same time track circuiting was provided to the new colour light advanced starter and outer home signals near Ranelagh.

In conjunction with the introduction of the DART system all of the signalling on the Amiens Street (Connolly) to Bray section was renewed in 1983-84 with continuous track circuiting and centralised train control based at Connolly, the old signal cabins being dispensed with.

Chapter Fifteen

PERSONNEL

WITH THE LINE almost ready for opening to Bray, a number of staff appointments were made in June 1854. On 6th June, Mortimer Harris was appointed Superintendent of Traffic at £250 per annum plus residence and Frederick Pemberton as Superintendent of Locomotives and Carriages, also at £250 but without a residence. Three Stationmasters were appointed, Robert Alcock to Harcourt Road at £100, Joseph Kennedy to Bray at £80 plus residence or an allowance in lieu, and John Upton to Dalkey at £50. Three weeks later Stationmasters were appointed at Dundrum, Stillorgan, Carrickmines, Shankill and Killiney at either £50 plus residence or £60.

Hardly had the line been opened but the Bray Stationmaster made a complaint against a porter there. This latter gentleman handed in his resignation which was accepted. In September there was a complaint of insubordination against another porter at Bray and he was dismissed. A saga which ran for almost three years also involved Bray station and first came to light in May 1856 when Harris was instructed to convey to the Stationmaster the censure of the board in connection with irregularities in his accounts. Arising out of this, Edward Badham, who had been appointed Secretary's clerk in June 1854, was ordered to visit stations occasionally for the purpose of testing the accuracy of the accounts. At the same board meeting, the Stillorgan Stationmaster was also censured, 'very strongly on the account of his neglect of duty complained of by Mr. Harris'. He was dismissed in June and granted a gratuity of £10 in consideration of his large family but from this was deducted the amount due by him to the company.

In the following October, Badham on one of his routine audits found further irregularities in the Bray station accounts. The board agreed that the Station Master Edward Carey should be admonished, 'but under the circumstances he should have a further trial period provided he pays the balance due from him'. What the circumstances were is not known unless it was his health as a further report at the end of November brought to light more irregularities. It was stated that Carey had not handed over the amount due but that he was absent on ill health. The directors appeared to be remarkably lenient towards Carey but when the accounts were audited again in February 1859, Carey was informed that any further discrepancies would bring about his dismissal. This is what happened in June 1859. His name was mentioned in another context in September 1858 as the result of his assault on a Mr Bolton at Bray. The directors were of opinion that they could not safely defend the case and suggested to Carey that he should settle himself with Bolton.

While these various events were unfolding at Bray, Robert Alcock approached the board in March 1856 seeking an additional £20 in his salary. Harris supported this application and confirmed Alcock's high character. Bearing in mind the additional duties and responsibilities which he would be expected to take on when goods traffic commenced operating from Harcourt Road, the board agreed to increase his salary to £120 as from 1st April. In October, Haughton was given responsibility as Locomotive Superintendent for both the Kingstown and Wicklow lines. Previous to this, in addition to being in charge of the D&KR locomotives after Pemberton's resignation in September 1856 on his appointment to the position of Locomotive Superintendent of the St Petersburg & Moscow Railway, he had been Superintendent of Stations and Traffic. Pim, who had been in charge of Locomotive and other works at Bray since October, resigned in February 1857 on his appointment as Locomotive Superintendent of the W&LR.

Also in February, it was reported that casks of beer were being tapped at Harcourt Road, the porter in charge being dismissed, while in December a driver was found in an intoxicated state on the platform at Harcourt Road and was, 'permitted to hand in his resignation'. The DW&WR appear to have transferred Stationmasters around for misdemeanours, as for example in July 1860, the Stationmaster at Dundrum was ordered to move to Ballybrack, the incumbent at the latter station moving to Dundrum. In this instance there was no difference in salary but there had recently been an accident at Dundrum and perhaps it was felt that discipline was lax there.

Other Stationmasters spent long periods in the one location. John Tozier was Station Master in Bray by August 1862 and remained there until he retired in March 1884, at which time he was granted a pension of £8.6s.8d per month. In August 1862 Tozier attended the board and reported on a dispute between two ticket takers at Shanganagh Junction. It was decided that the men should be separated and preferably both removed from the junction. When Tozier approached the board in June 1870 asking to be allowed to undertake the collection and delivery of parcels at Bray as a means of adding to his income, it was ordered that his pay be increased from £90 to £100 and he be informed that the company would not allow him to undertake any business outside that of his immediate position as a Stationmaster. Only a month before this, the Stationmaster at Booterstown had informed the board that he had become a cab proprietor. He was given a month to dispose of his car and licence. At about the same time it came to notice that the sister of the Stationmaster at Salthill, who resided with him there, had obtained a licence and become the proprietor of a cab. On this occasion the board decided not to intervene. When the company sought an assistant to the Traffic Manager in May 1873, Tozier applied for the position, but was informed that the vacancy had already been filled. On his retirement, he was replaced at Bray by Richard Ryan, who had been Stationmaster at Harcourt Street.

Some other amusing incidents came to light about this time. It was ordered that a guard on the Kingstown line be dismissed for insolence to the Assistant Stationmaster at Kingstown and subsequently to Payne, the Traffic Manager since Harris's resignation in September 1862, and finally for his conduct in the boardroom when called upon to answer the complaints against him. A report was received in September 1870 from the Booterstown Stationmaster regarding the arrest of a young boy for striking the driver of a train with a missile from the footbridge at Williamstown. It was ordered that the boy be summonsed but the summons was quickly dropped after it had come to light that the driver in question had thrown a lump of coal at the boy's kite. The Stationmaster at Carrickmines found himself before the board in October in connection with his neglect to return the amount paid for the carriage of a bag of apples to Wicklow. Unfortunately for him the apples never reached their destination, and he was ordered to pay the value of them. To add to his problem, the apples belonged to Mr Pim, who was a director at the time.

Following on the explosion of locomotive No 4's boiler at Bray in September 1872, it was decided to fit all of the company's engines with Ramsbottom safety valves which would prevent tampering by drivers. In the meantime, strict instructions were issued that drivers were not to increase the pressure on their engines by holding down safety valves. Only two months later, the locomotive foreman at Bray reported a driver for doing just that but a counter complaint was made against the foreman for being under the influence of drink. He was allowed to hand in his resignation, the driver being severely reprimanded and cautioned for, on his own admission, working his engine at too high a pressure. Within four months, he had started a train from Kingstown in the face of an incoming train for which he was dismissed. Another somewhat amusing incident was reported in July 1869 when a driver on the Shillelagh line and each of his three sons, who were in the employment of the company, were fined a week's pay for neglect of duty in the late starting of the early morning train from Shillelagh. They were informed that, 'any future neglect of the kind will be visited with dismissal'. It is not clear why all four men were targeted unless of course they comprised the entire crew of the train and also the steamraiser at Shillelagh. The Shillelagh branch was in the news again in October 1875 when a driver was fined 10s for running too fast. It was reported that only for his presence of mind when the leading wheels of his engine left the rails, his punishment would have been greater.

When a Stationmaster was moved, it generally created a ripple effect through the system. When the Dundrum Stationmaster was demoted to Ferns in November 1869, the senior booking clerk at Harcourt Street was appointed to take his place and he was replaced by the man in charge of the mineral tramway at Ovoca whose Stationmaster was then given the duties performed by the tramway man in return for a salary increase of £10 per annum. A ticket collector at Westland Row who was reported as being absent from his work, deputing his colleagues to stand in for him, was treated leniently by the Board. He was informed that he could not expect such behaviour to have the board's sanction, but if he was willing to devote his entire time to the business of the company, he would be appointed head ticket collector at Westland Row at wages of at least 25s per week. He was given time to consider the proposal and communicate his decision to Payne. As no further mention is made of the matter in the board minutes we can only assume that he decided to accept the board's generous offer.

In July 1870, a director complained of several irregularities regarding the use of the train staff and ticket and also of persons travelling on engines. It was ordered that employees be advised that strict adherence to the rules as laid down were expected. Also in July, a signalman at Westland Row was replaced for having on three occasions turned trains on to the wrong road. Three months later, a driver was fined £5 for starting the last up train from Kingstown against signals. The pointsman, who was asleep and neglected to turn the points on the same occasion, was dismissed.

The Stationmaster at Greystones was in trouble in December 1871, being threatened with removal to Carrickmines. A number of letters from local residents and the Greystones post master were sent to the board seeking his retention there. It was agreed that he should remain at Greystones, 'for the present', but later references in the board minutes show him at Carrickmines. When he retired in 1895, he petitioned the board for an addition to his meagre pension as he still had young children, and it was agreed that he be granted an additional 2s.6d per week for two years. This addition was extended for 12 months from December 1900, but was withdrawn in January 1902.

In July 1903, it was reported that a member of the Westland Row permanent way gang had been sent home until breakfast time as he was found, 'to be loitering his time away about 7am'. The individual in question stayed away from work for two weeks, turning up on pay-day to be informed that he was not wanted any more.

A Mr T Whiston came to the attention of Shannon in April 1904, apparently following an accident at work. Whilst off work following this accident, it appears that he was discovered to be working with his father painting railings on the Esplanade at Bray. Whilst entitled to half-pay allowance following his accident, he was believed to have been engaged in this painting job prior to his accident. He had a suit of oil clothes belonging to the company which he refused to return. Three months later, the suit had not been returned and he was informed that he would be prosecuted if he did not return it. This threat appears to have had the desired effect.

A complaint of a different kind came from a Miss Magan at Shanganagh in October 1904, when she reported that a ganger and a milesman had admitted trespass on her land by their poultry, but they stated that they were unaware that they or their fowl were doing any wrong.

Another incident worthy of mention concerned a ganger at Seapoint in April 1906. At that time, the company's practice to close the approach paths and roads to stations on one day each year to preserve their rights. During the course of carrying out this duty, the ganger was approached by a 'gentleman' who insulted him and tried to throw him to the ground. The gentleman in question then jumped over the wire which was across the path and refused to give his name and address. Another case of trespass on the railway itself occurred at Kilcool when two German brothers were apprehended and prosecuted at Bray court, each being fined 5s with costs. In this instance, the two brothers, who had a poor command of the English language, had previously been summonsed for shooting duck and had almost shot the Kilcool Stationmaster; the record does not state whether this was accidental or deliberate.

Hours of Work, Wages and Uniforms

There are few references in the board minutes to working hours. In November 1871, on Wakefield's recommendation, the Factory at Grand Canal Street went on a 54 hour, six-day week. At the same time, the hours in the Permanent Way Department were altered. Between 1st February and 1st November the men were to work from 06.00 to 18.00, with an hour allowed for breakfast and dinner, and for the remaining months, 06.45 to 17.15, with ¾ hour break, or if the majority of the men preferred, from 07.00 to 17.00 with one hour stopped for dinner. During the winter months, the pay of men in the Permanent Way Department was reduced by 1s.3d per week to reflect the shorter hours worked. Some gangers availed of company cottages. In February 1904, there were five such between Dundrum and Shanganagh, one paying 9d per week, the remaining four 1s.

In January 1876, it was ordered that three additional guards be appointed on the Kingstown line so as to reduce the hours of duty of the existing guards and provide Sunday relief. The BoT made the first of a number of enquiries regarding the working hours of staff in August 1890, following a collision at Westland Row the month before. Wakefield was ordered to report and put forward a plan for reducing the long hours of work of drivers and firemen. A month later, Wakefield reported on a scheme which would reduce the hours of work of the footplate crews, but would cost the company £640 per annum. This was ordered to be put into effect.

As the result of the accident at Ovoca some five years later, the BoT once again called attention to the long hours being worked by crews and requested detailed returns of booking-on times and actual hours worked by drivers, firemen and guards on each day during the two weeks ending 17th August 1895. Although the list was sent to the BoT, there is no further reference to this

correspondence in the board minutes. Again in March 1904, the BoT saw reason to draw the board's attention to the hours worked by the crews of the down day goods for the six days ended 16th January. The hope was expressed that steps would be taken to effect a reduction in the period of duty of the men in question.

Yet again, the BoT wrote in December 1907, on this occasion resulting from representations made to them regarding the hours worked by certain of the company's signalmen. A return of hours worked in all signal cabins from Wicklow to Dalkey was requested and in due course sent to the BoT. It is clear from a reference to letter books kept by Head Inspector George Archer at Bray that long hours were a problem as regards the ballast train crews. Frequent correspondence passed between Archer and Shannon in this regard. As an example, he referred in September 1907 to a ballast train having left Bray at 04.00 with rails for relaying at milepost 89. Delays were encountered at a number of places, the engine eventually arriving back in Bray at 21.00. The one crew was on duty throughout this time.

Following on the announcement by the IREC of the introduction of the eight-hour day, coupled with increases in salaries and wages at the beginning of 1919, a special Economies Committee was set up to consider how best the company could effect savings. It was recommended that at stations like Wexford, Enniscorthy and New Ross, where booking clerks had long spells of inactivity between trains, they should be employed in goods stores. This suggestion was approved. It was considered that certain categories of staff could not be included in the eight-hour day, these included Station-

masters, goods agents, locomotive foremen and District Inspectors. Likewise, it would be impossible to include crossing keepers. It appeared to Maguire that a considerable increase in staffing levels was inevitable. Other measures were also considered – the closing of some signal cabins, the running of the Shillelagh branch goods services by day rather than at night, which might bring about a reduction of four or five men.

A proposal for 24 additional men in the Permanent Way Department was agreed, this included two additional flagmen at Bray Head. On top of these, the Traffic Department required 81 men and the Locomotive Department 54, making a total of 159. Regarding the Factory, the hours of work were to remain at 08.00 to 17.15, with ¾ hour for dinner on Mondays to Fridays and 08.00 to 12.30 on Saturdays, making a total of 47 hours. At the time, five minutes grace was allowed in the mornings, after which the gate was closed and those arriving late lost a whole day's pay. In lieu of this arrangement, it was agreed to give ½ hour grace and where this was availed of, to deduct half a day's pay.

Over the years, a number of strikes occurred, some of a local nature, others having wider implications. At Arklow in September 1915, three members of the staff ceased work on account of not having received

2s.6d lodging money, an allowance which under the exceptional circumstances then prevailing in Arklow, had been granted to new porters in order to assist them in obtaining suitable lodgings. Coghlan recommended that the men, who were under suspension, be severely reprimanded and removed to other stations, and that men to be appointed to the vacancies at Arklow be granted the lodging allowance.

About the same time a strike of labourers occurred at the Factory. When this dispute was settled, bonuses were granted to certain members of staff who had loyally and energetically exerted themselves in carrying out the work of the company. Bonuses varied from £3 to £10, the latter to one of the Locomotive Inspectors.

When a carpenter employed at Ovoca died in December 1904, it was reported that he left a wife and seven children, with another expected within days. The only son capable of earning anything was aged 17. The deceased man had joined the company in 1877. It is not clear whether his widow was offered any assistance. When William Toole from Bray died in March 1905, his wife was given an amount of £2. Two permanent way men were killed in March 1914 whilst on duty. In moving aside to allow the up Wexford train to pass them near milepost 10½, they were knocked down and killed by the 10.15 down from Harcourt Street. In this instance, the company paid for the purchase of coffins.

The early uniforms were apparently green as it was resolved in May 1856 that police, guards and ticket collectors were in future to be dressed in blue instead of green. In December 1869, one of the directors, a Dr Waller, advised that he intended to bring before the board the propriety of every officer and servant of the company wearing a badge or other mark of distinction, but only a week later he withdrew the notice. In November 1882, Wakefield asked the board for permission to order coats for the enginemen. It must be remembered that engine cabs were primitive in the extreme and a trip on the goods from Bray to Wicklow on a stormy winter's night must have been exceptionally unpleasant. Also at that time, it was frequently necessary for footplate staff to leave their cabs to oil the motion while engines were on the move. Tenders were duly submitted for 61 enginemen's coats at £1.8s.6d each, 41 frieze coats at £1.4s.9d each, three moleskin suits at £1.0s.9d each and one cord suit, also at £1.0s.9d. These items were in due course ordered from Messrs Todd, Burns & Co of Dublin. The permanent way staff were provided with oil suits. It would appear that Stationmasters were not provided with uniforms as it was recommended that they be provided only at principal stations, and Coghlan was instructed to draw up a list.

Head Inspector (Permanent Way) Lynch was knocked down by a train leaving Bray on the morning of 29th December 1898. At the time, Lynch apparently stepped out of the way of a train departing for Westland Row, not realising that an engine was shunting a carriage parallel to it. Lynch was replaced by George Archer, who came from the L&NWR. Archer has left us an albeit incomplete set of letter books, which provide us with a good deal of information on events as they happened on the ground during the period March 1901 to December 1915. In particular, references are made to the proposed retirement of some of the elderly staff in the department. In January 1904, Archer wrote to Shannon regarding the case of Edward Kennedy, a labourer at Bray Yard. He was 78 years of age and had been in the employ of the company for more than 30 years. He was described as a total abstainer of good character, who had never married, but lived with his mother and three sisters, the last of whom had died some years previously. He was now in poor health, having been off work for the previous nine weeks, and not being a member of the Friendly Society, had nothing to keep him except a few shillings subscribed by his fellow workmen. Further correspondence in May 1906 listed a number of men whom Archer proposed should be pensioned. This included two men of 80 years of age and another of 74. One of the former claimed that he considered himself to be only 70. This throws an interesting light on birth records of the time. Yet another man of only 64, and who worked in the Rathdrum gang, although unfit for work in Archer's estimation, did not wish to be pensioned off as he had a wife ten years his junior and two teenage children.

The board received a letter from a member of the public in September 1901 to the effect that the permanent way gang at Newcastle were playing pitch and toss during working hours, and that four of the gang were drinking in Newcastle village between 09.00 and 10.00 on a specified date. Archer was instructed to investigate and his report comments that the correspondent was probably unaware that the gang, who were engaged in coast defence works, had at times to work according to the tides. He also pointed out that there was a ganger in charge, a timekeeper visited them once or twice daily and the local inspector visited them at least once a week. At no stage was there any hint that the men were idling their time away. As regards the drinking charge, on the date in question, the men had gone by train at 07.30 to Rathnew and did not return until 18.00. An amusing incident is related in January 1911 involving gang No 56E, who were ballasting near Woodbrook platform. On going to dinner, it appeared that the ganger's tea had been brewed in the wrong can. He commenced swearing at one of his colleagues, who told him to stop swearing and get his tea as all the cans were alike. The argument apparently escalated and a can of hot tea was thrown, badly scalding one of the participants on the neck, who then commenced to throw stones at his assailant. In connection with the workmen employed on the Bray Head diversion works, it was arranged in December 1915 that the 17.15 from Westland Row and the 18.10 from Greystones should stop at the new tunnel works to set down and pick up workmen. It was stressed that great care would be necessary to ensure that no passengers alighted from these trains.

With all the arrangements made for amalgamation into the GSR, a deputation from the staff attended the board meeting on 29th December 1924 to thank the directors for their past kindnesses, but pointing out that they were uneasy about their future position. They were informed that the board had received assurances in writing from the directors of the other amalgamating companies that the position of the D&SER staff would be carefully considered.

A composite of an original two-page notice issued by George Wild's office, giving details of the wages and hours of the various grades in the Locomotive Department. These conditions were introduced in 1919, following the imposition by the Irish Railways Executive Committee of the eight-hour working day. W E Shepherd collection

Top: **2-4-0WT No 41 of 1883 is seen, with employees, at Carlisle Pier, in its original condition prior to rebuilding with full side tanks in 1903.** H Fayle - IRRS collection)

Left: **A locomotive crew pose on the footplate of a Belpaire-boilered 4-4-0 at Harcourt Street.** IRRS collection

Bottom left: **The aftermath of the malicious triple collision and burning of trains at Macmine Junction on 23rd January 1923.** K A Murray - IRRS collection

Below: **The driver and several other members of staff pose with 2-4-0T Type 2 No 3, seen here in its post-1884 rebuilt state, at an unknown location. One of the first locomotives supplied to the Dublin & Wicklow for the opening of services in 1854, it was delivered from Fairbairn's of Manchester as a 2-4-0 tender locomotive.** K A Murray - IRRS collection

Chapter Sixteen

HOTELS, CATERING AND OTHER SERVICES

DESPITE running through the counties of Wicklow and Wexford, so famous for their scenery, the company did not become deeply involved in the tourist trade as far as hotels were concerned. Only two hotels were owned by the company and one of these was purchased for the purpose of obtaining additional land in connection with the proposed construction of a second platform at Bray station. As part of the extension of the line from Kilcommon to Rathdrum, the company awarded a contract to a Mr Cockburn for the construction of a hotel adjoining Rathdrum station at a cost of £3,400. The Royal Fitzwilliam opened for business on 26th October 1863, with the Misses Breslin in charge, presumably on behalf of Edward Breslin of Bray, who was involved in the provision of catering there. Following an inspection of the hotel by Smith in April 1872, it was ordered that the Breslins should be requested to give up possession after which the amount to be spent on restoration would be considered. The matter appears to have dragged on through the year, Breslin asking the company in the following November to take the blinds and fittings off his hands at a valuation to be agreed. He also requested that the hotel be advertised without his furniture being removed in order that any incoming tenant might have an opportunity of arranging for its purchase.

Offers were received in February 1873 for the tenancy of the hotel, William P Cunningham of Ovoca being the successful contender. As part of the agreement, Cunningham was obliged to maintain the land at the rear of the hotel as a pleasure ground for the use of visitors. For this he was to be paid £60 per annum. Seven months later, Breslin was ordered to remove his furniture. Cunningham's tenure was short as further proposals to rent the hotel were before the board in April 1874, the Secretary being requested to see a Mr John Wynne and arrange to give him the hotel on the best terms he could, but at not less than £50 per annum. Arrangements were made for a licence to be obtained in the company's name. Wynne agreed to take the lease of the hotel for five years. When he approached the board in May 1879, Wynne was granted a renewal of the lease to 1st May 1880, 'at the present

rent in consideration of the depressed state of business, but that he must be prepared after that date to pay an increased rent'. In October 1880, Wynne wrote offering to pay £70 per annum as the £100 requested by the board was more than the concern could afford to pay. It was therefore agreed to let him have a further year's lease at £70. Wynne in fact remained on as tenant of the hotel until the end of 1895 when the company took it back.

Another tenant in the person of a William James Alexander Fox took over the premises for a five year period from 1st July 1896 at a rent of £75 per annum, the tenant paying all taxes. In the following March, Fox requested the provision of additional bedrooms, agreeing to pay an additional 6% on his rent for the estimated outlay of between £200 and £250. When Fox's lease fell due for renewal in 1901, he was offered a ten year lease at a rent of £75 per annum plus one-third of gross receipts over £200 per annum. This latter figure was altered to £250 by agreement. Fox died in 1913 and the contents of the hotel were auctioned in November, the company purchasing curtains, blinds and other fittings at a cost of £18.8s.0d. It was decided in January 1914 to accept a surrender of the lease of the hotel from the representatives of the late Mr Fox on payment of the rent due to the next quarter day.

The hotel remained idle for upwards of twelve months as it was not until April 1915 that mention is made of negotiations being conducted with a Mr and Mrs Barry for letting of what was by then known as the Grand Central Hotel, prior to which it had been named the Railway Hotel. The Barrys offered a four year lease with no rent payable for the first year, £50 in the second, £55 in the third and £60 in the fourth year. The situation was to be reviewed at the end of the fourth year, the company to execute certain repairs and the tenants to pay all rates and taxes, licence duties and the like. These terms were accepted by the company, but within a year Mrs Barry stated that she could not meet the rent of £50 due to, 'the almost entire absence of tourist traffic'. It was ordered that the rent be remitted for the current year, at the close of which her account books were to be presented for inspection by the company and the matter

reconsidered. Once again, it is not quite clear when Mrs Barry vacated the premises, but in September 1919 the General Manager reported that he had interviewed Miss McGuinness, the company's Catering Manageress, and that it had been agreed to grant her the tenancy of the hotel for a five year period. The hotel remained in the ownership of the company and of the GSR, being finally closed in 1931. The building is still in existence although in poor condition. Rumours of its re-opening have been circulated on a number of occasions, but there have been no moves to date in this direction.

The Royal Marine Hotel, adjoining the Dublin end of the station at Bray, was built by Edward Breslin at the suggestion of William Dargan. Apart from his railway building activities, Dargan had taken a close interest in the development of the town of Bray. The coming of the railway combined with the Victorians' interest in the beneficial effects of seawater led to the rapid development of the town. Breslin, who was a friend of Dargan, purchased lands in the region of the station in 1854 and in addition to the hotel, built a terrace of exclusive villas. Dargan was responsible for the construction of the Esplanade at Bray, turning the town into the Brighton of Ireland. He also designed the Turkish Baths which were built in 1857 on the Quinnsborough Road. As a tribute to Dargan, the present Duncairn Terrace was originally named Dargan Terrace.

When it came to the notice of the board in March 1899 that the Royal Marine Hotel was about to be auctioned, it was suggested that the company should purchase the property. The idea was that the grounds adjoining the hotel might be utilised for the construction of a second platform at Bray station. Whilst powers were obtained in the Company's Act of 1900 for such a platform, the enlargement of Bray station had to wait until GSR days. At a special board meeting on 28th April 1899, the directors finally agreed to endeavour to purchase the hotel, putting in a bid of £14,000 which was successful. This purchase was to lead to complaints from shareholders regarding the use of capital for such purposes. The Chairman defended the directors' actions simply by reference to the 'serious detriment suffered in years gone by through the omission to acquire property adjoining stations, the directors (feeling) that they would have been inexcusable if they had not availed themselves of the opportunity offered by the sale of the Breslin estate to secure the power to extend and improve Bray station'.

Possession of the hotel was obtained as from 1st November 1899 and it was closed immediately to permit considerable improvements, although Breslin had agreed to continue to operate the hotel until the close of the tourist season at the end of October for a sum of £375. In October, it was agreed to retain certain of Breslin's staff, namely Miss Lloyd as caretaker, the housemaid, Kate Hand and porter William Sherbert at their present wages of £80 and £12 per annum and 10s weekly respectively. It was also agreed to re-employ William Jackson as gardener at his former wages of £20 per annum with the house Tower Cottage and coal free, as well as Byrne, the coachman at 12s per week. Miss Lloyd was additionally allowed a sum of 30s per week to cover board for herself and the two servants remaining. Communication had been made with Frank Bethell of the Grand Hotel in Malahide requesting him to undertake the working of the hotel on behalf of the company as from 1st January 1900. This he agreed to do but insisted that he be employed to oversee the renovations being carried out. He was employed in this capacity for twelve months from January 1900 at a figure of £200 plus a commission of 10% on net profits after deducting all outgoings, including the Manager's salary, rates, taxes and insurance.

In February 1900, the directors considered tenders for the various works required and accepted that of Messrs Meade at £4,060 for the building work, subject to it being completed by 5th May at the latest. Messrs Maguire & Gatchell successfully tendered for the sanitary work and kitchen fittings in an amount of £1,150 while electrical, painting and decorating work added a further £699. With his 12 month contract coming to a close, the Secretary approached Bethell in December 1900 seeking his views as to continuing to operate the hotel on behalf of the company. He offered to take the hotel and the station refreshment rooms for a sum of £1,000 per annum over and above rates and taxes. Attempts were made to improve on this offer and ultimately he agreed to a sum of £1,000 for the first year, £1,200 for the second year and £1,400 for the third and subsequent years. This was accepted by the board.

In April 1901, Bethell requested permission to alter the name of the hotel to the Marine Station Hotel, a request which was duly granted. Bethell sought to relinquish his tenancy early in 1904 and the hotel was offered to Frederick Koenigs who was at the time operating certain of the company's refreshment rooms. However, Bethell remained on at Bray and was still in charge on 22nd August 1916 when a serious fire occurred. The fire started in the south end of the east wing, completely destroying the roof and the third floor of the building as well as causing substantial damage to the second floor and water damage to the lower floors. The hotel accommodation was quoted as being seven sitting rooms and 44 bedrooms along with a fair garden. Gross receipts from the hotel, the Bray refreshment rooms and the catering cars were given in 1916 as being in excess of £6,500 per annum, although no breakdown is available. Arrangements had already been made about a month prior to the fire for Bethell to relinquish his interest in the various catering activities as from 1st February 1918. The building lay empty until October 1919 when it was advertised for sale. It was reported in February 1920 that a Mr Davis Frame was prepared to make an offer for the purchase of the damaged building but this appears to have fallen through as did a further offer made late in 1924 on behalf of a Mr Luke Brady of Cavan for £2,500 in cash for the company's interest in the property. Thus, the hotel passed into the ownership of the GSR in 1925.

Refreshment Rooms

At different periods the company operated refreshment rooms at various locations throughout the system. Some of these were short-lived as, for example, that at Wicklow which was ordered to be closed in 1858 due to the proprietor, Breslin, having provided alcohol to footplate crews. There also appears to have been a refreshment room at Rathdrum, although it is not clear whether or not this was part of the hotel. In April 1859, reference is made to a resolution to the effect that the rooms at Kingstown station, proposed to be let as refreshment rooms, should be advertised for letting. In the following month it was decided to accept the tender of Richard Polson for one year. Plans for the necessary work were duly submitted to the board and approved at an estimated cost of £500. All does not appear to have been well with the running of the rooms for in the July, the Chairman was instructed to speak to Polson on the management of the rooms, especially that for the third class. Two months later, Polson made application to the directors for a submission to the Kingstown Harbour Commissioners for a licence. It would appear that the Commissioners were not unduly impressed with Polson either as they announced their intention to oppose any request from him. Following further correspondence, it was confirmed that assent would be given to a licence for wine but not for beer or porter, provided it was in the name of the company.

In January 1860 it was decided to convert the third class room back to a waiting room. Six months later, the board agreed to renew Polson's lease at a rate of £100 per annum, payable quarterly. It is not clear what Polson was paying prior to this but he declined to renew the tenancy and requested the directors to forego a half year's rent due on 1st August. This they agreed to do. There is no further mention of Kingstown until October 1874 when a Bernard Murphy offered to rent rooms at Kingstown, Westland Row and Harcourt Street. His offer was declined and we must move on a further 23 years, when on 3rd June 1897, Grierson was ordered to look into the matter of a refreshment room at Kingstown and report to the board. Between then and January 1900, 'certain negotiations', took place with the DB Company (Dublin Bakery Company), leading to a decision to let the rooms to them on the basis of 10% of gross receipts, attendants and goods to be carried free. It was decided not to apply for a licence on this occasion.

Right: **A view of the fire-damaged Marine Station Hotel, taken after the building of the new 62-lever signal cabin in 1927. The sympathetic level crossing gates were operated from the signal cabin by a gate wheel.** K A Murray collection

Above: **Woodenbridge Junction, with the Ovoca River in the background. This appears to be a posed photograph - note the small amount of coal on No 67's tender. In the foreground is the Shillelagh branch face of the up platform upon which is a typical DW&WR signal cabin. Again, milk churns are in evidence, an important source of traffic for the company.**
Sean Kennedy collection

In September 1901, the tenants made application for additional accommodation and it was agreed that the necessary work should be done to render the back room and kitchen suitable in connection with the tea room. The DB Company advised in February 1903 that they would be surrendering their lease when it fell due for renewal on the following 1st October. What happened over the next four years is not clear, but we do know that the refreshment and tea rooms were let to a Mr E McGovern for one year from 1st March 1907 at a rent equivalent to 15% of gross receipts. McGovern's stay was short as a year later, the rooms were let on the same basis to a Miss Annie Timmons. Once again, no further mention is made of the rooms and we do not therefore know how long Miss Timmons remained in residence.

Edward Breslin, mentioned earlier in connection with the hotels at Rathdrum and Bray, was also closely involved with refreshment facilities at Bray. He had undertaken the catering for the directors and distinguished guests on the occasion of the first trial trip to Bray in 1853. A board minute of 20th May 1859 would appear to suggest that the Bray rooms were already open at that time as Breslin made application for certain repairs to be carried out. The Secretary reported in June 1869 that he had spoken to Breslin regarding the rooms at Bray and Woodenbridge, suggesting that Breslin pay an annual rent of £75 for the two. This he declined to do, offering £60 on condition that the company paint and paper the Bray rooms. The offer was accepted as regards

the monetary amount but the company declined to carry out the decoration work. When the directors suggested in December 1879 that the rent was too low, they also made reference to the fact that they were not satisfied with the way in which the rooms were being conducted and requested Breslin to surrender them. This he agreed to do on being paid for the licence and fixtures. This matter dragged on for quite a long period of time, agreement as to the amount to be paid not being reached until October 1884.

On obtaining possession, the directors carried out an inspection and decided on some alterations. The large saloon was to be divided in two so as to give a dining room separate from the bar, while a third class bar was to be opened on to the platform. In addition, a kitchen was to be built and sleeping accommodation provided. The works were duly carried out and in November 1884, it was decided to offer the rooms to Miss Marie Ryan, daughter of the Stationmaster, at £200 per annum, to be paid half yearly in advance. The Secretary was instructed to make full enquiries as to whether the representations made as to her experience and age were correct. She was also asked to produce a tariff of prices for prior approval. When an order was made in October 1886 for the rooms to be closed at 19.00 on Sundays, Miss Ryan requested a reduction in her rent, a request which was refused, although there was a change of heart in June 1887 when it was agreed that the rooms should remain open. Following on the death of her father, Miss Ryan applied

for a reduction in rent in June 1890, and it was reduced to £150. The board heard in 1895 and again in 1898 that summonses had been issued for the serving of drink to non *bona fide* patrons. In 1898 it was decided to increase the rent to £250 per annum and, despite protests from the tenant, this was enforced.

When Miss Ryan again appealed in 1900 for a reduction in her rent due to ill health, she was informed that the company had decided to terminate her agreement. Frank Bethell, who was now running the hotel, took over the rooms and he remained there until 1916. The company took over the Bray refreshment rooms and the buffet attached to the Marine Hotel and carried on the business under the direction of Miss McGuinness, Manageress of the saloons at Westland Row and Harcourt Street. It should be mentioned that a tea stall was erected at Bray early in 1885, but it appears to have been shortlived.

Brief mention has been made of a refreshment room at Woodenbridge. Breslin was in charge initially but he agreed to give it up in

October 1870 when it was decided to convert it into a waiting room. When the new station building was completed in 1876, plans were included for a refreshment room and this was in due course let to a Mrs Liza O'Brien at a rent of £45 per annum, payable in advance. When the company applied for a licence in 1879 this was opposed and the rooms were closed shortly afterwards. An even more short-lived room existed at Macmine Junction around 1897. This room was let to the Stationmaster at a nominal rent, with the necessary furniture being provided by the company.

The two remaining rooms were at Westland Row and Harcourt Street. The latter had been suggested in July 1875, the idea obviously being implanted following Murphy's offer of the previous year, when plans were drawn up for the proposed conversion of the parcels office. Whilst Smith was authorised to carry out the work, it was not done immediately and it was not until the following May that Bolton's tender of £482 was accepted. Work appears to have been expeditiously carried out as tenders for the renting of the rooms were before the Board on 15th June, that of Mrs Margaret Clarke being accepted. Sleeping accommodation was also provided and this was extended in 1877. Difficulties were encountered with undesirables frequenting the establishment and

when orders were given in July 1879 for the early closing of the rooms on Sundays, Mrs Clarke sought a reduction in her rent. She was in due course allowed £20 off. By September 1881, we find a Mrs Margaret O'Brien in charge and it would appear that she encountered the same problems and she was ordered to close at 19.00 on Sundays. When the company increased the rent in 1898 to £250, Mrs O'Brien applied for a reduction, but like her colleague in Bray, she was refused. In an attempt to curb the illegal use being made of the refreshment rooms, the directors requested Mrs O'Brien to use special nippers to ensure that tickets were not being used more than once to gain admittance. She refused to use these, and notice to terminate the agreement was issued. In due course, the rooms were taken over by Frederick Koenigs, who was already in charge of catering at Kingsbridge for the GS&WR. Further infringements of the regulations occurred.

In October 1914, a shareholder by the name of W U Hatte wrote to the company enquiring whether they were aware that the refreshment rooms were being leased to an alien and what steps were proposed to be taken in the matter. On enquiry, it turned out that Koenigs, who was a German, had become naturalised in 1902 and the legal advice was that the company could do noth-

ing to disturb his agreement which was not due to expire until 1916. The rooms in fact reverted to the company in June of that year. Whilst dealing with Harcourt Street, mention should be made of the fact that a tea stall was in operation from September 1880 under the management of Messrs Lepper & Company at an annual rent of £50. By 1898, this was being managed by Cooper, Cooper & Company, while in 1905 a Mr George O'Neill of the Belfast & Oriental Tea Company was operating it. In the following year, it was transferred to a Mr Corrn. A similar stall was opened at Westland Row in 1880, also under the care of Messrs Lepper & Company. A third stall was opened at Bray in 1885, all being discontinued around 1889.

As regards Westland Row, the first reference to an operational refreshment room was in March 1886 when an agreement was entered into with a Mrs Kavanagh at £300 per annum. Prior to this, approaches had been made in 1879 and 1882, the latter from

Below: **Rathdrum Station and Hotel.**
The running lines are hidden behind the wall, the tracks in the foreground being those into the goods yard. The footbridge is the one which collapsed under a crowd of racegoers on 26th April 1873.
W E Shepherd collection

Messrs Mitchell & Company, Wine Merchants of Dublin who are still in business. They offered a rent of £250 per annum, provided the company fitted up the rooms and obtained a wine and spirits licence. Consideration was postponed and the offer later declined. When Mrs Kavanagh complained of the high rent later in the year, it was suggested that she might apply for a spirit licence in her own name. It was ordered in August 1886 that application be made to the October Licensing Sessions for a retail spirit licence, provided the tenant sign an agreement that if the licence be obtained she would pay an extra £50 per annum after the first three years until it reached a maximum of £500 per annum. Mrs Kavanagh complained again in January 1887, requesting that the rent be reduced to £200 per annum from the previous 1st October, pending the obtaining of a spirit licence. It was ordered that a reduction of £100 be made and that a rent of £300 be charged from 1st October 1887. The reduction was only to be made on the understanding that the rooms were better conducted than 'they have hitherto been'.

Mrs Kavanagh apparently vacated the rooms during the next five year period, as reference is made to correspondence from a Miss Smith in July 1892, J C Smith, the Engineer, being requested to ascertain exactly what she required. Grierson was later requested to submit drawings of work proposed to be done, the work to be carried out at a cost not exceeding £75. Only a year later, Miss Smith asked to be released from her tenancy, the board deciding to offer a reduction in the rent, which she declined to accept. In April 1895, Grierson was instructed to draw up plans for a refreshment room at Westland Row. Agreement was reached in November 1896 as to the terms for the leasing of these rooms. Frederick Koenigs was to be appointed Manager for seven years at £50 per year and a share of the profits. On the first £500 gross receipts, the company were to take 25% and 15% thereafter. Light, fuel, hot and cold water were to be supplied by the company, who were also to be responsible for repairs, alterations and fixtures. Koenigs wrote in March 1898 requesting some alterations, Shannon being asked to see whether the room might be increased in size without too much cost. It was July 1899 before it was resolved that the room be extended so as to provide a suitable tea and dining rooms, and it was 10th May 1900 by the time the Secretary reported to the board that the rooms had been opened by Koenigs on 30th April. Koenigs' request to be allowed to relinquish the refreshment rooms in May 1916 has already been referred to under Harcourt Street. There was an additional complication at Westland Row, namely the occupancy of the rooms by the military due to the 1916 Rising. However in June, Koenigs was advised that a Mr Bennett had been appointed to value the fixtures, fittings and stocks of wine and spirits. It was agreed that the company would take over whatever stocks they required and they would retain the services of Miss McMahon, who was Koenigs' Manageress, at a salary of £60 per annum. Her stay was extremely short however, as in the following month she announced she was shortly to be married and requested that she be let go from 1st September. This was agreed to and in August, a Miss E McGuinness was appointed Manageress of the Catering Department at £5 per month. There are no further references to the Westland Row refreshment rooms, which remained open into GSR days.

A letter was received from the Womens' Temperance Association in December 1883 deprecating the sale of intoxicating drinks on railway stations. In a similar vein, the Assistant Secretary of the General Synod of the Church of Ireland wrote in May 1906 to the effect that the sale of strong drinks in railway refreshment rooms on Sundays, 'is mischievous and ought to be discontinued'. Receipt of the letter was simply noted. Further problems with supplying staff with strong drink, led to the board instructing the managers of the refreshment rooms to desist from such a practice.

On Board Catering

With the opening of the extension to Waterford in 1904, the decision was taken to provide catering on the mail trains. Details of the refreshment cars are given in Chapter Twelve and need not therefore be repeated here. The contract for the on-board catering was awarded to Frank Bethell from 1st January 1905, a payment of £15 to be made by him, out of which the company would provide one uniform suit for the attendant. In March 1906, terms were agreed for Bethell to pay 7½% of gross receipts for the year, increasing to 10% for 1907. In March 1907, instructions were given to Bethell that his staff on the up and down day mails were to be informed that liquor was to be served only in the restaurant cars. Complaints were made in April 1909 by Inspector Cushen of the Dublin Metropolitan Police in regard to the sale of drink in trains without a licence. This matter appears to have been amicably resolved. Catering services were discontinued in February 1917 at the request of the IREC as part of the wartime economy measures, but they were resumed some ten months later. As part of the settlement leading up to the transfer to the GSR, it was agreed in November 1924 to grant Miss McGuinness, Manageress of the Catering Department, a bonus of one year's salary, £400 free of tax, as a special recognition of the competent manner in which she had managed the department for the previous eight years. Further reference is made to Miss McGuinness in Chapter Eight.

Book Stalls and Advertising

As early as April 1857, tenders were received for the privilege of placing book stands for the sale of books and newspapers at Harcourt Road, Kingstown and Bray. The tender of W H Smith & Son for the foregoing, to include the free carriage of books and newspapers and a free pass for their Superintendent, a Mr Eason, was accepted. They were agreeable to pay £150 for three years, £200 for five years or £230 for seven years, with an addition of £50 if the bookstall at Westland Row was included. The tender for five years was accepted but the bookstall at Westland Row was let to a Mrs Connell at 10s per week, both agreements to operate from the first Friday in May.

When the agreement with Smiths came up for renewal in 1862, it was renewed for three years. At a later stage, Eason, who had become Manager for W H Smith in Ireland, took over the contract for the bookstalls and we find Messrs Eason & Son asking for a renewal of the agreement in June 1887. This was agreed to for a five year period, subject to them consenting to pay 60% of gross receipts from advertising, which had been included in the contract. They replied to the effect that they could not afford more than 50%, this being agreed to on condition the agreement run for six years.

When Messrs Eason expressed an interest in doing the company's bill posting in July 1897, this was agreed to subject to an allowance of 10% on bookstall receipts, stalls to be erected at Tara Street, Blackrock, Rathdrum and Woodenbridge. The bookstalls remained the preserve of Messrs Eason & Son up to and after the formation of the GSR in January 1925.

The stations at Harcourt Street and Westland Row being situated above the surrounding ground level, the company soon offered the vaults underneath to interested parties. Those at Harcourt Street were let to various tenants, the best known being Messrs W & A Gilbey as bonded warehouses. Complaints were made on a number of occasions regarding the wetness of these vaults. As regards Westland Row, the vaults were let to Sir John Power & Son in 1883. In October 1891, they wrote urging the purchase of a house in Cumberland Street for the purpose of ventilating the bonded stores and offered to subscribe £100 towards the cost. It was ordered that the necessary work be carried out.

At one point, the company was approached by the Dublin Laundry Company, whose premises were adjacent to the viaduct at Milltown, for a letting of the arches under the viaduct. They were given a tenancy for ten years. Various other commercial operations were introduced at the two Dublin termini, as for example a gramophone penny-in-the-slot machine at Harcourt Street, but these were generally short-lived.

Appendix A

CHAIRMEN & PRINCIPAL OFFICERS

CHAIRMEN
1854 Hon Frederick Ponsonby
1855 J Pennefather
1857 William F Darley
1858 Joseph Hone Jnr
1859 Hon George Handcock
1865 William Dargan
1867 Lawrence Waldron
1876 Sir James Power, Bt
1878 William Foot
1885 Sir Richard Martin
1892 Michael Murphy
1895 Lt Col J S Tighe
1897 Frederick W Pim
1917 Rt Hon Frank Brooke
1920 Sir Thomas Esmonde, Bt

SECRETARIES
1845 Richard M Muggeridge
1856 Arthur Moore
1862 E W Maunsell
1895 E M Cowan
1899 M F Keogh
1913 A G Reid
1916 R D Griffith

GENERAL MANAGERS
1900 A G Reid
1918 J Coghlan
1920 M J Maguire

TRAFFIC MANAGERS
1854 Mortimer Harris
1863 William L Payne
1895 D J Stewart
1899 J Coghlan
1919 G McDonald

**LOCOMOTIVE
SUPERINTENDENTS**
1854 Frederick Pemberton
1856 S Wilfred Haughton
1864 William Meikle
1865 John Wakefield
1882 William Wakefield
1894 T B Grierson
1897 Richard Cronin
1917 George H Wild

ENGINEERS

Consulting Engineers
1845 I K Brunel
1856 Barry Gibbons
1856 W R LeFanu
1863 Cotton & Flemyng

Chief Engineers
1875 John Challoner Smith
1895 T B Grierson
1899 Samuel J Shannon
1916 Courtney E Moore

Resident Engineers
1853   Purdon
1856 F Pemberton
1856   Lagan
1862   Talbot
1865 M Murphy
1868 John Challoner Smith

Appendix B

LOCOMOTIVE FACILITIES

Name of Station	Turntable Diameter	Capacity of Running Shed	Coal	Water Columns	Source of Water Supply	Quality of Water	Remarks
Amiens Street	44' 6"	Inspection pit	–	1	Grand Canal Street tank	Very bad, hard	Auxiliary water supply: Vartry
Westland Row	–	Inspection pit	–	1	Grand Canal Street tank	Very bad, hard	Auxiliary water supply: Vartry
Grand Canal Street	17' 4" 21' 4" 24' 0"	186' x 54' 15 engines –	Yes	1	Gravity and pump from canal	Very bad, hard	Locomotive Works
Dun Laoghaire (Carlisle Pier)	17' 3" 23' 4"	Inspection pit	–	4	Gravity	Hard	Auxiliary water supply: Vartry
Harcourt Street	46' 0" –	113' x 32' 4" 6 engines	Yes	2	Pumped from canal	Very bad, hard	Hydraulic buffers at Turntable Auxiliary water supply: Vartry
Carrickmines	–	–	–	2	Gravity	Excellent	
Bray	44' 7"	231' x 31' 16 engines	Yes	4	Pumped from river	Good quality	
Greystones	31' 6"	–	–	–	–	–	
Wicklow	–	–	–	2	Gravity	Fair	
Rathdrum	–	Inspection pit	–	2	Gravity	Fair	Water very dirty in rainy weather
Ovoca	–	–	–	1	Gravity	Good	
Woodenbridge	39' 5"	–	–	–	–	–	
Aughrim		–	–	From tank	Gravity	Excellent	
Shillelagh	41' 9"	88' x 30' 4 engines	–	1	Gravity and hand pump	Excellent	
Gorey	–	–	–	2	Steam pump from well	Good	
Enniscorthy	40' 0"	1 engine	–	2	Steam pump from River	Good	
Macmine Junction	45' 0"	–	–	2	Gravity	Excellent	
Wexford	49' 7"	156' x 43' 10 engines	Yes	1	Gravity	Contaminated by sewage sometimes	Auxiliary supply from town
Palace East	44' 7"	–	–	1	Steam pump from 2 wells	Fair	
Waterford	49' 8"	198' x 47' 12 engines	Yes	1	–	Fair	

Appendix C

LOCOMOTIVES

Type	No	Name	Builder/No	Built	Wdn	GSR No	GSR Cl
I	1	–	F	1854	1891		
	2	–	F	1854	1885		
II	3	–	F	1854 [1]	1898		
III	4	–	F	1855	1872		
	5 [2]	–	F	1855	1900		
IV	6 [3]	–	VF/392	1855	1903		
	7 [4]	–	VF/393	1855	1902		
	10 [5]	–	VF/407	1856	1902		
	11 [6]	–	VF/408	1856	1902		
V	8	–	VF/394	1855	1903		
	9	–	VF/395	1855	1890		
VI	12	–	F	1860	1902		
	13	–	F	1860	1904		
	14 [7]	–	F	1860	Rebuilt as Type VIa in 1907		
VIa	31	Glen of the Downs	GCS	1907	1923		
VII	15 [8]	Barrow	SS/1210	1860	1925		
	16	–	SS/1211	1860	Rebuilt as Type VIIa in 1901		
	37	Slaney	SS/2656	1877	1923		
VIIa	16	Killiney	GCS	1901	1922		
VIII	1(T) [10]	Hercules (?)	?	1861	1878		
	2(T) [10]	Pandora (?)	?	1861	1876		
	3(T) [11]	Hilda (?)	?	1863	1883		
IX	17	–	SS/1482	1864	1899		
	18	–	SS/1481	1864	1910		
	19	–	SS/1483	1864	1925	– [9]	
	20 [12]	–	SS/1490	1864	1925	– [36]	
	21	–	SS/1495	1864	Rebuilt as Type IXa in 1905		
	22	–	SS/1496	1864	1910		
	23	–	SS/1496	1864	1923		
	38	Nore	SS/2654	1877	1925	– [13]	
	39	Suir	SS/2655	1877	1925	– [13]	
	48	–	GCS	1889	1913		
IXa	21	Kilcoole	GCS	1905	1925	– [9]	
X	24	Glenmore	SS/1478	1864 [14]	1928	422	G7
	25	Glenart	SS/1479	1864	1925	– [13]	
	26	–	SS/1480	1864	Rebuilt as Type Xa in 1900		
	32	Glenmalure	SS/2304	1873	1925	– [13]	
	33	Glendalough	SS/2305	1873	1925	– [13]	
Xa	26	Blackrock	GCS	1900	1925	– [13]	
D&Ka	–	Vauxhall	GCS Reb	1840	1867		
	–	Princess	GCS	1841	1883		
	–	Belleisle	GCS	1841	1867		
	–	Shamrock	GCS	1842	1867		
	–	Erin	GCS	1843	1867		
	–	Albert	GCS	1844	1874		
	–	Comet	GCS	1851	1871		
D&Kb	–	Burgoyne	GCS	1845	1873		
	–	Cyclops	GCS	1847	Rebuilt as Type D&Kc in 1869		
	–	Vulcan	GCS	1848	Rebuilt as Type D&Kc in 1870		
	–	Jupiter	GCS	1848	1876		
D&Kc	27	–	GCS	1869	1887		
	28	–	GCS	1870	1887		
XI	–	Ariel	N/1122	1865	1894		
	–	Kelpie	N/1123	1865	1889		
	–	Kate Kearney	N/1124	1865	Rebuilt as Type XIa in 1887		
	–	Banshee	N/1125	1865	1894		
	–	Titania	N/1126	1865	1889		
	–	Oberon	N/1127	1865	1891		
	–	Elfin	N/1144	1865	1892		
XIa	27	–	GCS	1887	1906		
XII	29	–	GCS	1871	1906		
	30	–	GCS	1876	1902		
	31	–	GCS	1873	1905		
	4 [15]	–	GCS	1874	1908		
	36 [16]	–	GCS	1877	1902		
	40 [17]	–	GCS	1880	1905		
XIII	34	–	N/1782	1873	1923		
	35	–	N/1783	1873	1923		
XIV	41	Delgany	GCS	1882	1925	– [9]	
XV	42	Ballybrack	BP/2261	1883	1925	– [13]	
XV	43	Shanganagh	BP/2262	1883	1925	– [13]	
	44	Dunleary	BP/2263	1883	1927	– [13]	
XVI	2	Glenageary	GCS	1885	1925	– [13]	
	45	–	GCS	1886	Rebuilt as Type XXI in 1910		
	28	–	GCS	1887	Rebuilt as Type XXI in 1909		
	46	–	GCS	1888	Rebuilt as Type XXI in 1911		
	47	Stillorgan	GCS	1889	1953	425	G1
	9	Dalkey	GCS	1890	1952	424	G1
	49	Carrickmines	GCS	1891	1955	423	G1
	1	–	GCS	1893	1925	– [13]	–
	6	(Greystones)	GCS	1894	1925	– [13]	–
	7	(Foxrock)	GCS	1895	1926	(426)	G1
	10	–	GCS	1896	Modified to Type XXI in 1903		
	11	–	GCS	1897	Modified to Type XXI in 1900		
XVII	50	Arklow	VF/1310	1891 [18]	1930	447	J7
	51	New Ross	VF/1311	1891 [19]	1925	– [36]	–
XVIII	52	Duke of Connaught	SS/3909	1893	1955	458	C3
	53	Duke of Abercorn	SS/3910	1893	1960	460	C3
	54	Duke of Leinster	SS/3911	1893 [20]	1953	459	C3
XIX	55	Rathdown	VF/1448	1895	1929	450	D9
	56	Rathmines	VF/1449	1895	1934	451	D9
	57	Rathnew	VF/1455	1896	1933	452	D9
	58	Rathdrum	VF/1456	1896 [21]	1940	453	D9
XX	4	–	K/3686	1897	Rebuilt as Type XXa in 1908		
	5	–	K/3687	1897	Rebuilt as Type XXa in 1908		
XXa	4	Lismore	–	1908	1950	448	J1
	5	Clonmel	–	1908	1940	449	J1
XXI	3	St. Patrick	GCS	1898	1953	428	F2
	10	St. Senanus	GCS	1903 [22]	1925	(429)	F2
	11	St. Kevin	GCS	1900 [22]	1952	430	F2
	28	St. Laurence	GCS	1909 [23]	1950	431	F2
	45	St. Kieran	GCS	1910 [23]	1957	432	F2
	46	Princess Mary	GCS	1911 [23]	1957	433	F2
XXII	17	Wicklow	GCS	1899	1929	440	J20
XXIII	36	Wexford	GCS	1901 [24]	1935	441	J14
XXIV	8	St. Brendan	GCS	1903	1950	434	F1
	12	St. Brigid	GCS	1901	1950	435	F1
	40	St. Selskar	GCS	1902	1952	439	F1
XXIVa	27	St. Aidan	GCS	1907	1953	436	F1
	29	St. Mantan	GCS	1906	1951	437	F1
	30	St. Iberius	GCS	1909	1952	438	F1
XXV	59 [25]	Earl of Fitzwilliam	LNW/2856	1885	1917	–	–
	60 [26]	Earl of Courtown	LNW/2683	1883	1916	–	–
	61 [27]	Earl of Wicklow	LNW/2677	1883	1917	–	–
	62 [28]	Earl of Meath	LNW/3604	1895	1916	–	–
	63 [29]	Earl of Carysfort	LNW/2726	1884	1916	–	–
XXVI	64 [30]	Earl of Bessborough	LNW/3605	1896 [31]	1936	427	F3
XXVI	13	Waterford	GCS	1904	1930	442	J8
XXVIa	14	Limerick	GCS	1905	1955	443	J8
XXVIc	18	Enniscorthy	GCS	1910	1957	444	J8
XXVIb	65	Cork	BP/4647	1905	1957	445	J8
	66	Dublin	BP/4648	1905	1957	446	J8
XXVII	67	Rathmore	BP/4645	1905	1949	454	D8
	68	Rathcoole	BP/4646	1905	1925	– [36]	–
XXVIII	69 [32]	–	MW/1692	1906	1931	Elf	M2
	70 [33]	–	MW/1693	1906	1918	Sold to D&BST 1918	
XXIX	20	King George	GCS	1911	1959	455	C2
XXIXa	34	–	BP/6204	1924	1955	456	C2
	35	–	BP/6205	1924	1959	457	C2
XXX	–	Blackburn	MW/1099	1888 [34]	1925	–	–
XXXI	15	–	BP/6112	1922	1965 [35]	461	K2
	16	–	BP/6113	1922	1963	462	K2

KEY

[1] Rebuilt as 2-4-0T in 1884
[2] Renumbered 5A in 1897
[3] Renumbered 6A in 1894
[4] Renumbered 7A in 1895
[5] Renumbered 10A in 1896
[6] Renumbered 11A in 1896
[7] Renumbered 14A in 1905
[8] Rebuilt as 48 in 1922
[9] Ready for scrap in 1924
[10] Ex-Hodgson's Tramway
[11] Ex-Wicklow Copper Ming Coy.
[12] Renumbered 22 in 1911
[13] Passed to GSR and originally to have been numbered in the series 410 to 421, but nominally replaced by the 12 ex-MGWR Woolwich 2-6-0s assembled at Broadstone.
[14] Reconstructed at GCS in 1908
[15] Renumbered 4A in 1897 and 30 in 1902
[16] Renumbered 36A in 1900
[17] Renumbered 40A in 1902
[18] Rebuilt at GCS in 1912
[19] Rebuilt at GCS in 1915
[20] Rebuilt at GCS in 1913
[21] Rebuilt at GCS in 1916
[22] Modified from Type XVI
[23] Rebuilt from Type XVI
[24] Rebuilt at GCS in 1919
[25] Ex L&NWR No2070 in 1902
[26] Ex L&NWR No2502 in 1902
[27] Ex L&NWR No2496 in 1902
[28] Ex L&NWR No842 in 1902
[29] Ex L&NWR No1017 in 1902
[30] Ex L&NWR No2251 in 1902
[31] Rebuilt at GCS in 1914
[32] Ex Railmotor No1 in 1908
[33] Ex Railmotor No2 in 1907
[34] Ex Naylor Bros. in 1916
[35] Preserved by RPSI
[36] Maliciously damaged beyond economic repair in 1923.

LOCOMOTIVE BUILDERS

BP — Beyer Peacock & Co, Gorton, Manchester.
F — William Fairbairn & Sons, Manchester.
GCS — D&KR / DW&WR / D&SER, Grand Canal Street, Dublin.
K — Kitson & Co, Leeds.
LNW — London & North Western Railway, Crewe.
MW — Manning Wardle, Leeds.
N — Neilson & Co, Glasgow.
SS — Sharp Stewart & Co, Glasgow.
VF — Vulcan Foundry, Newton-le-Willows.

NOTE

Numbers and names in parentheses were allocated but never carried.

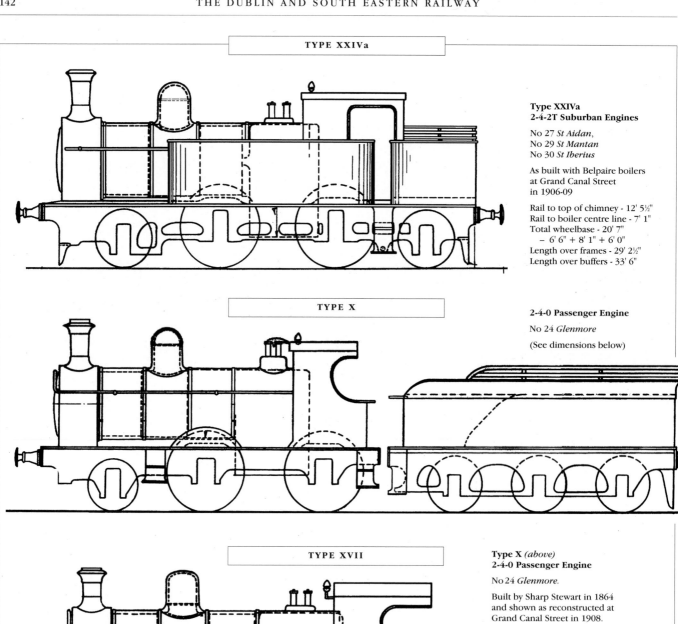

TYPE XXIVa

Type XXIVa
2-4-2T Suburban Engines

No 27 *St Aidan*,
No 29 *St Mantan*
No 30 *St Iberius*

As built with Belpaire boilers
at Grand Canal Street
in 1906-09

Rail to top of chimney - 12' 5½"
Rail to boiler centre line - 7' 1"
Total wheelbase - 20' 7"
   – 6' 6" + 8' 1" + 6' 0"
Length over frames - 29' 2½"
Length over buffers - 33' 6"

TYPE X

2-4-0 Passenger Engine

No 24 *Glenmore*

(See dimensions below)

TYPE XVII

Type X *(above)*
2-4-0 Passenger Engine

No 24 *Glenmore*.

Built by Sharp Stewart in 1864
and shown as reconstructed at
Grand Canal Street in 1908.

Rail to top of chimney - 12' 8"
Rail to boiler centre line - 7' 0"
Engine wheelbase - 6' 5" + 8' 1"
Tender wheelbase - 5' 9" + 5' 9"
Total overall wheelbase - 34' 10½"
Length over engine frames - 23' 0"
Length over tender frames - 19' 6"
Length over buffers - 46' 11"

Type XVII *(left)*
0-6-0 Goods Engine

Nos 50 and 51

Built in 1891
by the Vulcan Foundry
and shown as reconstructed
at Grand Canal Street
with Belpaire boilers.

Rail to top of chimney - 13' 2½"
Rail to boiler centre line - 7' 9"
Engine wheelbase - 7' 3" + 8' 9"
Tender wheelbase - 5' 9" + 5' 9"
Total overall wheelbase - 36' 10¼"
Length over engine frames - 25' 10"
Length over tender frames - 19' 6"
Length over buffers - 49' 9"

Appendix D

PRINCIPAL LOCOMOTIVE DIMENSIONS

Type	Wheels	Cylinders	Driving wheels	Boiler pressure	Heating surface	Grate area	Weight
				(psi)	(sq ft)	(sq ft)	tons/cwt
I	2-2-2WT	13"x18"	5' 0"				
II	2-4-0	13"x18"	5' 6"				
III	2-2-2WT	13"x20"	5' 3"				
IV	2-2-2ST	13"x20"	5' 3"				
V	2-4-0ST	15"x22"	5' 3"				
VI	2-4-0	14"x20"	5' 7"				
VIa	2-4-0 [1]	15½"x20"	5' 7½"	150	848	15	27.00
VII	0-4-2	15"x24"	5' 0"	140	1096	16	26.06
VIIa	0-4-2T	16"x24"	5' 0"	140	940	15	36.00
VIII	0-4-0	8"x12"	1' 6"	(3' 6" tramway engines)			
IX	0-4-2	17"x24"	4' 9"	150	1189	17	28.00
IXa	0-4-2T	17"x24"	4' 10½"	150	985	17.75	42.00
X	2-4-0	15"x22"	5' 3"		1032	14.8	
	2-4-0 [2]	16"x22"	5' 4½"	150	879	15.9	32.04
	As reconstructed 1908			150	888	15.9	34.17
Xa	2-4-0T	15"x22"	5' 3"	140	1032	15.9	38. 00
XI	2-2-2WT	14"x20"	5' 6½"	130	612	12	26.00
XIa	2-2-2WT	15"x20"					
XII	2-2-2WT	15"x20"	5' 6"				
XIII	2-2-2WT	15"x20"	5' 6"	120	843	12.2	
XIV	2-4-0WT [3]	16"x24"	5' 3"	140	987	15.15	38.10
XV	2-4-0T	16"x22"	5' 3"	140	1015	16.29	38.16
	New boilers 1901-03			145	962	17	38.00
XVI	2-4-0T	16"x24"	5' 6"	140	987	15.15	40.00
XVII	0-6-0	18"x26"	4' 9"	150	1028	18	39.10
	Belpaire boilers 1912-15			160	925	18.5	42.16
XVIII	4-4-2T	18"x26"	5' 3"	150	1227	17.8	55.00
	As reconstructed 1913			160	992	17	56.05

Type	Wheels	Cylinders	Driving wheels	Boiler pressure	Heating surface	Grate area	Weight
XIX	4-4-0	18"x26"	6' 1"	150	1027	19.68	41.00
	As reconstructed 1915			165	1020	19.7	48.03
XX	0-6-2T	18½"x26"	4' 9"	160	1249	21	64.00
XXa	0-6-0 [4]	18½"x26"	4' 9"	160	1249	21	47.00
XXI	2-4-2T	17"x24"	5' 6"	160	951	15	52.00
XXII	0-6-0	17"x24"	5' 0"	150	940	15	
	As reboilered 1920			160	894	17.75	37.16
XXIII	0-6-0	17½"x24"	5' 0"	150	940	15	
		18"x24" [5]	5' 0"	160	1110	17	41.00
XXIV	2-4-2T	17"x24"	5' 6"	150	951	15	52.00
XXIVa	2-4-2T	17"x24" [6]	5' 6"	160	958	17	53.01
XXV	2-4-2T	17"x20"	4' 8½"	150	972	14.2	45.18
	As reconstructed 1914			150	832	15.3	51.07
XXVI	0-6-0	18"x26"	5' 1"	160	1193	20	43.03
XXVIa	0-6-0	18½"x26"	5' 1"	160	1193	20	43.03
XXVIb	0-6-0	18¼"x26"	5' 1"	175	1193	20	43.06
XXVIc	0-6-0	18½"x26"	4' 11½"	175	1193	20	43.01
XXVII	4-4-0	18"x26"	6' 1"	175	1193	20	45.03
XXVIII	0-4-0T	12"x16" [7]	3' 7"	175	486	9.5	25.11
XXIX	4-4-2T	18"x26"	6' 1"	175	1193	20	61.10
XXIXa	4-4-2T	18"x26" [6]	6' 1"	175	1184	20	63.00
XXX	0-6-0T	14"x20"	3' 6"		655	8.5	27.00
XXXI	2-6-0	19"x26" [8]	5' 1"	175	1248	20	48.10

[1] As reconstructed 1907   [4] Belpaire boilers 1924/5   [7] Belpaire - outside valve gear
[2] As rebuilt 1898/9   [5] As reconstructed 1919
[3] As rebuilt in 1903   [6] Belpaire boilers   [8] Belpaire superheated

TENDERS

Type	Builder	Year	Wheels	Diam	W/base	Water	Coal	Weight	Engine Numbers
A	F	1855-60	4		8' 6"	1000 gal			3, 12, 13, 14
B	SS	1860	4	3' 6"	9' 6"	1400 gal		14t12cwt	15, 16
C	SS	1864-76	6	3' 6"	5' 9"+5' 9"	1600 gal		18t 3cwt	17-26, 32, 33, 38, 39
D	SS	1876	6	3' 6"	5' 6"+5' 6"	1600 gal		17t 2cwt	37
E	VF	1891	6	3' 6"	5' 9"+5' 9"	2000 gal	4 tons	25t15cwt	50, 51
F	VF	1895-96	6	3' 7½"	5' 3"+5' 3"	2000 gal	4 tons	27t 0cwt	55, 56, 57, 58
C Reb1	GCS	1898-99	6	3' 6"	5' 9"+5' 9"	1950 gal	4 tons	19t 0cwt	32, 33
C Reb2	GCS	1899-01	6	3' 6"	5' 9"+5' 9"	1850 gal	4 tons	22t 0cwt	17, 36
C Reb3	GCS	1903-05	6	3' 6"	5' 9"+5' 9"	2100 gal	4 tons	23t 0cwt	13, 14, 25, 39
G	VF	1905	6	3' 6"	5' 9"+5' 9"	2000 gal	4 tons	25t 0cwt	4, 5, 18
H	BP	1905	6	3' 8½"	5' 9"+5' 9"	2600 gal	4½ tons	30t10cwt	65, 66, 67, 68
C Reb4	GCS	1908	6	3' 6"	5' 9"+5' 9"	2250 gal	4 tons	23t 0cwt	24, 38
I	BP	1922	6	3' 8½"	6' 0"+6' 0"	2600 gal	5 tons	32t10cwt	15, 16

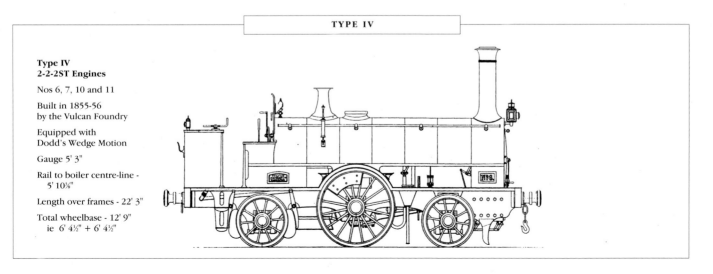

TYPE IV

Type IV
2-2-2ST Engines

Nos 6, 7, 10 and 11

Built in 1855-56
by the Vulcan Foundry

Equipped with
Dodd's Wedge Motion

Gauge 5' 3"

Rail to boiler centre-line -
5' 10⅜"

Length over frames - 22' 3"

Total wheelbase - 12' 9"
ie 6' 4½" + 6' 4½"

Appendix E

ROLLING STOCK

FIRST CLASS

No	Type	Builder	Cost	Intr	Wdn	Remarks
1	F01	DAW	£425	1854	1889	
2	F01	DAW	£425	1854	1889	
3	F01	DAW	£425	1854		To Third 84 in 1892
4	F02	B-M	£360	1855		To Van 6 in 1903
5	F02	B-M	£360	1855		To Van 14 in 1899
6	F02	B-M	£360	1855		To Van 15 in 1900
7	F02	B-M	£360	1855		To Van 17 in 1901
8	F01	DAW	£420	1860		To Van 7 in 1903
9	F01	DAW	£420	1860		To First 29 in 1903
10	F01	DAW	£420	1861		To Third 19 in 1892
11	F01	DAW	£420	1861		To Third 98 in 1894
12		Ex 2nd 13		1861		To Second 9 in 1903
13	F03	MCW	£442	1864		To First 29 in 1906
14	F03	MCW	£442	1864		To Van 8 in 1904
15	F03	MCW	£442	1864		To Compo 6 in 1906
16	F03	MCW	£442	1864		To Van 9 in 1906
17		Ex D&K		1866	1886	
18		Ex D&K		1866		To Third 74 in 1878
19		Ex D&K		1866	1887	
20		Ex D&K		1866	1883	
21		Ex D&K	£400	1866		(F01 DAW 1860); to 2nd 55 1881
22		Ex D&K		1866	1886	
23		Ex D&K		1866	1887	
24		Ex D&K		1866	1882	
25		Ex D&K		1866	1868	Either 25 or 26 destroyed in Westland
26		Ex D&K		1866	1879	Row fire 19-09-68; other replaced in 1879
27	F04	MCW	£422	1870		To Van 27 in 1913
28	F04	MCW	£422	1870		To Van 28 in 1913
25 or 26	F04	GCS		1871		25 to Van 25 in 1908 / 26 to Kitchen Van 201 in 1908
29	F04	GCS		1871		To Van 18 in 1903
30	F04	GCS		1872		Re-no'd 25 or 26 in 1879
31	F03	ASH	£550	1874		To Compo 1 in 1910/11
32	F03	ASH	£550	1874		To Compo 2 in 1910/11
33	F03	ASH	£550	1874	1925	Armoured Train 1923
34	F03	ASH	£550	1874		To Compo 3 in 1910/11
35	F04	CRA	£526	1876	1925	
36	F04	CRA	£526	1876	1926	Used on Cockle trains 1925-26
37	F04	CRA	£526	1876	1928	To 135A Tool Van, Wexford
38	F04	MCW	£465	1877	1936	Hut, Mallow Beet Factory
39	F04	MCW	£465	1877	1941	Hut, Grand Canal Street
40	F04	ASH	£421	1878	1928	
41	F04	ASH	£421	1878	1925	Armoured Train 1923
42	F04	ASH	£421	1878	c1921	
43	F04	ASH	£421	1878	1928	
18	F05	ASH	£350	1878		Re-no'd 18A and later 28 in 1918
30	F04	GCS	£450	1879	1937	Hut, Westland Row
21	F06	GCS	£400	1880	1943	Pupils' Hut, Inchicore
24	F04	GCS	£400	1882	1926	
20	F04	GCS	£356	1883	1925	
17	F04	GCS	£369	1886	1936	Hut, Tuam Beet Factory
22	F04	GCS	£369	1886	1926	
19	F04	GCS	£384	1887	1926	Used on Cockle Trains 1925-26
23	F04	GCS	£384	1887	1941	
1	F07	GCS	£352	1889	1936	Hut, Thurles Beet Factory
2	F07	GCS	£352	1889	1926	Used on Cockle Trains 1925-26
3	F08	GCS	£365	1892		To 200D Third in 1929
10	F08	GCS	£365	1892		To 215D Third in 1930
11	F08	GCS	£360	1894	1937	To 187A Accident Van, Bray
44	F08	GCS	£360	1894	1936	Hut, Thurles Beet Factory
45	F09	GCS	£443	1895	1947	Sold to HG Boardman Esq.
46	F09	GCS	£443	1895	1945	To Holding Van, Charleville
47	F08	GCS	£398	1896		To 210D Third in 1930
48	F08	GCS	£398	1896		To 217D Third in 1930
5	F10	GCS	£548	1899	1926	Used on Cockle Trains 1925-26
6	F10	GCS	£548	1900	1925	Malicious damage 1923
7		Ex 2nd 73		1903	1935	
8	F10	GCS	£367	1903		To 206D Third in 1929
9	F10	GCS	£367	1903		To 219D Third in 1931
12	B06	GCS	£1200	1903		To Compo 28 in 1918
29		Ex 1st 9		1903		To Second 14 in 1906
29		Ex 1st 13				To Van 18 in 1907
13	B10	GCS	£1386	1906		Re-numbered 18 in March 1918
15	F10	GCS	£506	1906	1959	

FIRST CLASS

No	Type	Builder	Cost	Intr	Wdn	Remarks
16	F10	GCS	£506	1906		To 201D Third in 1929
18		Ex 1st 13		1918		To Tea Car 74D in August 1927
28		Ex 1st 18A		1918	1936	Hut, Tuam Beet Factory
12		Ex Compo 28		1922	1957	
25		Ex Compo 15		1922		To 30D Compo in 1936
26		Ex Compo 16		1922		To 224D Compo in 1940
27		Ex Compo 5		1922	1936	Hut, Mallow Beet Factory
29		Ex Compo 10		1922	1964	To Kitchen Car 29D in 1938
31		Ex Compo 21		1922	1925	Malicious damage 1923
32		Ex 2nd 32		1922		To 208D Third in 1930
34		Ex 2nd 5		1922		To 213D Third in 1930
53		Ex 2nd 53		1922		To 216D Third in 1931
54		Ex 2nd 54		1922	1925	Malicious damage 1923
55		Ex 2nd 55		1922		To 55D Third in 1925
68		Ex 2nd 68		1922		To 204D Third in 1929
69		Ex 2nd 69		1922		To 218D Third in 1931
70		Ex 2nd 70		1922		To 211D Third in 1930
71		Ex 2nd 71		1922		To 205D Third in 1929
72		Ex 2nd 72		1922	1955	U/f to Flat Wagon for Ford Motor Co
73		Ex 2nd 73		1922	1954	
74D		Ex 1st 18D		1927	1962	Tea Car; to S&E tool van 462A
18D		Ex Compo 18D		1927		Back to 18D Compo in 1936
14D		Ex 2nd 14SD		1927		To 207D Third Brake in 1929
8D		Ex 3rd 206D		1935	1949	To 296A tool van
34D		Ex 3rd 213D		1935	1959	
53D		Ex 3rd 216D		1935	1953	
71D		Ex 3rd 205D		1935	1956	U/f to Flat Wagon for Ford Motor Co

SECOND CLASS

(* Atm = Atmospheric)

No	Type	Builder	Cost	Intr	Wdn	Remarks
1	S01	DAW	£325	1854		To Third 25 to 33 series 1885
2	S01	DAW	£325	1854		To Third 25 to 33 series 1885
3		Ex Atm*		1854	1868-69	
4		Ex Atm*		1854	1868-69	
5		Ex Atm*		1854	1864	
6		Ex Atm*		1854	1868-69	
7	S02	B-M		1854		To Third 53 to 59 series 1877
8	S02	B-M		1854		To Third 53 to 59 series 1877
9	S02	B-M		1854		To Third 53 to 59 series 1877
10	S02	B-M		1855		To Third 53 to 59 series 1877
11	S02	B-M		1855		To Third 53 to 59 series 1877
12	S02	B-M		1855		To Third 53 to 59 series 1877
13	S02	B-M		1855		To First 12 in 1861
14	S02	B-M		1855		To Third 53 to 59 series 1877
15	S02	B-M		1855		To Third 53 to 59 series 1877
13	S01	DAW	£418	1861		To Third 1888
16	S01	DAW	£418	1861		To Third 1884
17	S01	DAW	£418	1861		To Third 1887
18	S01	DAW	£418	1861		To Third 1888
5	S03	MCW	£365	1864		Rebuilt 1899; to 2nd 15 in 1901
41	S03	MCW	£365	1864		To Third 29 in 1902
49	S03	MCW	£365	1864		Rebuilt 1899; to 3rd 10 or 12 in 1905
50	S03	MCW	£365	1864		Rebuilt 1899; to 3rd 19 in 1915
19		Ex D&K		1866	1892	Rebuilt 1880 ?
20		Ex D&K		1866		To Third 25 to 33 series 1886
21		Ex D&K		1866		To Third 25 to 33 series 1886
22		Ex D&K		1866		To Third 25 to 33 series 1887
23		Ex D&K		1866	1874	Blackrock derailment 08/05/74
24		Ex D&K		1866		To Third 25 to 33 series 1884
25		Ex D&K		1866	1888	
26		Ex D&K		1866	1893	Rebuilt 1880 ?
27		Ex D&K		1866	1880	
28		Ex D&K		1866		To Third in 1877-78
29		Ex D&K		1866		To Third in 1877-78
30		Ex D&K		1866	1892	Rebuilt 1880 ?
31		Ex D&K		1866	1893	Rebuilt 1880 ?
32		Ex D&K		1866	1901	Preserved
33		Ex D&K		1866	1868	Westland Row Fire 09/68 ?
34		Ex D&K		1866		To Third in 1877-78
35		Ex D&K		1866		To Third in1877-78
36		Ex D&K		1866	1868	Westland Row Fire 09/68 ?
37		Ex D&K		1866	1882	
38		Ex D&K		1866	1868	Westland Row Fire 09/68 ?

SECOND CLASS

No	Type	Builder	Cost	Intr	Wdn	Remarks
39		Ex D&K		1866	1889	
40		Ex D&K		1866		To Third 25 to 33 series 1884
42		Ex D&K		1866	1875	
43		Ex D&K		1866	1882	
44		Ex D&K		1866	1888	
45		Ex D&K		1866		To Third in 1877/78
46		Ex D&K		1866	1889	
47		Ex D&K		1866	1889	
48		Ex D&K		1866	1889	
51		Ex D&K		1866	1887	
52		Ex D&K		1866	1887	
53		Ex D&K		1866	1870	
54		Ex D&K		1866	1870	
55		Ex D&K		1866		To Third 72 in 1881
56		Ex D&K		1866	1875	
57		Ex D&K		1866	1875	
58		Ex D&K		1866		To Third 1868
59		Ex D&K		1866		To Third 1868
60		Ex D&K		1866		To Third 1868
6	S03	GCS	£440	1868		Rebuilt 1882; to 3rd 29 in 1915
33	S03	GCS	£440	1868	1894	
36	S03	GCS	£440	1868	1894	
38	S03	GCS	£440	1868		Rebuilt 1883; to 3rd Bke 17 in 1914
53	S03	MCW	£350	1870		To Third 25 in 1902
54	S03	MCW	£350	1870		To Third 33 in 1902
7	S03	MCW	£521	1875		To Third 26 in 1907
9	S03	MCW	£521	1875		To Third 38 in 1903
15	S03	MCW	£521	1875		To Third 28 in 1901
42	S03	MCW	£521	1875		To Third 20 in 1903
56	S03	MCW	£521	1875		To Third 13 circa 1908-12
57	S03	MCW	£521	1875		To 3rd Brake 70 circa 1914
3	S03	CRA	£470	1876		To 3rd Brake 76 circa 1910-11
4	S03	CRA	£470	1876		To 3rd Bke 54/55/86 in 1909
14	S03	CRA	£470	1876		To Third 30 circa 1908-12
28	S03	CRA	£470	1876		To Third 25 circa 1908-12
34	S03	CRA	£470	1876		To 3rd Bke 54/55/86 in 1909
45	S03	CRA	£470	1876		To 3rd Bke 54/55/86 in 1909
8	S03	MCW	£454	1877		To 3rd Brake 21 circa 1910-11
10	S03	MCW	£454	1877		To 3rd Brake 31 circa 1908
11	S03	MCW	£454	1877		To 3rd Brake 69 circa 1914
12	S03	MCW	£454	1877		To Third 23 circa 1908-12
23	S03	MCW	£454	1877		To Third 39 circa 1908-12
29	S03	MCW	£454	1877		To Third 34 circa 1908-12
35	S03	MCW	£454	1877		To Third 15 circa 1908-12
27	S04	GCS	£500	1880		To Third 84 in 1918-19
55		Ex 1st 21		1881		To Third 13 in 1898
37	S04	GCS	£356	1882		To Third 71 in 1918-19
43	S04	GCS	£352	1882		To Third 89 in 1918-19
16	S04	GCS	£344	1884		To Third 16S in 1922
24	S04	GCS	£328	1884		To Third 24S in 1922
40	S04	GCS	£328	1884		To Third 98 in 1918-19
1	S05	GCS	£480	1885		To Third 1S in 1922
2	S05	GCS	£480	1885		To Third 2 S in 1922
21	S05	GCS	£325	1886		To Third 21S in 1922
20	S05	GCS	£398	1886		To Third 58 in 1918-19
22	S05	GCS	£398	1887		To Third 56 in 1918-19
51	S05	GCS	£375	1887		To Third 51S in 1922
52	S05	GCS	£375	1887		To Third 52S in 1922
17	S05	GCS	£375	1887		To Third 17S in 1922
18	S05	GCS	£375	1888		To Third 18S in 1922
13	S05	GCS	£397	1888		To Third 13S in 1922
25	S05	GCS	£330	1888		To Third 25S in 1922
44	S05	GCS	£330	1888		To Third 44S in 1922
46	S05	GCS	£350	1889		To Third 46S in 1922
47	S05	GCS	£378	1889		To Third 47S in 1922
48	S05	GCS	£378	1889		To Third 48S in 1922
39	S05	GCS	£378	1889		To Third 39S in 1922
58	S05	GCS	£359	1890		To Third 58S in 1922
59	S05	GCS	£359	1890		To Third 59S in 1922
60	S05	GCS	£350	1890		To Third 60S in 1922
61	S05	GCS	£350	1890		To Third 61S in 1922
62	S05	GCS	£357	1891		To Third 62S in 1922
63	S05	GCS	£357	1891		To Third 63S in 1922
64	S05	GCS	£353	1891		To Third 64S in 1922
65	S05	GCS	£353	1891		To Third 65S in 1922
19	S05	GCS	£350	1892		To Third 19S in 1922
30	S05	GCS	£350	1892		To Third 30S in 1922
31	S05	GCS	£343	1893		To Third 31S in 1922
26	S05	GCS	£343	1893		To Third 26S in 1922
33	S05	GCS	£330	1894		To Third 33S in 1922
36	S05	GCS	£330	1894		To Third 36S in 1922
66	S06	GCS	£334	1895		To 3rd Brake 40 in 1914
67	S06	GCS	£334	1895		To Third 43 in 1914
68	S07	BCW	£533	1896		To First 68 in 1922

SECOND CLASS

No	Type	Builder	Cost	Intr	Wdn	Remarks
69	S07	BCW	£533	1896		To First 69 in 1922
70	S07	BCW	£533	1896		To First 70 in 1922
71	S07	BCW	£533	1896		To First 71 in 1922
72	S07	BCW	£533	1896		To First 72 in 1922
73	S07	BCW	£533	1896		To First 7 in 1903
55	S08	GCS	£500	1898		To First 55 in 1922
5	S07	GCS	£347	1901		To First 34 in 1922
15		Ex 2nd 5		1901		To 3rd 10/12 in 1905
32	S07	GCS	£347	1901		To First 32 in 1922
53	S07	GCS	£350	1902		To First 53 in 1922
54	S07	GCS	£350	1902		To First 54 in 1922
41	B05	GCS	£908	1902		To Third 15 in 1920
9		Ex 1st 12		1903		To Compo 8 in 1914
73	S07	GCS	£353	1904		To First 73 in 1922
14		Ex 1st 29		1906	1910	
42	B15	GCS	£933	1909		To 3rd Brake 42S in 1922
14	B15	GCS	£933	1910		To 3rd Brake 14S in 1922
28	B23	GCS	£955	1914		To Compo 30 (Bus Coach) 1922

THIRD CLASS

(* Atm = Atmospheric)

No	Type	Builder	Cost	Intr	Wdn	Remarks
1	T01	B-M		1854		Re-numbered 85 in 1892
2	T01	B-M		1854		Convtd to 3rd Brake in 1882-83
3		Ex Atm*		1854	1860-61	
4		Ex Atm*		1854		To Brake Van 5 or 6 in 1859
5		Ex Atm*		1854	1860-61	
6		Ex Atm*		1854		To Brake Van 5 or 6 in 1859
7	T01	B-M		1854		Re-numbered 91 in 1892
8	T01	B-M		1854		Re-numbered 92 in 1892
9	T01	B-M		1854		Convtd to 3rd Brake in 1882-83
10	T01	B-M		1854		Re-numbered 94 in 1892
11	T01	B-M		1854		Re-numbered 95 in 1892
12	T01	B-M		1854		Re-numbered 96 in 1892
13	T01	B-M		1854		To Compo 3 in 1859
14	T01	B-M		1855		Convtd to 3rd Brake in 1882-83
15	T01	B-M		1855	1905-06	
16	T01	B-M		1855	1868	Possibly Bray Head accident 08/67
17	T01	B-M		1855	1868	Possibly Bray Head accident 08/67
18	T01	B-M		1855	1898	
19	T01	B-M		1855	1892	
20	T01	B-M		1855	1905	
21	T01	B-M		1855		Convtd to 3rd Brake in 1882-83
22	T02	DAW 1853		1855		Ex W&T. To 3rd Brake 1858-66
23	T02	DAW 1853		1855	1881	Ex W&T
24	T02	DAW 1853		1855		Ex W&T. To 3rd Brake 1858-66
25	T03	B-M		1856	1884-8	
26	T03	B-M		1856	1884-8	
27	T03	B-M		1856	1868	Possibly Bray Head accident 08/67
28	T03	B-M		1856	1884-88	
29	T03	B-M		1856	1884-88	
30	T03	B-M		1856	1884-88	
31	T03	B-M		1856	1884-88	
32	T03	B-M		1856	1884-88	
33	T03	B-M		1856	1884-88	
3	T02	DAW		1860-61	c1894	
4	T02	DAW		1860-61		To 3rd Brake 1858-66
5	T02	DAW		1860-61	c1893	
6	T02	DAW		1860-61		To 3rd Brake 1858-66
34		Ex D&K		1866	1890-91	
35		Ex D&K		1866	1878	
36		Ex D&K		1866	1878	
37		Ex D&K		1866	1891	
38		Ex D&K		1866	1901-03	
39		Ex D&K		1866	1875	
40		Ex D&K		1866	1875	
41		Ex D&K		1866	1873	
42		Ex D&K		1866	1884	
43		Ex D&K		1866	1875	
44		Ex D&K		1866	1891	
45		Ex D&K		1866	1901-03	
46		Ex D&K		1866	1881	
47		Ex D&K		1866	1901-03	
48		Ex D&K		1866	1900	
41		GCS		1873		Converted to 3rd Brake in 1882-83
39	T04	GCS		1875	c1908	
40	T04	GCS		1875		Converted to 3rd Brake in 1882-83
43	T04	GCS		1875		Converted to 3rd Brake in 1882-83
53		Ex 2nd 7/15		1877	1905-06	
54		Ex 2nd 7/15		1877		Converted to 3rd Brake in 1882-83
55		Ex 2nd 7/15		1877		Converted to 3rd Brake in 1882-83
56		Ex 2nd 7/15		1877	1905-6	
57		Ex 2nd 7/15		1877	1905-6	

THIRD CLASS

No	Type	Builder	Cost	Intr	Wdn	Remarks
58		Ex 2nd 7/15		1877	1905-6	
59		Ex 2nd 7/15		1877		Convtd to 3rd Brake, 1882-83
60		Ex 2nd		1877	1890	
61		Ex 2nd		1877	1898	
62		Ex 2nd		1877	1890	
73		Ex 2nd		1878	1883	
74		Ex 2nd		1878	c1904	
75		Ex 2nd		1878	1885	
76		Ex 2nd		1878	1905-06	
77		Ex 2nd		1878	1893	
35		Ex 2nd		1878	1900	
46		Ex Compo 3		1881	1905-06	
72		Ex 2nd 55		1881	1901-03	
23	T04	GCS		1881	1908-12	
13	T04	GCS		1882	1908-12	
73	T05	GCS	£300	1883	1928	
25		Ex D&K 2nd		1884-86	1901-03	
26		Ex D&K 2nd		1884-86	1901-03	
28		Ex D&K 2nd		1884-86	1901-03	
29		Ex D&K 2nd		1884-86	1890-01	
30		Ex D&K 2nd		1884-86	c1904	
31		Ex D&K 2nd		1884-86	1901-03	
32		Ex D&K 2nd		1884-86	1890-91	
33		Ex D&K 2nd		1884-86	1901-03	
80	T05	GCS	£318	1890	1927	
81	T05	GCS	£318	1890	1941	
37	T05	GCS	£293	1891	1926	Used on Cockle Trains 1925-26, to 113A
44	T05	GCS	£293	1891	1936	To Broadstone Tool Van 170A
82	T05	GCS	£321	1892	1926	Used on Cockle Trains 1925-26
83	T05	GCS	£321	1892	1927	To Mullingar Sleeping Van 137A
1	T05	B-M	£489	1892	1927	To Mullingar Sleeping Van 136A
2	T05	B-M	£489	1892	1926	Used on Cockle Trains 1925-26
3	T05	B-M	£489	1892	1957	
4	T05	B-M	£489	1892	1926	Used on Cockle Trains 1925-26
5	T05	B-M	£489	1892	1936	Shunters' Hut, North Wall, 1936
6	T05	B-M	£489	1892	1926	Used on Cockle Trains 1925/6
7	T05	B-M	£489	1892	1925	Malicious damage 1923
8	T05	B-M	£489	1892	1926	Used on Cockle Trains 1925/6
9	T05	B-M	£489	1892	1926	Used on Cockle Trains 1925/6
10	T05	B-M	£489	1892	1895	Wrecked in Ovoca collision 08/95
11	T05	B-M	£489	1892	1927	Hut, Newbridge Ballast Pit, 134A
12	T05	B-M	£489	1892	1895	Wrecked in Ovoca collision 08/95
19		Ex 1st 10		1892	1911-13	
84		Ex 1st 3		1892	1911-13	
85		Ex 3rd 1		1892	1893	
87		Ex 3rd 3		1892	1894	
89		Ex 3rd 5		1892	1893	
91		Ex 3rd 7		1892	1893	
92		Ex 3rd 8		1892	1893	
94		Ex 3rd 10		1892	1893	
95		Ex 3rd 11		1892	1893	
96		Ex 3rd 12		1892	1894	
96	T06	B-M 1874		1894	1911-13	Ex Finn Valley Railway
98		Ex 1st 11		1894	1911-13	
99	T07	BCW	£450	1896	1928	
100	T07	BCW	£450	1896	1941	To Turf Wagon
101	T07	BCW	£450	1896	1954	
102	T07	BCW	£450	1896	1949	
103	T07	BCW	£450	1896	1941	To Turf Wagon
104	T07	BCW	£450	1896	1941	To Turf Wagon
105	T07	BCW	£450	1896	1925	
106	T07	BCW	£450	1896	1941	To Turf Wagon
107	T07	BCW	£450	1896	1941	To Turf Wagon
108	T07	BCW	£450	1896	1936	To Kingsbridge Loco Tool Van 164A
109	T07	BCW	£450	1896	1925	Malicious damage 1923
110	T07	BCW	£450	1896	1942	To Turf Wagon
111	T07	BCW	£450	1896	1925	
112	T07	BCW	£450	1896	1926	Used on Cockle Trains 1925-26
35	B03	GCS	£642	1900	1957	
32	T07	GCS	£330	1901	1941	To Turf Wagon
48	T07	GCS	£330	1901	1931	Body sold to Mr Armstrong. Underframe convtd to Carrier Truck o.380
25		Ex 2nd 53		1902	1908-12	
29		Ex 2nd 41		1902	1914-15	
33		Ex 2nd 54		1902		To 3rd Brake 87 in 1916
28		Ex 2nd 15		1903		To 3rd Brake 64 in 1909 or 67 in 1913
38		Ex 2nd 9		1903		To 3rd Brake 64 in 1909 or 67 in 1913
45	T08	GCS	£334	1904	1941	To Turf Wagon
47	T08	GCS	£334	1904	1941	To Loco Dept. Turf Wagon 217A
10		Ex 2nd 5 or 49		1905	1941	To Turf Wagon
12		Ex 2nd 5 or 49		1905	1941	To Loco Dept. Turf Wagon 215A
20		Ex 2nd 42		1905	1926	Used on Cockle Trains 1925-26
74	B09	GCS	£1005	1905		To Restaurant Car stock 1913

THIRD CLASS

No	Type	Builder	Cost	Intr	Wdn	Remarks
57	B09	GCS	£834	1906		To Restaurant Car stock 1913
30		Ex 2nd 14		1906	1925	
46	T08	GCS	£328	1906	1956	
53	T08	GCS	£328	1906	1942	To Turf Wagon
38	B09	GCS	£834	1908		To Restaurant Car stock 1913
13		Ex 2nd 56		1908-12	1925	
15		Ex 2nd 35		1908-12		To Ballast Van 202 in 1915
23		Ex 2nd 12		1908-12	1926	
25		Ex 2nd 28		1908-12	1926	Used on Cockle Trains 1925/6
26		Ex 2nd 7		1908-12	1925	
34		Ex 2nd 29		1908-12	1931	To Sligo Breakdown Van 143A
39		Ex 2nd 23		1908-12	1927	
72	B19	GCS	£1130	1912	1925	Malicious Damage 1923
28	B21	GCS	£1080	1913	1960	
19		Ex 2nd 50		1914-15	1925	Malicious Damage 1923
29		Ex 2nd 6		1914-15	1935	Temp Stores, Inchicore Carriage Shop
43		Ex 2nd 67		1914-15	1926	
56		Ex 2nd 22		1918-19	1926	Used on Cockle Trains 1925-26
58		Ex 2nd 20		1918-19	1927	
71		Ex 2nd 37		1918-19	1926	Used on Cockle Trains 1925-26
84		Ex 2nd 27		1918-19	1926	Used on Cockle Trains 1925-26
89		Ex 2nd 43		1918-19	1928	
98		Ex 2nd 40		1918-19	1925	
15		Ex 2nd 41		1920	1957	
1S		Ex 2nd 1		1922	1935	Hut at Rocksavage
2S		Ex 2nd 2		1922		Re-numbered 151D in 1926
13S		Ex 2nd 13		1922	1936	To Road Freight Dept., 1936
16S		Ex 2nd 16		1922		Re-numbered 154D in 1926
17S		Ex 2nd 17		1922	1926	Used on Cockle Trains 1925/6
18S		Ex 2nd 18		1922		Re-numbered 156D in 1926
19S		Ex 2nd 19		1922	1925	
21S		Ex 2nd 21		1922	1935	Hut at Thurles
24S		Ex 2nd 24		1922		Re-numbered 159D in 1926
25S		Ex 2nd 25		1922		Re-numbered 160D in 1926
26S		Ex 2nd 26		1922	1926	Used on Cockle Trains 1925-26
30S		Ex 2nd 30		1922	1936	To GCS Breakdown Van 166A
31S		Ex 2nd 31		1922	1927	To Broadstone Running Dept 144A
33S		Ex 2nd 33		1922	1925	Malicious Damage 1923
36S		Ex 2nd 36		1922		Re-numbered 165D in 1926
39S		Ex 2nd 39		1922	1936	To Road Freight Dept, 1936
44S		Ex 2nd 44		1922	1936	To GCS Breakdown Van 167A
46S		Ex 2nd 46		1922		Re-numbered 168D in 1926
47S		Ex 2nd 47		1922	1926	Used on Cockle Trains 1925-26
48S		Ex 2nd 48		1922	1925	
51S		Ex 2nd 51		1922		Re-numbered 171D in 1926
52S		Ex 2nd 52		1922	1925	Malicious Damage 1923
58S		Ex 2nd 58		1922	1935	Hut, Broadstone Wagon Dept.
59S		Ex 2nd 59		1922	1926	Used on Cockle Trains 1925-26
60S		Ex 2nd 60		1922		Re-numbered 175D in 1926
61S		Ex 2nd 61		1922	1928	
62S		Ex 2nd 62		1922		Re-numbered 177D in 1926
63S		Ex 2nd 63		1922	1926	
64S		Ex 2nd 64		1922	1925	
65S		Ex 2nd 65		1922		Re-numbered 180D in 1926
38D		Ex Rest Car 38D		1925	1957	
55D		Ex 1st 55D		1925	1928	
74D		Ex Rest Car 74D		1925	1956	
114D		Ex Co Bus 23D		1926	1947	Dest'd in Newcastle West collision
116D		Ex Co Bus 27D		1926	1942	Destroyed in Athlone Fire
151D		Ex 3rd 2SD		1926	1935	To Office and Store GCS
154D		Ex 3rd 16SD		1926	1939	Hut at Mungret, 1939
156D		Ex 3rd 18SD		1926	1949	To Workmen's Train as 297A
159D		Ex 3rd 24SD		1926	1936	Hut, Permanent Way Dept.
160D		Ex 3rd 25SD		1926	1937	Train Lighting Hut, Westland Row.
165D		Ex 3rd 36SD		1926	1956	
168D		Ex 3rd 46SD		1926	1936	To Road Freight Dept, 1936
171D		Ex 3rd 51SD		1926	1936	To Mullingar Breakdown Van 169A
175D		Ex 3rd 60SD		1926	1928	
177D		Ex 3rd 62SD		1926	1936	To Limerick Breakdown Van 163A
180D		Ex 3rd 65SD		1926	1935	PWD Hut, Inchicore Concrete Bank
200D		Ex 1st 3D		1929	1948	Hut at Cahir
201D		Ex 1st 16D		1929	1941	To Loco Dept. Turf Wagon 212A
202D		Ex Compo 9D		1929	1959	
203D		Ex Compo 12D		1929	1956	
204D		Ex 1st 68D		1929	1949	Sold at Inchicore
205D		Ex 1st 71D		1929		To 71D First in 1935
206D		Ex 1st 8D		1929		To 8D First in 1935
208D		Ex 1st 32D		1930	1949	To Weighbridge Tool Van 294A
209D		Ex Compo 19D		1930	1959	
210D		Ex 1st 47D		1930	1949	To Wexford Tool Van 241A
211D		Ex 1st 70D		1930	1959	
212D		Ex Compo 20D		1930	1959	
213D		Ex 1st 34D		1930		To 34D First in 1935
214D		Ex Compo 14D		1930	1957	

THIRD CLASS

No	Type	Builder	Cost	Intr	Wdn	Remarks
215D		Ex 1st 10D		1930	1941	To Sleeping Van 224A in 1944
216D		Ex 1st 53D		1931		To 53D First in 1935
217D		Ex 1st 48D		1931	1958	
218D		Ex 1st 69D		1931	1941	To Turf Wagon
219D		Ex 1st 9D		1931	1958	
220D		Ex 3rd Bke 220D		1940	1942	Ambulance 1941. Destr Athlone Fire
221D		Ex 3rd Bke 221D		1940	1961	
222D		Ex 3rd Bke 222D		1940	1960	To Workmen's Train as 349A
223D		Ex 3rd Bke 223D		1940	1959	
226D		Ex Compo 17D		1954	1960	

THIRD CLASS BRAKES

No	Type	Builder	Cost	Intr	Wdn	Remarks
4		Ex 3rd		1858-66		Rebuilt 1879; re-no'd 88 in 1892
6		Ex 3rd		1858-66		Rebuilt 1881; re-no'd 90 in 1892
16		Ex 3rd		1858-66	1886	
17		Ex 3rd		1858-66	1908-11	Rebuilt 1875
22		Ex 3rd		1858-66	1885	
24		Ex 3rd		1858-66	1878	Wrecked, Glenageary collision 02/78
27		Ex 3rd		1858-66	1886	
49	TB1	GCS	£216	1875		Cattle Brake; to Goods Stock 1913
50	TB1	GCS	£216	1875		Cattle Brake; to Goods Stock 1913
51	TB1	GCS		1876		Cattle Brake; to Goods Stock 1913
52	TB1	GCS		1876		Cattle Brake; to Goods Stock 1913
63	TB2	MCW	£265	1878	1925	Workshop, Harcourt Street, 1930
64	TB2	MCW	£265	1878	1909	
65	TB2	MCW	£265	1878	1913	
66	TB2	MCW	£265	1878	1913	
67	TB3	MID	£262	1878	1913	
68	TB3	MID	£262	1878	1925	
69	TB3	MID	£262	1878	1914-15	
70	TB3	MID	£262	1878	1914-15	
71	TB3	MID	£262	1878	1918-19	
36	TB3	MID	£262	1878	1910	
24	TB3	GCS		1878	1918-19	
2		Ex 3rd		1882-3		Re-no'd 86 in 1892
9		Ex 3rd		1882-3		Re-no'd 93 in 1892
14		Ex 3rd		1882-3		To Brake Van 12 or 19 in 1904
21		Ex 3rd		1882-3	1906	
40		Ex 3rd		1882-3	1908-11	
41		Ex 3rd		1882-3	1908	
43		Ex 3rd		1882-3	1908-11	
54		Ex 3rd		1882-3	1906	
55		Ex 3rd		1882-3	1906	
59		Ex 3rd		1882-3		To Brake Van 12 or 19 in 1904
42	TB4	GCS	£318	1884	1925	Malicious Damage 1923
22	TB1	GCS		1885		Cattle Brake; to Goods Stock 1913
75	TB1	GCS		1885		Cattle Brake; to Goods Stock 1913
16	TB1	GCS	£171	1886		Cattle Brake; to Goods Stock 1913
27	TB1	GCS	£249	1886		Cattle Brake; to Goods Stock 1913
78	TB1	GCS		1888		Cattle Brake; to Goods Stock 1913
79	TB1	GCS		1888		Cattle Brake; to Goods Stock 1913
60	TB1	GCS	£282	1890		Cattle Brake; to Goods Stock 1913
62	TB1	GCS	£282	1890		Cattle Brake; to Goods Stock 1913
86		Ex 3rd Bke 2		1892		To Brake Van 13 or 16 in 1898
88		Ex 3rd Bke 4		1892	1906	
90		Ex 3rd Bke 6		1892		Cattle Brake; to Goods Stock 1913
93		Ex 3rd Bke 9		1892		To Brake Van 13 or 16 in 1898
77	TB4	LCW	£234	1893	1926	Used on Cockle Trains 1925-26 To 117A Traffic Dept., Carlow
85	TB4	LCW	£234	1893	1925	
87	TB5	B-M 1874		1894	1916	Ex Finn Valley Railway
97	TB5	B-M 1874		1894	1908	Ex Finn Valley Railway
18	TB6	GCS	£282	1898	1925	Malicious damage 1923
61	TB6	GCS	£282	1898	1956	
14	TB7	GCS	£336	1904	1949	
59	TB7	GCS	£336	1904	1925	Malicious damage 1923
97	TB8	GCS	£211	1908	1955	To 305A
31		Ex 2nd 10		1908	1926	
54		Ex 2nd 4/34/45		1909	1919-20	To PW Ballast Van 54 in 1920
55		Ex 2nd 4/34/45		1909	1925	Malicious damage 1923
86		Ex 2nd 4/34/45		1909		To 113A Examiners' Hut, Broadstone
41	B16	GCS	£928	1909	1960	
64		Ex 3rd 28 or 38		1909-13	1935	To 156A Tool Van
67		Ex 3rd 28 or 38		1909-13	1925	
36	B16	GCS	£858	1910	1956	
21		Ex 2nd 8		1910-11	1928	Used on Cockle Trains 1925-26
76		Ex 2nd 3		1910-11	1926	Used on Cockle Trains 1925-26
17		Ex 2nd 38		1914	1926	Used on Cockle Trains 1925-26
40		Ex 2nd 66		1914	1927	
69		Ex 2nd 11		1914	1935	To 161A Material Van
70		Ex 2nd 57		1914	1926	

THIRD CLASS BRAKES

No	Type	Builder	Cost	Intr	Wdn	Remarks
33	B24	GCS	£1034	1915		To Bus Coach 29 in 1922
87		Ex 3rd 33		1916	1925	
14S		Ex 2nd Brake		1922		To First Brake 14D in 1927
42S		Ex 2nd Brake		1922	1961	'S' Suffix dropped in 1925
207D		Ex 1st Bke 14D		1929	1960	To 355A Breakdown Van
220D		Ex Compo 22		1935		To 220D Third in 1940
221D		Ex Compo 24		1935		To 221D Third in 1940
222D		Ex Compo 28		1935		To 222D Third in 1940
223D		Ex Compo 29		1935		To 223D Third in 1940

COMPOSITES

(* Atm = Atmospheric)

No	Type	Builder	Cost	Intr	Wdn	Remarks
1	C01	DAW		1854	1882	
2		Ex Atm*		1854	1868	(* Atm = Atmospheric)
3		Ex 3rd		1859	1881	
4	C01	DAW	£350	1860	1894	
5	C01	DAW	£350	1861	1894	
6		Ex 2nd		1865	1906	
7	C02	GCS	£388	1869	1926	Used on Cockle Trains 1925-26
8	C02	GCS	£388	1869	1914	
2	C02	GCS	£388	1869	1911	Rebuilt 1883
3	C03	GCS	£480	1881	1910	
1	C03	GCS	£480	1882		To Van 10 in 1911
4	C04	GCS	£350	1894	1925	Malicious Damage 1923
5	C04	GCS	£350	1894		To First 27 in 1922
9	C05	B-M 1874		1894		Ex Finn Valley Rly; to Van 4 in 1901
10	C05	B-M 1874		1894		Ex Finn Valley Rly; to Van 3 in 1899
11	B01	BCW	£785	1895	1925	Malicious damage 1923
12	B01	BCW	£785	1895		To 203D Third in 1929
10	B02	GCS	£1000	1899		To First 29 in 1922
13	B04	GCS	£1033	1900	1925	
14	B08	GCS	£1142	1905		To Restaurant Car stock 1913
6		Ex 1st 15		1906	1928	
9	B11	GCS	£1103	1906		To 202D Third in 1929
15	C06	GCS	£688	1907		To First 25 in 1922
16	C06	GCS	£688	1907		To First 26 in 1922
17	B12	GCS	£1033	1908		To Restaurant Car stock 1913
18	B13	GCS	£1180	1908		To 18D First in 1927
19	B14	M-W		1908		Ex Railmotor; 209D Third 1930
20	B14	M-W		1908		Ex Railmotor; 212D Third 1931
21	B11	GCS	£1117	1909		To First 31 in 1922
22	B17	GCS	£1028	1910		To Bus Coach 1922
23	B17	GCS	£1028	1910		To Bus Coach 1922
3		Ex 1st 34		1910	1926	
1		Ex 1st 31		1911	1926	
2		Ex 1st 32		1911	1925	To 121A in 1927
24	B17	GCS	£1084	1911		To Bus Coach 1922
25	B18	GCS	£1203	1912	1960	Was to become 225D Third
26	B20	GCS	£1242	1913	1961	For Pier Train; Steam Heated
27	B22	GCS	£1158	1914		To Bus Coach 1922
8		Ex 2nd 9		1914	1925	
28		Ex 1st 12		1918		To First 12 in 1922
29		Ex 3rd Bke 33		1922		Bus Coach
30		Ex 2nd Bke 28		1922		Bus Coach; Re-no'd 28 in 1923
14D		Ex Restaurant		1925		To 214D Third in 1930
17D		Ex Restaurant		1925		To 226D Third in 1954
18D		Ex 1st 18D		1936	1961	
30D		Ex 1st 25D		1936	1949	
224D		Ex 1st 26D		1940	1953	

COMPOSITE BRAKES (Bus Coaches)

Compo Brake	Third 1926	3rd Bke 1935	G'ways fitted	Wdn	Remarks
22		220D	1940	1942	Destroyed in Athlone fire
23	114D		1939	1947	Newcastle West collision
24		221D	1951	1961	Guard's Compt removed 1940
27	116D		1939	1942	Destroyed in Athlone fire
28		222D	1951	1960	Guard's Compt removed 1940
29		223D	1951	1959	Guard's Compt removed 1940

RESTAURANT CARS

No	Type		Intr	Wdn	Remarks
14	From Composite list		1913		To 14D Compo 1925
17	From Composite list		1913		To 17D Compo 1925
38	From Third list		1913		To 38D Third 1925
57	From Third list		1913	1925	Malicious damage 1923
74	From Third list		1913		To 74D Third 1925

PASSENGER VANS

(* Atm = Atmospheric)

No	Type	Builder	Cost	Intr	Wdn	Remarks
1	V01	B-M	£205	1854	1897	Rebuilt 1869
2	V01	B-M	£205	1854	1892	Rebuilt 1869
3	V01	B-M		1856	1901	Rebuilt 1870
4	V01	B-M		1856	1899	Rebuilt 1879
5		Ex Atm* 3rd		1859	1861-63	
6		Ex Atm* 3rd		1859	1861-63	
5		GCS		1861-63	1891	
6		GCS		1861-63	1903	
7	V02	TCM	£325	1863	1903	Rebuilt 1879
8	V02	TCM	£325	1863	1904	Rebuilt 1880
9	V02	TCM	£325	1864	1906	Rebuilt 1880
10	V02	TCM	£325	1864	1911	Rebuilt 1881
11	V02	TCM	£325	1864	1904	Rebuilt 1878
12	V02	TCM	£325	1864	1904	Rebuilt 1878
13		Ex D&K		1866	1898	
14		Ex D&K		1866	1899	
15		Ex D&K		1866	1900	
16		Ex D&K		1866	1898	Rebuilt 1883
17		Ex D&K		1866	1901	
18		Ex D&K		1866	1903	Rebuilt 1882
19		Ex D&K		1866	1904	
20		Ex D&K		1866	1912	Rebuilt 1881
21		Ex D&K		1866	1910	Rebuilt 1883
22		Ex D&K		1866	1897	Rebuilt 1883; Pier Mails
23		Ex D&K		1866	1874	
23	V03	GCS		1874	1903	
24	V03	GCS		1874	1903	
25	V04	MCW	£252	1878	1908	Under-frame to Mortuary Van
26	V04	MCW	£252	1878	1910	
27	V05	GCS	£194	1886	1913	
28	V05	GCS	£194	1886	1913	
5	V06	GCS		1891	1955	Steamheated 1951
2	V07	GCS		1892	1941	Milk Van
32	V08	GCS	£461	1893	1958	Travelling Post Office
33	V08	GCS	£461	1893	1958	Travelling Post Office
36	V09	GCS	£464	1896	1949	
37	V09	GCS	£464	1896	1949	
38	V09	BCW	£419	1896	1949	
39	V09	BCW	£419	1896	1958	
40	V09	BCW	£419	1896	1949	To Trial Train Van 245A
41	V09	BCW	£419	1896	1960	
1	V10	GCS		1897	1926	Pier Mails; to 114A in 1926
22	V11	GCS		1897	1959	Milk Van
13		Ex 3rd Bke 86 or 93		1898	1941	New body on old under-frame
16		Ex 3rd Bke 86 or 93		1898	1912	New body on old under-frame
4		Ex Compo 9		1899	1927	
14		Ex 1st 5		1899	1941	New body on old under-frame
15		Ex 1st 6		1900	1958	New body on old under-frame
3		Ex Compo 10		1901	1925	
17		Ex 1st 7		1901	1926	New body on old under-frame
6		Ex 1st 4		1903	1925	New body on old u/f; to 111A
18		Ex 1st 29		1903		To Stores Van 18A in 1907
7		Ex 1st 8		1903	1925	Malicious damage 1923
23	V12	GCS		1903	1949	Low Roof; Gangways
24	V12	GCS		1903	1949	Low Roof; Gangways
11	B07	GCS		1904	1960	Kitchen Van - Gangways
8		Ex 1st 14		1904	1941	U/frame to Motor Truck, Rosslare
12		Ex 3rd Bke 14 or 59		1904	1941	New body on old under-frame
19		Ex 3rd Bke 14 or 59		1904	1925	New body on old under-frame
9		Ex 1st 16		1906	1927	
18		Ex 1st 29		1907	1922	Maliciously destroyed
25		Ex 1st 25		1908	1952	Paint Stores Van 304A
21	V13	GCS		1910	1960	High Roof
26	V13	GCS		1910	1960	High Roof
10		Ex Compo 1		1911	1925	
16	B07	GCS		1912	1956	Kitchen Van; Gangways Destroyed in Mallow crash
20		Ex Kitchen 201		1912	1925	Gangways; Malicious damage 1923
27		Ex 1st 27		1913	1941	
28		Ex 1st 28		1913	1925	To 109A in 1925
18		GCS		1922	1960	Gangways; Steamheated 1936

HORSEBOXES

No	Type	Builder	Cost	Intr	Wdn	Remarks
1		B-M	£130	1856	1909	Rebuilt 1881
2		B-M	£135	1857	1896	
3		B-M	£135	1857	1896	
4		Frith	£132	1863	1900	
5		Frith	£132	1863	1898	
6		Frith	£132	1863	1900	
7		ASH	£195	1872	1904	
8		ASH	£195	1872	1909	

HORSEBOXES

No	Type	Builder	Cost	Intr	Wdn	Remarks
9		ASH	£195	1872	1904	
10		ASH	£174	1879	1927	
11		ASH	£174	1879	1926	
12		ASH	£174	1879	1927	
13		ASH	£174	1879	1926	
14		ASH	£174	1879	1955	
15		ASH	£174	1879	1941	Rebuilt 1907
16		B-M 1872		1894	1928	Ex Finn Valley Railway
2		GCS		1896	1925	
3		GCS		1896	1926	
17		GCS		1896	1926	
18		GCS		1896	1926	
5		GCS		1898	1926	
4		GCS		1900	1941	
19		GCS		1900	1925	
20		GCS		1904	1941	
6		GCS		1904	1926	
7		GCS		1909	1958	
9		GCS		1909	1958	
1		GCS		1913	1961	
8		GCS		1913	1961	
21		GCS		1914	1928	Built in 1907 for 'Boss' Croker

NON-BOGIE CARRIAGE STOCK

Type	Class	Length	Wheels	Corrs	Compartments	Seating	Weight
C01	Composite	?	6	NC	?	?	?
C02	Composite	30' 0"	6	NC	2x1st + 3x2nd	16x1st + 30x2nd	12 tons
C03	Composite	24' 6"	6	NC	2x1st + 2x2nd	16x1st + 20x2nd	11 tons
C04	Composite	30' 0"	6	NC	2x1st + Lug + 2x2nd	16x1st + 20x2nd	12 tons
C05	Composite	27' 6"	6	NC	1x2nd + Saloon 1st + 1x2nd + 1x3rd	14x1st + 20x2nd + 12x3rd	11 tons
C06	Composite	34' 4"	6	SC	2x1st + Lav + 3x2nd	13x1st + 25x2nd	15 tons
F01	First	?	?	NC	4x1st	32x1st	?
F02	First	22' 0"	6	NC	1x1st + Saloon + 1x1st	30x1st	?
F03	First	25' 2"	6	NC	4x1st	32x1st	11 tons
F04	First	24' 6"	6	NC	4x1st	32x1st	11 tons
F05	First Brake	24' 6"	6	NC	3x1st + Guard	24x1st	11 tons
F06	Saloon	24' 6"	6	Open	2 Saloons	19x1st	11 tons
F07	First Luggage	24' 6"	6	NC	3x1st + Luggage	24x1st	10 tons
F08	First	28' 0"	6	NC	4x1st	32x1st	12 tons
F09	First	30' 0"	6	NC	2 Saloons	24x1st	12 tons
F10	First	33' 6"	6	NC	5x1st	40x1st	13 tons
S01	Second	?	?	?	?	?	?
S02	Second	22' 0"	4	NC	5x2nd	50x2nd	?
S03	Second	31' 4"	6	NC	6x2nd	60x2nd	12 tons
S04	Second	27' 6"	6	NC	5x2nd	50x2nd	11 tons
S05	Second	28' 0"	6	NC	5x2nd	50x2nd	11 tons
S06	Second	31' 0"	6	SC	3x2nd + Lav + 2x2nd	45x2nd	12 tons
S07	Second	33' 6"	6	NC	5x2nd	50x2nd	13 tons
S08	Second	30' 0"	6	NC	5x2nd	50x2nd	12 tons
T01	Third	22' 0"	4	NC	5x3rd	60x3rd	?
T02	Third	?	?	NC	?	?	?
T03	Third	?	?	NC	?	?	?
T04	Third	26' 3"	4	NC	5x3rd	60x3rd	?
T05	Third	28' 0"	6	NC	6x3rd	72x3rd	11 tons
T06	Third	27' 6"	6	NC	5x3rd	60x3rd	12 tons
T07	Third	33' 6"	6	NC	6x3rd	72x3rd	13 tons
T08	Third	34' 4"	6	NC	6x3rd	72x3rd	14 tons
TB1	Third Brake	?	?	NC	3x3rd + Guard	36x3rd	?
TB2	Third Brake	21' 6"	4	NC	1x3rd + Guard + 2x3rd	36x3rd	?
TB3	Third Brake	21' 6"	4	NC	1x3rd + Guard + 2x3rd	36x3rd	?
TB4	Third Brake	30' 0"	6	NC	4x3rd + Guard	48x3rd	12 tons
TB5	Third Brake	27' 6"	6	NC	4½x3rd + Guard	54x3rd	12 tons
TB6	Third Brake	30' 0"	6	NC	3x3rd + Guard	36x3rd	12 tons
TB7	Third Brake	34' 4"	6	NC	4x3rd + Guard	48x3rd	13 tons
TB8	Third Brake	27' 6"	6	NC	3x3rd + Guard	36x3rd	12 tons
V01	Pass Bke Van	?					
V02	Pass Bke Van	22' 0"	4				8 tons
V03	Pass Bke Van	20' 0"	4				?
V04	Pass Bke Van	21' 6"	4				8 tons
V05	Pass Bke Van	25' 0"	4				9 tons
V06	Pass Bke Van	27' 6"	6				11 tons
V07	Milk Van	27' 6"	6				11 tons
V08	TPO Van	28' 0"	6				12 tons
V09	Pass Bke Van	30' 0"	6				12 tons
V10	Mail Van	30' 0"	6				12 tons
V11	Milk Van	30' 0"	6				12 tons
V12	Pass Bke Van	34' 4"	6				13 tons
V13	Pass Bke Van	34' 4"	6				13 tons

8 - WHEEL BOGIE CARRIAGE STOCK

Type	Class	Length	G'wys	Corrs	Compartments	Seating	Wt
B01	Composite	44' 0"	–	NC	1 x 3rd + 2 x 2nd + 2 Lav +2 x 1st + 1 x 3rd	15 x 1st + 19 x 2nd +24 x 3rd	23 tons
B02	Composite	45' 0"	–	SC	2 x 1st + Lav + 3 x 1st + 1 x 2nd	31 x 1st + 9 x 2nd	23 tons
B03	Third	45' 0"	–	NC	4 x 3rd + 2 Lav + 4 x 3rd	92 x 3rd	22 tons
B04	Composite	45' 0"	–	NC	1 x 2nd + 2 Lav + 4 x 1st +2 Lav + 1 x 2nd	30 x 1st + 18 x 2nd	24 tons
B05	Second	45' 0"	2	OC	5 x 2nd + 2 Lav + 2 x 2nd	56 x 2nd	23 tons
B06	First	50' 0"	2	OC	5 x 1st + Lav + 1½ x 1st	37 x 1st	25 tons
B07	Kitchen Van	50' 0"	2		Kitchen + Van & Guard		21 tons
B08	Restaurant	50' 0"	2	OC	2 x 1st + Kitchen +2 x 2nd	12 x 1st +16 x 2nd	26 tons
B09	Restaurant	50' 0"	2	SC	Lav + 8 x 3rd + Lav	80 x 3rd	24 tons
B10	Saloon	50' 0"	2	OC	3 Saloons	25 x 1st	25 tons
B11	Composite	50' 0"	2	SC	Lav + 3 x 1st + 4 x 2nd + Lav	18 x 1st + 32 x 2nd	26 tons
B12	Restaurant	54' 0"	2	O&S	2 x 1st + Lav + 1 x 1st + 1 x 2nd + Lav + 2 x 2nd	18 x 1st + 24 x 2nd	28 tons
B13	Composite	54' 0"	–	NC	5 x 1st + 3 x 2nd	40 x 1st + 30 x 2nd	25 tons
B14	Composite	44' 0"	–	OC	2 x 1st + 5 x 2nd +1 x 3rd	18 x 1st + 44 x 2nd +12 x 3rd	22 tons
B15	Second Brake	54' 0"	–	NC	5 x 2nd + Van & Guard	50 x 2nd	24 tons
B16	Third Brake	54' 0"	–	NC	9 x 3rd + Guard	108 x 3rd	25 tons
B17	Composite	57' 0"	–	NC	4 x 1st + 5 x 2nd	32 x 1st + 50 x 2nd	26 tons
B18	Composite	58' 0"	2	SC	Lav + 4 x 1st + 4 x 2nd + Lav	24 x 1st + 32 x 2nd	29 tons
B19	Third	58' 0"	2	SC	Lav + 9 x 3rd + Lav	90 x 3rd	29 tons
B20	Composite	58' 0"	–	NC	5 x 1st + 4 x 2nd	50 x 1st + 48 x 2nd	28 tons
B21	Third	58' 0"	–	NC	10 x 3rd	120 x 3rd	27 tons
B22	Composite	58' 0"	–	NC	4 x 1st + 5 x 2nd	32 x 1st + 50 x 2nd	28 tons
B23	Second Brake	58' 0"	–	NC	5 x 2nd + Van & Guard	50 x 2nd	26 tons
B24	Third Brake	58' 0"	–	NC	9 x 3rd + Guard	108 x 3rd	27 tons

GOODS WAGONS

The original builds of the various types of wagon are given below. Covered goods wagons were of two types: those with open centre roofs designated cov and those with continuous roofs shown as van. Although numbered amongst the wagon stock, carriage trucks and fish vans were listed with the passenger stock in the company's reports. One mineral wagon destroyed by accident in 1868 was replaced by new covered wagon No 385 in 1870.

Wagon Nos	Intr	Capacity	Type	Builder	Cost
1 & 2	1855		COV	Ex MGWR ?	?
3 & 4	1856		COV	DAW	£105
5 to 12	1856		COV	B-M	£105
13 to 24	1857		COV	ASH	£115
25 to 48	1858		COV	DAW	£107
49 to 60	1860		OPE	DAW	£94
61 to 85	1861		COV	B-M	£123
86 to 125	1863		COV	MCW	£114
126 to 135	1863		OPE	MCW	£109
136 to 185	1863-64		COV	TCM	£114
186 to 195	1856-62		CT&TT	Renumbered to Wagon Stock	–
196 to 215	1862		TIP	MCW	£83
216 to 227	1863		MIN	MCW	£76
228 to 241	1856-59		LEAD	Renumbered Ballast Wagons	–
242 to 245	1864		MIN Bke	TCM	£89
246 to 271	1864		MIN	TCM	£84
272 to 294	1864		MIN	TCM	£84
295 to 297	1864		COV	?	?
298 & 299	1864		OPE	?	?

GOODS WAGONS

Wagon Nos	Intr	Capacity	Type	Builder	Cost
300 to 324	1864-65		MIN	TCM	£84
325 to 335	1864-65		TIP	TCM	£118
336 to 355	1867		MIN	TCM	£100
356 to 385	1867		MIN	TCM	£97
228 to 241	1870		COV	MCW	£112
385 to 390	1870		COV	MCW	£112
391 to 410	1872		COV	MCW	£112
411 to 430	1872	8 tons	OPE	MCW	£118
431 to 450	1873	8 tons	OPE	MID	£134
451 to 470	1873		COV	MCW	£146
471 to 520	1876	8 tons	COV	CRA	£133
521 to 561	1878	8 tons	COV	ASH	£130
562 to 566	1885	8 tons	OPE	GCS	£121
567 to 616	1887	8 tons	COV	MCW	£98
617 to 646	1891	8 tons	COV	MCW	£131
647 to 650	1892-93		FISH	GCS	?
651 to 690	1894	8 tons	VAN	MID	£115
691 to 715	1894	8 tons	COV	B-M 1872 Ex Finn Valley Rly	–
716 & 717	1894	8 tons	OPE	B-M 1872 Ex Finn Valley Rly	–
718	1894		CT	B-M 1872 Ex Finn Valley Rly	–
719 to 768	1895	8 tons	COV	BCW	£100
769 to 793	1895	10 tons	OPE	BCW	£85
794 to 796	1895	8 tons	OPE	GCS	£89
797 to 800	1895	8 tons	TT	GCS	£95
801 to 806	1895	8 tons	OPE	GCS	£92
807 to 831	1898	8 tons	LOCO	GCS	£97
832 & 833	1898		GAS	GCS	£92
834 to 845	1899	7 tons	MIN	Ex Parnell Quarry	£32
846	1900	8 tons	LOCO	GCS	£109
847	1902		CT	GCS	?
848 to 872	1902	8 tons	CAT	GCS	£86
873 to 897	1902	8 tons	VAN	ASH	£116
898 to 900	Not issued				–
901 to 915	1904	12 tons	OPE	GCS	£88
916 to 930	1904	12 tons	OPE	H-N	£94
931 to 934	1904	8 tons	TIM	GCS	£90
935	1904	15 tons	BOIL	GCS	£107
936 to 975	1906	8 tons	COV	GCS	£90
976 to 1010	1906		COV	Renumbered Duplicate Stock	–
1011 to 1045	1906	8 tons	CAT	H-N	£117
1046	1907	8 tons	LOCO	GCS	£94
1047 to 1064	1911	12 tons	OPE	GCS	£105
1065 to 1089	1914	12 tons	OPE	ChR	£101
1090 to 1114	1914-15	8 tons	CAT	GCS	£113

ROLLING STOCK BUILDERS

ASH	Ashbury Carriage & Iron Co, Manchester
BCW	Birmingham Carriage & Wagon Co
B-M	Brown Marshall & Co, Birmingham
ChR	Chas Roberts, Wakefield
CRA	Craven Brothers, Sheffield
DAW	J S Dawson (later Dawson & Russell), Dublin
Frith	Thomas Frith, Belfast
GCS	DW&WR/D&SER, Grand Canal Street, Dublin
H-N	Hurst Nelson, Motherwell
LCW	Lancaster Carriage & Wagon Co
MCW	Metropolitan Carriage & Wagon Co, Saltley
MID	Midland Carriage & Wagon Co
M-W	Manning Wardle, Leeds
TCM	T&C Martin, North Wall, Dublin

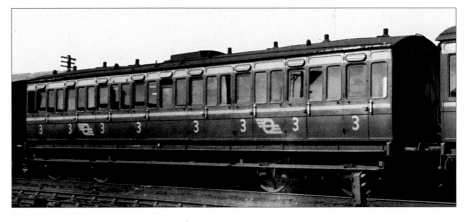

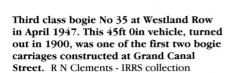

Third class bogie No 35 at Westland Row in April 1947. This 45ft 0in vehicle, turned out in 1900, was one of the first two bogie carriages constructed at Grand Canal Street. R N Clements - IRRS collection

METROPOLITAN 24'5" FIRST CLASS – 1870

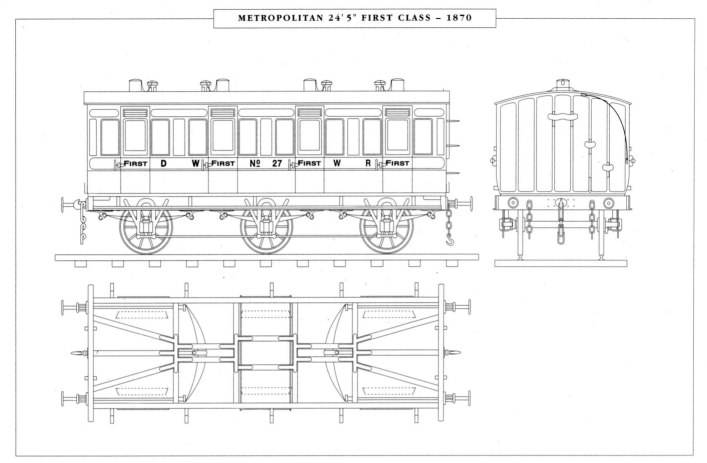

METROPOLITAN 31'4" SECOND CLASS – 1870

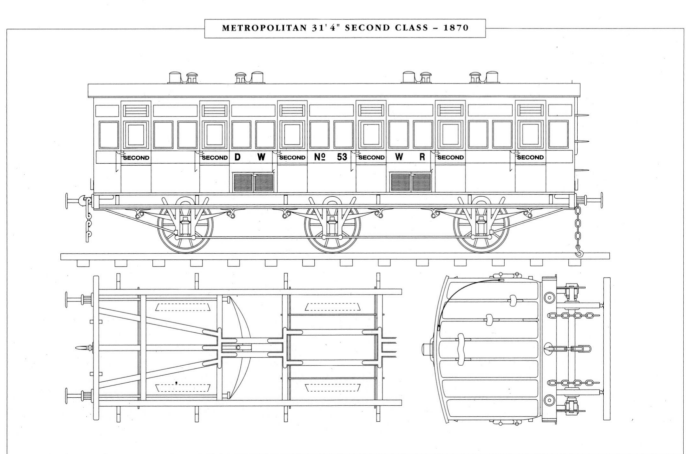

Based on drawings by Herbert Richards

33' 6" FIVE COMPARTMENT & 31' 4" THIRD BRAKE

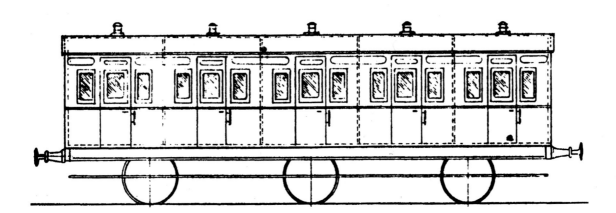

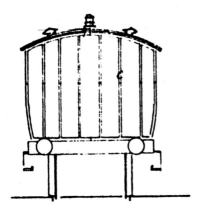

33' 6" Five Compartment

First Class
Nos 5, 6, 8, 15 and 16.

Second Class
Nos 5, 32, 53, 54 and 68 to 73,
built from 1896-1906.

Length over headstocks - 33' 6"
Wheelbase - 11' 0" + 11' 0"
Rail to buffer centres - 3' 6" unloaded
Rail to rooftop - 12' 3"
Rail to ventilators - 13' 1"
Carriage body width (excluding overhang) - 9' 0"
Width over steps - 9' 3"

31' 4" Third Brake
Nos 17, 21, 40, 64, 67,
76, 70, 86 and 87
as converted from
Second Class 1909-1916.

Length over headstocks - 31' 4"
Wheelbase - 9' 6½" + 9' 6½"
Rail to buffer centres - 3' 6" unloaded
Rail to rooftop - 11' 2"
Rail to ventilators - 12' 0"
Carriage body width (excluding overhang) - 9' 0"
Width over steps - 9' 6"

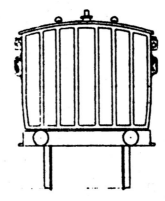

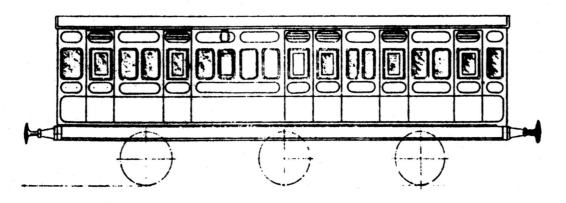

45'0" BOGIE THIRD & 50'0" BOGIE SALOON

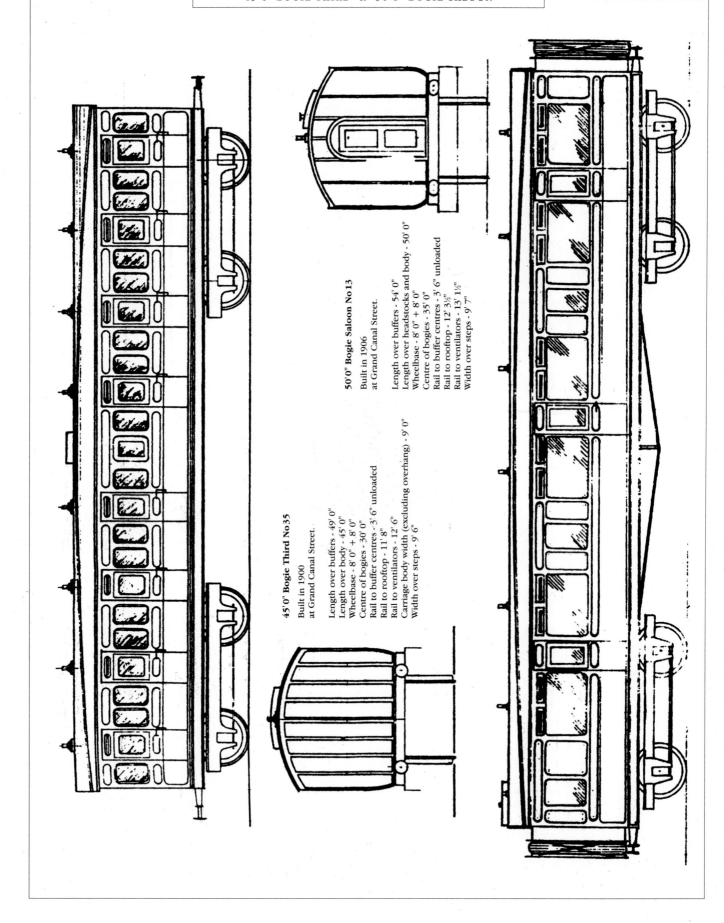

45'0" Bogie Third No 35

Built in 1900
at Grand Canal Street.

Length over buffers - 49' 0"
Length over body - 45' 0"
Wheelbase - 8' 0" + 8' 0"
Centre of bogies - 30' 0"
Rail to buffer centres - 3' 6" unloaded
Rail to rooftop - 11' 8"
Rail to ventilators - 12' 6"
Carriage body width (excluding overhang) - 9' 0"
Width over steps - 9' 6"

50'0" Bogie Saloon No 13

Built in 1906
at Grand Canal Street.

Length over buffers - 54' 0"
Length over headstocks and body - 50' 0"
Wheelbase - 8' 0" + 8' 0"
Centre of bogies - 35' 0"
Rail to buffer centres - 3' 6" unloaded
Rail to rooftop - 12' 3½"
Rail to ventilators - 13' 1½"
Width over steps - 9' 7"

ASHBURY 13'6" COVERED WAGON 1902

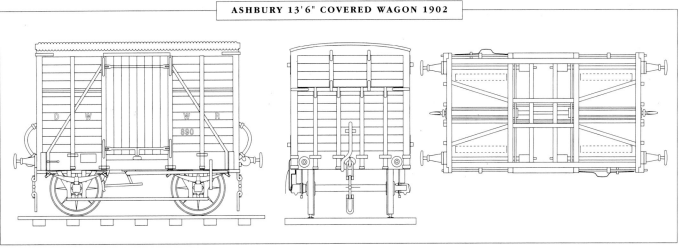

HURST NELSON 16'0" OPEN WAGON 1904

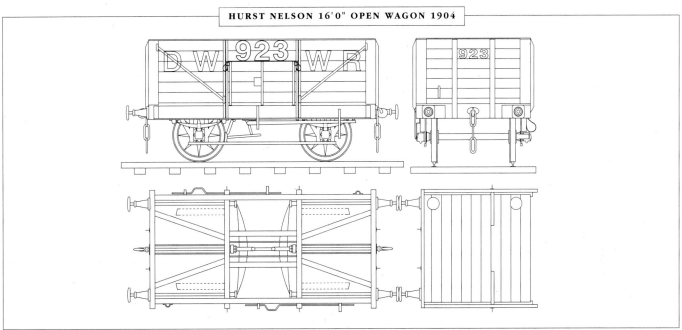

15'4" OPEN WAGON REBUILD c1920

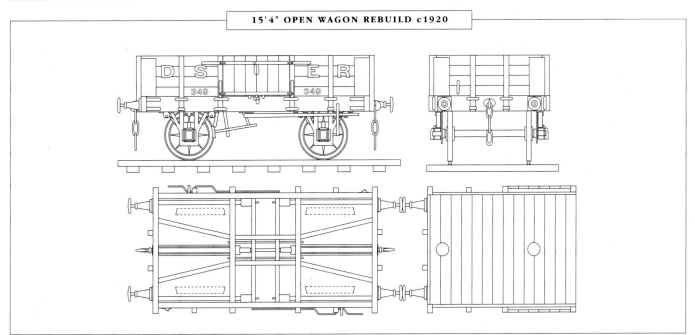

Based on drawings by Herbert Richards

Appendix F

LIST OF STATIONS, JUNCTIONS AND SIDINGS

DUBLIN - WEXFORD

Miles	Station	Open	Closed	Remarks
00.00	Harcourt Street	1859	1958	
00.10	Harcourt Road	1854	1859	
01.00	Rathmines & Ranelagh	1896	1958	
01.60	Milltown	1860	1958	
03.00	Dundrum	1854	1958	
05.20	Stillorgan	1854	1958	
06.10	Foxrock	1861	1958	Temporary platform provided in 1859
07.20	Carrickmines	1854	1958	
09.55	Shankill	1854	1958	
10.65	Shanganagh Junction	1854	1877	No junction 1877-1915.
10.42	Shanganagh Junction	1915	1961	New junction - no station.
11.10	Woodbrook	1910	1960	Repositioned with 1915 diversion.
12.20	Bray	1854	Open	
13.10	Bray Head Halt	1906	1907	
13.60	Worthington's Siding	1873	1882	
14.10	Stone Siding	c1860	?	
16.24	Jubilee Siding	1918	?	Site of Creosoting plant 1918-21.
17.05	Greystones & Delgany	1855	Open	
19.66	Kilcool	1855	Open	Closed 1964-80.
22.38	Newcastle	1856	1964	
25.44	Killoughter	1855	1867	
27.69	Wicklow Junction	1861	1989	No station - Chemical Works sidings.
(28.00)	Hibernian Brick Siding	1861	?	
(28.32)	Wicklow (original station)	1855	1989	Closed for passenger traffic 1885-1969 and from 1976.
28.20	Wicklow	1885	Open	
29.54	Rathnew	1866	1964	
30.37	Brickfields Siding	1896	1931	
32.54	Glenealy	1861	1866	
33.20	Glenealy	1866	1964	
36.09	Rathdrum (Kilcommon)	1861	1863	
37.24	Rathdrum	1863	Open	
38.17	Balleece Siding	1901	1937	
40.20	Connorree Siding	1865	1869	
41.30	Cronebane Siding	1874	1940	Also known as Tigroney siding.
42.66	Ovoca	1863	1964	Renamed Avoca, 1912.
44.60	Woodenbridge Junction	1865	1964	Sidings in use until 1968.
46.48	Shelton Abbey Sidings	1964	Open	Two connections with main line.
47.05	Glenart	18??	?	Private platform
49.00	Arklow	1863	Open	
50.60	Kish Siding	1886	c1940	
53.40	Inch	1885	1964	
59.44	Gorey	1863	Open	
67.08	Camolin	1867	1964	
69.71	Ferns	1863	1977	
73.20	Scarawalsh Ballast Pit	1918	c1925	
77.40	Enniscorthy	1863	Open	
77.52	Roche's Siding	1879	c1965	
78.40	St Johns Siding	1873	1965	Also served Kavanagh's cartway.
81.03	Edermine Ferry	1872	1964	
83.30	Macmine Junction	1873	1964	
86.16	Killurin	1872	1964	
87.00	Killurin Ballast Pit	?	?	Site of old ballast pit.
91.52	Park Siding	1872	18??	Temporary terminus.
92.12	Wexford (Carcur)	1872	1874	
92.54	Wexford	1874	Open	

MACMINE JUNCTION - WATERFORD

Miles	Station	Open	Closed	Remarks
83.30	Macmine Junction	1873	1964	
86.34	Sparrowsland	1870	1876	Siding in use until 1963.
89.69	Chapel	1876	1963	
93.69	Palace East	1870	1963	
96.55	Rathgarogue	1894	1963	
102.09	New Ross	1887	1963	Remained open for freight until 1993.
102.60	Stafford's Wharf	1927	19 . . ?	Fertiliser traffic 1964.
108.02	Glenmore & Aylwardstown	1904	1963	Remained open for goods until 1974.
115.57	Abbey Junction	1904	Open	No station.
116.17	Waterford	1906	Open	GS&WR station.

WOODENBRIDGE - SHILLELAGH

Miles	Station	Open	Closed	Remarks
44.60	Woodenbridge Junction	1865	1964	
49.25	Aughrim	1865	1944	Remained open for goods to 1947 and stone to 1952.
53.58	Ballinglen	1875	1944	
56.54	Tinahely	1865	1944	
61.16	Shillelagh	1865	1944	

WESTLAND ROW - SHANGANAGH JUNCTION

Miles	Station	Open	Closed	Remarks
00.00	Westland Row	1834	Open	Original terminus of D&KR.
00.25	Grand Canal Street	1837	1925	D&KR and D&SER Workshops.
01.07	Lansdowne Road & Ballsbridge	1870	Open	D&KR Engine Hospital located here 1834-39.
(01.39)	RDS Sidings	1893	1971	
01.40	Serpentine Avenue	1835	1835	
01.52	Sandymount	1835	Open	Closed 1841-60, 1862-82, 1901-28 & 1960-84.
02.20	Sydney Parade	1835	Open	Closed 1841-62 & 1960-72.
02.60	Merrion	1835	1934	Closed 1862-82 & 1901-28.
03.20	Booterstown	1835	Open	Closed 1960-75.
03.50	Williamstown	1835	1841	
04.07	Blackrock	1834	Open	
04.60	Seapoint	1862	Open	
05.26	Salthill & Monkstown	1837	Open	Closed 1960-84.
05.40	Kingstown	1834	1837	Original terminus.
06.04	Dun Laoghaire	1837	Open	Known as Kingstown until 1920.
06.15	Carlisle Pier Junction	1859	1980	No station.
(06.33)	Carlisle Pier	1859	1980	
06.58	Sandycove & Glasthule	1855	Open	
07.20	Glenageary	1867	Open	
07.55	Atmospheric Terminus	1844	1854	
07.57	Glenageary Siding	18??	1918	
08.05	Dalkey	1854	Open	
09.00	Obelisk Hill	1855	1857	
09.50	Killiney	1854	1882	Station building re-sited 1858.
09.74	Killiney & Ballybrack	1882	Open	
10.15	Ballybrack	1854	1857	
10.20	Ballybrack	1857	1882	
11.20	Shankill	1977	Open	New station at Corbawn Lane.
12.10	Shanganagh Junction	1861	1877	No junction 1877-1915.
11.77	Shanganagh Junction	1915	1961	New junction - no station.

WESTLAND ROW - NEWCOMEN JUNCTION

Miles	Station	Open	Closed	Remarks
00.00	Westland Row	1834	Open	
00.20	Tara Street & George's Quay	1891	Open	
01.01	Amiens Street Junction	1891	Open	Interchange with GNR(I)
01.23	Newcomen Junction	1891	Open	No station - junction with MGWR.

Note:
Distances are given in miles and chains.
Those mileages in brackets refer to facilities not on main line.

Appendix G

LEVEL CROSSINGS AS IN APPENDIX TO GSR WTT

Name of Crossing		Station to which attached	Harcourt St Miles/Yards		Signalling, Direction	Inter-locked	Cottage Attached
HARCOURT STREET TO WEXFORD							
Leopardstown	*	Stillorgan	5	880	Up Down	Yes	Yes
Tulla		Carrickmines	8	0	Up Down	Yes	Yes
Station Gates	C	Bray	12	300	Up Down	Yes	
Ennis Lane		Greystones	15	1,700	None		Yes
Station Gates		Kilcool	19	1,500	None		
Station Gates		Newcastle	22	880	None		
Five Mile Point		Newcastle	23	440	None		Yes
Killoughter		Wicklow	25	940	None		Yes
Chemical Yard.		Wicklow	27	1,580	None		Yes
Bolarney		Wicklow	28	360	None		Yes
Ballymerrigan		Rathnew	30	1,320	None		Yes
Ballymanus	C	Glenealy	32	1,190	Up Down		Yes
Kilcommon No.1		Rathdrum	35	1,320	None		Yes
Kilcommon No.2		Rathdrum	36	440	None		Yes
Station Gates		Woodenbridge	44	1,440	None		
Aske		Gorey	56	1,700	None		
Knockinagh		Gorey	57	730	None		Yes
Tullabeg		Camolin	65	630	None		Yes
Crory		Ferns	71	630	None		Yes
Station Gates	CX	Edermine	81	160	Up Down	Yes	
NEW ROSS AND WATERFORD							
Rathgarogue No.1	C	Rathgarogue	95	1,560	No		Yes
Rathgarogue No.2	C	Rathgarogue	96	750	Up Down	(H)	Yes
Station Gates	CX	New Ross	102	300	Up Down	Yes	
Ballyverneen		Glenmore	106	530	None		Yes
Carrigcloney	C	Glenmore	107	540	None		Yes
Glenmore No.1		Glenmore	107	1,370	None		Yes
Rathinure		Glenmore	109	580	None		Yes
Curraghmore	C	Waterford	111	680	Down		Yes

Name of Crossing		Station to which attached	Harcourt St Miles/Yards		Signalling, Direction	Inter-locked	Cottage Attached
NEW ROSS AND WATERFORD (continued)							
Luffney		Waterford	111	1,450	None		Yes
Rathpatrick	C	Waterford	112	800	Down		Yes
WOODENBRIDGE & SHILLELAGH							
Coolattin		Shillelagh	59	1,140	None		Yes
Shillelagh	C	Shillelagh	61	440	None		
WESTLAND ROW AND BRAY							
Station Gates	CX	Lansdowne Road	1	440	Up Down	Yes	
Serpentine Avenue	CX	Lansdowne Road	1	880	Up Down	Yes	
Sandymount	CX	Lansdowne Road	1	1,320	Up Down	Yes	
Station Gates	CX	Sydney Parade	2	440	Up Down	Yes	
Merrion	CX	Sydney Parade	2	1,320	Up Down	Yes	
Dunleary	CX	Salthill	5	880	Up Down	Yes	
Carlisle Pier	CX	Dun Laoghaire	6	440	Up Down	Yes	
Coal Quay	CX	Dun Laoghaire	–		Up Down	Yes	
Victoria Wharf	CX	Dun Laoghaire	–		None		
Shanganagh or Fields		Killiney	11	0	Up Down	Yes	Yes

Notes: C = Gates extend across railway line when open to public road traffic
CX = Gates are an exception to Rule 99
(H) = Operated by Gate Heel
* = Gates are an exception to Rule 99 but do not extend across Railway line.

Rule 99 states: Unless special authority be given to the contrary, the gates at level crossings must be kept closed across the roadway, except when required to be opened to allow the line to be crossed.

Appendix H

SIGNAL CABINS, 1924

Location	Built	Frame	Levers	Closed	Remarks
Harcourt Street	1878	Stevens	20	20-02-38	Replaced by new electric cabin
Ranelagh	1896	McK&H	9	10-09-28	Block post from 15-11-06
(Milltown)	1892	McK&H	7	-23	Instruments to Ranelagh 15-11-06
Dundrum	1886	McK&H	11	01-04-59	
Stillorgan	1892	McK&H	7	19-01-42	
Leopardstown	1892	McK&H	3	01-04-59	Not a block post
Foxrock	1924	WB&SS	28	01-04-59	Old cabin destroyed 1922 - new enlarged cabin opened 1924
Shankill	1893	McK&H	12	01-04-59	
Shanganagh Junction	1915	McK&H	20	10-07-61	Junction dispensed with
Bray (North)	1894	McK&H	31	16-09-27	Replaced by new cabin
Bray (South)	1894	McK&H	44	16-09-27	Replaced by above new cabin
Greystones	1888	McK&H	15	-26	Replaced by new cabin and 18 lever RSC frame
Newcastle	1924	WB&SS?	10	21-04-68	Old cabin destroyed 1922 - 21 lever frame 1938
Wicklow Junction	1877	Stevens?	14	07-08-27	
Wicklow	1884	McK&H	10	In use	22 lever frame 08-27
Glenealy	1893	McK&H	20	30-03-64	Cabin rebuilt 1923
Rathdrum	1888	McK&H	13	In use	
Avoca	1893	McK&H	16	12-01-31	
Woodenbridge	1889	McK&H	22	21-04-68	
Arklow	1893	McK&H	16	In use	
Gorey	1891	McK&H	18	In use	
Ferns	1893	McK&H	15	22-09-76	
Enniscorthy	1888	McK&H	18	In use	Cabin rebuilt 1923
Edermine	1919	?	7	?	Not a block post
Macmine Junction	1887	McK&H	31	01-04-64	Cabin rebuilt 1924
Killurin	1893	McK&H	14	-22?	
Wexford	1895	McK&H	24	In use	
Amiens Street (South)	1906	McK&H	40	28-10-34	Replaced by new electric cabin
Tara Street	1891	McK&H	?	25-06-25	Block post from 1901
Westland Row	1881	McK&H	40	26-01-36	Replaced by new electric cabin
Grand Canal Street	1894	McK&H	16	24-05-36	Replaced by above new cabin
Lansdowne Road	1871	S&F ?	19	02-85	
Serpentine Avenue	1910	McK&H	7	02-85	Cabin rebuilt 1923 - Not a block post
Sandymount	1871	S&F ?	9	03-11-37	Replaced by new electric cabin
Sydney Parade	1871	S&F ?	9	02-85	
Merrion	1871	S&F ?	10	11-03-84	13 levers from 06-05-36
Blackrock	1924	WB&SS ?	8	03-11-37	Old cabin destroyed 1923
Salthill	1888	?	6	21-03-26	
Dunleary	1893	McK&H	5	21-03-83	Block post 21-03-26 to 16-06-57
Dun Laoghaire (North)	1895	McK&H	34	14-03-26	Replaced by new cabin
Dun Laoghaire (South)	?	?	?	14-03-26	Replaced by above new cabin
Carlisle Pier	1891	McK&H	13	10-03-62	Replaced by new cabin
Sandycove	1900	McK&H	6	28-03-26	Cabin rebuilt 1923
Dalkey	1896	McK&H	17	21-03-83	Cabin rebuilt 1922
Killiney	1915	McK&H	14	04-08-83	Cabin rebuilt 1923
Aughrim	1893	McK&H	19	05-24	
Tinahely	1893	McK&H	21	05-24	
Shillelagh	1893	McK&H	10	24-04-44	Cabin rebuilt 1897
Palace East	1924	WB&SS	16	01-04-63	Old cabin destroyed 1923 - new enlarged cabin
New Ross	1904	McK&H	20	18-04-66	
Glenmore	1904	McK&H	16	29-07-29	

Appendix I

PRINCIPAL ACCIDENTS

Date	Location	Public K	Inj	Staff K	Inj	Description
20-12-57	Kingstown	–	–	–	1	Locomotive collided with carriages.
09-02-58	Sandycove	–	1	–	1	Down train collided with runaway wagons from Dalkey.
26-03-58	Harcourt Road	–	3	–	–	11.55 am from Wicklow collided with carriages at platform.
10-08-61	Greystones	–	1	–	–	Train collided with locomotive.
15-07-63	Kingstown	–	10	–	–	Collision between 5.45 pm Down and 6.0 pm Up trains.
17-11-63	Enniscorthy	–	1	–	–	Up Night Mail turned into siding.
25-03-65	Bray	–	5	–	–	5.0 pm Down overran signals and collided with wagons.
23-04-65	Bray Head	–	–	–	–	9.0 am Down passenger train derailed.
09-08-67	Bray Head	2	23	–	2	6.30 am Up train derailed and fell into ravine.
17-02-68	Bray	–	?	–	–	5.0 pm Down collided with ballast wagons.
25-09-68	Sydney Parade	–	–	–	–	6.30 pm Down Mail struck cow on crossing and derailed.
23-11-68	Serpentine Ave	–	2	–	–	Up Mail collided with van on level crossing.
31-01-70	Westland Row	–	–	–	–	6.30 pm Up Mail train derailed.
16-09-72	Bray	–	–	–	2	Boiler of locomotive No 4 exploded.
26-04-73	Rathdrum	–	2	–	–	Footbridge collapsed under weight of crowd.
24-11-73	Cronebane	–	–	–	–	Collision between 2.0 pm Down passenger and Mineral train.
08-05-74	Blackrock	–	–	–	3	7.0 pm Down Mail derailed due to broken tyre.
04-04-77	Ovoca	–	1	–	–	Collision between 1.10 pm Up goods train and Cattle Special.
04-07-77	Dalkey	1	7	–	–	7.55 pm Up train from Bray derailed on facing points.
27-02-78	Glenageary	1	16	–	1	11.45 am Down collided with runaway wagons from Dalkey.
19-04-78	Bray Head	–	–	–	–	2.0 pm Down passenger train turned into the Stone siding.
07-09-78	Dalkey	–	–	–	1	Collision between Mineral and Ballast trains.
17-06-81	Kingstown	–	–	–	–	Thirteen ballast wagons ran away into Harbour.
17-02-83	Scarawalsh	–	–	–	–	8.10 pm Down goods derailed due to washout of track.
19-07-83	Kingstown	–	1	–	–	10.45 am train derailed.
09-04-84	Blackrock	–	35	–	–	Light engine ran into rear of 6.0 am Down train.
24-08-84	Enniscorthy	–	2	–	–	Collision.
05-12-87	Seapoint.	–	–	–	–	Trailing locomotive of a pair of light engines derailed.
21-02-88	Enniscorthy	–	6	–	1	2.0 pm Down train collided with Cattle Special.
29-12-88	Woodenbridge	–	1	–	–	Shillelagh goods train pushed into field.
10-07-90	Westland Row	–	?	–	–	Shunting engine collided with rear of outgoing 10.10 pm train.
27-11-90	Shankill	–	1?	–	–	Collision between Wexford passenger and Bray goods trains.
23-04-91	Westland Row	–	2	–	–	Locomotive collided with train when backing down.
03-08-91	Leopardstown	1	–	–	–	Light engine collided with horse and cart on level crossing.
06-08-95	Ovoca	–	–	1	1	8.0 pm Down goods collided with Up empty carriage special.
06-12-95	New Ross	–	–	–	–	Train ran through end of terminal station.
03-12-97	Wicklow Jct	–	–	–	2	Engine collided with Ballast train van in Chemical sidings.
11-05-98	Tinahely	–	1	–	–	Derailment at points.
14-08-98	Greystones	–	2?	–	–	Engine backed down too quickly onto train.
27-12-98	Bray	–	–	1	–	P.W. Inspector knocked down and fatally injured.
03-11-99	Seapoint	–	3+	–	8?	Head-on collision between Up passenger and Breakdown train.
14-02-00	Harcourt Street	–	–	–	1	Up Enniscorthy Cattle Special ran through end wall of station.
17-03-00	Glenealy	–	2	–	–	Collision between 6.10 pm Down passenger and Up goods.
05-09-00	Tara Street	–	–	–	–	Light engine collided with rear of Down passenger train.
14-11-02	Westland Row	–	?	–	–	2.25 pm Up train from Bray collided with empty carriages.
16-04-07	Shankill	–	–	–	–	Down empty Cattle Special derailed on incomplete trackwork.
29-02-08	Bray	–	–	2	–	Two shunters struck by carriage.
24-03-09	North Wall	–	–	–	1	D&SER train collided with empty MGWR passenger train.
11-05-11	Kingstown	–	?	–	–	Derailment.
15-06-12	Foxrock	–	1	–	–	Derailment of Down Race Special.
28-03-14	Shanganagh	–	–	2	–	Two milesmen struck by 10.15 am Down train.
04-12-14	Avoca	–	–	–	–	Derailment of Down night goods train.
30-08-17	Harcourt Street	–	–	–	–	Engine ran through engine shed and fell into garden.
07-12-18	Edermine	–	–	1	–	Stationmaster fatally injured by train whilst opening gates.
05-08-21	Enniscorthy Tunnel	–	–	1	5	Enniscorthy shunting engine collided with P.W. trolley.
24-02-23	Bray Head	–	–	–	1	7.40 am Up Wexford passenger train ran into rock fall.
01-05-23	Amiens Street	–	2	–	–	Engine overran turntable and fell into Post Office cloakroom.
07-07-23	Carlisle Pier	–	5	–	–	Reversing train struck motor car on level crossing.

Appendix J

MALICIOUS DAMAGE & DESTRUCTION 1922-23

Date	Location	Details
02-07-22	Dalkey	Signal cabin destroyed by fire.
02-07-22	Killiney	Signal cabin destroyed by fire.
04-07-22	Inch	Bridge damaged.
06-07-22	Inch	Two bridges damaged.
10-07-22	Killurin	Bridge 399 blown up - train derailed and locomotive No 17 fell into River Slaney.
14-07-22	Bridge 457	Blown up.
16-07-22	Palace East	Signal cabin burnt down.
24-07-22	Killurin	Train ambushed.
27-07-22	New Ross	Bridge blown up.
31-07-22	Palace East	Bridge blown up.
15-08-22	Killurin	Down night mail hauled by loco No 14 derailed.
26-08-22	Shankill	Two bridges blown up.
06-09-22	Dalkey	Temporary signal cabin burnt down.
09-09-22	Macmine Jct.	Signal cabin & waiting room burnt down.
16-09-22	Enniscorthy	Signal cabin burnt down.
04-10-22	Inch	Station raided and considerable damage done.
14-10-22	Ballyanne	Train and locomotive No 36 derailed.
16-10-22	Newcastle	Signal cabin destroyed.
17-10-22	Glenealy	Signal cabin burnt down.
07-11-22	North Wall	MGW locomotive No 96 sent from Liffey Jct; 7 D&SE wagons destroyed.
09-11-22	Waterford	Carriage & Wagon shed damaged.
21-11-22	Foxrock	Attempt to wreck goods train.
23-11-22	Killurin	Train derailed; locomotive No 18 thrown into River Slaney.
25-11-22	Sparrowsland	Train derailed; locomotive No 36 damaged.
26-11-22	Foxrock	Signal cabin burnt to the ground.
28-11-22	Rathpatrick	Train held up and mails removed.
07-12-22	Killurin	Train derailed; locomotive No 32 thrown into River Slaney.
09-12-22	Serpentine Avenue	Signal cabin burnt down; signalman badly burnt.
10-12-22	Waterford	GS&W/D&SE goods sheds burnt down; 9 D&SE wagons destroyed.
17-12-22	Killiney	Temporary signal cabin burnt down.
23-12-22	Killiney	Attempt to burn train but little damage.

Date	Location	Details
03-01-23	Macmine Jct.	Station and signal cabin burnt down - damage estimated at £1,400.
08-01-23	Carrickmines	Raid on 07.15 down - mailbags removed.
10-01-23	Ballyanne	Collision between locomotives Nos 25 & 56.
16-01-23	Ballyanne	17.00 mixed ex Macmine derailed - locomotive No 17 damaged.
18-01-23	Scarawalsh	Mail train set on fire, 1 six-wheeled and 3 bogie carriages destroyed.
20-01-23	Palace East	Head-on collision; locomotives Nos 51 & 68 wrecked.
27-01-23	Macmine Jct.	Triple collision and fire; locomotive No 22 wrecked, 3 carriages completely destroyed and 4 seriously damaged, 1 other slightly damaged, 8 wagons destroyed and 6 seriously damaged.
29-01-23	Killiney	Four carriages destroyed by fire.
31-01-23	Dog's Road	Bridge 457 wrecked; locomotive No 39 damaged and 2 carriages destroyed.
01-02-23	Tinahely	Signal cabin burnt down.
02-02-23	Near Palace East	Locomotive removed from train and set off - ran out of steam.
03-02-23	Foxrock	Two carriages destroyed by fire and temporary signal cabin burnt.

Date	Location	Details
12-02-23	Ballinglen	Station burnt.
16-02-23	Tinahely	Raid on goods store.
19-02-23	Dalkey	Carriages burnt - 1 destroyed.
23-02-23	Bridge 367	Attempted derailment.
24-02-23	Sandycove	Signal cabin destroyed by fire.
01-03-23	Palace East	Engine and two carriages sent off - considerable track damage.
19-03-23	Palace East	Attack on station.
19-03-23	Blackrock	Signal cabin blown up.
22-03-23	Foxrock	Temporary signal cabin blown up.
23-03-23	Inch	Station burnt.
07-04-23	Grand Canal Street	Carriages blown up, 1 destroyed and 3 damaged.
12-04-23	Chapel	Station burnt down.
26-04-23	Amiens Street	Central signal cabin destroyed.

Note:
Apart from the signal cabins listed as having been destroyed, a number of others were damaged to varying degrees. These included Dundrum, Shankill, Shanganagh Junction (twice), Avoca, Woodenbridge, Edermine, Glenmore, Sandymount (twice), Sydney Parade and Salthill. Enniscorthy and Sandycove, which were subsequently destroyed, were also damaged in earlier incidents.

Appendix K

TICKETS

Very little is known about the tickets used prior to the formation of the DW&WR in 1860. They were certainly in use by 1854, for in that year Season ticket charges were being examined. Subscription tickets from 1st August to 1st November 1856 were ordered to be prepared between Kingstown and Dalkey, Obelisk Hill and Ballybrack stations. Simple card 6-month Season tickets Dublin to 'Rock' (Blackrock) for 1843 and 1844 are known to have existed. Conditions of issue include free 'Cold Sea Bathing at the company's bathing places'. In 1857 return tickets at single and a half fare were issued on the Wicklow line to main stations beyond Bray on Mondays only.

In 1857 again an offer was received from Messrs Moray & Lyons, paper dealers, proffering 4s.6d per hundredweight for old tickets and paper – an early example of the commendable practice of recycling waste paper. This was accepted by the company who resolved that old D&KR tickets and any other waste paper be sold to the firm. This agreement did not include old D&WR tickets. These latter were to be destroyed in the presence of the chairman and deputy-chairman. How this destruction was undertaken is not known for it was only in 1877 that the Secretary was authorised to purchase, on the best terms he could, a machine lately used by the Clearing House for cancelling and cutting collected tickets.

Still in 1857, the company examined the comparative economy of printing paper tickets for use on the Kingstown line in large numbers, possibly against the use of the more expensive Edmondson card ticket. Neither type have been seen. In any event, three million tickets in total of various kinds were printed.

After 1859 a clear pattern of ticket type and colour begins to emerge. First class singles were white in colour. However an up single issued from Dalkey to Glenageary was noted as being white with yellow horizontal stripes. First class returns were yellow and white or white with one central horizontal red stripe. Second class single tickets were blue, some again with the horizontal red stripe. Second class returns were pink and blue. Again the horizontal red stripe appears on some.

Third class single tickets were straw coloured, some with the red stripe. Blue third class single tickets were also in use but generally from stations outside the Dublin area. Third class returns were coloured straw and green or vice versa, again some having the central red stripe. Cheap Sunday third class return tickets for use on the Dublin suburban services were coloured white with brown horizontal stripes. Special tickets for events such as a booking from Westland Row to Sutton on the GNR(I) for Baldoyle Races were a colourful combination of white, orange and green. Golf and Evening tickets were coloured white, red and yellow.

Bicycle and Dog tickets were also issued, the former being either white or orange, the latter being yellow and red. Privilege tickets were similarly coloured to the latter. No cross-channel bookings appear as tickets. Through bookings to other Irish railways appear to have been confined to the GNR(I).

For the Dublin suburban services great use was made of small folding card tickets. These were described as Subscribers' or Subscription tickets. These latter were available for Gentlemen, Ladies, Governesses, Tutors (coloured blue) and Youths. Up to 1870, the price of a ticket was not printed on its face. Where appropriate, the CofDJR initials were printed in brackets on DW&WR tickets. Tickets solely issued by the CofDJR title have not been seen even for journeys between Amiens Street, Tara Street and Westland Row. Platform tickets are not known to have been used on the CofDJR.

With the title change to D&SER in 1907 ticket colours changed to come more in line with other Irish companies. First class single and return tickets became white in colour, second class singles blue, returns red and blue. Third class singles and returns became buff or straw. There were however certain small exceptions to these colours for unknown reasons.

Special dated trips for the Leopardstown Races and Locomotive Department excursions were multi-coloured with no discernable pattern to their issue. Bicycle and Dog ticket colours were unchanged. Cross-channel tickets now appear and they seem to have been white for all classes of travel.

Platform tickets appeared for the first time in 1916 and in that year, the Secretary reported that the sale of tickets for admission to the platform at Greystones had realised £4.15s.7d. during the month of July. It was recommended that the arrangement be put into operation at Arklow, Gorey, Enniscorthy and Wexford. These tickets were generally coloured with horizontal green and white stripes. Examples have been seen however from Ferns and Harcourt Street with these colours printed vertically to include yellow. One example from Greystones issued in July 1918 is coloured white with a thin red band transcending from left to right. A further ticket issued from Greystones in October 1920 is coloured white with a vertical red stripe.

In August 1916 the Company Secretary submitted a statement to the Board in to the effect that the cost of supplying Season tickets for the year 1915 amounted to £110.16s.3d. The Board was shown specimens of season tickets from the London Electric Railway and it was stated that if this type of ticket was adopted by the company the annual supply would cost about £10 (sic). It was recommended that the present type of Season ticket be substituted by card tickets, colours for each class to be considered later.

One extant third class six-day 1s.8d ticket of this type for use between Westland Row and Blackrock, not available by mail trains or on Sundays, is coloured white with two vertical green stripes, its size is 3¾in x 2in and it is printed on very stiff card. The obverse contained conditions of issue and a space for the user's signature.

The DW&WR was well aware of the tourist potential of the districts it served. During its period of operation use was made of thin card cascade folding tickets from stations in Dublin and Wicklow to the Vale of Avoca with tickets coloured white for first class, blue for second class and salmon for third class. Express tickets from Kingstown Pier to Westland Row, Amiens Street or Kingsbridge (GS&WR) were of thin paper coloured yellow, blue or green respectively.

To combat the DUTC tramway service between Dublin and Dalkey, the D&SER introduced in late 1922 a special rail service with what were known as 'Bus trains'. These consisted of a locomotive, one bogie coach with 76 bus-type seats and a van. Tickets were issued on board by a Travelling Conductor and were of tramway punch type, possibly printed by Williamson, Ashton but with no printer's name on them. These tickets used stage numbers rather than actual station names and appear solely for use on the Harcourt Street to Greystones service. The tickets had a maximum of 23 stage numbers and some tickets had a large 'X' overprinted on them, the purpose of which is not known as they do not appear to be return tickets.

There were at least two series of these punch tickets for although the colour and value remain unchanged, the conditions of issue and number of stages do change.

A further difference is that some have an eight digit number at the base and some do not. Known values are 1d olive, 2d blue, 4d salmon, 5d pink, 6d light olive, 7d yellow, 8d purple, 9d brick, 10d grey, 1s purple, 1s.4d pink, 1s.7d yellow and 1s.9d brick. In this series there is also a white ticket described as a 'Voucher issued in lieu of ordinary ticket'. These tickets are quite unlike the 'Ticket Barrier' punch tickets used by the later GSR and CIE which were purchased on the platform, whereas the D&SER tickets were purchased from a conductor on the 'Bus Train'.

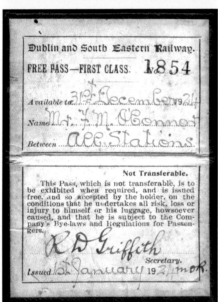

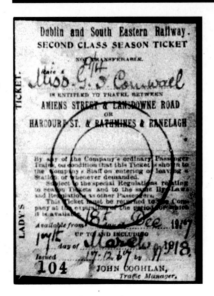

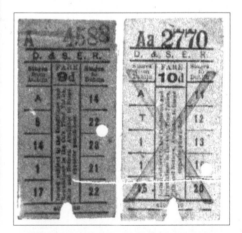

INDEX

Note:
Numbers in italics refer to illustrations.

Back cover illustration:
**The company crest, depicts in the first
quarter the arms of Wicklow. The second
quarter, consisting of three lymphads
flammant (heraldic ships on fire), are the
arms of Wexford, while the third quarter
(bottom left) showing the stag and
greyhound in full course towards the
sinister represents New Ross. The fourth
quarter shows the three English lions and
three seafaring ships of Waterford (the lions
are represented because King John granted
Waterford its charter). The escutcheon in
the centre carries the three burning castles
of Dublin. No alterations in colours, design
or dimensions were made when the
company's title was changed in 1907. The
transfer was mounted in a conventional
position below the waistline on coaching
stock while on locomotives, it was (with a
few exceptions) high up on the cab side.**

*Further railway titles from
Midland Publishing Limited*

**Irish Railways in Colour
From Steam to Diesel 1955-1967**
by Tom Ferris (200 colour illustrations)
ISBN 1 85780 000 1   £16.99 Stg

**Irish Railways in Colour
A Second Glance 1947-1970**
by Tom Ferris (350 colour illustrations)
ISBN 1 85780 019 2   £19.99 Stg

**Johnson's Atlas & Gazetteer
of the Railways of Ireland**
includes 36 colour maps and 160 pages
ISBN 1 85780 044 3   £19.99 Stg

The Irish Narrow Gauge
A Pictorial History by Tom Ferris
Volume One: From Cork to Cavan
Hbk, 250 b/w illustrations)
ISBN 1 85780 010 9   £15.99 Stg
Volume Two: The Ulster Lines
Hbk, 287 b/w illustrations)
ISBN 1 85780 017 6   £15.99 Stg

**The Midland Great Western Railway
of Ireland** by Ernie Shepherd
includes 287 b/w illustrations
ISBN 1 85780 008 7   £18.99 Stg

The *Irish Railway Pictorial* series:

The County Donegal Railway
by Steve Flanders
64pp, includes 158 b/w illustrations
ISBN 1 85780 054 0   £7.99 Stg

The Cavan & Leitrim Railway
by Tom Ferris & Patrick Flanagan
64pp, includes 160 b/w illustrations
ISBN 1 85780 073 7   £8.99 Stg

**The Londonderry & Lough Swilly Rail-
way** by Steve Flanders
64pp, includes 170 b/w illustrations
ISBN 1 85780 074 5   £8.99 Stg

The Belfast & County Down Railway
by Desmond Coakham
96pp, includes 240 b/w illustrations
ISBN 1 85780 076 1   £12.99 Stg

*Midland/OnLine
Irish Railways Video programmes:*

1: Irish Railways Miscellany 1950s-70s
    55min, colour and b/w.   £14.99 Stg
2: Swansong of Steam in Ulster '62-64
    55 min, all colour.   £14.99 Stg
3: Irish Narrow Gauge 1939-59
    50 min, all colour.   £16.99 Stg
4: Twilight of Steam in Ulster '62-64
    55 min, colour & b/w.   £15.99 Stg
5: Irish Railways in 1940s and '50s
    45 min, colour & b/w.   £14.99 Stg
6: The Peat Railways of Ireland
    55 min, all colour.   £16.99 Stg
7: Irish Railways in the 1960s
    55 min, colour & b/w.   £16.99 Stg
8: From Baltimore to Belfast
    53 min, colour & b/w.   £16.99 Stg

*All the above titles are available post-free to
UK and Irish addresses. Order from:*
    Midland Counties Publications
    Unit 3, Maizefield, Hinckley, LE10 1YF
    Tel: 01455 233 747 Fax: 01455 233 737